# Corporate Governance and Accountability

# Corporate Governance and Accountability

Second Edition

Jill Solomon

John Wiley & Sons, Ltd

Published by John Wiley & Sons, Ltd, The Atrium, Southern Gate, Chichester,
West Sussex PO19 8SQ, England
Telephone (+44) 1243 779777

Email (for orders and customer service enquiries): cs-books@wiley.co.uk
Visit our Home Page on www.wiley.com

Reprinted April and September 2007

*Other Wiley Editorial Offices*

John Wiley & Sons Inc., 111 River Street, Hoboken, NJ 07030, USA

Jossey-Bass, 989 Market Street, San Francisco, CA 94103-1741, USA

Wiley-VCH Verlag GmbH, Boschstr. 12, D-69469 Weinheim, Germany

John Wiley & Sons Australia Ltd, 42 McDougall Street, Milton, Queensland 4064, Australia

John Wiley & Sons (Asia) Pte Ltd, 2 Clementi Loop #02-01, Jin Xing Distripark, Singapore 129809

John Wiley & Sons Canada Ltd, 6045 Freemont Blvd, Mississauga, ONT, Canada L5R 4J3

Wiley also publishes its books in a variety of electronic formats. Some content that appears in print may not be available in electronic books.

*Library of Congress Cataloging-in-Publication Data*

Solomon, J. (Jill)
Corporate governance and accountability / Jill Solomon. – 2nd ed.
p. cm.
ISBN 0-470-03451-3
1. Corporate governance. 2. Boards of directors. 3. Disclosure in accounting. 4. Corporate governance–Great Britain. I. Title.
HD2741.S65 2007
338.6–dc22
2006028455

*British Library Cataloguing in Publication Data*

A catalogue record for this book is available from the British Library

ISBN – 13: 978-0-470-03451-4 (P/B)

Typeset in 10/13 pt Times by Thomson Digital
Printed and bound in Great Britain by Antony Rowe Ltd, Chippenham, Wiltshire
This book is printed on acid-free paper responsibly manufactured from sustainable forestry
in which at least two trees are planted for each one used for paper production.

*To my wonderful parents, Brenda and Derek,*
*my loving partner, Mike,*
*and my fabulous daughter, Zoe Clare*

# Contents

# Preface

Recent years have witnessed an exponential growth in corporate governance. Improvements in corporate governance practice are being orchestrated at a global level. International bodies such as the Organization for Economic Development (OECD) have developed internationally acceptable standards of corporate governance. In the UK, companies are continuing to strengthen their generally sound corporate governance systems, focusing on shareholder and stakeholder relations and accountability, improvements in the performance of boards of directors, auditors and the accounting function, and paying attention to the ways in which their companies are controlled and run. Similarly, institutional investors, accountants, auditors and the general public are increasingly aware of a continuing need to promote corporate governance reform. Scandals such as Enron and Parmalat have driven home this need for constant reform.

As a result of increasing interest in corporate governance matters within the practitioner community, academic research has burgeoned in the area. At universities across the UK, new modules are springing up on corporate governance-related issues, with corporate governance as a subject in its own right becoming central to many business-related degree courses. A general text on corporate governance and accountability is therefore in great demand and a second edition of this now established text was deemed necessary. Students need an up-to-date reference book covering theory and practice in the area. This text aims to provide an overview of corporate governance as a growing academic discipline. It attempts to give a flavour of the academic research in the field, with reference to theoretical frameworks. It also aims to demonstrate the close relationship between academic research and professional practice in the area. The text includes a number of contemporary illustrations and case studies, and provides readers with questions for reflection and discussion at the end of each chapter.

The text is designed specifically to accompany a one-semester module in corporate governance and is oriented toward undergraduates studying accounting and finance, business and management, as well as toward MBA (Master of Business Administration) and other postgraduate students taking modules with a corporate governance component. However, given the growing interest in corporate governance issues, it is hoped that a wide range of other readers may find the book useful. For example, given the growing emphasis on corporate governance training for pension fund trustees, following the Myners Review (2001) it is hoped that this book will be a useful guide for trustees on the many training courses that are being developed for them around the country, as well as for other professionals in the institutional investment community who require a reference text on corporate governance issues. Corporate secretaries are now playing a pivotal role in guiding companies on corporate governance issues and again, a general corporate governance text is likely to be of value to them. Further, as can be seen from the international orientation of the text, the book is intended for students of corporate governance around the world. It focuses on the relevance of corporate governance reform to countries all over the globe. Aims and learning outcomes are established at the beginning of each chapter so that students have a clear picture of what they are expected to assimilate and how their learning should progress at each stage of the book. There is also a summary at the end of each chapter bringing together the main concepts learned and providing continuity throughout the text.

This book represents the output of more than a decade of research into corporate governance and corporate accountability to stakeholders by the author and her colleagues. Throughout the book there are references to the results of the author's sole and collaborative research activities, including numerous postal questionnaires and a long-term series of in-depth research interviews. I am extremely grateful for the financial support I have received for research over the years, from a number of institutions including the ESRC-funded centre for Business Relationships, Accountability, Sustainability and Society (BRASS) at Cardiff University, the Nuffield Foundation and the ESRC.

## The Second Edition

Given the velocity of change in corporate governance globally since this text was first published in 2003, it was deemed necessary to update it. The second edition incorporates a series of new features as well as general updating. Rather than any dramatic changes or reforms, the UK has witnessed an overall fine-tuning and refining of corporate governance mechanisms since the first edition of this book was published. Attention has been given to improving institutional investor voting systems and widening the gene pool of non-executive directors. Corporate disclosures are also advancing and new sections devoted to narrative reporting (the Operating and Financial Review versus the Business Review), governance reporting and sustainability reporting, reflect these developments. These issues are discussed in the new edition. The new edition also includes more countries in the international section of the book, reflecting the ongoing globalization of corporate governance best practice standards. Several new figures have also been added to represent trends in corporate governance reform in the UK and elsewhere. Lastly, one area where significant changes in policy and attitudes have been experienced is that of socially responsible investment. Consequently, the second edition includes new sections on corporate governance ratings and the importance of risk, new reports on consideration of environmental, social and governance factors by institutional investors and the verification of social, environmental and sustainability reports. The latest research by the author and her colleagues is also summarized and discussed throughout the text.

# Acknowledgements

I am grateful to many people who have helped the development of both editions of this text and especially to my Mum, Brenda Ann Thompson for her regular reading of drafts and for her careful editing. I also thank her for her moral support, without which the book would never have been published in the first, let alone, the second edition. I also thank my partner, Michael John Jones, for his continual support and love, and for his encouragement in writing the second edition as well as in all areas of my life.

For the first edition of this book, I am extremely grateful to several close friends and colleagues at Cardiff Business School who have devoted time and energy to helping me write this text. Special thanks to Mark Clatworthy for his careful comments on the final draft, especially on style. Thanks to Howard Mellett for comments on structure and academic content, as well as some careful editing. I also thank Simon Norton for his careful reading of the final draft, his insightful comments and suggestions, and his continuing friendship and support.

I am also grateful to Nathan Joseph from Aston Business School for his comments and advice – as always, he has provided constant moral and academic support. Thanks to Linda Lewis (Sheffield University Management School) for her guidance and friendship over the years. Thanks are extended to David Owen (Nottingham Business School), Nikolaos Milonas (University of Athens and Cardiff Business School) and Nickolaos Travlos (ALBA, Greece and Cardiff Business School) for their comments on the book's structure and orientation. I am also grateful to a number of people who have acted (some anonymously) as reviewers on this book, especially to Michael Mumford (University of Lancaster) for his suggestions and for the extra literature he provided, especially his course notes on corporate governance, used at Lancaster University.

I am also grateful to many people from the UK institutional investment and corporate communities who have contributed to this book through their participation in research projects, especially questionnaire surveys and research interviews. This has provided the rich, in-depth knowledge of corporate governance developments and issues that are essential for any text on such a wide and far-reaching subject as corporate governance and accountability. Thanks also to students, who have attended the module 'Corporate Governance and Accountability' at Cardiff University in 2001–2002 and 2002–2003, for their feedback and suggestions on early drafts of the text. I am also grateful to my PhD student, Shih Wei Lin, for his comments on drafts of the book, and thank my MBA students who have commented on sections of the text. Special thanks to Monalisa Vora, who commented on Part II of the text. Thanks to Gil Powell for transcribing the interview data on which the empirical data are based and to Lauren Darby for research assistance. Thanks also to my Dad, Derek Thompson for his insightful comments on the historical sections of this text, as well as for expressing and debating views on corporate governance issues. I am also extremely grateful to the people at John Wiley & Sons who have worked hard to publish both editions, especially Steve Hardman and Mark Styles, who have provided support and guidance at every stage of the writing. Thanks also to the copy-editor, Bruce Shuttlewood of Originator, for his help and hard work in the final stages of the book's first edition.

In the writing of the second edition, I would like to add a number of people who have provided feedback from using the text, encouragement and suggestions for improvement of the text, namely, David Campbell (Newcastle University Business School), Rob Gray (University of St. Andrews), and Richard Laughlin (Kings College, University of London). I also want to thank Aris Solomon, the co-author of the first edition of this text, for his contribution to our joint work.

The *Combined Code on Corporate Governance* (2003) has been reproduced in full as an appendix to this book with the kind permission of the Financial Reporting Council. For further information regarding *The Combined Code* please contact the Financial Reporting Council on 020 7611 9700. To order a copy of *The Combined Code* please call 0870 777 2906.

# Introduction

Corporate governance is a central and dynamic aspect of business. The term 'governance' derives from the Latin *gubernare*, meaning 'to steer', usually applying to the steering of a ship, which implies that corporate governance involves the function of direction rather than control. There are many ways of defining corporate governance, ranging from narrow definitions that focus on companies and their shareholders, to broader definitions that incorporate the accountability of companies to many other groups of people, or 'stakeholders'. Chapter 1 discusses a large array of definitions, but for the purposes of this introduction corporate governance is taken as *the way in which companies are directed and controlled.*[1]

The importance of corporate governance for corporate success as well as for social welfare cannot be overstated. Examples of massive corporate collapses resulting from weak systems of corporate governance have highlighted the need to improve and reform corporate governance at an international level. In the wake of Enron, Parmalat and other similar cases, countries around the world have reacted quickly by pre-empting similar events domestically. As a speedy response to these corporate failures, the USA issued the Sarbanes–Oxley Act in July 2002, whereas in January 2003 the Higgs Report and the Smith Report were published in the UK, again in response to recent corporate governance failures. The impact of their recommendations are discussed throughout this book. The difference between the rules-based approach to corporate governance adopted by the USA and the comply or explain approach chosen by the UK is discussed. The main aim is to consider why such initiatives are being pursued and why continuing refinement and fine-tuning of the corporate governance system in the UK and elsewhere is necessary. In this introduction, the scene is set by placing the evolution of corporate governance in its historical and theoretical context, focusing mainly on the UK case. The contents of the chapters are now outlined in more detail.

## Part I Corporate governance: frameworks and mechanisms

### Defining corporate governance

Part I of this book examines the frameworks and mechanisms of corporate governance, mainly from a UK perspective. *Chapter 1* considers a range of definitions of corporate

---

[1] This definition is taken from the Cadbury Report (1992).

governance and provides a definition of corporate governance developed specifically for this text. A number of theoretical frameworks that have been used in the literature to analyse corporate governance issues are discussed. The study of corporate governance is principally the study of the mechanics of capitalist systems. As will become clear throughout this text, however, the US and UK forms of capitalism represent only one type of framework among many. There are as many variations of capitalism and corporate governance as there are countries in the world. However, corporate governance research has tended to focus predominantly on the Anglo-American (often termed the Anglo-Saxon) system of corporate governance, where companies are listed on stock exchanges and shareholders can trade freely in the shares. Traditionally, in this system, share ownership has been widely dispersed and management of companies has been distinctly separate from ownership. The development of the Anglo-American system of corporate governance is now discussed from a historical perspective.

## A historical perspective

Corporate ownership structure has been considered as having the strongest influence on systems of corporate governance, although many other factors affect corporate governance, including legal systems, cultural and religious traditions, political stability and economic events. All business enterprises need funding in order to grow, and it is the ways in which companies are financed which determine their ownership structure. It became clear centuries ago that individual entrepreneurs and their families could not provide the finance necessary to undertake developments required to fuel economic and industrial growth. The sale of company shares in order to raise the necessary capital was an innovation that has proved a cornerstone in the development of economies worldwide. However, the road toward the type of stock market seen in the UK and the US today has been long and complicated. Listed companies in their present form originate from the earliest form of corporate entity, namely the sole trader. From the Middle Ages, such traders were regulated by merchant guilds, which oversaw a diversity of trades.[2] The internationalization of trade, with traders venturing overseas, led gradually to regulated companies arising from the mediaeval guild system. Members of these early companies could trade their own shares in the company, which led ultimately to the formation of joint stock companies.[3]

The first company to combine incorporation, overseas trade and joint stock was the East India Company, which was granted a Royal Charter in 1600, for Merchants of London trading into the East Indies. The early governance structures of this company

[2]  See Farrar and Hannigan (1998) for a detailed history of the development of companies in the UK from a legal perspective.

[3]  Joint stock companies have been defined as companies consisting of individuals organized to conduct a business for gain and having a joint stock of capital represented by shares owned individually by the members and transferable without the consent of the group (Longman, 1984).

were reminiscent of corporate governance structures and mechanisms in today's companies (see Farrar and Hannigan, 1998; Cadbury, 2002). International trade and interest in investment overseas led to the infamous South Sea Bubble of 1720, where the general public in Britain, who had invested in 'shares' in the Company of Merchants of Great Britain Trading to the South Seas, realized they had lost their hard-earned money in the first stock market overvaluation and subsequent collapse. At one point during the Bubble's growth the amount invested in companies involved in the South Seas reached £500 million, double the value of all the land in England at the time. Investors did not realize the lack of solid foundation underlying their investment. The bubble in UK information technology ('Dot Com') stocks in the late 1990s was another example of investor irrationality and the ways in which the markets could be fooled. The Bubble Act, which followed the bursting of the South Sea Bubble, prevented companies from acting as a body corporate and from raising money by selling shares, without the legal authority of an Act of Parliament or Royal Charter. Inevitably, this halted the development of joint stock companies. It was the development of the railway network in Britain in the 1800s that again instigated the development of companies as we know them today, as they needed to attract funds to feed their growth.

A total of 910 companies were registered from the introduction of the first modern Joint Stock Companies Act in 1844 (Farrar and Hannigan, 1998). However, these companies were 'unlimited'. This implied that their shareholders bore unlimited liability for their investee company's debts, and this was not an effective means of encouraging people to place their monies into the hands of company management. Greater enticement was required. This came with the Limited Liability Act of 1855. Limited liability implied that shareholders could only lose the amount they had invested in the company, rather than be liable for their entire wealth, as had been the case with unlimited companies. These events represented a major breakthrough for the growth of capitalism. This was introduced as a progressive reform measure aimed at revitalizing British business, as at that time companies were seeking incorporation in the USA and France in preference to the UK, in order to obtain limited liability for their shareholders. The number of incorporations rose dramatically following these changes.

In the USA the managerially controlled corporation evolved at a similar time, following the Civil War in the second half of the 19th century. It was from this time that the notorious 'divorce' of ownership and control began to emerge. This corporate malaise was first outlined in Berle and Means' (1932) seminal work, *The Modern Corporation and Private Property*, which showed that the separation of ownership from control had engendered a situation where the true owners of companies, the shareholders, had little influence over company management and were rendered impotent by the wide dispersion of ownership and by a general apathy among shareholders toward the activities of investee company management. It was the dispersion of ownership that created the root of the problem rather than the separation *per se*. The influence of companies was growing at the time of Berle and Means' work and many feared the potential impact of their influence on society, unless their power was checked by their owners, the shareholders. They considered that companies were growing to such an extent that they were almost becoming 'social institutions'. Yet, there was little incentive for shareholders to involve themselves in their investee companies. They held relatively small shares in a broad portfolio of companies. If they were dissatisfied with the companies' behaviour they could sell their shares. This approach to share ownership has been termed 'exit' as opposed to a more proactive approach of using their 'voice'. The 'problem' revealed in Berle and Means formed the basis of the 'agency problem', where shareholders (the principals) struggle to control and monitor the activities of managers (the agents) in order to align managerial interests and objectives with their own. An important implication of these observations was to focus increasing attention on the role of companies' boards of directors, as a mechanism for ensuring effective corporate governance.

Although the ownership structure underlying the traditional agency problem was prevalent in the USA, the situation was extremely similar in the UK, where share ownership flourished following the introduction of the Joint Stock Companies Act of 1844 and the Limited Liability Act of 1855. Problems arising from separation of ownership and control were recognized in Adam Smith's *The Wealth of Nations* (Smith, 1838). In his discussion of joint stock companies, he explained that company directors were the managers of their shareholders' money, and not their own. He considered it likely that these directors would be less concerned about someone else's investment than they would be about their own and that this situation could easily result in 'negligence and profusion' in the management of company affairs. Further, in his personal exposition of corporate governance, Sir Adrian Cadbury (Cadbury, 2002) pointed out that there were allusions to the 'agency problem' in the UK that predated Berle and Means' writing. Indeed, Cadbury explained that in the Liberal Industrial Inquiry of 1926–1928 in the UK, a significant problem was detected because management and responsibility were in different hands from the provision of funds, the risk taking and the financial rewards. A study by Florence (1961) also suggested similarity between the UK system of corporate governance and that of the USA, as he showed that two-thirds of large companies were not controlled by their owners.

When companies within the capitalist system of the UK and the USA demonstrate effective systems of corporate governance, they can be productive and efficient, and can have a positive impact on society as a whole. Efficiently functioning capital markets can, theoretically at least, lead to efficient allocation of resources and a situation of optimal social welfare. However, ineffective, weak corporate governance can have the opposite result. The 'yin and yang' of the capitalist system are widely known. On the positive side, capitalism is associated with wealth production, economic prosperity and corporate success. On the negative side, capitalism is associated with greed, despotism, abuse of power, opaqueness, social inequality and unfair distribution of wealth. The negative aspects of global capitalism and its impact on society have been explored at some length in the literature (Hutton, 1995; Hutton and Giddens, 2001). It is the functioning of internal and external corporate governance that determines whether a company, or even a country, displays more of the negative or the positive aspects of the capitalist system. The level of inherent trust within the business sector and within society as a whole has been questioned in recent times, with a general acknowledgement by sociologists of a decline in social cohesion[4] and community. Specifically, there has been a decline in society's confidence in institutions, such as corporations and institutional investment organizations.[5] This decline in trust, so prevalent in UK society, and its implications for financial institutions are alluded to throughout this text, as they represent one major driving force behind corporate governance reform. Many aspects of corporate governance reform may be interpreted as attempts to rebuild society's trust in companies, investment institutions and other organizations.

The traditional Anglo-American system of corporate governance described above has not remained stable and has undergone dramatic changes in recent years. The main aspect of change has involved transformation of ownership structure in the UK and the USA. The rise of the global institutional investor as a powerful and dominant force in corporate governance has transformed the relationship between companies and their shareholders and has created a completely different system of corporate governance from that described above. Ownership structure is no longer widely dispersed, as in the model presented by Berle and Means, but is now becoming increasingly concentrated in the hands of a few major institutional investors. Some of these dominant investment institutions may now be seen as insiders, rather than outsiders, influencing company management directly.

## Corporate Governance Failure

*Chapter 2* provides a case study focusing on the fall of Enron. This was a salient case of corporate governance failure, which led to the collapse of one of the most successful companies in the world. The case study shows that corporate governance mechanisms such as the function of non-executive directors, auditors, the internal audit committee and the board of directors all failed in certain respects. The discussion also highlights the importance of ethical behaviour in business, explaining that corporate governance checks and balances serve only to detect, not cure, unethical activity. Clearly, the fall of Enron accelerated the worldwide agenda for corporate governance reform. This detailed case is followed by analysis of the 'European Enron', Parmalat and the corporate governance weaknesses involved in this Italian company's crisis.

## Corporate governance reform: a UK perspective

*Chapter 3* outlines the principal codes of practice and policy documents that have been developed within the UK agenda for corporate governance reform, considering their

---

[4] McCann et al. (2003) defined social cohesion as the degree of integration and bondedness of a society at large. They considered that social cohesion involves face-to-face interactive connections and the integration of shared values. To measure social cohesion is to measure the degree to which members of a society feel connected and integrated into communities and to general norms and values of the social world. Social cohesion is the opposite state to Durkheim's *anomie*, see Durkheim (1952).

[5] Giddens (1991) and Fukuyama (1995) discussed the decline in social cohesion and trust in society.

motivation and main objectives. *Chapter 4* examines the role of boards of directors in corporate governance. Within the context of the preceding historical discussion, the need for a well-functioning board at the head of companies became evident as companies grew in size and their owners became more dispersed and less involved in companies' operations. The discussion focuses on initiatives that have been implemented to maximize board effectiveness, such as splitting the role of chairman and chief executive, as well as the extent to which they have been successful in improving corporate governance in the UK and elsewhere. *Chapter 5* investigates the role of institutional investors in UK corporate governance, focusing on the instruments of shareholder activism, especially voting and engagement. *Chapter 6* considers the role of transparency in corporate governance, examining the importance of corporate disclosure, internal control and auditing to effective corporate governance. Having analysed corporate governance reform within a UK context, the discussion turns to considering approaches to corporate governance reform in different countries around the world.

# Part II Global corporate governance

The Anglo-American model of corporate governance is by no means the only model, despite suggestions and indeed concerns that it is becoming dominant internationally. In fact, it is the least common model historically, when all countries are considered. The second part of this book considers the various categorizations used to describe and analyse different systems of corporate governance around the world. There are many more forms of corporate governance, based on different structures of ownership and influenced by vast variations on cultural and religious background, legal framework and political climate. For example, some systems of corporate governance are characterized traditionally by state ownership influence. These are typical of countries such as Russia and China, which have experienced hefty state control due to their political climates. Further, corporate governance in many East Asian countries has been influenced heavily by cultural and legal factors. Confucian ethics has had a significant and lasting impact on the development of business in South Korea, for example. Countries in the Middle East, such as Saudi Arabia, feature corporate governance which is influenced largely by family ownership and religious beliefs and values. Corporate governance in the other countries in the European Union also represents a patchwork of different systems, with many countries characterized by founding family ownership structures, and extremely different legal structures from that in the UK. Other corporate governance systems have been characterized traditionally by bank relationships, such as Japan and Germany, as well as by 'pyramidal' ownership structures, where companies are ultimately owned, through complicated chains, by other companies. Specifically, *Chapter 7* discusses the 'insider–outsider' categorization of corporate governance, examining the characteristics of the most extreme forms of these systems. *Chapter 8* provides a 'Reference Dictionary' of a selection of corporate governance systems around the world. Given the number of countries in existence, it is impossible to provide exhaustive coverage of global corporate governance, as that would represent a book *per se*. However, the main characteristics of corporate governance in a number of countries are summarized in order to illustrate the diversity of corporate governance systems around the world.

## Part III Broadening the corporate governance agenda

Part III examines ways in which the concept of corporate governance has broadened to incorporate stakeholder concerns as well as shareholder accountability. In *Chapter 9* we consider the development of corporate social responsibility and the ways in which companies are discharging a broader accountability. Corporate failures such as Enron have rocked global confidence in business activities and have only served to fan the flames of distrust in the integrity of executives and management. Corporate governance weaknesses, which perhaps passed unnoticed in earlier times, have led to massive corporate collapses, affecting countries around the world. How many Enrons would it take to destroy global capitalism by leading shareholders to withdraw their financial support for the corporate community? Clearly, corporate governance systems require urgent attention and companies need to smarten up their act. Investor confidence and trust in institutions must be regained if society in its current form is to endure.

We are in a climate of change with corporate governance at the centre of this transformation. Not only is there a worldwide effort to improve corporate governance, but even countries that have been long-term communist states, such as China and Russia, are embracing a market-oriented system with shareholder accountability and greater corporate transparency, as can be seen from the discussion in *Chapter 8*. Capitalism has survived into the 21st century and seems to be becoming the dominant system in corporate governance. This is a difficult political issue, as it implies dominance of one political and economic system over another. This is not necessarily the most appropriate route for many countries in the world, as they need to retain their own character and culture in the face of change. However, this is not the only trend. The whole corporate discourse is metamorphosing. Whereas the shareholder-based model of corporate governance has dominated the 20th century, with attention being focused principally on making companies more accountable to their shareholders, there is now an increasing emphasis on satisfying the needs of a broad range of stakeholders. A far greater focus on ethics and on stakeholder inclusion is now an essential element of business strategy and activity.

Stakeholder concerns are gradually taking on a central position in corporate governance across the globe. Even countries with developing stock markets are concentrating not only on improving shareholder accountability but also on embracing stakeholder concerns. A new reality is dawning in the corporate world. The directors' discourse for the 21st century is very different from that of 20th century directors. Directors are being forced to concern themselves with far more than simply running their business and increasing shareholder value. Directors now have far-reaching responsibilities to wide stakeholder groups. Directors worry about pollution, social issues, stakeholder engagement and the impact of their company's operations in countries at the other side of the world. And if they don't they are being forced to at least discuss and consider these issues due to pressure from institutional investors and other stakeholder groups. Companies that do not take account of social and environmental issues are faced with direct shareholder and stakeholder action. Corporate social responsibility is becoming a primary concern of business, whether through a desire to be ethical or through a belief that being ethical actually improves profitability. Social and environmental issues have become significant risks requiring careful management. With global warming from carbon emissions and business activity becoming a threat to the survival of humanity, corporate social responsibility is arguably one of the most salient issues for economies worldwide. The contribution of businesses toward advancing ecological catastrophe is now acknowledged and has to be taken seriously. Sustainability has become a primary objective for businesses in the UK and elsewhere. There is now a growing body of empirical evidence that suggests that companies which are more socially responsible are also more profitable in the long-run, as we see from empirical evidence presented throughout this text. There is strong evidence of a negative relationship between corporate social responsibility and shareholder value, as social responsibility risks can destroy company value, not just in the long-run but also in the short-run. *Chapter 9* explores ways in which businesses are becoming more socially responsible and we examine the metamorphosis of the directors' discourse in the UK and elsewhere. Accountability is increasing in importance, not only to shareholders but to a wide range of stakeholders.

*Chapter 10* is concerned with the rise of socially responsible investment, whereby institutional investors are realizing the impact of social, ethical and environmental issues on their investment return and are therefore encouraging companies to treat these issues with more gravity. The book considers the dawning of a new corporate reality in the 21st century, involving a complete paradigm shift away from individual introvert corporate groups toward a global corporate community that is outward-looking and all-encompassing. Companies are assuming a role in society, by embracing corporate social responsibility and actively pursuing improvements in social welfare, by discharging greater accountability to a broad range of stakeholders. Furthermore, they are pursuing this inclusive approach with the full endorsement of their primary shareholders, the institutional investors. Environmental, social and governance (ESG) issues are now among the main considerations in mainstream institutional investment.

*Chapter 11* concludes the text with a discussion of the possible future route that corporate governance and accountability may take in the UK and elsewhere. A number of suggestions for policy makers, as well as a series of general observations and reflections are made.

**Part I**

# Corporate governance: frameworks and mechanisms

# Chapter 1

# Defining corporate governance

## Aims and objectives

This chapter provides an introduction to the corporate governance discipline, predominantly from a UK perspective. The specific objectives of this chapter are to:

- discuss a range of definitions of corporate governance in order to arrive at a definition that is appropriate for this text;

- appreciate the development of corporate governance from a historical perspective;

- compare and contrast several theoretical frameworks that are applied to the corporate governance discipline.

## Introduction

'Corporate governance' has become one of the most commonly used phrases in the current global business vocabulary. The notorious collapse of Enron in 2001, one of America's largest companies, has focused international attention on company failures and the role that strong corporate governance needs to play to prevent them. The UK responded by producing the Higgs Report (2003) and the Smith Report (2003), whereas the US produced the Sarbanes–Oxley Act (2002). Nations around the world are instigating far-reaching programmes for corporate governance reform, as evidenced by the proliferation of corporate governance codes and policy documents, voluntary or mandatory, both at the national and supra-national level. See Figure 7.1 in Chapter 7 for an illustration of how corporate governance best practice is being diffused around the world through the gradual development of codes of practice in a profusion of countries. In my view the present focus on corporate governance will be maintained into the future and over time. The phenomenal growth of interest in corporate governance has been accompanied by a growing body of academic research. As the discipline matures, far greater definition and clarity are being achieved concerning the nature of corporate governance. This chapter considers the broad-ranging nature of corporate governance and the many ways of defining the subject. Corporate governance is now discussed from a theoretical perspective, setting the scene for the following chapters.

## What is corporate governance?

There is no single, accepted definition of corporate governance. There are substantial differences in definition according to which country is considered. The main focus of this chapter and the following five is the agenda for corporate governance reform, mainly from a UK perspective. However, corporate governance failures in the USA and Italy are used in Chapter 2 to demonstrate the need to improve corporate governance mechanisms. However, even within the confines of one country's system, such as the UK, arriving at 'a' definition of corporate governance is no easy task. Corporate governance as a discipline in its own right is relatively new. The subject may be treated in a narrow or a broad manner, depending on the viewpoint of the policy maker, practitioner, researcher or theorist. It seems that existing definitions of corporate governance fall along a spectrum, with 'narrow' views at one end and more inclusive, 'broad' views placed at the other. One approach toward corporate governance adopts a narrow view, where corporate govern-ance is restricted to the relationship between a company and its shareholders. This is the traditional finance paradigm, expressed in 'agency theory'. At the other end of the spectrum, corporate governance may be seen as a web of relationships, not only between a company and its owners (shareholders) but also between a company and a broad range of other 'stakeholders': employees, customers, suppliers, bondholders, to name but a few. Such a view tends to be expressed in 'stakeholder theory'. This is a more inclusive and broad way of treating the subject of corporate governance and one which is gradually attracting greater attention, as issues of accountability and corporate social responsibility are brought to the forefront of policy and practice in the UK and elsewhere.

Table 1.1 considers some published definitions of corporate governance, each of which adopts a different view of the subject, and provides a consensus on the relative importance of these definitions. The consensus derives from a questionnaire survey that sampled a large number of UK institutional investors (Solomon et al., 2000b).[1] The questionnaire survey evaluated institutional investors' views of corporate governance. They were pre-sented with a number of established definitions of corporate governance. These defini-tions were not intended to discriminate completely between different views, but rather each was chosen to emphasize slightly different interpretations of the corporate govern-ance function. The selection represents a range of definitions, starting from the narrowest which described the basic role of corporate governance (The Cadbury Report, 1992; see also, Cadbury, 2002), to a solely finance perspective involving only shareholders and company management (Parkinson, 1994) and extending to a broader definition that encompassed corporate accountability to a wide range of stakeholders and society

---

[1] This survey is one of a number carried out by the author in collaboration with colleagues, the findings of which are referred to throughout the text.

**Table [1.1]**  Definitions of corporate governance: institutional investors' views

| Rank | Corporate governance is . . . | Average response |
|---|---|---|
| 1 | . . . the process of supervision and control intended to ensure that the company's management acts in accordance with the interests of shareholders (Parkinson, 1994). | Strongly agree |
| 2 | . . . the governance role is not concerned with the running of the business of the company *per se*, but with giving overall direction to the enterprise, with overseeing and controlling the executive actions of management and with satisfying legitimate expectations of accountability and regulation by interests beyond the corporate boundaries (Tricker, 1984). | Agree |
| 3 | . . . the governance of an enterprise is the sum of those activities that make up the internal regulation of the business in compliance with the obligations placed on the firm by legislation, ownership and control. It incorporates the trusteeship of assets, their management and their deployment (Cannon, 1994). | Agree |
| 4 | . . . the relationship between shareholders and their companies and the way in which shareholders act to encourage best practice (e.g., by voting at AGMs and by regular meetings with companies' senior management). Increasingly, this includes shareholder 'activism' which involves a campaign by a shareholder or a group of shareholders to achieve change in companies (The Corporate Governance Handbook, 1996). | Some agreement |
| 5 | . . . the structures, process, cultures and systems that engender the successful operation of the organization (Keasey and Wright, 1993). | Some agreement |
| 6 | . . . the system by which companies are directed and controlled (The Cadbury Report, 1992). | Slight agreement |

Reproduced by permission of Academic Press

at large (Tricker, 1984). A definition was also included which emphasized the importance of shareholder activism, as this allowed an evaluation of the institutional investors' views on their own role in corporate governance (The Corporate Governance Handbook, 1996). The selection also included definitions that were regulation-centred (Cannon, 1994) or focused on corporate success (Keasey and Wright, 1993). The definitions in Table 1.1 are ranked according to the institutional investors' views of their relative importance.[2] The table illustrates that the finance paradigm is probably the most easily

---

[2]  Specifically, the ranking was achieved by calculating the mean average response to a question in the questionnaire asking institutional investors the extent to which they agreed or disagreed with each definition. Institutional investors were asked to select a score from 1 (strongly disagree) to 7 (strongly agree).

acceptable to UK institutional investors, as Parkinson's (1994) shareholder-oriented definition received strongest support. This is not surprising as they are major shareholders and are likely to give themselves priority in terms of corporate governance relationships.

In general the definitions of corporate governance found in the literature tend to share certain characteristics, one of which is the notion of accountability. Narrow definitions are oriented around corporate accountability to shareholders. Some narrower, shareholder-oriented definitions of corporate governance focus specifically on the ability of a country's legal system to protect minority shareholder rights (e.g., La Porta et al., 1998). However, such definitions are mainly applicable to cross-country comparisons of corporate governance, and at present we are focusing on corporate governance within the UK. We return to the legal influence on different systems of corporate governance around the world in Chapters 7 and 8. Broader definitions of corporate governance stress a broader level of accountability to shareholders and other stakeholders. Tricker's (1984) definition, encompassing accountability to a broader group of people than just the shareholders, was also supported strongly by institutional investors from the results in Table 1.1. This demonstrates an interest within the financial community in a broader, stakeholder-oriented approach to corporate governance. The broadest definitions consider that companies are accountable to the whole of society, future generations and the natural world. This text presents a relatively broad definition of corporate governance for the purposes of this book, based on my own view of corporate governance issues. For the purposes of this book, corporate governance is defined as *the system of checks and balances, both internal and external to companies, which ensures that companies discharge their accountability to all their stakeholders and act in a socially responsible way in all areas of their business activity.*

This text attempts to show throughout that theoretical frameworks suggesting that companies should be accountable only to their shareholders are not necessarily inconsistent with theoretical frameworks which champion stakeholder accountability. The reason underlying this argument is that shareholders' interests can only be satisfied by taking account of stakeholder interests, as companies that are accountable to all of their stakeholders are over the long term more successful and more prosperous. The above definition of corporate governance therefore rests on the perception that companies can maximize value creation over the long term, by discharging their accountability to all of their stakeholders and by optimizing their system of corporate governance. This view is supported by the emerging literature. Some of this literature is discussed in Chapters 9 and 10, specifically. Indeed, my own[3] empirical research has provided substantial support for the view that corporate financial performance is positively related to corporate governance. The research findings provide substantial evidence to suggest a growing perception among institutional investors in the City of London and within the corporate

---

[3] I refer to my own research throughout the book, which is mostly work that I have done with colleagues.

community, that there is a corporate governance dividend as well as a dividend attached to stakeholder accountability. Indeed, I have found from my research that one reason 'good' corporate governance, as well as corporate social responsibility, are linked significantly to good corporate financial performance is its link with management quality. Better managers instigate better corporate governance and pay attention to their stakeholders. Better managers also manage companies more effectively and produce higher financial returns. This view was expressed by an investment analyst in a large UK investment institution, who commented that:

> I feel that organisations that demonstrate a commitment to a broad range of stakeholders are likely to show better management skills than those that do not...[4]

The Higgs Report (1993) reflected a similar sentiment, emphasizing a strong link between good corporate governance, accountability and value creation, in the following:

> ...the UK framework of corporate governance...can clearly be improved...progressive strengthening of the existing architecture is strongly desirable, both to increase corporate accountability and to maximise sustainable wealth creation.
> (Higgs Report, p. 12, para. 1.13)

Overall, this perception is growing among the professional community, and academic research is beginning to provide empirical evidence in support of this view of corporate governance, accountability and corporate profitability. However, this is the 'business case' for corporate governance and, more generally, for corporate social responsibility. Should companies improve corporate governance and discharge accountability to all of their stakeholders purely because it is ethical? These ethical issues are discussed in the subsection on stakeholder theory on p. 24. In the real world, it is unlikely that businessmen and investors will be interested in acting ethically unless there are positive financial returns to be made from so doing. As there appears to be a strong business case underlying corporate governance reform and stakeholder accountability, then the corporate and financial communities are more likely to embrace these approaches. Having provided an introduction to corporate governance and a sample of the many approaches to defining the subject, it is time to discuss a number of theoretical frameworks that are used to analyse corporate governance issues.

---

[4] This view was expressed in a questionnaire arising from a collaborative research project I was involved in. The questionnaire survey was conducted in January 2003 and was distributed to all of the members of the Society of Investment Professionals, who amount to over 4,000 investment analysts, fund managers, trustees, *inter alia*. The survey focused specifically on social, ethical and environmental disclosure and socially responsible investment, as an important aspect of corporate governance.

## Theoretical frameworks

A number of different theoretical frameworks have evolved to explain and analyse corporate governance. Each of these frameworks approaches corporate governance in a slightly different way, using different terminology, and views corporate governance from a different perspective, arising from a different discipline (e.g., the agency theory paradigm arises from the fields of finance and economics, whereas transaction cost theory arises from economics and organizational theory). Other frameworks, such as stakeholder theory, arise from a more social-orientated perspective on corporate governance. Although there are marked differences between the various theoretical frameworks, as they each attempt to analyse the same problems but from different perspectives, they do share significant commonalities. Further, the frameworks overlap theoretically. This section aims to outline some of the most commonly used theoretical frameworks in accounting and finance-related disciplines and to specify some of the commonalities and differences between these competing paradigms. Agency theory, transaction cost theory and stakeholder theory are examined. Other approaches include organization theory and stewardship theory (see Tricker, 1998). It is also important to recognize that there are cultural and legal influences on corporate governance, which are considered in Part II, where relevant.

To appreciate fully the various theories of corporate governance, it is useful to review briefly the development of stock markets, as their structure and operations have led to the development of agency theory. The introductory chapter summarized the historical development of corporate governance in the UK. For the purposes of this chapter, the development of limited liability is revisited, with the aim of laying the foundations of agency theory.[5] Before stock markets developed, companies relied on finance from wealthy individuals, usually relatives of the entrepreneur. Companies were owned and run by the same people. For economies to grow, it was necessary to find a large number of different investors to provide money for companies, so that they could expand. The principal element of today's stock markets, which has encouraged investors to buy shares, thereby ensuring a steady flow of external finance for companies, is known as limited liability. This was developed in 1855 and means that *shareholders are not responsible for the debts* of the companies in which they invest. The development of limited liability meant that investors were more prepared to buy shares, as all they would risk was their investment – not their entire wealth. A stock market is a means by which a company can raise capital by selling shares to investors, who become shareholders. Not only can investors buy shares but also these financial securities may be traded on the stock market. It is important to remember that the only time the company receives any funds is when the shares are sold for the first time. The important issue from a theoretical viewpoint is that in buying a share, even though an investor does not jeopardize his entire wealth, he is

---

[5]  Arnold (1998) provided a detailed history of the development of stock markets as a way for companies to obtain finance and is a useful text for students to read in order to appreciate the links between the development of UK capitalism and corporate finance.

becoming an 'owner' of the company. However, although the majority of shareholders own, in part, the investee company, they have little to do with running the company, as this is the job of the company directors, to whom they entrust their funds.

## Agency theory

The introduction of limited liability and the opening up of corporate ownership to the general public through share ownership had a dramatic impact on the way in which companies were controlled. The market system in the UK and the USA, *inter alia*, is organized in such a way that the owners, who are principally the shareholders of listed companies, delegate the running of the company to the company management. There is a separation of ownership and control that has led to the notorious 'agency problem'. Berle and Means (1932) discussed the extent to which there was a dispersion of shareholding, which consequently led to a separation of ownership and control in the USA. Prais (1976) showed that a similar structure of ownership and control operated in the UK. The agency problem was first explored in Ross (1973), with the first detailed theoretical exposition of agency theory presented in Jensen and Meckling (1976). They defined the managers of the company as the 'agents' and the shareholder as the 'principal' (in their analysis there is one shareholder versus the 'managers'). In other words, the shareholder, who is the owner or 'principal' of the company, delegates day-to-day decision making in the company to the directors, who are the shareholder's 'agents'. The problem that arises as a result of this system of corporate ownership is that the agents do not necessarily make decisions in the best interests of the principal. One of the principal assumptions of agency theory is that the goals of the principal and agent conflict. In finance theory, a basic assumption is that the primary objective for companies is shareholder wealth maximization. In practice this is not necessarily the case. It is likely that company managers prefer to pursue their own personal objectives, such as aiming to gain the highest bonuses possible. Managers are likely to display a tendency towards 'egoism' (i.e., behaviour that leads them to maximize their own perceived self-interest: Boatright, 1999). This can result in a tendency to focus on project and company investments that provide high short-run profits (where managers' pay is related to this variable), rather than the maximization of long-term shareholder wealth through investment in projects that are long-term in nature. Hence British industry has been notorious for 'short-termism'.

Short-termism has been defined as a tendency to foreshorten the time horizon applied to investment decisions, or raise the discount rate above that appropriate to the firm's opportunity cost of capital (Demirag and Tylecote, 1992). It is considered to characterize countries that are classified generally as 'outsider-dominated' (see Franks and Mayer, 1994; Short et al., 1998) where this means that the economy is not only dominated by large firms controlled directly by their managers but also indirectly through the actions of outsiders, such as institutional investors. This categorization of corporate governance systems is discussed in more detail in Chapter 7. Further, short-term pressure on companies has arisen from the institutional investment community, who have been more interested in gaining quick profits from portfolio investment than in the long-term survival and growth of their investee companies. They have been accused of 'churning' shares in order to make high returns on investment, regardless of the effects of their actions on managers, who as a consequence have been under pressure to focus on short-term performance (Sykes, 1994). This aspect of institutional investment is covered in more depth in Chapter 5.

In this corporate governance environment, managers are tempted to supplement their salaries with as many perquisites (such as holidays through the company, office equipment and the like) as possible – again leading to a reduction in shareholder value. The reduction in shareholder's welfare is known as the 'residual loss' in agency theory terminology. Overall, we can see that the ownership structure in the UK (and in other countries with similar market systems) leads to a significant problem of divergent objectives. This 'agency problem' presents shareholders with a need to control company management.

An important question is therefore, 'how can shareholders exercise control over company management?' Another important and basic assumption of agency theory is that it is expensive and difficult for the principal to verify what the agent is doing (see Eisenhardt, 1989). There are a number of ways in which shareholders' and managers' interests may be aligned, but these are costly. Agency costs arise from attempts by the shareholder to 'monitor' company management. Monitoring by the shareholder is expensive, as it involves initiating activities such as shareholder engagement (expensive on resources and time-consuming). Incentive schemes and contracts are examples of monitoring techniques. The literature shows that solutions to agency problems involve establishing a 'nexus' of optimal contracts (both explicit and implicit) between manage-ment and the company's shareholders. These include remuneration contracts for manage-ment and debt contracts. These contracts seek to align the interests of the management with those of the shareholder. Although agency costs arise from establishing these contracts, costs are also incurred from the agents' side. Managers are keen to demonstrate to the shareholder that they are accountable and that they are following the shareholder wealth maximization objective. They may provide extra information about risk manage-ment in their annual reports, for example, which will add costs to the accounting process. They may expend additional resources in arranging meetings with primary shareholders. The costs associated with such initiatives are referred to as *ex-ante* bonding costs. The total agency cost arising from the agency problem has been summarized as comprising of: the sum of the principal's monitoring expenditures; the agent's bonding expenditures; and any remaining residual loss (see Hill and Jones, 1992). One of the main reasons that the desired actions of principal and agent diverge is their different attitude toward risk. This is referred to as the problem of 'risk sharing', as managers and shareholders prefer different courses of action because of their different attitudes toward risk (see Shankman, 1999).

We now consider the direct ways in which shareholders can 'monitor' company management and help to resolve agency conflicts. These methods of shareholder activism and their impact are discussed in more detail in Chapter 5. First, as owners of the company, shareholders have a right to influence the way in which the company is run, through voting at AGMs. The shareholder's voting right is an important part of his or her financial asset. An area of the finance literature is devoted to investigating the use of voting rights by shareholders, particularly institutional investors, and some of this literature is discussed in Chapter 5. Shareholders can influence the composition of the board of directors in their investee companies (the companies in which they invest) through voting at AGMs. There is also a range of other issues on which shareholders may vote. Voting by shareholders constitutes 'shareholder activism'. Although the voting right is seen to constitute part of a shareholder's financial asset, institutional investors do not necessarily consider it to be a benefit, but rather an albatross around their necks. One pension fund director interviewed by the author commented that:

> There is a weakness in the present system of corporate governance in that respon-
> sibility for ownership rests with people who don't want it and are not seeking it. We are
> investing in shares because they give us a good return and it is coincidental really that
> they bring with them this responsibility. I am not saying we don't want this responsi-
> bility. I am just saying it is difficult to handle that sort of thing.

However, the same interviewee also suggested that one important result from the most recent code of corporate governance practice in the UK (the Combined Code, 1998) was that fund managers are taking more interest in corporate governance and in particular are voting at AGMs. As we see in Chapter 5, new initiatives in the UK are aimed at improving the voting mechanism for institutional investors by, for example, facilitating electronic voting systems.

Connected to shareholder voting rights is the takeover mechanism, which represents another means of controlling company management. Jensen and Ruback (1983) empha-size the importance of the stock market as a means of disciplining company management through the takeover mechanism. If shareholders are dissatisfied with a company's management structure they can vote in favour of a takeover. Clearly, the threat of takeover is *per se* a disciplining force on managers, as they are unlikely to want to lose their jobs. Directors' contracts represent one means by which they can gain some security, although lengthy contracts are becoming less popular as corporate governance reform continues.

Another way in which shareholders may attempt to align managers' interests with their own is through the passing of shareholder resolutions, where a group of shareholders collectively lobby the company on issues with which they are dissatisfied. This is an extreme form of shareholder activism which has been employed infrequently in the UK. An illustration of shareholder activism can be seen in the BP-Amoco case in Chapter 10 (see Illustration 10.2). Of course, shareholders also have the option of divesting (selling their shares). This is the ultimate action and represents a failure on the part of the company to retain investors, where the divestment is due to dissatisfaction with manage-ment activities. An example of this was the case of Huntingdon Life Sciences, a company that conducts scientific research through animal experimentation. Not only did this com-pany lose its principal UK institutional investors, as they were forced to divest following lobbying by animal rights groups, but it also lost investment from institutions in the USA. There has, however, been a recent backlash, with industry lobbies in the UK retaliating against animal rights extremists by demanding greater police protection from the government for their employees and shareholders. This case is discussed in more detail in Chapter 10 in the context of socially responsible investment (see Illustration 10.1). Clearly, if companies lose major shareholders, the market loses confidence in the company, more shareholders sell their shares and the share price plummets. Without financial support the company will fail. It is in the interests of listed companies not only to attract potential investors but also to retain them. Divestment is the ultimate threat.

Another way in which core institutional investors can influence investee company management is through one-to-one meetings between a representative from the invest-ment institution and a manager from the company. Such meetings are taking place more and more frequently and seem to be influencing corporate behaviour in a significant way. Holland (1998) considered the function of such meetings from a financial reporting perspective, showing that private disclosure through engagement and dialogue was developing to supplement public corporate disclosure. There is a distinct link between these one-to-one meetings and managerial decision making, although the Hampel Report (1998)[6] suggested that institutional investors do not want to be involved in companies' business decisions. However, there are important legal issues involved in the content and results of these meetings. If any price-sensitive information is revealed by company management (i.e., information which, if traded on, could affect share prices) to the institutional investors, then it is against the law for the investor to trade on this information until it becomes publicly available. This has led to many controversies in the past and occasionally results in 'insider dealing', where an investor (or a member of the family of an investment manager, for example) sells or buys shares in a company on receipt of private information, in order to make personal profit. Such events are high profile and result in court cases, if information becomes public. For example, the recent Enron trials found one of the former directors guilty of insider dealing, as will be discussed in Chapter 2. The legal framework relating to insider dealing is dealt with in more detail in Chapter 5.

If the market mechanism and shareholders' ability to express themselves are not enough to monitor and control managerial behaviour, some sort of regulation or formal guidance is needed. Indeed, if markets were perfectly efficient and companies could compete in an efficient market for funds, artificial initiatives aimed at reforming corporate governance would be redundant, as:

> ...we should not worry about governance reform, since, in the long run, product market competition would force firms to minimize costs, and as part of this cost minimization to adopt rules, including corporate governance mechanisms, enabling them to raise external capital at the lowest cost...competition would take care of corporate governance.
>
> (Shleifer and Vishny, 1997, p. 738)

---

[6] This Report is the third significant report on corporate governance in the UK. It is discussed in detail in Chapter 3.

However, markets are not perfectly competitive and therefore intervention is necessary in order to improve corporate governance, help companies to raise finance and make companies more accountable to their shareholders and other stakeholders. Agency problems do exist between companies and their shareholders throughout the world, and governments are intervening by producing policy documents and codes of corporate governance best practice at an amazing rate, as can be seen from Figure 7.1.

Since the early 1990s several 'voluntary' codes of practice and policy documents have been developed in the UK to help companies improve their standards of corporate governance – to make companies more accountable to shareholders and other stake-holders. The Cadbury Report, the Greenbury Report, the Hampel Report, the Turnbull Report, the Higgs Report, the Smith Report, the Tyson Report and their accompanying codes of practice are introduced in Chapter 3. Although the codes of conduct and recommendations contained in the related policy documents are voluntary, companies that are listed on the stock exchange have to disclose the extent to which they comply with the codes. Fears of damage to companies' reputation arising from the potential exposure of corporate governance weaknesses renders it difficult for listed companies not to comply. A good example of this relates to the separation of chairman and chief executive. UK companies not complying with the Combined Code (1998) in this area will be branded as having weak corporate governance checks and balances. Similarly, peer pressure has an effect with companies competing to be seen as compliant. The 'comply or explain' approach to corporate governance is explored in Chapter 3. We now turn to discuss a different theoretical framework for corporate governance, namely transaction cost theory.

## Transaction cost theory

An exposition of transaction cost theory, describing its historical development, may be found in Williamson (1996). He stated that transaction cost theory was, '... an inter-disciplinary alliance of law, economics, and organization...' (Williamson, 1996, p. 25). This discipline was initiated by Cyert and March's (1963) *A Behavioural Theory of the Firm*, a work that has become one of the cornerstones of industrial economics and finance theory. Theirs was an attempt to view the firm not as an impersonal economic unit in a world of perfect markets and equilibria but rather as an organization comprising people with differing views and objectives. Transaction cost theory is based on the fact that firms have become so large that they, in effect, substitute for the market in determining the allocation of resources. Indeed, companies are so large and so complex that price movements outside companies direct production and the markets co-ordinate transactions. Within companies, such market transactions are removed and management co-ordinates and controls production (Coase, 1937). The organization of a company (e.g., the extent of vertical integration) seems to determine the boundaries beyond which the company can determine price and production. In other words, it is the way in which the company is organized that determines its control over transactions.

Clearly, it is in the interests of company management to internalize transactions as much as possible. The main reason for this is that such internalization removes risks and uncertainties about future product prices and quality. It allows companies to remove risks of dealing with suppliers to some extent (e.g., by owning both breweries and public houses, a beer company removes the problems of negotiating prices between supplier and retailer). Any way of removing such information asymmetries is advantageous to company management and leads to reduction in business risk for a company. There are non-trivial and prohibitive costs in carrying out transactions in the marketplace, and it is therefore cheaper for companies to do it for themselves through vertical integration. The same analysis applies equally well to the case of oil companies in their various stages of production, from oil exploration, to refining and eventual retail distribution.

Traditional economics considers all economic agents to be rational and profit maximization to be the primary objective of business. Conversely, transaction cost economics attempts to incorporate human behaviour in a more realistic way. In this paradigm, managers and other economic agents practise 'bounded rationality'. Simon (1957) defined bounded rationality as behaviour that was intentionally rational but only limitedly so. Transaction cost economics also makes the assumption of 'opportunism'. This means that managers are opportunistic by nature. The theory assumes that some individuals are opportunistic, some of the time. The result of assuming bounded rationality and opportunism is that companies must:

> ...organize transactions so as to economize on bounded rationality while simultaneously safeguarding the transactions in question against the hazards of opportunism.
>
> (Williamson, 1996, p. 48)

Opportunism has been defined as 'self-interest seeking with guile' and as 'the active tendency of the human agent to take advantage, in any circumstances, of all available means to further his own privileges' (Crozier, 1964, p. 265). Given the problems of bounded rationality and opportunism, managers organize transactions in their best interests, and this activity needs to be controlled. Such opportunistic behaviour could have dire consequences on corporate finance as it would discourage potential investors from investing in companies. Immediately, we can see similarities here between agency theory and transaction cost economics, as both theories present a rationale for management to be controlled by shareholders. We now examine the ways in which transaction cost theory and agency theory are similar.

## Transaction cost theory versus agency theory

Difficulties in disentangling agency theory and transaction cost economics have been acknowledged in the literature (see, e.g., Gilson and Mnookin, 1985). Williamson (1996) addressed the extent to which agency theory and transaction cost theory provided different views of the theory of the firm and of managerial behaviour. He concluded that one of the main differences between agency theory and transaction cost theory was simply the use of a different taxonomy (i.e., using different terminology to describe essentially the same issues and problems). For example, transaction cost theory assumes people are often opportunistic, whereas agency theory discusses moral hazard and agency costs. Agency theory considers managers pursue perquisites whereas in transaction cost theory managers opportunistically arrange their transactions. Another difference is that the unit of analysis in agency theory is the individual agent, whereas in transaction cost theory the unit of analysis is the transaction. However, both theories attempt to tackle the same problem: 'how do we persuade company management to pursue shareholders' interests and company/shareholder profit maximization, rather than their self-interest?' They are simply different lenses through which the same problems may be observed and analysed. We now consider a third 'lens', that of stakeholder theory.

## Stakeholder theory

Stakeholder theory has developed gradually since the 1970s. One of the first expositions of stakeholder theory, couched in the management discipline, was presented by Freeman (1984), who proposed a general theory of the firm, incorporating corporate accountability to a broad range of stakeholders. Since then, there has been an abundance of writing based on stakeholder theory, across a wide array of disciplines (see, e.g., Donaldson and Preston, 1995). The role of companies in society has received increasing attention over time, with their impacts on employees, the environment, local communities, as well as their shareholders, becoming the focus of debate. Social and environmental lobby groups have gathered information on business activities and have targeted companies that have treated their stakeholders in an unethical manner.

Stakeholder theory may be viewed as a conceptual cocktail, concocted from a variety of disciplines and producing a blend of appealing sociological and organizational flavours. Indeed, stakeholder 'theory' is less of a formal unified theory and more of a broad research tradition, incorporating philosophy, ethics, political theory, economics, law and organizational social science (Wheeler et al., 2002). A basis for stakeholder theory is that companies are so large, and their impact on society so pervasive that they should discharge an accountability to many more sectors of society than solely their shareholders. There are many ways of defining stakeholder theory and 'stakeholders', depending on the user's disciplinary perspective. One commonality characterizing all definitions of stakeholders is to acknowledge their involvement in an 'exchange' relationship (Pearch, 1982; Freeman, 1984; Hill and Jones, 1992). Not only are stakeholders affected by companies but they in turn affect companies in some way. They hold a 'stake' rather than simply a 'share' in companies. Stakeholders include shareholders, employees, suppliers, customers, creditors, communities in the vicinity of the company's operations and the general public. The most extreme proponents of stakeholder theory suggest that the environment, animal species and future generations should be included as stakeholders. Indeed, the stakeholder relationship has been described as one of exchange, where the stakeholder groups supply companies with 'contributions' and expect their own interests to be satisfied via 'inducements' (March and Simon, 1958). Using this analytical framework, the general public may be viewed as corporate stakeholders because they are taxpayers, thereby providing companies with a national infrastructure in which to operate. In exchange they expect companies as 'corporate citizens' to enhance, not degrade, their quality of life (Hill and Jones, 1992). Indeed, every stakeholder represents part of the nexus of implicit and explicit contracts that constitutes a company. However, many writers refer to 'stakeholders' simply as those who have a legitimate stake in the company, in the broadest sense (Farrar and Hannigan, 1998).

In the UK the Corporate Report (ASSC, 1975) was a radical accounting proposal for its time, which suggested that companies should be made accountable for their impact on a wide group of stakeholders. The way that the Corporate Report hoped to achieve this was by encouraging companies to disclose voluntarily a range of statements aimed for stakeholder use, in addition to the traditional profit and loss account, and balance sheet. The additional statements included a statement of value added, an employment report, a statement of money exchanges with government, a statement of transactions and foreign currency, a statement of future prospects and a statement of corporate objectives. This was the first time that such an all encompassing approach to financial reporting was considered seriously by a professional UK accounting body. The report excited substantial controversy, although its impact was negligible at the time. One reason for the apparent dismissal of the Corporate Report was the change of government, with the Conservative Party coming to power in 1979 and advocating a more free market approach than the Labour Party. In more recent years, however, a stakeholder approach to accounting and finance has become more acceptable, particularly in light of the change of government from Conservative to Labour in 1997 and the growing emphasis on an 'inclusive' society. Indeed, Wheeler and Sillanpää (1997) explained the importance of developing a stakeholder society and highlighted the need for companies to be accountable to a wide range of stakeholders. Their book was endorsed by Tony Blair, the UK Prime Minister, as the 'right' approach to industrial activity.

Linked to stakeholder theory is the idea of corporate social responsibility, which is explored more fully in Chapter 9. This is becoming a major issue for companies in the current political and social climate. Companies are being actively encouraged by social and environmental lobby groups to improve their attitudes toward stakeholders and to act in a socially responsible manner. One motivation for encouraging corporate social responsibility derives from a belief that companies have a purely moral responsibility to act in an ethical manner. This 'pure ethics' view assumes that companies should behave in a socially responsible way, satisfying the interests of all of their stakeholders, because this is 'good'. This is intuitively appealing. Quinn and Jones (1995) defined this approach as 'noninstrumental ethics', arguing that company managers have no special rules that allow them to ignore their moral obligations as human beings and that, whether ethical behaviour is profitable or not, it must be adhered to. They provided strong analytical arguments that agency theory could only be applied effectively if four moral principles were adhered to: avoiding harm to others; respecting the autonomy of others; avoiding lying; and honouring agreements. Indeed, they claimed that the principal–agent model could only hold if it was embedded in the setting of these four moral principles. Why should the 'moral obligation' to 'keep a promise' to maximize shareholder wealth be any more important, or supersede, basic human principles, such as avoiding harm to others? In other words:

> How can one be morally bound to an agreement to ignore one's other moral obligations?
>
> (Quinn and Jones, 1995, p. 36)

This argument formed the basis of their exposition of 'agent morality', where agents must first attend to their basic moral duties as human beings, as they have no special dispensation from moral obligations. Only after meeting these moral obligations could they attend to their obligation to maximize shareholder wealth.

Company law, however, makes a purely ethics-motivated approach to business impractical, as companies have a legal and fiduciary obligation to shareholder wealth maximization.[7] Similarly, institutional investors have a legal, fiduciary obligation to maximize the returns of their clients. The issue of fiduciary duty and the growing relevance of environmental, social and governance considerations for institutional investors is discussed in Chapter 10. These legal obligations mean that the 'business case' for corporate social responsibility is the only realistic approach for company management. The legal system has been shown to be a significant barrier to the noninstrumental ethics case for business in the US (Quinn and Jones, 1995). The basic philosophy of separate legal personality of companies, as famously encapsulated in the *Salomon versus A. Salomon & Co. Ltd* decision (see Farrar and Hannigan, 1998), is incompatible with a framework that makes directors personally accountable for their behaviour. Even the latest review of company law in the UK, which has attempted in its various drafts to stress the needs for business to be accountable to stakeholders, has ultimately resigned corporate social responsibility to a back seat, based on the 'materiality' of social, environmental and ethical risks to the business. In other words, companies should only take account of these factors, in so far as they affect the bottom line. The implications of the Modernising Company Law (2002) review for corporate social responsibility and socially responsible investment are discussed, within the context of corporate governance, in Chapter 9. It is almost impossible to pursue ethical business unless it is demonstrated to be profitable, not only because of the attitudes of managers and shareholders but also because of our legal system and corporate governance structures. There has to be a strong business case for corporate social responsibility if companies are going to pursue it enthusiastically. It would take more than a change in attitude to reconstitute company law in the UK and elsewhere. A typical illustration of the

---

[7] A 'pure ethics' motive attracts derision from many members of both the professional and academic community, who view it as completely impractical and unrealistic. For example, one of our academic colleagues, who will remain nameless, dismisses a pure ethics approach as the 'pink fluffy bunny' view of corporate governance.

'business case' or 'instrumental ethics', approach to social responsibility may be found in a recent report produced by Rio Tinto,

> The business case underpinning our commitment to sustainable development has become more compelling. Companies that maintain high standards across the full spectrum of their social, environmental and economic performance have shown that they attract the best people, enhance the motivation and commitment of their employees and sustain the loyalty of their customers. They typically enjoy strong relationships with other stakeholders and benefit from a stronger corporate reputation. All these add to shareholder value.
>
> (Report to Society, Rio Tinto, 2004, p. 2)

This illustration is used by Jones (2006), who contrasts the pure ethics case, encapsulated in a subjective framework for environmental responsibility, with the 'real-life business case' demonstrated through corporate social reporting. He shows that companies are reporting on the environment unequivocally for 'business case' motives. The extent to which stakeholder theory and agency theory may be considered together, rather than be viewed as mutually exclusive is now assessed.

## Stakeholder versus agency theory

Is it possible that companies can maximize shareholder wealth, in an agency theory framework, at the same time as satisfying a broad range of stakeholder needs? In other words, 'is there any consistency between stakeholder theory and agency theory?' The importance of this question, and related questions, cannot be overstated, given the pervasive impact that businesses have on society in our consumer-led, multinational-driven world. Yet the answer remains elusive. New frameworks for business which depict a 'sustainable organization' culture within a corporate community and which also recognize the interdependencies and synergies between the company, its stakeholders, value-based networks[8] and society are emerging from the academic literature. Such an approach to business seeks to maximize value creation, through simultaneous maximization of economic, social and ecological welfare. Some academic work has provided empirical evidence that stakeholder management leads to improved shareholder value (Hillman and Keim, 2001).[9] However, stakeholder theory has long been vilified as the anathema of shareholder based agency theory (e.g., Sternberg, 1998). We revisit this perspective, embodied in the work of Milton Friedman, in Chapter 9. From this

---

[8]  Wheeler et al. (2002) used the term Value Based Networks (VBNs) to refer to new communities that are being created from a desire (or need) to create and increase value.

[9]  Hillman and Keim (2001) used an index to measure stakeholder performance for companies, known as the Kinder, Lydenburg, Domini Index. This Index was compiled by an independent rating service that focuses exclusively on ranking approximately 800 companies according to nine areas of social performance.

viewpoint, the only moral obligation facing managers is to maximize shareholder return, as this results (in an efficient market) in the 'best' allocation of social resources (see, e.g., Drucker, 1982; Jensen, 1991). The continual friction between these two theoretical frameworks was discussed by Shankman (1999), who pointed out that agency theory has for a long time represented the dominant paradigm for business and that the conflict between agency and stakeholder theories of the firm can be characterized as:

> ...an ongoing struggle between economic views of the firm which are decidedly silent on the moral implications of the modern corporation, and ethicists who place the need for understanding ethical implications in a central role in the field of business ethics.
>
> (Shankman, 1999, p. 319)

Indeed, on a theoretical basis, there are significant differences between the two theoretical paradigms, which at first sight render the two theories irreconcilable. For example, Shankman (1999) described stakeholder theory, but not agency theory, as normative in orientation, showing that the whole theoretical and philosophical underpinnings of the two theories were at variance. Nevertheless, there is a growing perception among theorists and practitioners that these two paradigms may be compatible (Wheeler et al., 2002) and that an altered approach to their theoretical derivation may allow them to be treated within one framework. For example, Shankman (1999) argued that agency theory may be subsumed within a general stakeholder model of companies, as:

**(i)** stakeholder theory is the necessary outcome of agency theory and is thus a more appropriate way to conceptualize theories of the firm;

**(ii)** agency theory, when properly modified, is at best a narrow form of stakeholder theory;

**(iii)** the assumptions about human behaviour and motivation implicit in agency theory are contradictory; and

**(iv)** all theories of the firm must uphold an implicit moral minimum that includes certain fundamental rights and principles and assumptions of human behaviour that may very well require other traditional theories of the firm to be modified or even reconceived.

Similarities between the theoretical standpoints are evident on close examination. For example, it is the manager group of stakeholders who are in a position of ultimate control, as they have decision-making powers allowing them to allocate the company's resources in a manner most consistent with the claims of other stakeholder groups (Hill and Jones, 1992). This means that it is company management who are ultimately responsible for satisfying stakeholders' needs and expectations. Using agency theory terminology, given their unique position of responsibility and accountability, managers' interests need to be aligned not only with shareholders' interests but also with the interests of all other stakeholder groups. As stated in Hill and Jones (1992):

> ...there is a parallel between the general class of stakeholder–agent relationships and the principal–agent relationships articulated by agency theory. Both stakeholder–agent and principal–agent relationships involve an implicit or explicit contract, the purpose of which is to try and reconcile divergent interests. In addition, both relation-ships are policed by governance structure.
>
> (Hill and Jones, 1992, p. 134)

Balancing the needs and interests of different stakeholder groups is notoriously difficult. This should not however be used as an excuse for making no effort to achieve such a balance. Hill and Jones (1992) also pointed out that many of the concepts and language of agency theory could be applied equally well to stakeholder–agency relationships. Overall, they argued that principal–agent relationships, as defined by agency theory, could be viewed as a subset of the more general class of stakeholder–agent relationships. Indeed, in developing 'stakeholder–agency theory' they sought to develop a modification of agency theory aimed at accommodating theories of power arising from a stakeholder perspective. They argued that stakeholder-derived and agency theory perspectives on organizational phenomena, which have been viewed as mutually exclusive interpretations, may indeed be interpreted in one model, by making a series of assumptions about market efficiency.

The moral discourse for company management implied by agency theory and stakeholder theory is vastly different. As Quinn and Jones (1995) explained, adopting one perspective (that of agency) leads to a discourse based on self-interest, whereas adoption of the other leads to a discourse of 'duty' and social responsibility. Unless these two perspectives can be merged in some way, the managerial discourse cannot be expected to combine fully the extremes of profit-seeking self-interest and moral responsibility to society.

As discussed above, the only realistic compromise solution to this problem is to adopt the business case, rather than the pure ethics case. The business case for managers to adopt a stakeholder-oriented approach is based on the notion that 'good ethics' is 'good business' and that employing ethics as a strategic management tool increases the present value of the firm (Blanchard and Peale, 1988; Kotter and Heskett, 1992; Quinn and Jones, 1995). This is, according to Quinn and Jones (1995), an example of 'instrumental ethics' whereby managers choose an approach of corporate social responsibility in order to maximize shareholder wealth. As argued earlier, this is really the only approach to ethics that makes sense in the modern world, given the extant legal and regulatory environment confronting businesses. Unless corporate social responsibility and accountability enhance shareholder wealth, neither company management nor large institutional investors, nor small-scale shareholders would ever endorse it as a realistic approach to corporate activity. It is more realistic to accept that ethics have to be profitable in order to be acceptable to businesses. But why should this not be the case? People are generally ethical, therefore ethical behaviour should be rewarded in a free market and unethical behaviour punished in an Adam Smith environment (see, e.g., Boatright, 1999).[10] This was certainly the case with Enron when managerial, unethical behaviour became public knowledge, as we can see from the case study in Chapter 2.[11]

It seems increasingly likely that creating value for stakeholders by businesses focusing attention on maximizing value for local communities, employees and environmental impacts (to name but a few) may be synonymous with creating financial value for shareholders. Ignoring the needs of stakeholders can lead to lower financial performance and even corporate failure. Corporate social, ethical and environmental performance are being viewed increasingly by investors as indicators of management quality and proxies for performance in other areas of the business. A company that is well managed is likely to have a good environmental management system and high levels of stakeholder dialogue and engagement. Indeed, the efforts made by many companies to increase the quality and quantity of cross-stakeholder dialogue are impressive. Camelot plc is a salient example of a company attempting to demonstrate an eagerness to embrace stakeholder dialogue and active engagement with diverse stakeholder groups (see Illustration 9.3 for a full discussion of this company's approach to stakeholders). However, this may be due to the company's heightened vulnerability in the area of ethics, given its core business of gambling. Nevertheless, any company with bad stakeholder relations could be characterized by poor management and consequently poor financial performance. This is one scenario – and one that is being accepted more widely in practice. There is, however, a large element of scepticism concerning the genuine improvements in stakeholder accountability arising from the increase in dialogue, as we see from the discussion in Chapter 9 (e.g., Owen et al., 2001).

An essential aspect of this debate is the extent to which satisfying the needs of a divergent group of stakeholders can also lead to satisfaction of the ultimate objective of shareholder wealth maximization. Part III of this book attempts to demonstrate that in the long term there is little inconsistency between the ultimate objective of agency theory and the practice of a stakeholder approach. It is only by taking account of stakeholder as well as shareholder interests that companies can achieve long-term profit maximization and, ultimately, shareholder wealth maximization. This belief is principally based on a growing body of literature and empirical evidence that suggests that corporate accountability which takes into account a broad range of social, ethical and environmental factors is conducive to financial performance. This text attempts to show that businesses can be

---

[10] Boatright (1999) explains that Adam Smith's invisible hand may, in an ethical environment, distribute wealth to socially responsible, ethical companies and distribute wealth away from unethical companies, through the free market mechanism.

[11] There are, however, problems with the instrumental ethics case, or business case, for corporate social responsibility, as it is difficult to see how a company is being truly 'moral' if it is only pursuing ethicality for reasons of self-interest. See Quinn and Jones, 1995, for an in-depth discussion of this dilemma. For example, they comment that, 'Discussions about stock price movements, instrumental ethics, and shareholder wealth maximization obscure the true moral argument' (p. 28). They also make the point that ethics is 'hard to fake'.

ethical and profitable, by considering the growing wealth of literature endorsing a positive relationship between corporate social responsibility and corporate financial performance.

## Chapter summary

In this chapter we have discussed the broad spectrum of definitions of corporate governance that exist in the literature, ranging from a narrow, agency theory definition to broader, stakeholder-oriented definitions. The definition for the purposes of this book adopts a stakeholder-oriented approach to corporate governance but one which does not necessarily contradict an agency theory approach. The chapter has also outlined three theoretical frameworks used for discussing and analysing corporate governance and has examined the extent to which they overlap. Having outlined some theoretical issues in corporate governance, we now turn to a discussion of the practical agenda for corporate governance reform. Our first task is to look at what happens when corporate governance fails, as in the cases of Enron and Parmalat. These cases clearly demonstrate a need for corporate governance reform. The next task is to examine the ways in which corporate governance may be improved by targeting a range of mechanisms, checks and balances.

## Questions for reflection and discussion

1   Read the definitions of corporate governance provided in this chapter. What would be your own, preferred definition of 'corporate governance'?

2   Which theoretical framework discussed in this chapter do you believe presents the most appropriate explicit framework for corporate governance, and why?

3   Do you think that agency theory and stakeholder theory are striving toward the same goal?

4   Read the discussion on the instrumental and non-instrumental ethics case for corporate social responsibility. Do you think either of these approaches is viable in today's business environment?

5   Look through a selection of corporate social responsibility/sustainability reports from UK listed companies. What reasons do the companies give for producing the report? Do their reasons coincide with a business case or a pure ethics motive for corporate social responsibility?

# Chapter 2

# Corporate governance failure

## Aim and objectives

This chapter presents a case study of the Enron saga and the case of the 'European Enron', Parmalat, in order to highlight the consequences that arise from the failure of corporate governance mechanisms. The specific objectives of this chapter are to:

- appreciate the importance of effective corporate governance and the consequences of weak corporate governance;

- consider the factors that led to the collapse of Enron;

- explain why the case of Enron has encouraged corporate governance reform worldwide;

- examine the case of the 'European Enron', Parmalat.

## Introduction

The previous chapter defined corporate governance and introduced a number of theoretical frameworks that have been used to analyse corporate governance issues. This chapter now provides a detailed case study of the collapse of Enron, in order to enhance the reader's appreciation of why corporate governance is essential to successful business and social welfare. The Enron saga presents a poignant illustration of what happens when corporate governance is weak and when the checks and balances are ineffective. Both Enron and Parmalat illustrate the problems of controlling human nature. However good corporate governance is from a cosmetic point of view, and however good a company's apparent financial performance, if there is unethical behaviour at the highest level, little if anything, can avoid eventual disaster.

## The collapse of Enron

In 2001 Enron became a household name – and probably in most households in most countries around the world! On 2 December 2001 Enron, one of the 10 largest companies in the USA, filed for Chapter 11 bankruptcy (a type of court protection giving the company management time to make arrangements with their creditors). In the following months, more and more evidence emerged of corporate governance weaknesses and fraudulent activity. Countries across the world have been unsettled and disturbed by the shock of this event and are now examining their own corporate governance systems in micro-detail, looking for similar weaknesses and potential Enrons. 'Enronitis' has spread across the globe like a lethal virus, infecting every company and every shareholding institution, worrying even the smallest shareholder and unnerving the financial markets. In this case study we examine the downfall of Enron in detail, looking at the reasons for the collapse and commenting on the corporate governance problems that were rife within the company.

Corporate governance failure and corporate collapse can happen in the strongest company. Investors, employees and creditors can be seduced by a company's reputation and success and can throw caution to the wind. If economic agents were rational, as they should be according to economic and finance theory, this sort of blindness could never happen. But it does. Investors do not always behave rationally, and human behaviour and psychology are factors that are difficult to incorporate in a finance model or an economic theory. Polly Peck and Coloroll were cases of irrational behaviour in the UK in the 1980s, when investors missed vital information in the accounts of these companies, pertaining to huge contingent liabilities. As soon as this information became public knowledge, both companies collapsed (Smith, 1996b). We first consider the way in which Enron built up its glittering reputation and the success that it encountered before crashing in such a monumental fashion.

## Laying the foundations

Enron was a Houston-based energy company founded by a brilliant entrepreneur, Kenneth Lay. The company was created in 1985 by a merger of two American gas pipeline companies. In a period of 16 years the company was transformed from a relatively small concern, involved in gas pipelines, and oil and gas exploration, to the world's largest energy trading company (*The Economist*, 28 November 2002). Deregulation of the energy market in the USA allowed utilities to choose their energy supplier. The 1980s saw deregulation of the market for natural gas in the USA, and deregulation of the wholesale electricity market followed in 1992 (*The Economist*, 26 February 1998). Deregulation had a far-reaching impact, allowing energy providers to diversify into other areas of the industry and become more competitive. Deregulation of energy in the UK had a similar effect, forcing providers to compete on price in order to attract supply contracts. One of the effects of deregulation was to create a market in energy trading, similar to a futures and options trading floor, where deals were struck between suppliers and clients on a continual basis.

## Glittering success

Enron's success was phenomenal. By 1998 Enron had eight divisions including Enron Energy Services (EES) and Enron Capital & Trade (ECT). In 1994 ECT sold

$ 10 million of electricity. By 1997 the company was selling $ 4 billion, which constituted almost a fifth of the North American wholesale market. Yet it only produced a small proportion of this itself. In 1998 Enron held $ 23 billion in assets (see *The Economist*, 26 February 1998 for these and other figures). In January 1998, Enron sold a 7 % share of EES to two pension funds for $ 130 million. From 1990 Enron's total return to shareholders ran far in advance of the index. In July 1998 Enron announced a $ 2.3 billion takeover of Wessex Water in the UK. Indeed, Rebecca Mark, then in charge of Enron's new water business, commented that they intended to be one of the two or three dominant players in the business (*The Economist*, 30 July 1998). In 1999 Enron's sales reached $ 40.1 billion. By 2000 the company's revenues reached over $ 100 billion (*The Economist*, 8 February 2001). In February 2001 the company's stock market value was $ 60 billion (*The Economist*, 29 November 2001). Enron became famous for its dexterity in handling risk management derivatives, as well as for its abilities in the area of commodity trading derivatives. Indeed, the company was proud of having 'invented' weather derivatives in 1997 (*The Economist*, 15 June 2000). Another area where Enron was praised for its innovation and success was in Internet-based business. At the end of 1999, Enron launched its Internet-based trading platform, EnronOnline. The venture was massively successful with 5,000 trades taking place online every day valuing about $ 3 billion (*The Economist*, 28 June 2001). However, the chief executive of Enron, Jeffrey Skilling, dismissed this success by saying that the Internet business was just a better form of telephone, which was the way the company did business successfully before.

Toward the end of its life, Enron had transformed itself from an energy company to a predominantly financial and energy trading company, trading financial derivatives as well as energy contracts and effectively running a gas pipeline on the side (*The Economist*, 29 November 2001). Success was so great at Enron that the words over the door as visitors entered the Houston headquarters were changed in 2001 from:

The world's leading energy company

to:

The world's leading company

Perhaps a quote from Dante would have been better:

Lasclate ogni sparanza voi ch'entratc![1]

This sort of self-confidence and pride is a clear example of counting chickens before they are hatched.

---

[1]  The translation of this is 'Abandon all hope ye who enter here!' It is the last sentence of the inscription over the entrance to Hell in the *Divina Commedia*, 'Inferno' canto 3, 1.

## Early worries

An article in *The Economist* (26 February 1998) raised queries as to the permanency of Enron's success. Causes for concern were, first, the differing speeds of deregulation in different states in America and, therefore, the ability to achieve free competition in all of the states·relatively quickly. Second, there were growing concerns that Enron may not have been well enough equipped to deal with the smaller customers it was taking on. Another main concern, expressed in many newspapers and professional literature, was that the company's management team were arrogant, overambitious and even sycophantic. Some even suggested that Kenneth Lay was like a cult leader with staff and employees fawning over his every word and following him slavishly (*The Economist*, 1 June 2000). This is not a healthy way to do business and indicates an ethical and moral problem at the head of the company. Such cases of unethical behaviour are associated with bad corporate governance and should be taken as warning signs. A prophetic, ironic and almost visionary comment begs quotation:

> Arrogance … is Enron's great failing … And how does Mr. Lay respond to this charge? … Mr. Lay speaks glowingly of the heyday of Drexel and of its star trader Michael Milken, whom he counts as a friend: they were accused of arrogance … but they were just being 'very innovative and very aggressive'. The comparison is not especially well chosen, for it is worth recalling what then happened: Mr. Milken ended up in jail for pushing the law too far, and the arrogant Drexel collapsed in a heap of bad debts and ignominy. For all its arrogance, Enron is hardly likely to share that fate: but hubris can lead to nemesis, even so.
>
> (*The Economist*, 1 June 2000)

This quotation proved to be a poignant forecast of later events at Enron, as well as prophetic in terms of the reasons for the company's downfall.

## Signs of distress

In 1997 Enron wrote off $ 537 million, mainly in order to settle a contract dispute over North Sea Gas. The company also became notorious for relying too heavily on non-recurring items, such as asset sales, to reach its target of 15 % annual growth in earnings. The company purchased Portland General Electric, a utility company in Oregon that held access to the California market. By buying into the Californian retail electricity market when the state deregulated electricity, the company seemed to be expanding too far. Furthermore, they had little success in penetrating the market and were only able to attract about 30,000 new customers in the whole state. This was not enough to merit their massive advertising campaign (*The Economist*, 23 April 1998). It seems that Enron's success in controlling the energy market came more from its dexterity in energy derivatives trading than its abilities in the core business. The company seems to have overstretched itself as a trader in commodities. In 2001, Dynegy, a competitor in the energy industry, was committed to a merger with Enron but backed out when Enron's accounting problems began to emerge. Indeed, not everyone was seduced by Enron's success. One investment firm, Reed Wasden, had been sceptical of Enron for a number of years. They pointed out that the company's trading margins had collapsed from 5.3 % in 1998 to under 1.7 % in 2001 (*The Economist*, 6 December 2001).

## The fall ... and fall ... of Enron

In August 2001 the chief executive, Jeffrey Skilling, left the company following concerns about the company's management and about his outburst of 'asshole' at an analyst who dared ask him a tricky question (*The Economist*, 6 December 2001). By late autumn it became clear that Enron was suffering serious financial problems with discussion over a takeover or bankruptcy (*The Economist*, 1 November 2001). Toward the end of October 2001, Moody's credit rating agency cut Enron's rating to barely above that of junk bonds. In November 2001 Standard & Poor's downgraded Enron's debt to junk bond status. Unfortunately, Enron's debt contracts included clauses stipulating that the company would have to make additional payments to debtholders if the company was downgraded (*The Economist*, 6 December 2001). On one day alone, 30 October 2001, Enron's shares fell by 19 % (*The Economist*, 1 November 2001).

Enron's brilliance in derivatives trading fuelled its demise, as the company lost $ 1.2 billion in capital from a failed hedging deal with a private equity fund. The company had to sell 55 million shares. A severe lack of transparency in Enron's balance sheet meant that no one was aware of this and other off-balance-sheet liabilities until it was too late. Despite such serious problems, even as late as November 2001, there was a general perception that the company was too big to fail and would weather the storm (*The Economist*, 1 November 2001). However, by the middle of November 2001 it was clear that the company was doomed. More than 20 class action lawsuits had already been filed. The main accusations covered fraud and material misstatement in the company's financial reports. Kenneth Lay himself commented that the company had been over-geared, with extensive use of debt capital on the balance sheet (*The Economist*, 15 November 2001). Furthermore, the company was accused of insider trading. Indeed, Enron top executives sold over $ 1 billion of Enron shares to other investors. Even though Enron's annual reports indicated financial prosperity, it was clear that Enron's management knew a lot more than they were letting on, making hay while the sun shone. This is a clear illustration of information asymmetry and agency problems, with insider investors profiting from better information than outsiders.

On 2 December 2001, the great Enron filed for Chapter 11 bankruptcy. Kenneth Lay resigned in January 2002. In August 2002, Michael Kopper, an assistant to the former finance director of Enron, pleaded guilty to charges of wire fraud and money laundering. On 2 October 2002, Andrew Fastow, former finance director of Enron, was charged with money laundering securities, wire and mail fraud; and conspiracy to inflate Enron's profits and enrich himself at the company's expense (*The Economist*, 3 October 2002).

## Creative accounting at Enron and its impact on the accounting profession

Transparency is an essential ingredient for a sound system of corporate governance. In Chapter 6 we examine the role of transparency in corporate governance in more detail. The USA has been dubbed the strongest capital market in the world, with the highest standards of integrity and ethicality. What went wrong? Both the audit function and the accounting function in Enron were fraudulent and opaque. However, Enron's collapse has had repercussions on the whole of the accounting and auditing profession, not just in the USA but worldwide. Enron's accounting was anything but transparent. Confidence in the company collapsed in 2001, when it became clear that their accounts were not only unreliable but fraudulent. Arthur Andersen, one of the Big Five, has now disappeared, partly as a result of its involvement in Enron's fraudulent accounting and auditing. However, Enron was not Andersen's first major problem. They had already paid out millions of dollars in settlements following inaccurate and weak auditing on a number of companies including Sunbeam, Waste Management and Discovery Zone (*The Economist*, 15 November 2001). In 2000, Andersen collected $ 25 million for auditing Enron's books in addition to $ 27 million for consulting services. This seems excessive and demonstrates a notorious problem of conflicts of interest between the auditing and consultancy arms of accounting firms. We return to this issue in more detail below.

Examples of Enron's devious accounting abound. The company recorded profits, for example, from a joint venture with Blockbuster Video that never materialized (*The Economist*, 7 February 2002). In 2002, Enron restated its accounts, a bad sign in itself and a process that reduced reported profits by $ 600 million (*The Economist*, 6 December 2001). Indeed, the process resulted in a cumulative profit reduction of $ 591 million and a rise in debt of $ 628 million for the financial statements from 1997 to 2000. This triggered an investigation by the Securities & Exchange Commission (SEC) into the auditing work of Andersen, Enron's auditors. The difference between the profit figures was mainly attributable to the earlier omission of three off-balance sheet entities. Such profit inflation allowed the company to increase its earnings per share figure (EPS). EPS is simply the total earnings figure divided by the number of shares. The company's exaggerated focus on its EPS was certainly a factor in its eventual decline, as Enron stated in its 2000 annual report that this main aim was to focus on EPS. This is a common strategy and one which can lead to manipulation of accounting numbers in attempts to inflate the EPS figure (*The Economist*, 6 December 2001). The pressure on companies in the USA and elsewhere to increase their EPS year on year has been blamed for corporate short-termism (see Chapter 1 for a discussion of short-termism, p. 17). It also provides directors with an irresistible temptation to cheat the figures! Not only did the company clearly manipulate the accounting numbers to inflate the earnings figure, but it was found to have removed substantial amounts of debt from its accounts by setting up a number of off-balance sheet entities. Such special purpose entities are non-consolidated, off-balance-sheet vehicles that have some legitimate uses, such as the financing of a research and development partnership with another company. However, they can also be used to hide a company's liabilities from the balance sheet, in order to make the financial statements look much better than they really are (*The Economist*, 2 May 2002). This was certainly the case for Enron. It meant that significant liabilities did not have to be disclosed on Enron's financial statements, as they were almost attributable to another legal entity (but not quite). To anyone, this is an obvious example of fraudulent, premeditated and unethical management. Furthermore, about 28 % of Enron's EPS was shown to have come from gains on sales of securitized assets to third parties connected to Enron (*The Economist*, 6 December 2001).

All this begs the question, 'why did Enron's auditor allow this type of activity?' They had to have been aware of it. Perhaps Andersen considered the transactions were relatively too small to be considered material. However, this is becoming less of a reasonable excuse (*The Economist*, 6 December 2001). In December 2001 the chief executive of Andersen, Joseph Berardino, stated that the firm had made an error of judgement over one of the off-balance-sheet entities created by Enron (*The Economist*, 20 December 2001). One 'special purpose' vehicle in particular, called Chewco, again created by Enron to offload liabilities for off-balance-sheet financing purposes, was cited as being a chief culprit, as it did not provide Andersen with adequate information. Clearly, had Andersen had this additional information, they would have forced Enron to consolidate Chewco into their accounts. However, such ignorance on the part of Andersen may not be adequate support for its lack of action. According to Enron, Andersen had been carrying out a detailed audit of the main structured finance vehicles, which made the auditing firm guilty of acting too slowly and inadequately (*The Economist*, 20 December 2001).

In January 2002, Andersen fired the partner in charge of Enron's audit, David Duncan, as he was found to have ordered the disposal of documents even after the SEC had subpoenaed the firm as part of its investigation into Enron. However, David Duncan clarified that he was not working in isolation, but was in constant contact with Andersen's headquarters. Furthermore, Enron itself ordered the shredding of vast quantities of documentation concerning the company's financial liabilities. The firm was criminally indicted by the Department of Justice for shredding documents relating to Enron. In March 2002, Andersen pleaded not guilty in a federal court to charges of obstruction of justice by document shredding (*The Economist*, 21 May 2002). Documents pertaining to Enron were not only shredded in Houston but also in London! Berardino resigned as chief executive of Andersen in March 2002. On 15 June 2002, Andersen was convicted of obstruction of justice. It is difficult for some to see how a company (as opposed to a person) can be found guilty of a crime, but certainly in the USA there is a perception that companies may be associated with unethical behaviour, in the same way as individuals (see *The Economist*, 13 June 2002, for a discussion of this issue). Such an approach makes corporate social responsibility a moral, human obligation, as companies are considered to be equivalent to people in a moral sense. This issue is explored in more detail in Chapter 9. The fall of Enron was the biggest corporate collapse ever, and the downfall of Andersen the most significant death of an accounting firm ever.

Conflicts of interest are a frequent problem in the audit profession. Independent appointment of the company's auditors by the company's shareholders is frequently replaced by subjective appointment by company bosses, where the auditor is all too often beholden to the company's senior management. Further, there are conflicts of interest arising from interwoven functions of audit and consultancy. Special, cosy relationships are built over time between companies and their auditors, which can again compromise independent judgement and cloud the auditing function. Such conflicts of interest impinge on the corporate governance function. Improvements in the audit function are clearly emphasized by the Enron case (*The Economist*, 7 February 2002). Creating a division between the auditing and consultancy arms of auditing firms may help. Indeed, a complete ban on auditing firms offering both services to the same client may be implemented. KPMG and Ernst & Young, PricewaterhouseCoopers and Deloitte Touche Tohmatsu have all decided to separate their auditing and consulting arms (*The Economist*, 7 February 2002). Another solution may be to instigate the rotation of auditors so that special relationships between auditors and their companies may not be allowed to develop. These possible routes to ensuring the effectiveness of the audit function are discussed in Chapter 6. Until now audit companies have been essentially self-regulated. They have used a process of peer review to check their procedures. The oversight bodies have been weak and lacking in regulative clout (*The Economist*, 7 February 2002). The Sarbanes–Oxley Act of July 2002 has taken a hard line on the regulation of auditing. The new Act restricts the consulting work that accounting firms are allowed to carry out for their audit clients. The Smith Report (2003) has also attempted to deal with these issues, as we see in Chapters 3 and 6.

The Financial Accounting Standards Board (FASB) in the USA has been forced to reconsider its position on off-balance-sheet financing, a subject that has troubled them for years. Especially, the FASB is reviewing its rules on how to account for special purpose entities (financing vehicles), such as those created and used by Enron. Attempts to address such issues in the past have been halted by aggressive lobbying (*The Economist*, 7 February 2002). Not surprisingly, one important lobbyist was Richard Causey, Enron's former chief accountant (*The Economist*, 2 May 2002). The FASB rule in place at the time of Enron's fall was that a company could keep a special purpose vehicle off its balance sheet, as long as an independent third party owned a controlling equity interest equivalent to at least 3 % of the fair value of its assets. The FASB has, post-Enron, considered raising that number to 10 % (*The Economist*, 2 May 2002). The Enron saga has added fuel to the process of international harmonization of accounting standards. The International Accounting Standards Board (IASB) is in the process of developing internationally acceptable standards for accounting worldwide. The strong card that the USA has traditionally played, in setting the agenda for international accounting, has been severely weakened by the shock waves from Enron. Under international accounting standards, the removal of material liabilities from Enron's balance sheet via its special purpose entities would not have been allowed, as the rules are harsher. The rules-based approach to accounting traditionally applied by the USA has also come under fire, as it provides companies with an incentive to comply with the letter but avoid the spirit of the rules. A more principles-based approach, such as that adopted in the UK, would probably encourage companies to comply more in substance than in form.

Further, there are two accounting standards in the UK that protect investors from the type of creative accounting practised by Enron. First, there is the fifth accounting standard 'Reporting the Substance of Transactions'. This ensures that quasi-subsidiaries, such as Enron's special purpose entities, are presented in the group's accounts so that the commercial effects of controlling operations, not owned by the company in a technical sense, are clarified. Second, there is the twelfth accounting standard, which deals with contingent liabilities. Companies in the UK have to disclose a description and a quantification of the effect of each and every contingent liability (see Ryland, 2002). Having suffered severely from Polly Peck and Coloroll, the UK has ensured that these potential black holes in accounting are dealt with. Surely this is encouraging for UK investors, as these two standards make a UK Enron less likely.

The Sarbanes–Oxley Act, brought in quickly in July 2002, also attempted to address accounting fraud through regulation. Chief executives and chief financial officers now have to 'swear' that to the best of their knowledge their latest annual reports and quarterly reports neither contain untrue statements, nor omit any material fact (*The Economist*, 15 August 2002). Such new legislation should encourage directors to act ethically and monitor their own financial accounting practices more carefully. They are now personally liable for cases of fraudulent, creative accounting. But is regulation really the answer? Is it not more worrying for shareholders to feel that the directors of companies they 'own' are so untrustworthy that they have to be tied down in this way, not having the integrity to regulate themselves?

## The aftermath

There are distinct similarities between the downfall of Enron and the collapse of Long Term Capital Management, an infamous hedge fund in the USA run by Nobel Prize-winning financial economists. Both companies demonstrated financial wizardry, trading immense quantities of derivative contracts and becoming excessively confident, indeed arrogant, about their abilities to beat the market. Indeed, although Enron had substantial abilities in the hedging field, these can collapse – and did – when the market started to fall. The general decline in stock markets around the world in 2001 had a negative influence on Enron's hedging success. The collapse of Enron also bore similarities to those of Maxwell and Polly Peck in the UK, as these companies also revealed significant audit failures. The personal suffering caused by Enron's collapse has been extensive. When Enron filed for bankruptcy many employees lost their savings as well as their jobs (*The Economist*, 28 November 2002). The pensions of Enron's employees were invested in Enron shares, so massive loss in future income for such pensioners is another important consideration. This emphasizes the social implications of corporate collapse and weak corporate governance.

One of the main effects of Enron's collapse has been on the general confidence of the government, corporate and professional bodies, and investors in companies' activities and management integrity. The effects of Enron have been so far-reaching that the term 'Enronmania' has been coined to refer to the reaction among company bosses and investors to fear (indeed terror!) that companies with characteristics similar to Enron may share its fate (Ryland, 2002). Indeed, the whole case raises the question, 'how could such a huge and successful company have avoided scrutiny for so long and managed to fool investors and creditors?' For the Federal Reserve, the concern was 'how could a company with such huge debts avoid regulatory checks and balances?' The immediate remedy for this situation was the Sarbanes–Oxley Act, which was produced and signed by the President in July 2002. However, an ongoing cause for concern is the choice between a regulated or a more voluntary corporate governance environment. As some countries, such as the USA, adopt a regulated approach to corporate governance reform and react in a regulative manner to corporate governance problems, other countries, such as the UK, consider that a more principles-driven and voluntary approach is more appropriate. The Higgs Report (2003) reviewed corporate governance in the UK and made proposals for improvements in boardroom practice, but avoided any attempt to introduce regulation. This is typical of the UK's more voluntary approach to corporate governance reform and is the UK's response to Enron, *inter alia* (see, e.g., *The Economist*, 31 October 2002). We discuss the 'comply and explain approach' to corporate governance in Chapter 3.

## The trial and the human dimension

The trials of Enron's top ex-directors began in earnest in January 2006 – five years after the company's collapse! The American government's case against chairman Kenneth Lay and Chief Executive, Jeffrey Skilling, was based on allegations that they conspired to mislead the general public about Enron's financial condition, lied to employees, investors and credit-rating companies and knowingly filed false financial reports (Mulligan, 2006). Indeed, the Federal investigators were convinced that the company's top directors were directly responsible for the use of creative accounting to conceal debt and massage reported profits, in order to bolster the company's share price. Worse still, when employees were about to lose their entire pension savings, it seems that top directors were pocketing immense profits from selling their shares when prices were sailing high. In Lay's case these profits amounted to $ 217 million and in the case of Skilling, $ 89 million. Skilling was charged with 31 counts of fraud, conspiracy and insider trading whereas Lay was charged with seven counts of fraud and conspiracy.

Before the trials began, the prosecutors received guilty pleas from 16 people, including Andrew Fastow, the Chief Financial Officer and Richard Causey, the company's chief accounting officer. The directors all appeared to be passing the buck, with Lay and Skilling trying to lay blame on others such as Fastow, who had already pleaded guilty.

Sean Berkowitz led the prosecution. One of the problems for the prosecution was the relative weighting they placed on details of the accounting fraud and on evidence of false statements by the defendants. Although evidence of fraudulent accounting activity was clearly important to the case, the prosecution were concerned about blinding the jurors with incomprehensible technical accounting details. The prosecutors therefore focused on a simple story of lies, greed and evil, taking the complexities out of the accounting aspects (Waldmeir, 2006). Indeed, John Coffee, from Columbia Law School, described the Enron saga as as long and complex as the famous novel, *War and Peace*, commenting that only scenes from the saga could be brought into the courtroom.

At the opening of the trial, the prosecution asserted that the

> two men at the helm of Enron told lie after lie about the true financial condition of that company.
>
> (Mulligan and Sanchez, 2006)

This was immediately met with the following retort from the defence lawyer,

> This is not a case of hear no evil, see no evil. This is a case of there was no evil...Skilling never broke the law he didn't lie, he didn't cheat, he didn't steal.

As with all court cases, one of these two viewpoints has to be wrong! Putting together the 'right' jury was one of the most difficult tasks, as it was essential to try and find people who were in no way personally affected by the Enron collapse, and who were impartial as to the eventual verdict.[2] From 100 potential jurors only 12 were chosen for the trial. As the US District Judge Sim Lake said to the jury,

> We are not looking for people who want to right a wrong or provide remedies for people who suffered because of the collapse of Enron...No one expects you to be able to blot out everything you have heard or read about this case...However, jurors must make their judgements based solely on the evidence they hear in the courtroom.
>
> (Mulligan and Sanchez, 2006)

Overall, the strategy adopted by the defence was to undermine all of the prosecution's witnesses by suggesting they lacked credibility (McNulty, 2006c).

There was a poignant human element to the whole trial. Emotions ran high. Near the beginning of the trial, Mark Koenig, the former head of investor relations at Enron, broke down in the courtroom because the defence lawyer asked him the age of his three children when he decided to plead guilty in August 2004 and agreed to cooperate with the prosecution (Barrionuievo and Evans, 2006). It was accounts such as Mr Koenig's which enforced the view that Lay and Skilling were concealing the company's true financial situation. Mr Fastow also broke down in tears when he testified, saying he had been extremely greedy, had lost his moral compass and had destroyed his life (McNulty, 2006b).

Predictions that if convicted, both Enron chiefs could spend the rest of their lives in prison (Barrionuievo and Evans, 2006) were borne out by events. On 25 May 2006,

---

[2] Potential jurors not only completed a lengthy questionnaire but also underwent a face-to-face interview before selection.

Lay and Skilling were convicted on fraud charges. Lay was found guilty on all six charges of fraud and conspiracy filed against him. Skilling was found guilty on 19 charges made against him of fraud, conspiracy, insider trading and making false statements. It took the jurors five days and two hours of deliberations to come to a verdict (Teather and Bates, 2006). The maximum technical time that each man could be sentenced for was estimated at 165 years for Lay and 275 years for Skilling! Even after the conclusion of the jury, Skilling maintained his innocence as he came out of the court room, despite being pale with shock.

## A reflection on the corporate governance problems in Enron

Severe corporate governance problems emerge from the Enron wreckage. Unfettered power in the hand of the chief executive is an obvious problem and one that characterized Enron's management. Separation of the chairman and chief executive role is not common in the USA, although this is starting to change (see Illustration 4.1 on Disney). This is a technique that is so successful in the UK as a means of improving the effectiveness of a company's board of directors that its application in the USA would benefit American companies and particularly American shareholders! As we see from Chapters 3 and 4, the Higgs Report (2003) has further strengthened the relevance of this initiative to corporate governance in the UK. The function of the non-executive directors in Enron was weak as they did not detect fraudulent accounting activities through their internal audit function. Indeed, the internal audit committee failed completely in policing their auditors. Serious conflicts of interest have arisen involving members of Enron's internal audit committee. For example, Wendy Gramm was the chairman of Enron's audit committee and her husband, Phil Gramm, a senator, received substantial political donations from Enron. Also, Lord Wakeham was on the audit committee at the same time as having a consulting contract with Enron (*The Economist*, 7 February 2002). These examples show that people in responsible positions, who should have detected unethical activities, were themselves not independent.

There were numerous illustrations of unethical activity within the Enron organization that continued to come to light long after its downfall. For example, in May 2002 it became clear from documents released by the Federal Energy Regulatory Commission that Enron's energy traders developed and used strategies, or tricks, to manipulate the markets in which California bought electricity. One trick, the 'Death Star', involved arranging power sales to flow in opposite directions, so that Enron could collect fees for transporting electricity when it had not done so! (*The Economist*, 9 May 2002).

Overall, corporate governance in Enron was weak in almost all respects. The board of directors was composed of a number of people who have been shown to be of poor moral character and willing to conduct fraudulent activity. This was the genuine root of the company's corporate governance failure. If the leadership is rotten how can the rest of the company succeed in the long run? Also, the non-executive directors were compromised by conflicts of interest. The internal audit committee did not perform its functions of internal control and of checking the external auditing function. Furthermore, the company's accounting and financial reporting function failed miserably. Both the financial director and the chief executive were prepared to produce fraudulent accounts for the company. The corporate crimes perpetrated by members of the Enron hierarchy are unnerving. How could the company survive so long with such unethical activities being carried out at the highest level? Why did no one notice? Where they did notice problems, why did they not report the company? How could the company's auditors allow such a travesty of justice? The questions raised by the Enron saga are far more numerous than the solutions offered.

There has been a proliferation of books on the downfall of Enron, seeking to explain why events transpired as they did.[3] As we have seen, the USA and the UK reacted strongly to Enron's collapse and corporate governance has been hurled to centre stage, as a result of the weaknesses at the heart of Enron's corporate governance system. The long-term effects of Enron will hopefully be a cleaner and more ethical corporate environment across the globe. Continuous updating of corporate governance codes of practice and systematic review of corporate governance checks and balances are necessary to avoid other Enrons in the future. In the famous (or infamous) UK novel, *The Clockwork Orange* (by Anthony Burgess), systems of controlling juvenile delinquents only worked super-ficially, as they forced a change in behaviour but did not alter the individuals' character and attitudes. The chief miscreant in the novel still wanted to behave amorally, but could not due to the treatment he had received. In a similar way, preventing unethical behaviour within companies through cold, legalistic and mechanistic means cannot alter a person's general approach. My own research into the attitudes of institutional investors and companies toward corporate governance issues, found that fund managers and directors considered unethical behaviour could not be controlled easily. For example, one corporate governance representative in a large investment institution in the City of London commented that:

> ...if people want to be fraudulent there is nothing in the current system to stop them – and if they are clever and fraudulent then they will get away with it for even longer and probably get rich on it.

Clearly, corporate governance checks and balances can only serve to detect, not cure, unethical practices. A complicating factor in issues of fraud and ethical breakdown is the intangible nature of fraud. It is difficult to determine exactly what constitutes fraud. There is a grey area surrounding what is 'right or wrong', 'good or bad' in human behaviour. Some comments from Sheldon Zenner, an American white-collar

---

[3]  The following represent just a few of the titles that have arisen as a result of the Enron debacle: Barreveld (2002), Cruver (2002), Elliott and Schroth (2002), Fox (2003) and Fusaro and Miller (2002).

criminal and civil lawyer, when speaking of the Enron trial, help to illuminate this issue,

> It's not like people sit around a table and say, 'Let's commit fraud on the investors'. It's people being asked to do something that their gut tells them is wrong. We all have an innate ability to rationalize our conduct. Nonetheless, if you tell the investing public X, when you knew it was really Y, then you still are committing fraud, whether you believed you were engaged in a conspiracy or not. If all these people knew it was wrong, it was wrong. If you tell the public something that is 'too good to be true', then it usually is just that – too good to be true. That's fraud.
>
> (McNulty, 2006)

We now turn to consider a European scandal, that of Parmalat.

## The 'European Enron': Parmalat

In December 2003, questions began to be asked about Parmalat, an Italian company founded by Calisto Tanzi, which specializes in long-life milk. The company had grown exponentially since the 1970s, moving into 30 countries and employing 36,000 people (Tran and Jay, 2004). The company's expansion was accompanied by rising debts, leading to the founding family giving up 49 % of its control over the company in 1990 in order to recover from debt. However, Parmalat quickly began to expand again, buying Beatrice Foods in 1997.

An immense black hole appeared in the company's accounts, after Parmalat struggled to make a € 150 million bond payment, when the company was, according to the books, cash rich. However, it was found that € 3.9 billion of the company's funds, which were held in a Bank of America subsidiary (Bonlat) account in the Cayman Islands did not exist. Letters from the Bank of America concerning Bonlat were found to have been forged. Parmalat was being audited by both Deloitte & Touche and Grant Thornton. The company has now admitted to £ 10 billion worth of debt. Enrico Bondi was appointed as special administrator in December 2003. Parmalat shares, once holding a market value of € 1.8 billion were worthless by the end of 2004. However, unlike Enron, Parmalat has survived the crisis and by February 2005 was managing to make pre-tax earnings of € 77 million (*Accountancy Age*, 4 February, 2005).

Further, Parmalat filed a lawsuit against Deloitte Touche Tohmatsu and Grant Thornton international in order to recover funds, in August 2004 (Moher, 2004). Parmalat described Grant Thornton as 'active conspirators' with the company's former management. Parmalat believed that Deloitte failed many times to blow the whistle on frauds that were plain to see, and which they must have been privy to. Lorenzo Penca, the Italian chairman for Grant Thornton, and Maurizio Bianchi, a partner, were attested and suspended from the audit firm, as a result of their misdoings concerning Parmalat (Rae, 2004). Almost two years after Parmalat's collapse, the fraud trials began in Italy

(Tran, 2005). Grant Thornton demonstrated self-preservation by threatening to sever its Italian arm if wrongdoings relating to Parmalat were uncovered (*Accountancy Age*, 5 January, 2004).

## Corporate governance failure in Parmalat

The media have termed Parmalat a particularly Italian scandal and have suggested that the situation was more likely to arise in a country like Italy than elsewhere (Mulligan and Munchau, 2003; Melis, 2005). Given the criticisms of Italian corporate governance in the literature, this is not surprising (Melis, 2005; La Porta et al., 1997). Whether it is true is a different matter. The same scenario arose in Enron where corporate governance is allegedly stronger. We discuss the Italian system of corporate governance in Chapter 6, showing that it falls into a family-dominated, insider framework. Such systems of corporate governance tend to be easy prey to abuse of power and fraud, where temptations arise.

Parmalat was owned by a complex group of companies, controlled by one strong blockholder (the founding Tanzi family) through a pyramidal structure (see Melis, 2005). Indeed, Melis (1999) explained that such ownership structures with opaque patterns of ownership and control are not uncommon in Italian companies. Melis (2000) stated that whereas the weaknesses of Anglo-Saxon systems of corporate governance were traditionally 'strong managers: weak owners', the key corporate governance problem in Italy was 'weak managers: strong blockholders and unprotected minority shareholders'. The case of Parmalat was typical of this form of corporate governance, with the controlling Tanzi shareholders channelling corporate resources illegally to themselves, at the expense of minority shareholders (Melis, 2005).

Although Italian corporate governance is characterized by monitors, namely the statutory auditors and the external auditing firm, these did not manage to protect the company from self-destruction. A direct analogy may be drawn between the cases of Enron and Parmalat, in terms of the fraudulent activities of the companies' audit firms. However, whereas Enron ceased to exist, Parmalat has survived its ordeal and has turned on the auditors in order to recover funds. Another difference is in the way that the auditing firms involved with Parmalat managed to extricate themselves from the crisis, whereas Arthur Andersen was destroyed in the aftermath of Enron.

Melis (2005) highlights a series of other serious corporate governance failures which led to Parmalat's crisis. Firstly, one of the non-executive directors in Parmalat was clearly not independent as he had been working in Parmalat as a senior manager since 1963. Secondly, the chairman and chief executive positions were not separated, as recommended by corporate governance codes of practice, in Parmalat Finanziara. Both positions were held by Tanzi. Thirdly, the Preda corporate governance code in Italy specified that where a group of shareholders controls a company, it is even more important for some directors to be independent from the controlling shareholders. This was certainly not upheld by Parmalat and no adequate explanation was given by the company for this lack of compliance.

As in the case of Enron, the failure of Parmalat to establish careful checking and monitoring structures within the company's governance framework laid it bare to abuse of power and fraudulent activity. Unless these devices for detecting fraud and misdoing are in place, it is relatively easy for Enron-like situations to arise.

## Chapter summary

In this chapter we have used the case of Enron's downfall to illustrate the importance of 'good' corporate governance. We have also outlined the saga of Parmalat, the 'European Enron'. The Enron case study has shown that not only does weak corporate governance affect the company it also affects society as a whole. The system of checks and balances that supports corporate governance needs to function effectively. Both Enron and Parmalat highlight the essential functions of non-executive directors, audit and disclosure, as well as ethicality of management. Indeed, all the checks and balances within the corporate governance system should have the ultimate aim of controlling and monitoring company management. Corporate governance mechanisms cannot prevent unethical activity by top management, but they can at least act as a means of detecting such activity before it is too late. When an apple is rotten there is no cure, but at least the rotten apple can be removed before the contagion spreads and infects the whole barrel. It is interesting that an analysis of both the Enron and Parmalat cases shows that both US and Italian corporate governance systems, so different in character, can be vulnerable to abuse and corporate governance weaknesses which are similar in nature. This is really what effective corporate governance is about. The rest of this text aims to explore the various checks and balances, and mechanisms by which good corporate governance ensures successful business and social welfare maximization.

## Questions for reflection and discussion

1   Read a selection of newspaper articles and academic writings on the collapse of Enron. Do you think that the Enron management behaved in an unethical manner? If so, do you think that a better system of corporate governance checks and balances would have detected their unethical behaviour before it was too late and avoided the company's collapse?

2   Do you think that the role of non-executive directors, auditors, the internal audit committee and the board of directors are all equally important as mechanisms of 'good' corporate governance? If not, which mechanism do you consider is the most important?

3   To what extent do you agree that 'When an apple is rotten there is no cure, but at least the rotten apple can be removed before the contagion spreads and infects the whole barrel. This is really what corporate governance is about.' Discuss your views.

**4**  Summarize the corporate governance problems in Enron. Do you think they are all of equal importance? If not, which corporate governance problem do you feel contributed the most to the company's downfall?

**5**  The response to Enron (and other recent corporate collapses) from the UK and from the USA are extremely different. Which approach do you prefer? Which do you think will be more effective in the long run? Explain your answer with reference to academic and/or professional articles you have read.

**6**  To what extent do you think a UK Enron is likely to occur? Discuss the reasons for your answer.

**7**  To what extent do you consider Parmalat was a purely Italian case of corporate governance failure? Consider similarities and differences between Enron and Parmalat in your answer. What do you think was at the root of both of these failures? Was the root cause of failure the same in both cases?

# Chapter 3

# Corporate governance reform in the UK

## Aim and objectives

This chapter considers the process of corporate governance reform within the UK environment. The specific objectives of this chapter are to:

- introduce the UK corporate governance codes of practice and policy documents;

- appreciate the importance of the 'comply or explain' approach to corporate governance reform adopted in the UK;

- discuss the importance of a link between corporate governance and corporate financial performance, especially in relation to the role of risk in corporate governance;

- consider the important development of corporate governance ratings.

## Introduction

Chapter 2 considered two salient cases of corporate failure related to corporate governance failure, and the case they presented for corporate governance reform. Although Enron has initiated further changes to UK corporate governance, a process of reform has been under way for over a decade. This does not imply, however, that inherent corporate governance problems do not persist in UK business. Directors continue to be rewarded for poor performance and even failure, as will be discussed in Chapter 4. Nevertheless, the UK is generally acknowledged as a world leader in corporate governance reform. This was not a predetermined strategy but the result of a growing interest in corporate governance issues within the boardroom, the institutional investment community and the Government. It was in part a reaction to scandals, such as the Maxwell case (see Illustration 3.1), and in part a result of introspection by boards and shareholders following economic decline in the early 1990s. The publication of the Cadbury Report (1992) represented the first attempt to formalize corporate governance best practice in a written document and to make explicit the system of corporate governance that was implicit in many UK companies. The renowned Cadbury Report has set the agenda for corporate governance reform in the UK and is the forerunner of numerous policy documents, principles, guidelines and codes of practice in the UK and elsewhere.

From a finance or 'agency theory' perspective, the corporate governance problem involves aligning managers' interests with those of their shareholders. As we saw in Chapter 1 there are a number of ways in which a shareholder (the principal) can monitor and control company management (the agent) including: shareholder voting at AGMs; one-to-one meetings between a representative fund manager and an investee company director; the takeover mechanism; shareholder resolutions; the threat of divestment. The important role of institutional investors in monitoring UK company management was also mentioned. Their stake in UK listed companies is expanding continuously, amounting to about 70 % at the end of the 20th century (the Hampel Report, 1998). As will be discussed in Chapter 5 the potential role that institutional investors can play in corporate governance has been emphasized in UK policy documents and accompanying codes of best practice since the early 1990s. However, shareholder activism is not the only way in which company management is controlled and governed. There are a number of other ways including: the fiduciary responsibility that is imposed on directors by company law; the legal requirement for an annual independent external audit of the accounts of the company; the overseeing by the Financial Services Authority (FSA); the Stock Exchange 'model code' on directors' share dealings; the Companies Act regulations on directors' transactions; the 'City Code' on takeovers and mergers; and voluntary corporate governance codes of practice. There were some spectacular cases of company failure and corporate abuse of power in the late 1980s and early 1990s, which created an incentive for corporate governance reform in the UK. One example is summarized in Illustration 3.1, where we discuss the corporate governance failures associated with the Maxwell case. Despite these regulatory checks and balances, and the efforts of shareholders, it has been deemed necessary to provide a series of corporate governance policy documents and codes of best practice in the UK, to help companies and institutional investors improve corporate governance.

The literature discusses the UK's approach to dealing with corporate governance issues, describing it as one involving the creation of committees (Jones and Pollitt, 2002; 2004). Each committee operates against a background of a business ethics environment where a number of potentially important stakeholders are involved in the consultation process. Jones and Pollitt (2002) label the key stages in the development of corporate governance reports as: initial interest; formation of a committee; writing terms of reference; deliberation of the committee; compilation of the report; presentation of findings; subsequent debate; and implementation. Further, they identify three phases in the development of corporate governance issues, namely: an education phase, where people become aware of the specific issue; an education phase, when the issue is analysed and solutions are suggested; and an implementation phase, where recommended solutions are implemented. Jones and Pollitt (2002) held up the Cadbury Committee as an ideal model of how to manage a corporate governance investigation, given the high quality of its process of investigation, conclusions and implementation of recommendations. Jones and Pollitt (2004) identified four features of the Cadbury process which made it exemplary:

**(i)** Sir Adrian Cadbury was a visionary chair who energetically promoted the committee's recommendations.

**(ii)** The committee reflected the main stakeholders.

**(iii)** The investigation produced a draft report followed by an extensive process of consultation.

**(iv)** A final report was produced whose recommendations were widely accepted and adopted.

The strength of the Cadbury consultation and ensuing code of practice may be the reason for its influence on the development of corporate governance throughout the world, as we see in Chapter 7, especially from looking at Figure 7.1. Indeed, it seems that not only has the Cadbury code spawned a far-reaching agenda for corporate governance reform in the UK, but its recommendations are also being disseminated throughout the rest of the world.

We now turn to considering each of the initiatives within the agenda of UK corporate governance reform. It is not necessary at this point to delve into the detailed content of each report and set of recommendations, as they are covered in later chapters when individual initiatives are explored in more depth. Figure 3.1 represents the development of codes of practice and policy documents in the UK along a time line. By looking at this diagram, we can see how corporate governance reform has evolved in the UK since 1992, from the early comprehensive codes of practice to more specific documents aimed at refining the solid architecture of UK corporate governance in more recent years.

### Illustration 3.1

### The Maxwell affair 1991

Robert Maxwell's abuse of power resulted in a scandal that was named the greatest fraud of the 20th century (Stiles and Taylor, 1993). Maxwell built up his corporate empire over time, but took on too much debt and pursued fraudulent activities in order to survive. The empire was founded mainly on two companies which were publicly quoted: Maxwell Communication Corporation and Mirror Group Newspapers, as well as a large number of private companies. After Maxwell's assumed suicide it emerged that he had taken money out of the pension funds of his public companies in order to finance his other activities. He was estimated to have stolen £727 million from the pension funds of the two public companies, as well as from the companies' assets. Also, an estimated £1 billion was lost from shareholder value after the public companies crashed.

There were a number of corporate governance problems relating to the Maxwell affair that have been flagged up as reasons why Maxwell was able to abuse his position so spectacularly. One problem was the lack of segregation of positions of power. Robert

Maxwell was both *chief executive and chairman* of Maxwell Communication Corporation from 1981 to 1991. He also held the positions of chairman and chief executive in Macmillan Publishers from 1988 to 1991. Such undivided control is now considered to represent inarguable corporate governance weakness. A second problem was that although Maxwell appointed *non-executive directors* to the board, they did not appear to perform a truly useful and independent function. The non-executive directors were reputable people and helped to give the company an aura of respectability. However, they did not alert shareholders to lack of transparency in Maxwell's financial activities. Furthermore, the *audit function* did not perform effectively. The auditors were in a position to observe movements of funds from the pension fund to the company, but did not seem to notice such activities in practice. Although there is an acknowledged expectations gap in auditing, this sort of audit failure is not acceptable. The *pension fund trustees* also failed to examine Maxwell's financial activities in sufficient detail. Clearly, trustees are responsible for pension fund monies and should have been in direct control of transferral of funds between the pension fund and the sponsoring company. So why did they allow money to be moved from one source to the other? Similarly, the pension fund *regulators* failed to investigate and control Maxwell's activities, probably as a result of the complexity of the 'empire'.

However, the Maxwell case raises another important issue that is central to corporate governance, that of ethics. No amount of corporate governance checks, balances, codes of practice or even regulation can change a person's character. In 1969 Robert Maxwell agreed a takeover bid for his company at the time, Pergamon Press, from Leasco, a US financial and data-processing group. However, the discussions collapsed after Leasco questioned the profits at Pergamon Press. An enquiry by the Department of Trade & Industry ensued which revealed that the profits depended on transactions with the Maxwell family's private companies. The resultant report by the Department of Trade & Industry concluded that ... '*notwithstanding Mr. Maxwell's acknowledged abilities and energy, he is not in our opinion a person who can be relied on to exercise proper stewardship of a publicly quoted company*'. Nevertheless, Maxwell rose from the ashes and went on to set up another business concern. But leopards do not change their spots. How can ethics in the boardroom be monitored and controlled? The latest efforts to sharpen the function of the audit committee in UK listed companies (Smith Report, 2003) and to improve the role and effectiveness of non-executive directors (Higgs Report, 2003) may help to monitor and control directors' activities more closely in the future.

# The UK experience

### The Cadbury Report 1992

As a result of public concern over the way in which companies were being run and fears concerning the type of abuse of power prevalent in the Maxwell case *inter alia*, corporate governance became the subject for discussion among policy makers. In this sense the formation of the Cadbury Committee may be seen as reactive rather than proactive. However, it is important to remember that the Cadbury Report was compiled on the basic assumption that the existing, implicit system of corporate governance in the UK was sound and that many of the recommendations were merely making explicit a good implicit system (see Cadbury Report, 1992, p. 12, para. 1.7). The Cadbury Report and its accompanying Cadbury Code (1992) derived their names from Sir Adrian Cadbury, who chaired the committee that produced them. The Council of the Stock Exchange and the Accountancy

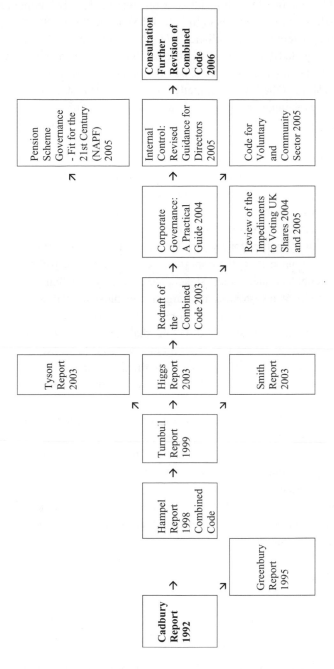

**Figure [3.1]**  The UK Experience

Profession set about establishing the Cadbury Committee, *The Committee on the Financial Aspects of Corporate Governance* which produced its report and accompanying Code of Best Practice at the end of 1992. The Cadbury Code was not legally binding on boards of directors. Nevertheless, one of the rules in the Stock Exchange *Yellow Book*[1] at the time of its publication was a 'statement of compliance' with the Code. The result of this was that all companies publicly quoted on the Stock Exchange had to state in their annual reports whether or not they had implemented the Code in all respects. If they had not complied with the whole Code, then they were compelled to make a clear statement of the reasons why, detailing and explaining the points of noncompliance. This, as we discuss later, formed the basis of the 'comply or explain' approach chosen for the whole UK corporate governance framework. The implication was that the companies' shareholders then had the opportunity of deciding whether or not they were satisfied with the companies' corporate governance system. Three general areas were covered by the Cadbury Report and its accompanying Code, namely: the board of directors; auditing; and the shareholders. The Cadbury Report focused attention on the board of directors as being the most important corporate governance mechanism, requiring constant monitoring and assessment. However, the accounting and auditing functions were also shown to play an essential role in good corporate governance, emphasizing the importance of corporate transparency and communication with shareholders and other stakeholders. Lastly, Cadbury's focus on the importance of institutional investors as the largest and most influential group of shareholders has had a lasting impact. This, more than any other initiative in corporate governance reform, has led to the shift of directors' dialogue toward greater accountability and engagement with shareholders. Further, we consider that this move to greater shareholder engagement has generated the more significant metamorphosis of corporate responsibility toward a range of stakeholders, encouraging greater corporate social responsibility in general. There is no denying the substantial impact that the Cadbury Code has had on corporate Britain and, indeed, on companies around the world. By the late 1990s there was strong evidence to show a high level of compliance with the Cadbury Code's recommendations (see, e.g., Conyon and Mallin, 1997). Similarly, Jones and Pollitt (2002; 2004) have championed the quality of Sir Adrian Cadbury's efforts in producing a worthwhile code for corporate governance.

Figure 3.1 shows the influence of the Cadbury Report (1992) by providing a timeline of corporate governance codes of practice and policy recommendations which have arisen from Cadbury's initial committee.

## The Greenbury Report 1995

A second corporate governance committee was created in response to public and shareholder concerns about directors' remuneration. There have been endless cases flagged up over recent years of excessive executive remuneration. *Fat Cat* incidents

---

[1] The *Yellow Book* provided the requirements of the Stock Exchange with which all listed companies had to comply. This has now been superseded by the overarching responsibilities of the FSA.

such as the notorious case of British Gas in the mid-1990s (see Illustration 3.2) attracted substantial media attention and distressed shareholders of large public companies. The phrase 'fat cats' was coined to refer to directors who orchestrated huge remuneration packages for themselves, which bore little (if any) relation to performance. Shareholders in general have become extremely concerned about unseemly pay increases for company directors. My own research into institutional investors' attitudes toward corporate governance has revealed executive remuneration to be one of the areas of greatest concern. For example, one pension fund director I interviewed commented that:

> What's different in corporate governance? Fat Cattery's different in the last few years and the publicity that goes with it. All these boards giving themselves big pay rises even when they fail. . .Ultimately, we are partly responsible because we have got some votes and some shares.

It is interesting to see from the above quotation that institutional investors are beginning to appreciate more sharply their own responsibilities as owners for corporate excesses and lack of accountability, as well as their ability to influence corporate decision making.

### Illustration 3.2

### Fat cats at British Gas 1995

The British Gas case is notorious both as a case of excessive executive remuneration and as a case of minority shareholder dissatisfaction. At the British Gas AGM on 30 May 1995 the views of individual shareholders were quashed by proxy votes from the company's institutional investors, in relation to the suitability of the company director, Cedric Brown, to run the company. One chief criticism was on his remuneration. Indeed, remuneration and compensation packages have attracted much attention in the UK, especially among minority shareholders. Despite strong sentiments among the smaller shareholders who attended the company's AGM in order to express their views and vote against the board, the votes of institutional investors supported the board, via proxy votes, even though their representatives did not attend. This was seen as unfair by many of the shareholders who attended and caused an outcry at the time. The case is especially memorable because a pig named Cedric, after Cedric Brown, was paraded outside the company during the AGM. The British Gas case is discussed in detail in a case study in the journal, *Corporate Governance: An International Review* (1996).

At this point it is important to note that the aim of the Greenbury Report was not necessarily to reduce directors' salaries. Rather, it was to provide a means of establishing a balance between directors' salaries and their performance. The report recognized the importance for companies of offering salaries that were high enough to attract directors of adequate calibre, capable of running large, multinational organizations. However, the report also highlighted deep concerns with directors' pay packages, especially in relation to share options and other additional sources of remuneration. The issue of executive remuneration and the impact of the Greenbury Report, as well as its successor, is considered in detail in Chapter 4.

## The Hampel Report 1998

The Hampel Committee was the successor to both the Cadbury and the Greenbury Committees, taking on both the financial aspects of corporate governance and directors' remuneration. The Hampel Report was published in 1998 and the Combined Code (1998) arose from it. This Code brought together all the issues covered in Cadbury and Greenbury, hence its name. The Combined Code (although redrafted since its original publication) is the currently applicable code of best corporate governance practice for UK listed companies. The recommendations of Hampel were along similar lines and on similar issues to Cadbury. An important contribution made by the Hampel Report was the emphasis attributed to avoiding a prescriptive approach to corporate governance. The Cadbury Report highlighted the importance of focusing on the spirit of corporate governance reform, and Hampel reinforced this by stipulating that companies and shareholders needed to avoid a 'box-ticking' approach to corporate governance. The Hampel Report emphasized the need to maintain a principles-based, voluntary approach to corporate governance rather than a more regulated and possibly superficial approach. This is typical of the UK approach to corporate governance and accounting as opposed to the US style of legislation, the rules-based approach. Indeed, the report stated:

> Good corporate governance is not just a matter of prescribing particular corporate structures and complying with a number of hard and fast rules. *There is a need for broad principles.* All concerned should then apply these flexibly and with common sense to the varying circumstances of individual companies. This is how the Cadbury and Greenbury committees intended their recommendations to be implemented... Companies' experience of the Cadbury and Greenbury codes has been rather different. Too often they believe that the codes have been treated as sets of prescriptive rules. The shareholders or their advisers would be interested *only in whether the letter of the rule had been complied with* – yes or no. A 'yes' would receive a tick, hence the expression '*box ticking*' for this approach.
>
> (The Hampel Report, 1998, p. 10, paras 1.11–1.12, emphasis added)

In some ways (such as the role of institutional investors in corporate governance) Hampel could be interpreted as being less demanding than Cadbury. Indeed, there is a widely held perception that the report represented the interests of company directors more than those of shareholders and that much of the positive impact from the Cadbury Report was diluted by the Hampel Report. Certainly, in the area of corporate social responsibility and corporate accountability to a broad range of stakeholders, there was a significant change in tack between the Cadbury Report and the Hampel Report. The Hampel Report clearly felt the need to redress the balance between shareholders and stakeholders and made strong statements on these issues. For example, the Hampel Committee stated that:

> The importance of corporate governance lies in its contribution both to business prosperity and to accountability. In the UK the latter has preoccupied much public

debate over the past few years. *We would wish to see the balance corrected.* Public companies are now among the most accountable organisations in society...We strongly endorse this accountability and we recognise the contribution made by the Cadbury and Greenbury committees. *But the emphasis on accountability has tended to obscure a board's first responsibility* – to enhance the prosperity of the business over time.

(The Hampel Report, 1998, p. 7, para. 1.1, emphasis added)

Although I agree that corporate governance in UK companies is exemplary in general and that the UK provides a benchmark for good corporate governance, such comments are suggestive of resting on laurels! UK companies should not be complacent. Accountability is one area where the corporate success of the future will be measured. Generally, it seems that Hampel was misguided in this area and in its perception of public, corporate and shareholder sentiment. As discussed in Chapter 1, there is a strong demand for greater accountability and there is also a growing perception that companies that are accountable to a broad range of stakeholders display better long-term performance. Although further research is required to demonstrate this link unequivocally, evidence is emerging that demonstrates that the approach of the Hampel Report was outdated and retrograde in this respect. These issues are revisited throughout the book, but especially in Part III.

An important contribution made by the Hampel Report related to pension fund trustees, as pension funds are the largest group of investors. Pension fund trustees were targeted by the report as a group who needed to take their corporate governance responsibilities more seriously. In particular, pension funds (and their trustees) were encouraged by the Hampel Committee to adopt a more long-term approach to institutional investment, in order to avoid short-termism for which UK companies are notorious. Pension funds were highlighted as the main culprits in placing short-term pressure on their investee companies. This discussion in the Hampel Report has been instrumental in encouraging an overhaul in the pension fund trustee's role, culminating in the recent Myners Review of the trustee's role and responsibilities (Myners, 2001). These issues are covered in more detail in Chapter 5. In this area, the Hampel Committee clearly picked up on and developed the spirit of the original Cadbury Report.

Generally speaking, the Combined Code readdressed all the issues raised in previous reports, bringing the major points together and concluding with basic principles and provisions. The first draft of the Combined Code contained a series of Principles of Good Corporate Governance. It then detailed a series of provisions that represented ways in which the general principles may be achieved. The Code was structured in two parts. The first part dealt with companies and includes four sections of Principles covering: (A) Directors; (B) Directors' Remuneration; (C) Relations with Shareholders; (D) Accountability and Audit. The second part dealt with institutional shareholders and included three sections covering: (E) 1. Shareholder Voting; 2. Dialogue with Companies; and 3. Evaluation of Governance Disclosures. We can immediately see that all of these issues were dealt with in Cadbury and in Greenbury. However, the emphasis of the Combined Code was slightly different and the aim was to consolidate previous views into a consensus on what constituted 'good' corporate governance. Under each main principle there was a list of provisions, giving details of how the Principles may be attained.

The impact of the Combined Code (and its predecessors) on UK company directors and institutional investors has been far-reaching, especially in the area of investor relations and shareholder activism. My own research into institutional investor attitudes toward corporate governance and accountability issues has highlighted the substantial effects that the process of corporate governance reform has had on institutional investor relations. Since 1992, corporate attitudes toward their core investors have been transformed from relative secrecy to greater transparency. Similarly, the attitudes of institutional investors have been transformed from relative apathy toward their investee companies' activities to an active interest. The impact of the Combined Code on UK companies and shareholders is considered in Chapters 4–6.

As was the case for Cadbury and Greenbury, the Hampel Report could also be seen as reactive rather than proactive, as further significant UK corporate failures arose from weak corporate governance structures between the publication of the Cadbury Report and the Hampel Report. One of these was the fall of a major UK bank, Barings, which created shock waves through the corporate and financial communities throughout the UK and, indeed, across the world. Corporate governance failure has, in hindsight, been blamed as the main cause for the company's collapse. The fall of Barings is summarized in Illustration 3.3. Read it to get a feel for the type of corporate governance problems that may arise in companies unless the necessary checks and balances are in place.

## Illustration 3.3

### The fall of Barings 1995

The case of Barings Bank is important as it highlights the importance of 'good' corporate governance in the banking sector in the same way as the Maxwell case in the publishing industry. You will probably recall that Nick Leeson, a young trader at Barings in Singapore, destroyed the company by losing more than $1 billion by unauthorized trading of futures contracts (a type of financial derivative). He took them out speculatively, but the Japanese market turned the opposite direction from that expected at the time. He was released from jail a few years ago and the film, *Rogue Trader* (based on a book by Leeson himself) was produced. The film covers the whole story leading to the downfall of Barings and gives a useful and interesting insight into the way in which derivatives trading happens. The film depicts Leeson as a young man, coming from a very different educational and social background from most employees at Barings. He was thrown into the Singapore market (SIMEX) with relatively little experience. He was given the *dual position* of General Manager and Head Trader, being in charge of the actual trading (on the stock exchange floor) and of the trading accounts. This was against generally accepted principles, as it gave him too much control – it is similar to the problems of the same person acting as chief executive and chairman of a company. Indeed, lack of segregation of these roles is seen as one of the main failings leading to the fall of Barings. In the film he was placed in a favourable light – almost as an innocent who became more and more entangled in financial problems, unable to tell anyone. However, it is unlikely that he was behaving as innocently as the film makes out. It seems he made no financial gains for himself, but the temptations of gambling on the stock market – not using his own funds – were irresistible. On his arrival in Singapore he set up an 'errors and omissions' account, number 88888, which would take any differences in trading balances at the end of the month. After a couple of mistakes by his similarly young and inadequately trained trading staff he tried to 'trade out' of the losses, using money from the bank's clients, so that he would not be in trouble for the losses incurred. Luckily, the first couple of times he managed to clear the losses in the bank's errors account (about a million pounds!) and made huge speculative profits over and over again. It is important at this point to realize that he was only allowed to trade for the bank's clients and not on the bank's own account. No one (except his secretary) knew that he was trading for the bank, using clients' money. Here there is a parallel between Leeson and Maxwell (see Illustration 3.1), as Maxwell was illegally using funds from the pension fund. His confidence soared as he did not seem to be able to lose on the many gambles he made on yen options.

Leeson then started to take bigger risks. A large French client wanted to buy options contracts on the yen for a ridiculously low price, and in order to keep the client Leeson made the deal. It resulted in a massive loss which he transferred to the secret errors account. The client left anyway and went to Société Générale in France – he was obviously playing brokers off against each other. This left Leeson in a very difficult position. He had acted illegally and now decided to cover his losses by trading on the bank's account, as before, but this time it did not work. He made huge unauthorized trades on the Nikkei 225 stock index using the 'mystery account'. He made loss after loss against the yen, following the Kobe Earthquake in Japan, which rocked the stock exchange. He could not make up the losses. He eventually ran up a debt in yen options of about 400 million dollars. He escaped to a holiday resort leaving a message for Barings' managers to close the losing position – but they did not and the losses increased to about £830 million by February 1995. He thought they would solve it and never considered the bank may collapse. The police picked him up at an airport in Germany as he was flying back to the UK. Although Nick Leeson behaved unethically, it was the bank itself that was chiefly to blame for allowing him to act in this way.

The bank's controls and monitoring procedures were insufficient. The management team in the UK seemed to have an unfounded confidence in their 'young star', and although they had the feeling there were problems they did not act to sort the situation out. They knew there was a very large client making huge losses and that Leeson was trading on the client's behalf with huge sums of money, but they did not realize that client 88888 was actually them! Leeson requested more and more funds from the UK London office to support his trading, but they believed he was covering margin payments for clients, not using the funds for his own trading. Still, if the bank had exercised the correct level of control, the situation could not have arisen. The *auditor* who visited was called back to London before she had finished the audit – so he escaped notice. There was a clear failure of the audit function. Although it was noted that he should not have been acting as manager of the trading floor as well as manager of the accounts, no moves were made to change this. The director in Singapore was keen on cost savings and did not want to pay out more salaries. Further, the director would not allow Leeson to have traders under him who were well qualified. He instead insisted that the staff were young and inexperienced and that Leeson could train them as they worked. This was another loophole in the system. By the time the London centre of Barings realized that there was a serious problem it was too late. The reasons for the fall of Barings and the Leeson affair can be summarized as:

- *On the part of Nick Leeson*: unethical behaviour, trading unlawfully.

- *On the part of Barings' senior management*: lack of segregation of Nick Leeson's duties; lack of supervision; lack of recognition of unusual profits; lack of understanding (London did simply not understand what happened in Singapore – the senior management did not understand the technicalities of derivatives trading); failure to conduct further investigations (audits not thorough enough and evident inefficiencies on the part of the auditor).

In a way we could say that Leeson was the scapegoat for Barings' lack of attention to detail. Although Leeson behaved unethically by trading without authorization and on the bank's account (absolutely against the rules) the bank was also much to blame for not having the internal control mechanism to constrain Leeson's activities. Since this affair (and others) there have been big moves to improve risk management within the banking sector. The corporate governance initiatives that have been adopted by companies in the UK to improve accountability and transparency have also been taken on by banks. Disclosure of risk-related information is immensely important for banks, as it is for other companies. Although we may not see the bank's 'lack of internal controls' as unethical behaviour, it is actually a *lack of responsible behaviour that is in itself unethical*. Therefore, the whole Leeson affair is not attributable solely to one individual's lack of ethics but to the corporate governance failure of the bank.

Not only did the Barings case focus attention on corporate governance reform in a general sense but, due to the specific nature of the case, attention was also channelled toward the area of risk management and internal control. As a result, the Turnbull Committee was formed which published a report at the end of the 1990s devoted entirely to these issues.

## The Turnbull Report 1999

The Combined Code (1998) dealt with internal control in Provisions D.2.1 and D.2.2. In these Provisions, the Code stated that company directors should conduct a review of the effectiveness of their internal control systems and should report this information to shareholders. The Turnbull Committee was established specifically to address the issue of internal control and to respond to these Provisions in the Combined Code. The report provided an overview of the systems of internal control in existence in UK companies and made clear recommendations for improvements, without taking a prescriptive approach. The Turnbull Report was revolutionary in terms of corporate governance reform. It represented an attempt to formalize an explicit framework for internal control in companies. Even though many other countries are now focusing attention on the systems of internal control and corporate risk disclosure within their listed companies, few have established a specific policy document or code of best practice dedicated to this issue. The USA, with its Treadway Commission (1987), paid attention to internal control, but the Turnbull Report has focused worldwide attention on this aspect of corporate governance. The Turnbull Report sought to provide an explicit frame of reference, against which companies and boards could model their individual systems of internal control. The framework was not meant to be prescriptive, given the problems of providing a common framework to companies in diverse industries that face an innumerable series of different risks and uncertainties. The aim was to provide companies with general guidance on how to develop and maintain their internal control systems and not to specify the details of such a system. The elements of the explicit framework for internal control presented by the Turnbull Report are examined in Chapter 6.

## The Higgs Report 2003

Although the Cadbury Report and the Hampel Report stimulated substantial improvements in corporate governance in UK listed companies, certain areas have been highlighted for further examination. The fall of Enron spurred the UK and other countries into re-evaluating corporate governance issues, such as the role and effectiveness of non-executive directors. As can be seen from the cases of Enron and Parmalat discussed in Chapter 2, the non-executive directors were ineffective in performing their corporate governance role of monitoring the company's directors and were subject to conflicts of interest. Even though the emphasis on non-executive directors in the UK has represented an improvement in UK corporate governance, the UK government post-Enron felt obliged to set up an enquiry to examine their effectiveness. My own research has detected an element of disillusionment with the effectiveness of non-executive directors as corporate monitors. One reason why non-executive directors are not fulfilling their potential is the difficulties of retaining their position. For example, one pension fund director I interviewed suggested that:

> There is a feeling that somebody ought to exercise constraint on boards. I don't think the system of non-executive directors is terribly successful. It is very difficult being a non-executive director because you actually have got to let the chief executive run the show – you cannot keep interfering, and that is the trouble. You don't want to interfere – you will get yourself voted out if you are too awkward.

The Higgs Report dealt specifically with the role and effectiveness of non-executive directors, making recommendations for changes to the Combined Code. The general recommendations included a greater proportion of non-executive directors on boards (at least half of the board) and more apt remuneration for non-executive directors. The report also concluded that stronger links needed to be established between non-executive directors and companies' principal shareholders. This would help to foster more effective monitoring of the notorious agency problem, as it would enhance the abilities of non-executive directors to represent shareholder interests and align the interests of shareholders and directors. One important practical recommendation of the Higgs Report was that one non-executive director should assume chief responsibility as a champion of shareholder interests. We return to the detailed implications and impact of the Higgs Report in Chapter 4.

## The Tyson Report 2003

The Tyson Report on the Recruitment and Development of Non-Executive Directors, published in June 2003, was commissioned by the Department of Trade & Industry (DTI) following the publication of the Higgs Review of the Role and Effectiveness of Non-Executive Directors in January 2003. The Higgs Report had called for a group to be created consisting of business leaders *inter alia*, who would examine ways in which companies could broaden the gene pool of board membership. As a result, the Department of Trade and Industry invited Dean Laura D'Andrea Tyson, from the London Business School, to chair the group. The resulting Tyson Report found that diversity in backgrounds, skills and experience of non-executive directors enhanced board effectiveness by bringing a wider range of knowledge and viewpoints to bear on issues relating to corporate performance, strategy and risk. Further, the report indicated that greater boardroom diversity improved relationships with corporate stakeholders, such as customers, employees and shareholders. These groups would welcome broader board membership as it should imply that boards would have a better understanding of stakeholder needs and their importance to corporate success. In these ways, the Tyson Report emphasized the need for stakeholder inclusion in corporate decision-making.

## The Smith Report 2003

As an accompaniment to the Higgs Report, another review was commissioned by the UK Government in response to the Enron scandal, *inter alia*, with the aim of examining the role of the audit committee in UK corporate governance. This Report was published in January 2003. The main issues dealt with in the Report concerned the relationship between the external auditor and the companies they audit, as well as the role and responsibilities of companies' audit committees. The creation of audit committees was a recommendation of the Cadbury Report and represented a clear means of monitoring company directors' activities. In the case of Enron, the failure of the audit committee and internal audit function were one of the principal causes of the company's collapse. Improvements in this area represent one way of keeping a check on the production of reliable and honest accounts. Nevertheless, some have suggested that the Report did not go far enough. It has been suggested that a more prescriptive approach would have been preferable, which would, for example, prevent auditing companies from offering other professional services, such as consultancy or IT services, to client companies that they audit. However, the Smith Report preserved the UK tradition of a principles-based approach, attempting not to create a 'one size fits all' set of rules for listed companies. This would be counterproductive as not all companies would be in a position to comply. The detailed recommendations of the Smith Report are discussed in Chapter 6. Further, in Chapter 6, we draw comparisons between the UK's approach to improving the audit function and that adopted by the USA through the Sarbanes–Oxley Act. ⟶

## Redraft of the Combined Code 2003

In July 2003 the Financial Reporting Council approved a new draft of the Combined Code, as intended from the Higgs Report in January 2003. It was referred to as 'the biggest shake-up of boardroom culture in more than a decade' (Tassell, 24 July 2003). Although the redrafted Code was not as prescriptive as Higgs' original recommendations, it retained much of the flavour of his concerns. Indeed, the redrafting was welcomed by both the corporate and institutional investment communities, despite their initial reactions to the Higgs Report. The revised Code in fact retained almost all of the 50 recommendations contained in Higgs' original report. The language, not the message, was altered. The main reforms of the new Code included the following:

- at least half the board of directors should comprise independent non-executive directors;

- a company's chief executive should not become chairman of the same company, except in exceptional circumstances;

- the board's chairman should be independent at appointment;

- a Senior Independent Director (SID) should be appointed to be available to the company's shareholders, if they have unresolved concerns;

- boards should undertake a formal and rigorous evaluation of their own performance, considering especially the performance and effectiveness of its committees and individual directors;

- institutional investors should avoid box ticking when assessing investee companies' corporate governance;

- companies should adopt rigorous, formal and transparent procedures when recruiting new directors;

- non-executive directors should only be reappointed after six years service, following 'a particularly rigorous review';

- non-executive directors can only continue after nine years' service following annual re-elections and should be considered no longer independent;

- boards should not agree to a full-time executive director accepting more than one non-executive directorship, or chairmanship, in a Top 100 company.

One of the main targets of the redrafted Code was to readdress executive remuneration, as the new version of the Code focused on forcing companies to avoid excessive remuneration which displayed little relation to corporate performance. The revised Code also placed an emphasis on shareholder activism as a means of furthering corporate accountability and transparency. The most up-to-date draft of the Combined Code is provided in Appendix A.

## Corporate Governance: A Practical Guide

This document was developed by the London Stock Exchange and RSM Robson Rhodes LLP (a leading firm of chartered accountants and business advisors) and was published on 24 August 2004. Its aim was to provide guidance on corporate governance issues for board members and other interested parties.

### Pension Scheme Governance – Fit for the 21st Century: A Discussion Paper from the National Association of Pension Funds (NAPF)

This NAPF discussion paper was published in July 2005. The paper issued from a review by the NAPF of the governance arrangements for pension schemes. The report concluded that there was no effective mechanism in place to represent the collective interests of the millions of pension scheme members after they enter their schemes. In other words, the report concluded there was a 'governance vacuum' in pensions governance. Consequently, the paper recommends the formation of three potential governance structures to fill this gap: a trust board, a Pensions Management Committee, or a Pensions Committee.

### Internal Control: Revised Guidance for Directors on the Combined Code

In 2004, the Financial Reporting Council (FRC) established the Turnbull Review Group to consider the impact of *'Internal control: Guidance for Directors on the Combined Code'* and to determine whether the guidance should be updated. As a result, *Internal Control: Revised Guidance for Directors on the Combined Code* was published by the FRC in October 2005. The review concluded that the substantial improvements in internal control initiated by application of the Turnbull framework had been achieved without the need for more prescriptive guidance. The comply or explain, principles-based approach seems to have been enough to set about genuine improvements in internal control. Overall, the review strongly recommended maintaining the flexible, principles-based approach of the original Turnbull Report (1999) and made only minor amendments. We consider these specific recommendations in Chapter 6.

### Consultation on Further Revision of the Combined Code

In January 2006, the FRC began consultation on the possibility of making a small number of changes to the Combined Code. This follows a review by the FRC of progress in implementing the 2003 Combined Code. Their report found that the Code was being adopted effectively and that significant changes were not necessary. The main areas where the FRC considered changes may be necessary are:

- relaxing the current guidance such that the company chairman may be allowed to sit on the remuneration committee;

- adding new provisions regarding companies including a 'vote withheld' box on AGM proxy voting forms;

- publishing the results of resolutions voted on a show of hands.

The consultation process closed on 21 April 2006. Any changes should be integrated into practice from 1 November 2006.

We now consider the regulatory environment within which the UK codes of practice have been introduced.

## Comply or explain

From the beginning of the process of corporate governance reform in the UK, a voluntary approach of 'comply or explain' has been chosen. This has been in keeping with the preferred approach of company law in the UK, which is one of self-regulation of the City of London financial institutions, as expressed in the Financial Services Act 1986 (Farrar and Hannigan, 1998). The Cadbury Report emphasized the importance of adopting an approach that encouraged compliance with a voluntary code of best practice. As we saw from our discussion of the reports above, this approach was preferred to a statutory code mainly because it would be more likely to develop a 'good' corporate governance culture within UK companies. They would be encouraged to comply in spirit rather than in letter (Cadbury Report, 1992, p. 12, para. 1.10). This is an approach that has continued to the present day. It is not, however, an approach that has been adopted at a global level. The choice by many countries to adopt a more legalistic and statutory approach to corporate governance reform rests in part on the legal framework already in place in the countries themselves. This is an important issue that has generated a wealth of theoretical and empirical literature in the finance field and one to which we will return in some depth in Chapter 7. However, there is also a cultural influence on the choice of regulatory environment. The USA, as discussed earlier, prefers a more regulated, rules-based environment. This UK/US dichotomy is an important issue that is highlighted throughout this book, wherever relevant. In the UK, companies disclose details of non-compliance and provide a general compliance statement. For example, the Corus annual report of 2001 provided the following information:

> The board believes that during the period it has complied with the provisions of the Code of Best Practice with the following exceptions: (i) The reduction of notice periods for directors to one year or less. (ii) Currently the roles of chairman and chief executive are combined. This is a temporary situation, arising as a result of the resignation of the joint chief executives in December 2000.

Looking at a more recent example, the comply or explain approach continues to result in detailed disclosures such as the following from BP's 2005 annual report:

> BP complied throughout 2005 with the provisions of the Combined Code Principles of Good Governance and Code of Best Practice, except in the following aspects:
>
> A.4.4  Letters of appointment do not set out fixed time commitments since the schedule of board and committee meetings is subject to change according to the exigencies of the business. All directors are expected to demonstrate their commitment to the work of the board on an ongoing basis. This is reviewed by the nomination committee in recommending candidates for annual re-election.

B.1.4  The amount of fees received by executive directors in respect of their service on outside boards is not disclosed since this information is not considered relevant to BP.

B.2.2  The remuneration of the chairman is fixed by the board as a whole (rather than the remuneration committee) within the limits set by shareholders, since the chairman's performance is a matter for the whole board.

(BP, 2005, p. 163)

There is, however, a lacuna perceived by investors in reporting on governance compliance. Instead of simply disclosing instances of non-compliance, shareholders feel that companies should be taking the opportunity to report the positive ways in which they are meeting the governance challenge (Independent Audit Limited, 2006). The new initiatives in the area of governance reporting are discussed in Chapter 6. Some companies are providing far more detail in their reports than before, on the ways in which they ensure they have good corporate governance. For example, in BP's 2005 report, there are more than five pages of narrative describing governance in BP and the role of the board. This disclosure covers issues such as: accountability to shareholders; how the board governs the company; accountability in the business; who sits on the board; directors' appointments; board independence; committees; and induction, training and evaluation of directors.

In 2001 the FSA assumed control of company oversight, taking over the powers of the stock exchange listing rules. The FSA is an umbrella organization with the heavy responsibility of overseeing the activities of companies and financial institutions. The FSA is essentially the 'City watchdog'. However, the key issue for legislators concerning the future direction of corporate governance reform is the extent to which civil sanctions, such as the imposition of fines and the removal of director status for a predetermined time, should be supplemented by a 'heavier stick', namely the imposition of criminal sanctions, such as a period of imprisonment.

## Applying the codes of practice to small companies

The Combined Code recognized that smaller listed companies may initially have difficulty in complying with some aspects of the Code. The boards of smaller listed companies who cannot, for the time being, comply with parts of the Code should note that they may instead give their reasons for non-compliance. However, the Hampel Committee also believed that full compliance by small companies would be beneficial. In particular, the appointment of appropriate non-executive directors should make a positive contribution to the development of their businesses. A report from the Department of Trade and Industry (DTI, 1999) entitled *Creating Quality Dialogue between Smaller Quoted Companies and Fund Managers* focused attention on the transferability of standards for 'good' corporate governance to smaller companies, especially the recommendations for better and more effective shareholder relationships.

The Generally Accepted Accounting Practice in the UK (GAAP, 2001) detailed the relevance of corporate governance for smaller quoted companies. The Cadbury Code made no distinction in its recommendations between larger and smaller listed companies. Hampel discussed whether a distinction should be made but concluded it should not, stressing that high standards of governance were as important for smaller listed companies as for larger ones. GAAP concluded that each company should be able to determine its corporate governance procedures in the best interests of the company. Smaller listed companies should not be forced to adopt corporate governance principles as this may be difficult for them. The Combined Code should not be prescriptive, but smaller quoted companies need to inform their shareholders of any ways in which they are not complying with the Code. Communication is the most important issue.

The Quoted Companies Alliance (QCA)[2] fights for the interests of thousands of companies that are not among the top 350 listed UK companies. It includes smaller companies, such as those in the Alternative Investment Market (AIM) and OFEX. In 2000 the Annual QCA Smaller Company Analyst Survey showed that the number of institutional investors prepared to invest in UK smaller quoted companies was declining for the second consecutive year. Improving corporate governance may be one way for smaller listed companies to attract more equity finance. This group prepared guidance in 1994 for smaller quoted companies aimed at identifying areas of the Cadbury Code that could prove difficult for smaller companies to implement. They suggested alternative recommendations that were more feasible. In April 2001 the QCA revised this guidance, providing alternative recommendations in the following areas: the role and number of non-executive directors, the constitution of audit committees, board meetings, the identification of a senior independent non-executive director, the size of the board and nomination committees. The QCA have recently produced an updated corporate governance guide for AIM companies and are preparing guidance for smaller quoted companies on how they should respond to demands to report in the operating and financial review (OFR) and now the Business Review.

## Ranking corporate governance initiatives

As we can see from our above discussion, a broad range of corporate governance initiatives have arisen from the corporate governance policy documents and codes. However, there is little evidence relating to the relative importance of these initiatives. Are they all of equal importance to investors, for example? Solomon et al. (2000a) provided some empirical evidence that attempted to rank the various initiatives. They examined which corporate governance initiatives were considered to be of most importance to UK institutional investors. Table 3.1 summarizes the results.

These results were obtained from a questionnaire survey sent to an extensive sample of UK institutional investors. The investors were asked the extent to which they agreed

[2] The QCA was formerly known as the City Group for Smaller Companies (CISCO).

**Table [3.1]**  Institutional investors' views on specific corporate governance initiatives

| Ranking | Initiatives | Average response |
|---------|-------------|------------------|
| 1 | Appointment of non-executive directors | Strong agreement |
| 2 | Splitting of chairman/chief executive roles | Strong agreement |
| 3 | Appointment of audit committees | Strong agreement |
| 4 | Removing rolling three-year contracts for executive directors | Strong agreement |
| 5 | Company directors who deliberately produce misleading information should be made personally liable for their actions | Strong agreement |
| 6 | Establishment of remuneration committees | Strong agreement |
| 7 | The role of the audit committee in policing negligence and fraud | Strong agreement |
| 8 | Restrictions on contract severance compensation for directors | Strong agreement |
| 9 | Increased voting rights for shareholders | Strong agreement |
| 10 | Increased disclosure of internal control mechanisms | Agreement |
| 11 | Training programmes for newly appointed executive directors | Agreement |
| 12 | Enhanced shareholder powers | Agreement |
| 13 | Declaration of voting policy by institutional investors | Agreement |
| 14 | Greater transparency in proxy voting by institutional investors, concerning share ownership declaration | Some agreement |
| 15 | Restrictions on executive directors' remuneration | Some disagreement |
| 16 | Limitations on proxy voting by institutional investors | Strong disagreement |

that each of the various initiatives had led to an improvement in corporate governance.[3] We can see that from the institutional investors' viewpoint, the appointment of non-executive directors was considered the most important and effective corporate governance initiative. Interestingly, this has been the target of the most recent review of corporate governance, the Higgs Report (2003), which endorses my research findings. In second place came the splitting of the chief executive and chairman role. These, from an agency theory perspective, represent effective ways of controlling the agents

---

[3]  The respondents selected a score from 1 (strongly disagree) to 7 (strongly agree).

and are therefore likely to be seen as important by shareh
investors themselves concerning their own role in corp
agreement as declaration of voting policy by ins
transparency in their voting, as well as limitations on ,
toward the end of Table 3.1. The institutional investors who resp
company management to be accountable, but were not as interested in
own accountability. This attitude has been reflected recently in calls by ind.
for institutional investors to 'practise what they preach' and become more au
encouraging corporate governance reform. Interestingly, those initiatives ranked ,
first, second and third place in Table 3.1 have been shown in practice to represent areas
where weaknesses can lead to corporate failure. The Enron and Parmalat cases
(presented in Chapter 2) involved serious flaws regarding the independence of non-
executive directors, power held at the top, and the audit function. Similarly, the Barings
case (see Illustration 3.3) displayed significant weaknesses in the areas of power
distribution and audit. Other recent cases of corporate failure, such as WorldCom, were
also attributable to weaknesses in the accounting and audit function. These findings
therefore show that investors are most concerned about these areas of corporate
governance, and with good cause.

## Why is good corporate governance important?

Policy makers, practitioners and theorists have adopted the general stance that
corporate governance reform is worth pursuing, supporting such initiatives as splitting
the role of chairman/chief executive, introducing non-executive directors to boards,
curbing excessive executive performance-related remuneration, improving institutional
investor relations, increasing the quality and quantity of corporate disclosure, *inter
alia*. However, is there really evidence to support these initiatives? Do they really
improve the effectiveness of corporations and their accountability? There are certainly
those who are opposed to the ongoing process of corporate governance reform. Many
company directors oppose the loss of individual decision-making power, which comes
from the presence of non-executive directors and independent directors on their boards.
They refute the growing pressure to communicate their strategies and policies to their
primary institutional investors. They consider that the many initiatives aimed at
'improving' corporate governance in the UK have simply slowed down decision
making and added an unnecessary level of bureaucracy and red tape. As an example,
read the short summary of Richard Branson's experiment with the stock market in
Illustration 3.4. Such concerns need to be noted and debated. The Cadbury Report
emphasized the importance of avoiding excessive control and recognized that no
system of control can completely eliminate the risk of fraud (such as in the case of
Maxwell, Illustration 3.1) without hindering companies' ability to compete in a free
market (Cadbury Report, 1992, p. 12, para. 1.9). This is an important point, because
human nature cannot be altered through regulation, checks and balances, as discussed
in previous chapters.

## Illustration 3.4

### Branson's flotation experiment in the 1980s

Richard Branson's affair with the accountability and corporate governance practices recommended by Cadbury was short-lived and tempestuous. Branson was the primary owner of his Virgin company from its creation. After some years, he was persuaded to gain a listing on the London Stock Exchange as this would provide him with valuable funds for his varied business ventures and endless new projects. However, the regular trips to the City of London to meet with institutional shareholders and discharge accountability to his shareholders cramped his style of business management. He withdrew from the stock market as soon as he could in the mid-1980s! He found that 'excessive' corporate governance hindered his decision making, slowing down his ability to 'make things happen'. For Branson, the problems of accountability to shareholders severely outweighed the benefits. Indeed, a common criticism wielded against corporate governance codes of practice and corporate governance reform in general is that it slows down decisions at company board level and makes running a company unnecessarily difficult, hindering innovation and creativity. These criticisms cannot be ignored. A balance needs to be achieved between accountability and transparency of operations and the ability of entrepreneurs to operate competitively and efficiently. However, Branson has once again been seduced by the City of London as he was considering floating a number of his Virgin firms raising as much as £2 billion in funds from shareholders in 2002.

Nevertheless, there is a growing perception in the financial markets that good corporate governance is associated with prosperous companies. My own research has provided some evidence to support the agenda for corporate governance reform. The findings indicated that the institutional investment community considered both company directors and institutional investors welcomed corporate governance reform, viewing the reform process as a 'help rather than a hindrance'. Specifically, the focus was on the attitudes of an extensive sample of UK unit trust fund managers toward corporate governance reform (see Solomon and Solomon, 1999). Table 3.2 provides the consensus of the institutional investors surveyed concerning corporate governance reform.

These findings endorse many of the issues discussed in this chapter relating to the agenda for corporate governance reform in the UK. They show, for example, that institutional investors agreed strongly with the Hampel view that corporate governance is as important for small companies as for larger ones. The results also indicated significant support from the institutional investment community for the continuance of a voluntary environment for corporate governance. The respondents' agreement that there should be further reform in their investee companies also added support to the ongoing reform process. Lastly, the institutional investors perceived a role for themselves in corporate governance reform, as they agreed that the institutional investment community should adopt a more activist stance. This is all encouraging. However, we now turn to the essential issue of whether improvements in corporate governance engender better corporate financial performance.

**Table [3.2]**  Institutional investors' attitudes toward corporate governance reform

| Rank | Statements | Average response |
|---|---|---|
| 1 | I believe that high standards of corporate governance are as important for smaller listed companies as for larger | Strong agreement |
| 2 | I believe that corporate governance reforms should remain within a voluntary framework | Agreement |
| 3 | I believe that institutional investors should adopt a more activist stance | Agreement |
| 4 | I believe that there should be further reforms in corporate governance in our investee companies | Agreement |
| 5 | I believe that the directors of our investee companies are presently overburdened with corporate governance reforms | Slight disagreement |
| 6 | I believe that corporate governance reforms are more of a hindrance than a help for UK company directors | Disagreement |
| 7 | I believe that corporate governance reforms should be regulated through Government | Disagreement |
| 8 | I believe that corporate governance reforms are more of a hindrance than a help for UK institutional investors | Strong disagreement |

## Corporate governance and corporate performance

The ultimate test of whether or not corporate governance reform is having a positive impact on UK industry is whether or not there is a positive relationship between corporate financial performance and corporate governance. There is growing academic evidence to indicate that there is a significant statistical relationship between bad corporate governance and poor corporate financial performance. Indeed, it has been shown that US companies with weaker corporate governance structures (indicated by substantial agency problems) perform less well than companies with better corporate governance structures (see, e.g., Core et al., 1999). Some institutional investors have taken on the role of 'corporate governance doctors' and have profited from it. Lens (an American investment institution) experimented with the link between corporate governance and corporate performance in its approach to institutional investment. Lens is a fund established by Robert Monks and Nell Minow in the USA. This fund was set up as a vehicle for collective action. The fund was invested in companies with acknowledged weak corporate governance structures. Using extensive shareholder activism, the investee companies have been forced to improve their internal corporate governance, which has resulted in substantial increases in share valuation. This has led to excess returns to portfolio investment, well above the average market indices. Lens uses a strategy of investing in a company's shares, then negotiating and effecting change within the company. The fund has targeted such companies as Sears and Eastman Kodak (see Monks and Minow, 2001, for a discussion of Lens' successes). Lens joined forces with a major UK institutional investor, Hermes, and established a similar fund in the European market, which has also succeeded in achieving excess returns.

A study by McKinsey & Company (2000) found that global investors were willing to pay a significant premium for companies which are well-governed. This was a salient finding as it indicates that the institutional investment community attaches a value to corporate governance and that corporate governance factors are therefore decision-useful. Similarly, a study by Harvard found that the best governed S&P 500 companies outperformed the worst governed by 8.5 % per annum between 1990 and 1999 (MacKenzie, 2004). Further, research by Deutsche Bank Securities found that investment in the FTSE 100's best governed companies would have produced 35 % higher returns than investment in the worst governed over a three year period.

Another recent study has examined the link between corporate governance and wealth creation by canvassing the views of company chairmen and finance directors on the purpose of corporate governance (Moxey, 2004). The survey also investigated their views about the influence of good practice on aspects of corporate effectiveness related to wealth creation, their opinions of the Combined Code and which aspects of corporate governance they considered were the most important. The results of this research were extremely mixed in terms of supporting the ongoing agenda for UK corporate governance reform. The canvassing revealed divergent views, with some directors seeing corporate governance as a time-consuming, wasteful exercise. Indeed, some directors felt that some aspects of corporate governance reform could harm the competitiveness of UK companies. Others did, however, link good corporate governance positively with wealth creation. The research raised probably more questions than answers. The primary outcome of the survey was to identify a need to adopt a more holistic approach towards corporate governance reform. Such an approach should help companies and their stakeholders to understand the links between accountability and performance, and to avoid viewing corporate governance as an exercise in box-ticking and compliance. The backlash to corporate governance has come from a number of quarters, where corporate governance reform has been questioned and criticised. See Illustration 3.5 for a commentary. However, it seems that criticisms of corporate governance reform arise mainly from the people whose behaviour is most likely to be altered as a result of the various initiatives, rather than those parties who will benefit from the reforms. Criticisms relate more to the pain of change than to a genuine belief that good corporate governance does not engender wealth creation.

**Illustration 3.5**

**Negative Views on Corporate Governance Reform**

As we saw from the attitude of Richard Branson (Illustration 3.4), not everyone is in favour of corporate governance reform. In the corporate community there is still a feeling that corporate governance mechanisms slow down decision-making and stifle entrepreneurship. A recent survey of company secretaries has revealed concerns that satisfying corporate governance codes and guidelines is limiting shareholder value (Burgess, 2006). The survey, conducted by KPMG and Lintstock found that companies were fairly unanimous in their view that their expenditure on corporate governance compliance was not adding much value for shareholders. Although companies felt their level of dialogue and engagement with institutional investors had improved, they were not convinced that this was actually adding value. They felt that their efforts to communicate more effectively with institutional investors were being wasted, as the information was not being read or analysed adequately.

Again, these arguments may be viewed from a risk perspective. Although companies may not feel corporate governance compliance is adding value for shareholders, the important issue is whether it is reducing the risks of potentially huge losses to shareholders. By putting careful mechanisms in place to control and monitor corporate governance, there should be less risk of corporate governance weaknesses and failures leading to corporate failure or financial distress. This view was acknowledged in the survey, as respondents did state that a discount would be associated with companies notable for having weak corporate governance.

## A risk perspective on corporate governance

As we can see from the previous section, there is some indication from practitioner evidence that improvements in corporate governance are linked to better financial performance. However, there is no conclusive, persuasive evidence from research that this is definitely the case. There is, nevertheless, a strong and more convincing negative relationship. It is now pretty much indisputable that there is a risk-related motivation for monitoring and improving corporate governance. In other words, weak corporate governance has been shown unequivocally to lead to financial losses.

As we saw in Chapter 2, extreme cases of corporate governance failure, such as Enron and Parmalat, are inarguably the cause of corporate failure. In less extreme cases, corporate governance weaknesses have led to reduced, less than optimal, financial performance. This risk-related motivation for corporate governance can be seen in the recent focus on improving internal control systems and risk management practices within companies in the UK and elsewhere. As we shall see in Chapter 6, the Enron debacle initiated Sarbanes–Oxley and the Smith Report, which focused heavily on the internal audit function and the role of audit committees in improving corporate governance.

## Corporate governance ratings

A variety of organizations have, over the last few years, taken it upon themselves to provide corporate governance ratings. This is partly inspired by institutional investor demand for quick and easy measurements of companies' corporate governance, which is comparable across international boundaries and between companies (see Van den Berghe and Levrau, 2004). There are similarities and differences among the wide range of rating systems now available to investors and other interested parties. Similarities include reference, by most, to international corporate governance guidelines such as those produced by the OECD (1999; 2004, see Chapter 7). According to an analysis performed by Van den Berghe and Levrau (2004), the main criteria used in rating systems appear to fall into three categories: (i) criteria used by (almost) all; (ii) criteria used by some, and; (iii) criteria used in exceptional cases. The first category includes the requirement for independent non-executive directors, the need for effective board committees and attention to executive remuneration. Category two includes limiting the maximum number of board members, and board leadership structure. Frequency of board meetings also falls into this category. In category three fall issues such as age limits on directors, board review and directors' training.

According to a survey by Mercer Investment Consulting (2006) more than half of investment managers worldwide believe that corporate governance is a material issue for the performance of individual assets. In other words, corporate governance factors can significantly impact on shareholder wealth. This means that neither company directors nor the institutional investment community can ignore key corporate governance issues. As we see in Chapter 10, institutional investors are now considering environmental, social and governance factors (ESG factors) in their investment decision-making.

# Chapter summary

In this chapter we have considered the development of policy documents and codes of practice for corporate governance in the UK, focusing on the work of the Cadbury Report, the Greenbury Report, the Hampel Report, the Turnbull Report, the Higgs Report and the Smith Report. However, complacency is not an option for companies. The proliferation of codes of practice and the close attention paid to UK corporate governance since 1992, does not mean that no more needs to be done. There are many dissenting voices, rallying against corporations and accusing them of making little genuine change in terms of accountability. Illustration 3.6 cameos corporate governance problems in the UK and examines inherent weaknesses in the UK system. Good corporate governance involves far more than adherence to codes of practice. It involves a clear mandate to encourage companies in their quest for greater accountability to their shareholders and other stakeholders. It is also important at this stage to note that corporate governance reform is not solely a UK issue but has taken centre stage in the international arena. Many countries around the world have followed in the footsteps of the Cadbury Committee and have developed corporate governance policy documents and codes of practice for 'good' corporate governance. Further, there have been several attempts to produce internationally acceptable standards of corporate governance at a global level, as we discuss in Part II. However, in the next chapter we turn to a discussion of the UK agenda for corporate governance reform in more detail, by examining the essential role played by boards of directors in corporate governance.

## Illustration 3.6

### A Critique of UK Corporate Governance Reform

Despite the proliferation of codes of practice and policy recommendations since 1992, which have targeted UK corporate governance, there are dissenting voices. An influential paper by Mitchell and Sikka (2005) has raised serious concerns about the genuine changes to corporate governance in practice. The authors have made it their business to act as a conscience for society and are adamant in their pursuit of corporate social responsibility. They characterize corporations as being,

> ...accountable to no one. Company executives play their selfish games, enriching a few and impoverishing many. Shareholders, employees and consumers are routinely ripped-off, sold worthless pensions, endowment mortgages and other financial products.
>
> (Mitchell and Sikka, 2005, p. 2)

They accuse companies of being,

> ...the playthings of their directors, bankers, accountants and lawyers and accountable to no one (p. 30)

Mitchell and Sikka (2005) believe that companies are failing to discharge a genuine accountability to society and are practising bad corporate governance, as follows:

(i) 'Chairman and CEOs determine their own remuneration, sitting on each other's remuneration committees as non-executive directors' and 'non-executive directors are the chums of company directors and don't bite the hand that feeds them' (p. 30)

(ii) Companies are avoiding tax, and are therefore reducing social investment by cheating the government out of billions of pounds of tax.

(iii) Companies are putting profits before people, despite their attempts to look socially responsible and caring.

(iv) Auditors are producing reports which 'are not worth the paper they are written on' (p. 26) and British accounting practices 'have more holes than Swiss Cheese' (p. 28)

(v) Individual shareholders do not have enough information, or political and economic resources necessary to hold corporate management accountable.

(vi) Institutional investors have the resources, but not enough interest, to become significantly involved in investee companies' corporate governance.

Their monograph represents a call to arms to force companies to improve corporate governance in a genuine way:

> The necessary precondition for good corporate governance is to invigorate the institutions of democracy, and this needs to be accompanied by reforms relating

to the governance of corporations and rights for all stakeholders to call
companies to account.

(Mitchell and Sikka, 2005, p. 2)

The authors of this evangelical work propose an agenda which involves educating
children and students through school and university in order to raise their awareness
of the need for social responsibility, ethical conduct, compassion, care for the
community and the environment. They conclude that,

Scandals, abuses and exploitation have now made the time ripe to bring
corporations under democratic control ... and to develop practical measures
based on independence, regulation, public accountability and democracy to
strengthen the public interest and rebalance power between the people and
the corporations. This should be the basis of a new social settlement which is
neither corporate chaos nor state control, but allowing companies and stakeholders to work in partnership for the benefit of each.

(p. 53)

## Questions for reflection and discussion

1   Analyse and debate the extent to which you consider the initiatives aimed at corporate
    governance reform in the UK represent an improvement to the system of corporate
    governance.

2   Read Illustration 3.4. Do you think that Richard Branson was right in his concerns
    that corporate governance reform slows down decision making and creates time-
    wasting, unnecessary bureaucracy?

3   How important do you think it is that the UK institutional investment community
    supports the agenda for corporate governance reform?

4   Do you agree with the view encapsulated in the Hampel Report that corporate
    governance reform is as important for smaller listed companies as for larger ones?

5   Discuss the critical view of corporate governance presented in Illustration 3.5. Do you
    agree with this point of view?

6   To what extent do you feel the views presented in Illustration 3.6 are realistic? Are the
    authors unnecessarily cynical? If not, do you feel change is possible? How would you
    suggest changes could be made?

## Chapter 4

# The role of boards in corporate governance

## Aim and objectives

This chapter examines the role of boards of directors in corporate governance, mainly from a UK perspective. The specific objectives of this chapter are to:

- explain the main initiatives introduced in the UK to improve the effectiveness of boards of directors;

- evaluate the impact of these initiatives on board function;

- discuss the findings of academic research relating to the effectiveness of boards as a corporate governance mechanism.

## Introduction: Enhancing Board Effectiveness

Chapter 3 discussed the series of UK policy documents and codes of practice aimed at reforming corporate governance, initiated by the Cadbury Report (1992). The primary emphasis of the Cadbury Report was on the need for boards of directors within listed companies to be effective. This was considered by the Cadbury Committee as being a quintessential ingredient determining the UK's competitive position. The Cadbury Report reviewed the structure of the board and the responsibilities of company directors, making recommendations for best practice. The report recommended that company boards should meet frequently and should monitor executive management.

For a company to be successful it must be well governed. A well-functioning and effective board of directors is the holy grail sought by every ambitious company. A company's board is its heart and as a heart it needs to be healthy, fit and carefully nurtured for the company to run effectively. Signs of fatigue, lack of energy, lack of interest and general ill health within the board's functioning require urgent attention. The free and accurate flow of information in and out of the board is as essential to the healthy operating of the corporate body as the free and unhindered flow of blood is to the healthy functioning of the human body.

A light-hearted approach to recommending the key characteristics of board effectiveness was adopted in *Corporate Governance: A Practical Guide* (2004). The guide summarized seven types of board in a circular diagram, in order to help boards identify whether they are successful and effective, or not. From the seven types, only one is an effective board demonstrating the following characteristics:

- clear strategy aligned to capabilities;

- vigorous implementation of strategy;

- key performance drivers monitored;

- effective risk management;

- sharp focus on views of City and other key stakeholders;

- regular evaluation of board performance.

The other six types of board were labelled, 'The Rubber Stamp', 'The Talking Shop', 'The Dreamers', 'The Adrenalin Groupies', 'The Number Crunchers' and 'The Semi-Detached'. It is easy to ascertain from these titles that boards falling into any of these six categories have got serious problems that they need to address!

An individual and interesting insight into board effectiveness was also presented in *The Fish Rots from the Head* (Garratt, 1996). Garratt drew on his experiences on company boards as well as his experience as an academic to highlight problems within boards and make recommendations for corporate governance improvements in this essential area. One criticism he made was that boards spent too much time 'managing' (being professional managers) and insufficient time 'directing'. He defined 'directing' as showing the way ahead and providing leadership.

There are numerous ways in which the effectiveness of the direction provided by a company's board can be improved. Below, we consider the many initiatives that have been recommended in order to ensure board effectiveness.

## Unitary and two-tier board structures

Boards fall into two general models, a unitary board or a two-tier board. Unitary boards tend to be the most common form, especially in countries which have been influenced by the Anglo-Saxon style of corporate governance. Unitary boards include both executive and non-executive directors and tend to make decisions as a unified group. On the other hand, two-tier boards have two separate boards, a management board and a supervisory board. The management board generally includes only executives, focuses on operational issues of major importance and is headed by the chief executive. The supervisory board deals with other strategic decisions and oversees the management board. The chairman of the company sits on the supervisory board as a non-executive. Supervisory boards consist exclusively of non-executive directors. The supervisory board is often used as a vehicle for introducing diverse stakeholder groups into corporate governance, by including representatives on the board, such as employees or environmental consultants. This is an area where two-tier boards provide a much greater opportunity for stakeholder inclusivity than unitary boards. Two-tier boards are, however, only effective where there is an effective relationship between the chief executive, heading the management board, and the chairman, heading the supervisory board.

## Splitting the role of chairman and chief executive

The Cadbury Report recommended that there should be a balance of power between board members such that no individual could gain 'unfettered' control of the decision-making process. Further, there should be a clear division of responsibility at the top of the company, ensuring this balance of power and authority. The Cadbury Report stipulated that if the roles of chairman and chief executive were not filled by two individuals, then a senior member of the board should be present who was independent. In 2003 the Higgs Report re-emphasized the importance of splitting the chairman and chief executive roles in UK listed companies. Higgs stated that, as a result of the Cadbury recommendations, approximately 90 % of listed companies had actually split the roles of chairman and chief executive at the time of his report. This was indicative of Cadbury's lasting impact on the UK corporate community. However, Higgs recommended a change from Provision A.2.1 in the Combined Code which stipulated that:

> A decision to combine the posts of chairman and chief executive officer in one person should be publicly justified.
>
> (The Combined Code, 1998, p. 14)

to the far more rigorous version:

> The roles of chairman and chief executive should not be exercised by the same individual.
>
> (Suggested revisions to the Combined Code, 1998, Annex A of the Higgs Report, 2003, p. 80)

The essence of these recommendations, among others made by Higgs, was incorporated in the Combined Code in July 2003.

The importance of splitting the roles of chairman and chief executive derives from the extremely different functions which someone in each of these positions should carry out. The essential role of the chairman in ensuring board effectiveness cannot be overstated. As stated in *Corporate Governance: A Practical Guide* (2004), the chairman has a pivotal role to play in helping the board to achieve its potential, being responsible for leading the board, setting the board agenda and ensuring its effectiveness. According to Parker

(1990), the intangible quality of personal leadership issuing from the chairman is the most important factor in achieving board effectiveness. Cadbury (2002) drew an analogy between the chairman of a board and the conductor of an orchestra. However good an orchestra is, and however brilliant the individual players, it is the conductor who brings them together, leads them, sets the pace and highlights their individual prowess against the backdrop of the whole team of players. We now look at evidence from the academic literature relating to the importance of these initiatives for effective corporate governance.

## Research into split roles

According to the academic literature, splitting the role of chairman and chief executive is a corporate governance initiative that can reduce agency problems and result in improved corporate performance because of more independent decision making (Donaldson and Davies, 1994). In Chapter 1, we considered that agency problems could be lessened by mechanisms that aided monitoring of boards in order to align shareholder and management interests. Some studies have shown that splitting the role has indeed led to significantly higher financial performance (Peel and O'Donnell, 1995). However, it has been suggested that such improvements may be a case of wishful thinking and that the evidence is not persuasive enough to engender splitting the roles in practice (Daily and Dalton, 1997).

One area of the academic literature has focused on the relationship between top management turnover, corporate financial performance and the introduction of corporate governance initiatives, such as split roles into companies. In such studies, top management turnover has been used as a proxy for corporate governance quality, as a well-governed company is considered likely to remove ineffectual directors before they can do harm. A company with 'good' corporate governance mechanisms, such as split roles or an optimal balance of executive and non-executive directors, is likely to display more effective monitoring of management. However, high turnover of directors may not always involve replacing poor managers with better ones. There may be ulterior motives behind such replacements, which do not result in better people on the board. Nevertheless, if 'good' managers replace 'bad' ones, then we would assume that companies with higher top management turnover, better corporate governance mechanisms and more effective board members would display superior financial performance. Basing their analysis on these assumptions, Dahya et al. (2002) found that top management turnover was higher after Cadbury than before, but only in companies that had altered their board structure as a result of Cadbury. They also found that higher turnover of top management was statistically related to poorer financial performance, for an extensive sample of UK companies around the time of the Cadbury Report. They therefore deduced that:

> These results indicate that the increase in CEO turnover is not random; rather it is (inversely) correlated with performance: After controlling for performance, the likelihood

that the CEO will depart his position is greater once a poorly performing firm comes into compliance with the key provisions of the Code. *The answer to the question of whether the 'right' managers are leaving the firms appears to be yes*, assuming, of course, that our measures of performance properly identify the right managers.

(Dahya et al., 2002, p. 478, emphasis added)

These results provide a powerful mandate for corporate governance reform in the UK, as they endorse the positive impact of the chief Cadbury recommendations.

In the USA, boards of directors have been harshly criticized for not attaining a balance of power and therefore reducing board effectiveness. The board culture in the USA is considered to discourage conflict. This implies that the CEO (usually also the company chairman) wields excessive power and has ultimate control over decision making. Further, it is typical that US boards are excessively large, also reducing board effectiveness (see Jensen, 1993). Indeed, statistical evidence has shown that corporate performance and value were a decreasing function of board size (Yermack, 1996). For most companies, the CEO and chairman tend to be the same person. There is an emerging consensus opposing this practice, as expressed in the following statement:

Some of the Sarbanes–Oxley rules for bosses and directors may be too cumbersome or prescriptive ... A more useful idea is a toughening of checks and balances for bosses. Best of all, *American companies should adopt the common European practice of separating the jobs of chairman and chief executive, entrenching a check at the heart of their corporate governance systems.*

(*The Economist*, 28 November 2002, emphasis added)

This is one area of corporate governance where the UK is significantly more proactive than the USA, although senior independent directors substitute for split roles to some extent on American boards. However, gradually things are changing, as can be seen from Illustration 4.1 on Walt Disney's change of heart.

### Illustration 4.1

#### A Triumph for Shareholder Activism: Split Roles at Disney

Although UK companies have generally institutionalized split roles for their chairmen and chief executives, as a result of corporate governance reform, the US has been slower to initiate change in this area. However, change is on its way. In January 2005, Walt Disney made the separation of its chairman and chief executive roles (Parkes, 2005). Michael Eisner had held both positions since 1984. George Mitchell replaced him as chairman as a result of institutional investor activism in the March 2004 annual general meeting. However, the company only decided to make the split roles permanent in 2005. Following an institutional investor revolt in March 2004, over the company's corporate governance, the board of directors felt this was a necessary reform. The change was deemed a significant victory for shareholders.

# The role of non-executive directors in corporate governance

As we saw from the case study in Chapter 2, the collapse of Enron during 2001 focused attention on the effectiveness of the non-executive director function. The Higgs Report (2003) in the UK, and the related Tyson Report, were clearly knee-jerk responses to the considerable impact of ineffective non-executive directors in such companies as Enron. From an agency theory perspective, the presence of independent non-executive directors (frequently referred to as NEDs) on company boards, should help to reduce the notorious conflicts of interest between shareholders and company management, as they perform a monitoring function by introducing an independent voice to the boardroom. However, it needs to be borne in mind that inside directors have an essential role to play in achieving the appropriate balance between outside and inside directors on boards, which is an essential ingredient for an effective board, as:

> The inside directors provide valuable information about the firm's activities, while outside directors may contribute both expertise and objectivity in evaluating the managers' decisions. The corporate board, with its mix of expertise, independence, and legal power, is a potentially powerful governance mechanism.
>
> (Byrd and Hickman, 1992, p. 196)

The Tyson Report specified that the role of a non-executive director was to:

- provide advice and direction to a company's management in the development and evaluation of its strategy;
- monitor the company's management in strategy implementation and performance;
- monitor the company's legal and ethical performance;
- monitor the veracity and adequacy of the financial and other company information provided to investors and other stakeholders;
- assume responsibility for appointing, evaluating and, where necessary, removing senior management; and
- plan succession for top management positions.

However, the Higgs Report emphasized that non-executive directors needed to have more than simply the experience and ability necessary to perform these functions. The report stipulated that non-executive directors also needed to have integrity and high ethical standards, sound judgement, the ability and willingness to challenge and probe on issues, as well as strong interpersonal skills. Indeed, the search for an ideal non-executive director should include '*no crooks, no cronies, no cowards*'![1]

---

[1] This phrase was suggested for the selection of non-executive directors by the Aviva Chairman, Pehr Gyllenhammar, as quoted in the Tyson Report (2003, p. 5).

Another issue, discussed in Spira and Bender (2004), is the acknowledged tension between the strategic and monitoring roles which non-executive directors are expected to play in boardrooms. In other words, how do non-executive directors balance their need to monitor insider directors, at the same time contributing to corporate strategy?[2] It is essential that they attain this balance in order to be effective.

The Cadbury Report recommended that the board of directors should include a minimum of three non-executive directors who are able to influence the board's decisions. It stipulated that non-executive directors should provide an independent view on corporate strategy, performance, resources, appointments and standards of conduct. Further, the majority of non-executive directors should be independent of management and free from any relationship that could affect their independence (except their fees and shareholdings). Indeed, the Report stated that at least two of the minimum requirement of three non-executive directors should be independent. Several ways of ensuring the independence of non-executive directors have been suggested. For example, the Cadbury Report discussed the fees payable to non-executive directors, stipulating that a balance needed to be struck between recognizing the value of the contribution made by non-executive directors and avoiding compromising their independence. Another way was to encourage non-executive directors not to take part in share option schemes as this could also compromise their independence. The Cadbury Report also stressed that the appointment of non-executive directors was an important decision that should be taken via a formal selection process (using a nomination committee), again strengthening their independence. As well as the problem of independence, the Cadbury Report aired concerns about the supply of adequately qualified non-executive directors. This is an issue which has become increasingly problematic as more non-executive directors have been deemed necessary on boards.

The Hampel Report (1998) readdressed the role of non-executive directors but did not increase the desirable number of non-executives on the board. The balance of non-executive and executive directors recommended by the accompanying Combined Code (1998) remained unchanged from the number suggested in the earlier Cadbury Code. Both Codes stipulated that non-executive directors should comprise not less than one-third of the board. Indeed, it seems that the comments made in the Hampel Report, pertaining to the 'excessive' emphasis placed on the monitoring role of non-executive directors, was misguided. Specifically, the Report noted that:

> An unintended side effect has been to overemphasise the monitoring role [of non-executive directors].
>
> (The Hampel Report, 1998, p. 25, para. 3.7)

Such cases as Enron and Parmalat have underlined the dangers of an ineffective group of non-executive directors and the severe problems that can arise when their independence is compromised through conflicts of interest (see Chapter 2).

---

[2] This issue is also analysed in Ezzamel and Watson (1997) and Stiles and Taylor (2001).

In April 2002 Patricia Hewitt, the UK Secretary of State, and Gordon Brown, the Chancellor of the Exchequer, commissioned Derek Higgs to prepare a review on the role of independent directors. This represented the UK equivalent of the Sarbanes–Oxley Act (2002), as it provided a response to the problems highlighted by Enron. The consultation document was published in June 2002 and requested responses from interested parties (such as the Stock Exchange, major institutional investors, the Institute of Directors). The terms of reference for the Higgs Review were set out in this consultation document. They specified that the objective of the review was to provide a short, independent investigation into the role and effectiveness of non-executive directors in the UK. The terms of reference also stated that, from the perspective of UK productivity performance, progressive strengthening of the quality and role of non-executive directors was strongly desirable. The terms of reference specified that the review should:

- provide a picture of the population of non-executive directors in the UK at that time, focusing on who the non-executive directors were, how they were appointed and how a broader pool of prospective non-executive directors may be found;

- assess the extent to which the non-executive directors were 'independent' in practice;

- assess the effectiveness of non-executive directors in UK listed companies;

- assess the accountability of non-executive directors (i.e., their actual and potential relationship with institutional investors);

- assess a variety of issues relating to non-executive directors' remuneration;

- most importantly, proffer appropriate recommendations for strengthening the quality, independence and effectiveness of non-executive directors.

Lastly, the terms of reference stated that the review should:

- build and publish an accurate image of the status quo relating to non-executive directors;

- lead debate on non-executive director-related issues;

- make appropriate recommendations to the Government, or other relevant parties.

In keeping with the typical UK approach to corporate governance reform, we can see from the Higgs consultation document that the Government intended to maintain a voluntary environment in the area of non-executive directors, avoiding regulation or legislation. The Government considered (in the terms of reference) that they required someone who was a leading figure in the City of London and who would provide an independent assessment of the current role and effectiveness of non-executive directors in UK listed companies. *The Economist*'s description of the man selected for the job was entertaining and evocative:

Except that he is a devoted reader of the left-leaning *Guardian* newspaper, Derek Higgs is a typical member of the City of London elite. As astute deal-maker at the Warburg investment bank, an engaging dinner companion and comfortably rich, ... The sort of chap that British governments down the years have got to run committees to defuse political bombs with some sensible proposals ... If, as has been suggested this week, ministers are worried that he 'has not come up with anything radical enough', the surprise is that they expected anything else.

*(The Economist*, 31 October 2002)

However, the final Higgs Report was published on 20 January 2003 and, contrary to expectations such as those expressed in the above quotation, it delivered some quite 'radical' suggestions. The full text can be viewed on the Department of Trade & Industry (DTI) website. Higgs' review was based on three pieces of primary research, specifically:[3]

- data on the size, composition and membership of boards and committees in the 2,200 UK listed companies, as well as the age and gender of their directors;

- a survey of 605 executive directors, non-executive directors and chairmen of UK listed companies conducted by MORI (the national polling agency) in August 2002;

- interviews of 40 directors in top UK listed companies carried out by academics in the field.[4]

First and foremost the Higgs Report recommended that at least half of a company's board of directors should be independent non-executive directors. This is a definitive development from the earlier codes of practice and one that conflicts with the Hampel Report's suggestion that the monitoring role of non-executive directors had been 'overemphasized'. He considered non-executive directors needed all the support possible to ensure they perform their role effectively and called for more non-executive director training. In many quarters this call was answered by discontent, as we can see from Illustration 4.2.

## Illustration 4.2

### Educating NEDs

Cranfield School of Management and Henley Management College both offer training programmes for non-executive directors. However, despite calls from Derek Higgs for greater provision of training for non-executive directors (NEDs) both colleges are finding it difficult to fill their courses. Indeed, Cranfield had to cancel their two-day training seminar on the responsibilities of NEDs three times due to insufficient demand. Similarly, Henley abandoned a similar course for similar reasons. One reason certainly seems to be a feeling among board members that NEDs have no need for training. They are ready for

[3] The data were supplied to the Higgs Committee by Hemscott Group Limited.
[4] They were Dr Terry McNulty (University of Leeds), Dr John Roberts and Dr Philip Stiles (both of the University of Cambridge).

the job in hand and have the adequate experience already. Forcing them to take courses and attend training sessions may simply be a time-wasting exercise, detracting from their main aim of serving on company boards. This attitude does, however, display a certain level of arrogance. To what extent can anyone ever claim to know everything about what they do? There is always more to learn. Some research findings have led some to the conclusion that the way NEDs are appointed represents the 'last Bastion of great British managerial amateurism' (Maitland, 2003). Such amateurism is a thing of the past in most areas of business today, as top management tend to be trained better than they have ever been. NEDs need just as much encouragement to take courses and receive training as anyone else with an important, responsible role to play in business. Certainly, another of Higgs' recommendations, to 'widen the gene pool' of NEDs, will be hard to meet unless adequate training is available and the encouragement to attend courses exists.

Another section of the Higgs Report was devoted to relationships with shareholders and contained a number of far-reaching (and controversial) recommendations, emphasizing that:

The role of the non-executive director includes an important and inescapable relationship with shareholders.

(Higgs Report, 2003, p. 67, para. 15.1)

This aspect of the Higgs Report made probably the most advanced and progressive recommendations, as he encouraged the linkage of two essential corporate governance mechanisms, namely the role of non-executive directors and the role of institutional investors. Such a linkage should be synergistic, as the combination of the two mechanisms should result in a much stronger monitoring instrument than when they function separately. The report recommended that one (or several) non-executive director(s) should take direct responsibility for shareholder concerns, effectively championing shareholder interests at board level. A related recommendation from the Higgs Report was for this senior non-executive director to attend regular meetings with the company's shareholders and for non-executive directors to be more closely involved with the process of shareholder engagement, which is continually evolving between companies and their core institutional investors. Clearly, this is another way of augmenting the monitoring role of both non-executive directors and institutional investors. This recommendation arose from the impression that these two groups were operating separately and that they were missing an opportunity to strengthen their effectiveness by combining forces, as:

...only rarely do non-executive directors hear at first hand the views of major shareholders.

(Higgs Report, 2003, p. 67, para. 15.5)

As soon as the Higgs Report was published there was a strong reaction from some members of the business community, specifically in relation to this recommendation. A senior representative from the Confederation of British Industry (CBI) was clearly concerned about potential conflicts of interest that may arise from this recommendation, when he commented that:

> This could lead to multiple splits in the board which every man and wife could come along and exploit. And that would be a madhouse.
>
> (Tassell et al., 2003, p. 1)

Adverse reaction to the Report seemed to be widespread throughout the business community, with Higgs' calls for greater accountability viewed as an infringement on company operations. For example, a poll of company directors in the Top 30 listed companies, immediately after the publication of the Report, indicated that the majority viewed this recommendation as potentially divisive and destructive in the boardroom (Tassell, 31 January 2003).

Another weighty recommendation in the Higgs Report was that executives should be indemnified against defending themselves from legal action by their own company. This recommendation also received an immediate negative response from insurance brokers who predicted a possible increase in insurance fees of 50 % following its adoption (Tassell et al., 2003). However, from my own research involving interviews with institutional investors, this recommendation has inspired little confidence. There was a general attitude among people interviewed that such insurance would represent a waste of resources as it would simply involve executives insuring themselves against events that would never transpire.

There was also a call in the Higgs Report for modest pay rises for non-executive directors to reflect their growing range of responsibilities. The report stated that non-executive directors in the FTSE 100 companies were earning on average £ 44,000 per annum whereas those in companies outside the FTSE 350 were earning an average of £ 23,000 per annum. 'Low' levels of pay (in relation to the responsibilities and workload of non-executive directors) were cited by Higgs as a chief reason why the task of recruiting non-executive directors of sufficient calibre had become onerous. Indeed, the Higgs Report indicated that there was no evidence of a 'magic circle' of non-executive directors, with boards controlled by a few individuals. Recent research has shown that only 95 directors of the 2,800 in the FTSE 350 held two or more posts on boards (Tassell et al., 2003).

The independence of the majority of non-executive directors on a board, introduced by the Cadbury Report, was re-emphasized by the Higgs Report, which sought to develop the Combined Code definition of independence to encompass the following general statement, accompanied by a detailed list of requirements:

> A non-executive director is considered independent when the board determines that the director is independent in character and judgement and there are no relationships or circumstances which could affect, or appear to affect, the director's judgement.
>
> (Higgs Report, 2003, p. 37)

This is a further example of the far-reaching and ambitious nature of the Higgs review. It seems that, although the Higgs Report was conducted partly in response to such corporate governance failures as Enron and was therefore partly reactive in nature, the recommendations contained in Higgs were far-reaching and therefore more proactive than its predecessors. This was probably the reason why the Report caused such a stir in UK companies! In other words, whereas previous corporate governance reports and codes caused systems that were already implicit in UK listed companies to become explicit, the Higgs Report made recommendations for change that were not based solely on the existing, implicit framework of UK corporate governance. Generally, policy recommendations that require changes to the status quo are likely to meet with opposition, as they seek to transform people's attitudes.[5] Illustration 4.3 provides a cameo of some of the initial reactions to the Higgs Report, which demonstrated that the status quo within the City was being threatened.

---

### Illustration 4.3

### Initial reactions to Higgs

The Higgs Report was published in January 2003. Higgs was invited by the Government to review the role and effectiveness of non-executive directors in UK corporate governance. From an agency theory perspective, the function of non-executive directors is to monitor company directors in order to improve their accountability to the company's shareholders and align the interests of these two groups.

*Reactions from the corporate community*

There was an immediate adverse reaction to the report within the business community, with Higgs' calls for greater accountability being viewed as an infringement on company operations. A poll of company directors in the top 30 listed companies, immediately after the introduction of the Report, showed they saw some recommendations as potentially divisive and destructive in the boardroom (Tassell, 31 January 2003). The aspect of Higgs that caused the greatest stir was the recommendation that there should be a senior independent director (a SID) to champion shareholder interests. Accompanying this concept was the suggestion that this shareholder-friendly non-executive director should attend the meetings between executives and their institutional investors. Higgs considered that non-executive directors should be more closely involved in the engagement process and that their monitoring role would be enhanced through greater contact with core investors. Fears that this could be divisive represent exactly the executive attitudes that Higgs sought to change. Resistance to such recommendations highlights a lack of alignment between executives and their shareholders at the heart of corporate decision making, which is reminiscent of an agency problem. If more shareholder representation is seen as divisive, this could be a sign that directors are still far away in their objectives from their shareholders.

The recommendation by Higgs that the nomination committee of the board should be chaired by a SID rather than the chairman also sparked fiery corporate opposition. This was clearly a radical monitoring device that would prevent cronyism

---

[5]   See Solomon and Solomon (2000) for a discussion of conceptual frameworks that may or may not challenge the status quo.

in appointments. Representatives from both the CBI and the Institute of Directors (ID) expressed serious concerns that this and other recommendations could be divisive. Again, if there were no agency problems inherent in businesses, this type of knee-jerk reaction would be less likely.

Another recommendation of the Higgs Report was that the largest UK listed companies should not appoint retiring chief executives as chairmen, as this could encourage boardroom complacency. Companies generally ignored this recommendation, with John Sainsbury being an outstanding example in their appointment of Sir Peter Davis in March 2003 (Flanagan, 2003). However, the director of the voting agency, Manifest, considered that removing Sir Peter, at the same time as the chairman was retiring, would create too much instability in the company. There are clearly two sides to this, and even the institutional shareholders were not in favour of Higgs' recommendations in this case (Tassell and Voyle, 2003). There was, however, suspicion in the press that chairmen of Top 100 companies who criticized Higgs' recommendations had not actually read the Report (Plender, 16 March 2003). Such apathy and complacency are symptomatic of an inherent corporate governance problem.

### Reactions from institutional investors

Surprisingly, it was not just the corporate community that reacted against Higgs' recommendations, even though his intentions were clearly to improve corporate accountability to shareholders. Strong reactions to the recommendations of the Higgs Report from the institutional investor community were voiced at the conference of one of the largest investor groups, the National Association of Pension Funds (NAPF), in Edinburgh in March 2003. Pension fund managers and pension fund trustees, who together represent the weight of the institutional investors community in the UK, expressed their opposition to one of Higgs' recommendations that at least half the board of a company should comprise independent non-executive directors, as 40 % of the conference delegates voted against it (Tassell, 14 March 2003a). The head of investment of another large investor group, the Association of British Insurers (ABI), considered that without a 'critical mass of support' the revisions to the Combined Code suggested by the Higgs Report would not be advisable. Qualifying this, he commented that, although the 'comply or explain' approach to corporate governance reform provided a solid basis for change, it would become impotent without a critical mass of support. Companies would simply 'comply or do nothing!' This accompanied Higgs' own concerns, also voiced at the conference, that companies would either 'comply or breach' or 'comply and have their trousers taken down in the press'! (Tassell, 14 March 2003b).

Clearly, the initial reactions to Higgs' recommendations were strong and varied, coming from both the corporate and the institutional investor community. The amount of discussion and the level of dissatisfaction were considerable. But change is never easy: no pain no gain. Accountability will only improve if changes are made.

Another recommendation of the Higgs Report was to widen the 'gene pool' from which non-executive directors were selected. This suggestion was taken up in the Tyson Report, published later in 2003. The Tyson Report explored how greater diversity in the boardroom, in terms of background, skills, experience of members, could lead to better relationships with stakeholders and improved board effectiveness.

Possible sources of non-executive director recruitment considered by the Tyson Report included candidates from unlisted companies, private equity firms, business services and consultancies, organizations in the non-commercial sector and the layer of corporate management just below board level, known as the '*marzipan layer*'. The Higgs Report had found that the majority of non-executive directors were white, middle-aged males of British origin, with previous director experience in listed companies ('male, pale and stale', as described in Garratt, 2005, p. 123). However, the emerging literature suggests this is not an optimal situation for boards. Boardroom diversity is increasingly viewed as valuable to board effectiveness, according to the academic literature (Milliken and Martins, 1996; Conger and Lawler, 2001). Indeed, the Tyson Report heralded the need to employ more transparent and more rigorous searches for non-executive directors in order to enhance board talent and effectiveness. Consequently, this would also foster greater diversity in knowledge, skills, experience, gender, race, nationality and age of non-executive directors.

The Tyson Report stressed that widening boardroom diversity would help companies improve their reputation by engendering trust among their stakeholders. The diverse constituencies underpinning corporate activity would be likely to be more confident in a company whose board was more representative of broader groups with broader knowledge and understanding. For example, social and environmental lobby groups would have greater confidence in a company with a non-executive director whose background was in environmental regulation or human resource management. The Tyson Report does, however, stress that in casting a wider net, companies have to consider their individual size, age, customers, employees, international involvement and strategies. In other, words, there was no optimum formula for appointing non-executive directors. Each company would have its own specific, individual optimal profile for non-executive board membership. The Tyson Report also identified a number of constraints on creating more diverse boards. These included board size, existing board membership, growing responsibilities and liabilities facing non-executive directors and the potential conflict between independence and non-executive remuneration. See Illustration 4.4 for a discussion of Race for Opportunity's activities. This group is lobbying companies regarding ethnic diversity in boardrooms, on a business case argument.

## Illustration 4.4

### Race for Opportunity

Race for Opportunity is a UK network of private and public sector organizations whose aim is to promote the business case for race and diversity. They challenge organizations to improve diversity by focusing on the following issues:

- employment of ethnic minorities;
- marketing to ethnic minorities;
- engaging ethnic minority business and supply chains and as business partners;
- including ethnic minority individuals and communities in their activities.

The business case argument employed by Race for Opportunity rests on evidence that a significant and growing proportion of the UK's population consists of ethnic minorities, of whom almost a half are under 25 years of age. Furthermore, 12 % of university graduates are from ethnic minorities. Not only can UK businesses employ high quality employees from ethnic minorities but also they need to be targeting these groups in their strategic marketing and reputation enhancement. This, the group argues, will lead to better financial performance in the long run. Indeed, the emerging view is that failure to deal with inequality within organizations in the UK could seriously damage the economy.

Race for Opportunity produced a Benchmarking Report (RfO, 2004) which benchmarked the performance of UK organizations on race.

The survey produced a list of top performers on the basis of self-assessment, evidence provided by the organizations, interviews and site visits. 113 organizations completed the survey. The top performers were:

*Private Sector*

1. BT

2. Lloyds TSB Group

3. West Bromwich Building Society

4. HSBC Bank

5. HBOS

6. Barclays Bank

7. B & Q

8. McDonald's Restaurants

9. Britannia Group

10. Ford Motor Company

*Public Sector*

1. The Army

2. Department of Trade and Industry

3. Royal Air Force

4. Department for Work and Pensions

5. West Midlands Police

6. Royal Navy

7. Ministry of Defence

8. Inland Revenue

9. Devon Fire and Rescue

10. Middlesex University

The report concluded that progress is being made, with more ethnic minority people progressing to senior positions than in past surveys. 65 % of the respondents to the survey said that their work on diversity was good for brand reputation, supporting the business case. Further, 43 % of respondents said that their marketing and race diversity actions had had a measurable impact on their bottom line.

The Tyson Report also recommended training programmes for all board members, but especially for non-executive directors. All newly-appointed non-executive directors should undergo thorough induction programmes. Training should also be available to incumbent non-executive directors (see Illustration 4.2 for further discussion).

There has been some criticism of the Higgs Report in the corporate governance literature. It has been suggested that the Higgs Report fell far short of the Cadbury Report, in that it did not call for a broad consultation process and the author of the final report was one person (Higgs) rather than a committee, as,

> Clearly something is lost if reviews are not subject to review by other members of a committee.
>
> (Jones and Pollitt, 2004, p. 169)

One suggestion following on from the work of the Higgs Report is the extent to which the non-executive directors' monitoring role can be made more effective through the introduction of 'gatekeeper liability' (Kirkbride and Letza, 2005). They suggest that as a natural progression from Higgs' recommendations, a structure of gatekeeper liability should be designed. This would imply that non-executive directors could be made personally liable for the misdeeds of executive directors. An interesting outcome of the Higgs Report was the recommendation that corporate secretaries should play a leading role in corporate governance affairs, stating that they should provide a source of corporate governance information and should support the effective performance of non-executive directors.

We now turn to considering evidence from the academic literature concerning the usefulness of the non-executive director function.

## Research into the role of non-executive directors

There is a growing body of academic literature relating to the function of non-executive directors and their contribution to 'good' corporate governance. However, there is no clear consensus in the literature concerning whether or not non-executive directors play a useful corporate governance role and whether or not they enhance shareholder wealth and financial performance. We look now at a selection of empirical evidence from the academic research in favour of the presence of non-executive directors on boards, as well as evidence against it.

### Evidence in favour

From an agency theory perspective, non-executive directors may be perceived as playing a monitoring role on the rest of the board. There is a substantial quantity of academic literature indicating that boards of directors perform an important corporate governance function and that non-executive directors act as necessary monitors of management (e.g., Fama, 1980; Fama and Jensen, 1983). Our own research has shown that a high degree of importance is attached to the non-executive director function by the UK institutional investment community. We surveyed a large sample of investment institutions and the respondents ranked the presence of non-executives on boards as the most important corporate governance mechanism recommended in successive policy documents (see Table 3.1). Without the monitoring function of non-executive directors it would be more likely that inside executive directors would be able to manipulate their position by gaining complete control over their own remuneration packages and securing their jobs (Morck et al., 1988).

Some academic studies have shown that non-executive directors have monitored management effectively. An indicator that has been used to proxy for such monitoring efficiency is chief executive turnover, the implication being that more frequent turnover of chief executives leads to better corporate financial performance. Further, this may in turn be related to a greater proportion of non-executive directors on company boards. We saw earlier in this chapter that similar assumptions are made in testing the effectiveness of splitting the roles of chairman and chief executive. Their independent influence on the board should in such cases lead to the removal of ineffective chief executives. Indeed, Weisbach (1988) found evidence that the turnover of chief executives was more strongly related to company performance in companies characterized by a majority of non-executive directors.

The presence of outsiders on company boards is also thought to be positively related to corporate control activity, as outsiders can facilitate takeovers, thereby activating the takeover constraint that disciplines company management (Agrawal and Knoeber, 1996). In relation to hostile takeover bids, empirical evidence has been provided, showing that boards with a significant independent contingent benefit shareholders in the bidding process (Byrd and Hickman, 1992). Again, this endorses the presence of non-executive, outside directors on boards. Also, in relation to the positive effects for shareholders of non-executive directors' involvement on boards, Rosenstein and Wyatt (1990) found evidence of a positive share price reaction to their appointment.

### Evidence against

Another school of thought in the academic literature considers that boards of directors *per se* are superfluous, as the market provides a natural solution to the notorious agency problem rendering internal mechanisms unnecessary (e.g., Hart, 1983). If boards are superfluous then, from this theoretical viewpoint, non-executive directors are merely another impotent element in an unnecessary structure. Proponents of this view consider that the 'market' disciplines company management naturally (e.g., through the threat of hostile takeovers and shareholder voting), thereby aligning managers' interests with those of shareholders.

In relation to the relevance of non-executive directors versus the relevance of executive directors, there is considerable debate in the academic literature. Some evidence endorses the position of executives in preference to non-executives on boards. For example, one empirical study investigated the wealth effects of inside, executive director appointments by management (Rosenstein and Wyatt, 1990). Using event study methodology, the paper reported a positive share price reaction to the announcement of inside director appointments. The findings stressed the important role that inside directors played in ratifying material corporate decisions and endorsing corporate strategies. However, the study also highlighted the relevance of the existing board composition to the effect of new appointments on share price, as they found that the market reacted more favourably to insider appointments, where there was a board imbalance displaying a high proportion of non-executive directors, and less favourably when the balance was skewed more to insiders. The paper concluded that the benefits associated with the appointment of a new inside director only outweighed the costs of such an appointment when managerial and shareholder interests were closely aligned (i.e., when there was no significant agency problem).

There is also a perception among some academics and practitioners that the involvement of non-executive, outside directors on boards can damage corporate governance by reducing entrepreneurship in the business and by weakening board unity. This was certainly the view expressed by many board directors in their initial response to the Higgs recommendations to broaden the role and effectiveness of non-executive directors in the UK. Higgs' suggestion to make non-executive directors the champions of shareholder interests met with immediate opposition. Despite supporters of the non-executive director role, such as Derek Higgs, some leading figures in the City of London consider that non-executive directors can do more harm than good and that their role should be abolished! (*The Economist*, 13 June 2002). Indeed, there is a potential for the appointment of non-executive directors to result in more cronyism and a more comfortable network of close ties and cosy relationships between directors of leading companies. Furthermore, accusations are made that the relatively new level of non-executive directors in UK business provides just more 'jobs for the boys' and the opportunity for an even firmer golden handshake than retiring directors receive already.

There is also evidence suggesting that non-executive directors have a negative, rather than a positive impact on corporate financial performance. The presence of outside directors on US boards represented one of seven mechanisms used to control agency problems examined by Agrawal and Knoeber (1996). They found persistent evidence of a negative relationship between the proportion of outside directors and the companies' financial performance. Their conclusion was that companies had too many outside directors on their boards. This is not encouraging evidence for supporters of the UK Higgs Report. However, the authors were 'puzzled' by this result. One explanation they proffered was that outside directors were often added to boards in companies that were already performing badly, in order to improve performance (a result also presented in Hermalin and Weisbach, 1988). The authors examined their findings and concluded that the causality ran from board composition to performance, and not in the opposite direction, dispelling this explanation. They commented that:

> One possible rationale is that boards are expanded for political reasons, perhaps to include politicians, environmental activists, or consumer representatives, and that these additional outside directors either reduce firm performance or proxy for the underlying political constraints that led to their receiving board seats.
>
> (Agrawal and Knoeber, 1996, p. 394)

Clearly, these authors would be unlikely to support the hypothesis that wider stakeholder accountability improves corporate financial performance. However, their results are interesting and beg further investigation. They emphasized the interdependence of various control mechanisms, such as the non-executive director function, and took account of such interrelationships in their analysis in order to avoid spurious results.

### Getting the balance right

Overall, it seems that the majority of empirical evidence endorses the roles of both non-executive and executive directors, even though some results are conflicting. Both groups of directors bring different but essential skills to the boardroom. An effective board attains the appropriate balance between the two. The weight of evidence seems to endorse the monitoring role played by non-executive directors and supports the current UK and US policy of encouraging their effectiveness. This view is emphasized by Mace (1986), for example, who stated that many chief executives considered the most effective boards were those with a 'balance' of inside and outside directors. Too great a proportion of insiders or outsiders can swing the balance in the wrong direction, for example:

> If there are too many insiders, the management team can become excessively cohesive. This sets up a very dangerous situation because the directors tend to derive their judgement only from colleagues. The scarcity of outside directors restricts outside influence and leads to close-minded decisions. On the other hand, the addition of many outsiders brings new information and ideas and allows the entire board to make sound decisions. Outside directors provoke an independent and fresh review of long-term decisions, effectuate impartial, uncontaminated audits of managerial performance, and counterbalance the influence of top management. *Companies need strong, knowledgeable insider directors as well as independent outsiders in order to represent stockholders most effectively.*
>
> (Alkhafaji, 1989, p. 54, emphasis added)

In practice, although the market offers real incentives to solve the agency problem, they are not sufficient to satisfy fully the needs of shareholders and other stakeholder groups. Such corporate governance mechanisms as the presence of independent, non-executive directors are necessary to improve the quality of governance in listed companies.

Another question addressed in the academic literature asks whether or not non-executive directors who are alleged to be independent are truly independent, or whether their independence is debatable. Indeed, a degree of scepticism is displayed by many authors concerning non-executive directors' independence. One of the major problems highlighted in the literature arises from the role played by executive directors in appointing non-executives. This could clearly compromise their independence if the appointment process is affected unduly by cronyism (see, e.g., Waldo, 1985; Mace, 1986; Vancil, 1987). Short (1996) also debated this issue, concluding that far more research was required.

*Who wants the job anyway?*

As in many other areas of UK industry, recommendations for improvements, greater accountability on remuneration and many other factors are making such positions as that of a non-executive director less attractive to prospective newcomers. As we mentioned above, this was a concern detected in the Cadbury Report and covered in the Higgs Report. Indeed, there appears to be a growing reluctance to become a non-executive director (*The Economist*, 31 October 2002). This is also the case in the USA where people are less and less inclined to become involved in companies as either inside or outside directors, given the potentially frightening repercussions from Sarbanes–Oxley. If non-executive directors are meant to bring impartiality into the boardroom, the question for legislators is the extent to which legal liability, including criminal sanctions, should attach to the role of non-executive directors. Clearly, it would be a significant disincentive to people considering a position as a non-executive director.

Such organizations as ProNED act as a type of professional dating service, matching prospective non-executive directors to suitable company boards. Their role is essential in ensuring the non-executive director function operates efficiently. The Tyson Report (2005) lists a whole host of organizations dedicated to providing a broader source of non-executive directors, including the Association of Executive Search Consultants, Charity and Fundraising Appointments, High Tech Women and the City Women's Network.

# Executive remuneration

In the early 1990s people were not as familiar with the term 'corporate governance' as they are today. Even in leading business schools, discussion of corporate governance tended to centre around directors' pay and 'fat cats'. As we can see from this textbook, corporate governance is a far broader subject than that! However, the contentious issue of executive remuneration and the problems of setting pay at appropriate levels is an extremely important aspect of corporate governance. The need to establish directors' pay at a level that incentivizes management to pursue shareholder interests has been emphasized in the academic literature (Jensen, 1993). In this sense, executive remuneration is one more mechanism that can be refined to improve corporate governance.

The gap between executives' pay and that of workers on the factory floor has been shown to have widened in the past 20 years (see, e.g., *The Economist*, 15 November 2002). The Higgs Report quoted research findings that, on average, company chairmen in the FTSE 100 companies were earning £ 426,000 per annum at that time. This gives an indication of the salaries earned by senior board members. A scatter of contentious salary packages is collated in Illustration 4.5. Directors have received unreasonable amounts of additional benefit (e.g., in the form of stock options), which has generated controversy. Further, some people have felt that such high rewards have not been accompanied by high performance. An opinion poll in 2003 performed by MORI revealed that 78 % of those members of the public surveyed considered that directors of large companies were paid too much (Blitz, 2003).

## Illustration 4.5

### Is remuneration excessive?

Just a few tasty morsels of pay to chew on. Rose Marie Bravo at Burberry, the maker of fashionable raincoats, received a £6 million salary in 2002. Despite her hard work in transforming the company, the NAPF felt they could not condone the 'sheer largesse' of the executives' salaries in Burberry and the lack of any relation to performance (Boxell, 14 July 2003). The ABI expressed similar concerns. Ben Verwaayen, the chief executive of BT earned £3 million in 2002. Also in 2002, four executives at AWG, the utilities group, received special bonuses totalling £475,000 for their role in debt restructuring (Bream, 2003). Vittorio Radice, the ex-boss of Selfridges, was given a 'golden hello' of £1.15 million by Marks and Spencer. In April 2003 Alistair Dales received compensation of £889,457 when he agreed to retire early from Nationwide, on top of his basic salary of £301,000 and bonuses (Croft, 24 July 2003). But the problem doesn't seem to end when they leave the company. Sir Iain Vallance, the former chairman of BT, received almost £1.1 million over two years following his resignation as executive and appointment as 'president emeritus'. These are just a random handful of cases. A cursory glance at the media would reveal many more. The problem is by no means restricted to the UK. Frits Bolkestein, the EU Commissioner for the Internal Market and Taxation, has taken a hard line on executive remuneration at a pan-European level, commenting that, '... the remuneration for top dogs (and fat cats) in industry is out of all proportion ... I find the pay packages excessive.' He considers that prompt action is necessary for annual disclosure of remuneration policy, with shareholder approval of the policy, for listed companies throughout EU member states (see European Financial Services Regulation, 2003). What do you think about these levels of pay?

The Cadbury Report devoted some attention to executive remuneration, but it was the Greenbury Report and its accompanying Code of Practice, produced in 1995, that focused specifically on issues relating to directors' pay. As with the Cadbury Code, the Greenbury Committee proposed that all listed companies registered in the UK should comply with the code and report annually to shareholders on their level of compliance. The Code aimed to establish best practice in determining and accounting for directors' remuneration. The Greenbury Report (1995) may be seen as reactive rather than proactive in nature, as it responded to public sentiment. The Greenbury Committee consisted of leading investors and industrialists and the chairman was Sir Richard Greenbury. The group's terms of reference were: *To identify good practice in determining directors' remuneration and prepare a code of such practice for use by UK plcs*, with the aim of increasing accountability and enhancing performance. Also, full disclosure of remuneration and other related information was raised as requiring attention. One important aim of the Committee (and of the earlier Cadbury Code of best practice) was to create remuneration committees that would *determine pay packages needed to attract, retain and motivate directors of the quality required but should avoid paying more than is necessary for this purpose*. This was an initiative intended to improve transparency in this area. Such remuneration committees of (mainly) non-executive directors were established to determine the company's policy on executive remuneration and specific remuneration packages for the executive directors, including pension rights and any compensation payments. Clearly, the intention was to prevent executive directors from designing their own pay packages. The need for an independent remuneration committee has been highlighted in the academic literature as an essential mechanism to prevent executives writing and signing their own pay cheques (Williamson, 1985). The members of the remuneration committee should be listed each year in the committee's report to share-holders and the committee should make a report each year to the shareholders on behalf of the board. This report should also include full details of all elements in the remuneration package of each individual director by name, such as basic salary, benefits in kind, annual bonuses and long-term incentive schemes including share options, as well as pension entitlements earned by each individual director during the year.

Since Greenbury, there have been significant improvements in the quality and quantity of disclosure relating to directors' remuneration, with companies providing substantial quantities of information relating to their directors' remuneration in their annual reports. The revision of the Combined Code in July 2003, in the wake of the Higgs review on non-executive directors, incorporated a series of provisions aimed at preventing excessive executive pay (Tassell, 22 July 2003). The new draft aimed to avoid the upward ratchet of pay levels that do not correspond to performance. We now turn to the academic literature for evidence relating to issues of directors' remuneration.

## Research into executive remuneration

There is a vast quantity of literature relating to executive remuneration. Clearly, it is not the intention of this text to provide comprehensive coverage of this literature, but rather to give a flavour of the issues addressed and some of the salient findings. As for the relationship between remuneration and corporate performance, one academic study found strong statistical evidence linking excessive executive remuneration with 'bad' corporate governance and poor corporate performance in the USA (Core et al., 1999). Indeed a significant negative association was found between remuneration (arising from board and ownership structure) and corporate operating and share price performance, indicating that companies fared less well when their board structure allowed an imbalance of power leading to excessive chief executive remuneration. This paper made a policy recommendation that US boards should split the roles of CEO and chairman, in line with the recommendations of Cadbury, *inter alia*. Academic research has also shown a significant relationship between CEO compensation and the manner in which members of the board are appointed. Generally, the more control the CEO has over appointing other board members, the higher their remuneration tends to be (Lambert et al., 1993).

With respect to remuneration committees, Bostock (1995) found that the recommendation to establish remuneration committees produced a speedy response, with a large number of UK company boards establishing committees comprising relatively few executive directors. Further, Conyon and Mallin (1997) reported that by 1995, 98 % of companies responding to a questionnaire survey had established a remuneration commit-tee in response to the initial Cadbury recommendations.

In relation to the level of executive remuneration in different countries, another paper examined the progressive globalization of executive remuneration (Cheffins, 2003). The author debated that not only was remuneration harmonizing at an international level but it was also following US levels, which are traditionally higher than in other parts of the world. The paper reviewed the data on the remuneration of US executives, concluding that the pay packages of US chief executives were far more lucrative than those of executives in other countries around the world. The paper discussed a number of market-oriented drivers for executive pay convergence and linked this evolution to the steady convergence of global corporate systems toward a market-based structure: a more market-driven global corporate governance system may be characterized by more lucrative executive pay structures. One of the main issues raised was disclosure of executive remuneration. Cheffins (2003) considered that if tougher laws on disclosure of executive pay packages were introduced internationally this would advance the 'Americanization' of executive pay. Moreover, shareholders would be able to see the remuneration that incentivizes executives to maximize shareholder value. This would in turn help to reduce the 'agency cost' in those companies. Cheffins (2003) argued that a strong relationship between pay and performance could reduce the costs associated with shareholder monitoring. Such changes are certainly occurring at present, with the UK Government's introduction of legislation committing institutional investors to vote on directors' remuneration and requiring companies to make far more detailed disclosure on their policies on director remuneration. Nevertheless, it appears that 'Americanization' of pay may become a reality in the UK if Cheffins' (2003) model holds. Certainly, the remuneration package given to the director of US operations at HSBC in May 2003, which included a multimillion dollar pay-off if he was ever ousted, and totalled $ 37.5 million over three years, is evidence of American-style remuneration packages crossing the Atlantic (Croft, 12 May 2003). However, unless such appealing packages are offered, it will be impossible to attract talent from the USA, which many UK companies are attempting to do (Gimbel, 2003). Indeed, equalization of executive remuneration is likely to occur at a higher, rather than a lower level. Illustration 4.6 discusses the latest conflicting empirical evidence on current levels of executive remuneration in the UK. Interestingly, Cheffins' (2003) predictions seem to be vindicated by the findings.

## Illustration 4.6

### Fat Cats Leaner or Fatter?

There has been mixed evidence on whether directors' remuneration has risen or fallen as a result of corporate governance reform.

*Leaner?*

Recent survey evidence presented by Watson Wyatt pointed to a fall in top directors' remuneration of 18 % in 2005 (Burgess, 2005). The survey examined pay packages for executive directors in FTSE100 companies. As the survey considered packages including salaries, bonuses and future share and performance-related share-option awards, the findings reflect principally the impact of performance-related changes to remuneration. The drive by institutional investors to ensure that directors' remuneration is related directly to actual corporate performance, rather than performance of the market, has clearly had an effect. Performance criteria for awarding share options have become far more exacting. In the past, directors had been awarded options if their earnings rose by 3 % above inflation. Now, they only receive share options if earnings rise 10 % above inflation.

*Fatter?*

A survey of 903 companies, conducted by Independent Remuneration Solutions (a consultancy) and Manifest (the proxy voting agency) found that total chief executive remuneration had risen 208 % since 1998, while their salaries had increased by 58 % (Moules, 2005). Further, directors of the largest companies were attracting 'superstar' levels of remuneration, with their pay being on average 63 % above the next person down in the corporate hierarchy. There is clear evidence now that the sort of globalization of pay along US levels is starting to take place in the UK, as predicted by Cheffins (2003).

*Comment*

As with all statistical evidence, the data set selected, the time period and the variables chosen all affect the outcome. These findings give diametrically opposite results. On balance, it seems that executives at the very top of the ladder have perhaps suffered some decrease in their overall earnings, but executives overall are continuing to do very well. Another element is the increasing complexity of pay packages. It seems that by making them more complex, the actual ingredients of huge payouts are less transparent, making critique of remuneration more difficult. Sarah Wilson from Manifest has commented that although this growing complexity is delivering value to directors, it may not be delivering value for shareholders (Moules, 2005).

There has also been some attempt in the literature to evaluate the extent to which corporate governance reform in the UK has been effective in curbing excessive executive remuneration. Thompson (2005) found that the various initiatives that have been implemented to make the setting of executive remuneration more transparent have not had much impact on the relationship between executive pay and performance. The paper speculates that the City of London is to blame for the low impact of reform initiatives. Thompson argues that the reform of executive remuneration policy has been motivated by the media and politics, rather than by financial institutions, saying that,

City institutions, themselves no strangers to high pay, do not appear to have been overly concerned, except perhaps where pay increases seem to generate damaging publicity.

(Thompson, 2005, p. 24)

In Chapter 6 the literature that links the disclosure of financial accounting information with remuneration policies is discussed, in order to demonstrate the importance of establishing a positive relationship between remuneration and performance.

## Voting on directors' remuneration

Despite the concerns aired above, that the City has not supported initiatives to reform executive remuneration policy, one substantial change effected in UK corporate governance and accountability was the decision by many companies (following pressure from shareholders and lobbyists, *inter alia*) to allow their shareholders to vote on directors' remuneration. In October 2001 the Government announced proposals to produce an annual directors' remuneration report that would be approved by shareholders. There has been a significant increase in UK listed companies that have allowed their shareholders to vote on directors' pay. Indeed, a survey indicated that 37 % of blue-chip companies were considering allowing their shareholders to vote on directors' remuneration at their AGMs in 2002, compared with only 13 % in 2001 (see Jones, 2002). The Government's Trade and Industry Secretary, Patricia Hewitt, produced a consultative document in 2002 dealing with directors' remuneration, which called for enhanced shareholder powers in this area. However, the actual powers shareholders gained by such a change were perhaps less far-reaching than one might imagine. The vote is only advisory. In other words, the company does not have to take any notice of the outcome, should it prefer not to. Shareholders do not have the opportunity to vote on the remuneration of individual directors. Further, some institutional investors have reacted negatively to the proposal, as they see it as a means of passing the buck from directors to shareholders, forcing them to discharge accountability and responsibility rather than the companies, for pay levels (Mayo and Young, 2002). Nevertheless, as with many 'voluntary' areas of corporate governance, it would be unlikely for companies with good reputations to ignore such a demonstration of discontent from their shareholders. This greater level of shareholder involvement should result in improved accountability and more reasonable remuneration packages.

The emerging evidence indicates that shareholder activism in this area is having a significant impact on company management, with remuneration policies being altered following shareholder protests. We discuss the evidence in detail in Chapter 5, when we consider the effectiveness of institutional investor activism in monitoring managerial behaviour. Specifically, Illustration 5.2 looks at a number of cases of shareholder activism on remuneration policies.

In the wake of these changes, the UK Government decided that there is no need to change company law, as institutional investor activism seems to have worked in demanding higher standards from companies on remuneration (*Financial Times*, 26 January 2005). The Government feels that there has been sufficient progress in the disclosure of remuneration by companies and in the involvement of institutional investors, to avoid legislative changes. There is also evidence that directors' remuneration is being more closely linked to corporate financial performance (Burgess, 2005).

## Directors' training

Another board-related issue that has been the focus of policy recommendations is directors' training. Education and qualifications are becoming increasingly important in today's society. The required specific knowledge to play a role within an institution is essential if the organization is to operate efficiently. In order to create a dynamic 'learning' board (Garratt, 1996) that has a lively approach, conducive to good corporate governance, directors are encouraged to attend training courses. Indeed, this was a recommendation of the Cadbury Report, which stated that:

> The weight of responsibility carried by all directors and the increasing commitment which their duties require emphasise the importance of the way in which they prepare themselves for their posts. Given the varying backgrounds, qualifications and experience of directors, it is highly desirable that they should all undertake some form of internal or external training.
>
> (Cadbury Report, 1992, p. 24, para. 4.19)

The Hampel Report reaffirmed the Cadbury emphasis on directors' training, especially in the case of new directors who have relatively little experience. Hampel also highlighted the necessity of training for directors on relevant new laws, regulations and evolving business risks. As suggested in Cadbury, there is an important role for business schools to play in providing high-quality training and corporate governance education for company directors. This also presents an opportunity for further research, as it would be interesting to find whether there is a significant statistical link between director training and corporate financial performance.

## A sympathetic viewpoint

Having reviewed the many areas where corporate governance reform has targeted boardroom practice, we may wonder if such changes have started to discourage people from entering the boardroom. It could be said that a director's job, certainly in the UK, is getting tougher. It is no longer enough to have 'come up through the company', 'learned from Dad' or 'have experience of the trade'. Training, qualifications and evidence of the ability to direct are now required. Worse still for directors, any whiff of fraudulent or unsavoury thoughts, let alone actions, may now lead to prosecution and even jail, as directors' liabilities have become more carefully spelled out in the aftermath of Enron and other corporate collapses. Corporate reputation, built up over decades, can be destroyed overnight. The Sarbanes–Oxley Act (2002) represented a turning point for directors as it specified personal liability and prison for directors found guilty of corporate crime. Although the Act applies directly to the USA, it has severe implications for directors in other countries who may have any business connections with US companies. However, liabilities acted as a deterrent to prospective board members before the Enron debacle. Alkhafaji (1989) argued that in 1980s' America, candidates were turning down board positions because of the liabilities involved, given a significant increase in lawsuits against boards of directors. However, he also considered that such lawsuits may have been self-inflicted, in terms of the following analogy:

...if board members do not use their expertise and knowledge in the best interest of the corporation and shareholders, then they are guilty of malpractice – just like negligent doctors. From a business viewpoint, the patient is the corporation, the doctor is the board, and the shareholders are the family that sues the board for malpractice.

(Alkhafaji, 1989, p. 69)

Nevertheless, in today's environment, directors can no longer be confident of receiving a bulky pay package to compensate for their considerable liabilities. Director remuneration is forced further under the microscope, with investors in the UK now possessing the right to vote on directors' pay. Every detail of pay packages is disclosed in the annual reports – no stone is left unturned. In fact, with such an increasingly difficult job and such far-reaching responsibilities, it is amazing that there are still volunteers! However, even if remuneration has been curbed, or at least observed, it is not a pittance. Indeed, who would turn down such a large salary, however difficult the job and far-reaching the responsibilities?

## Other factors contributing to board effectiveness

A whole host of other issues are now considered to improve board effectiveness as well as the primary three discussed above. Board size is an important factor which is included in most corporate governance rating systems, as seen in Chapter 3. Boards should be,

...small enough to be effective, more cohesive and to enable more participation and discussion.

(Van den Berghe and Levrau, 2004, p. 464)

Constraining board size in order to achieve a more effective board seems to be the preferred choice. From the burgeoning academic and practitioner literature on boards of directors, as well as from the recommendations of the various codes of practice, we have compiled a lighthearted 'recipe' for a 'good board' as follows:

**Recipe for a 'good board'**

*The board should meet frequently*

*The board should maintain a good balance of power*

*An individual should not be allowed to dominate board meetings and decision making*

*Members of the board should be open to other members' suggestions*

*There should be a high level of trust between board members*

*Board members should be ethical and have a high level of integrity*

*There must be a high level of effective communication between members of the board*

*The board should be responsible for the financial statements*

> Non-executive directors should (generally) provide an independent viewpoint
>
> The board should be open to new ideas and strategies (a 'learning board', Garratt, 1996)
>
> Board members should not be opposed to change
>
> The board must possess an in-depth understanding of the company's business
>
> The board must be dynamic in nature
>
> The board must understand the inherent risks of the business
>
> The board must be prepared to take calculated risks: no risk no return
>
> The board must communicate with shareholders, be aware of shareholder needs and translate them into management strategy
>
> The board must be aware of stakeholder issues and be prepared to engage actively with their stakeholders
>
> As education becomes increasingly important, board members should not be averse to attending training courses
>
> Keep on a low heat and stir frequently!

# Alternative models for enhancing board effectiveness

In the literature a number of alternative models have been proposed for improving the effectiveness of boards in corporate governance. Most of the literature discussed in this chapter has derived from an agency theory, finance paradigm of corporate governance and boardroom effectiveness. However, other disciplines, such as management science, have illuminated our understanding of boards as corporate governance mechanisms.

For example, Nicholson and Kiel (2004) move the focus away from the issue of independence within the boardroom, towards a more holistic view of the board as a group of individuals. They argue that corporate governance reform has become largely preoccupied with an agency approach, stressing the need for greater independence in the boardroom, whereas their proposed model draws on the broader concept of board intellectual capital. In their framework they attempt to incorporate the complexity of board function in a systems view of the relation between boards and performance, arguing that the following factors constrain a board's composition, powers and actions, including the company's institutional and historical factors and the capability 'set' of the board members as a group. For example, the paper explains that major phases throughout a company's development have a significant impact on current corporate governance expectations within the boardroom. Their framework conceptualizes the board as a 'social phenomenon'.[6]

---

[6] Their framework builds on the analogy between a board of directors and a natural system, as theorized in Katz and Kahn (1978).

The basic premise is that an effective board achieves an appropriate 'fit' between the various elements of its intellectual capital and the various functions of the board. The authors define intellectual capital with respect to four components: human capital (individual directors' skills, abilities and knowledge); social capital (implicit and tangible set of resources arising from social relationships of board members); structural capital (procedures, policies and processes developed by the board over time); and cultural capital (external societal expectations of the board and the company). The authors believe that group dynamics are far too complex to be simplified into an agency theory analysis and that many 'partial' models of corporate governance fail to capture the complexities of board dynamics and do not represent an adequate version of reality. Further, the paper highlights a gap between corporate governance theory building in the academic literature and corporate governance practice, as they suggest that models arising from the literature are more holistic but are ignored by corporate governance policies which tend to take a myopic, agency-theoretic perspective on the whole. Nicholson and Kiel (2004) suggest that their model may be implemented as a diagnostic tool, such that boards may diagnose common corporate governance problems by evaluating their board's capabilities in relation to the various components of the proposed framework.

## Brave new boardrooms?

Although the agenda for corporate governance reform since the early 1990s has made significant inroads into enhancing board effectiveness, work remains to be done. As mentioned throughout this text, it is not a time for practitioners, policy makers and corporate governance actors, such as board directors, to rest on their laurels.

Garratt (2005) provided a colourful portrait of boardrooms in 2015. In this futuristic boardroom, a number of changes had occurred, some seemingly against the current best practice in UK corporate governance. For example, the remuneration committee had been abolished. The members of the board faced the shareholders and were willing to argue for linking their own salaries to performance indicators. The board demonstrated their commitment to the company by each agreeing to buy a minimum of £ 100,000 in the company's equity and dropping all stock options.

Another radical action, against the recommendations of the Higgs Report, was to reject the terms 'executive' and 'non-executive' director, as they propounded a belief that they were all equally liable and accountable to their shareholders. They also espoused themselves to a common one-year contract for services for all directors. There was an overall desire by the board to be genuinely altruistic, driven by ethics and an attempt to be 'professional'. Indeed, in Garratt's portrait a new law had allowed a new board to sue the previous board for lack of care and general incompetence.

For the most part, Garratt's predictions built on his model of the learning board. To develop their skills and 'learn' actively, the futuristic board had regular 'awaydays' devoted to subjects such as policy, strategy and accountability. Mere compliance with the letter of the Combined Code had gone out of the window by 2015, with UK law making directors liable under a range of criminal laws. This has concentrated directors' minds towards complying more in spirit, which was the original battlecry of the Cadbury Report (1992). Improvements in boardroom accountability included, for example, mandatory board appraisals every year.

Fictional? Maybe. Embedded in fact? Possibly. It certainly seems that Garratt's (2005) prophesies for UK boardrooms are founded on the message arising from practitioners and research in corporate governance at the moment. Complacency needs to be avoided, ethics and accountability require more attention and directors must focus on applying corporate governance best practice in spirit as well as to the letter.

## Chapter summary

In this chapter we have considered the role of boards of directors in corporate governance, focusing mainly on UK listed companies. We have looked at the evolution of their role and the evolution of the UK codes of best practice in corporate governance and their accompanying policy documents, from the Cadbury Report in 1992 to the Higgs Report in 2003. Specifically, we have considered the importance of achieving a balance of power in company boards and drawn the similarity between a company board and the heart of the human body, its effective and healthy function being essential to the healthy functioning of a company. We have highlighted the growing importance of the role of independent non-executive directors in corporate governance, as they provide an independent view on corporate strategy and help to attain a balance of power. We have also discussed ways in which the Tyson Report has presented a route for companies to broaden their gene pool of potential non-executive directors. The contentious issue of executive remuneration has been discussed, as has the empirical evidence linking excessive pay packages to weak corporate governance structures and poor corporate performance.

In the UK, corporate governance has a sound base, but there is always room for improvement. Companies should not rest on their laurels and should aspire constantly to fine-tuning their corporate governance checks and balances, in order to avoid a UK Enron and to improve accountability. Garratt's (2005) predictions for the way in which board-rooms may develop in the future were presented in the last section and provide an insight into continuing problems. The main issues seem to revolve around an urgent need to nurture more accountability and genuine ethical behaviour within the boardroom. Amendments to UK company law, making board members personally liable with associated criminal charges, would help to nurture a more responsible corporate environment. The academic research in this area has provided mixed results on all issues relating to boards of directors. We saw, for example, the divergent evidence on the effectiveness of the non-executive director function in monitoring company management. There is clearly room for further research and a need to clarify the advantages and disadvantages of the various corporate governance initiatives in this area in order to inform policy.

## Questions for reflection and discussion

**1**   Has the Higgs Report produced recommendations that are feasible in practice? Do you agree with critics who have suggested that the recommendations are divisive?

**2**   Do you consider that non-executive directors play a useful role in company boards? To what extent do you think the academic research has clarified this issue?

**3**   Do you think that there will be an 'Americanization' of executive remuneration? Support your arguments with examples from the press.

**4**   Compare and contrast the recommendations contained in the original Higgs Report (January 2003) with the revised Combined Code (July 2003). To what extent do you think the revised code is less prescriptive than Higgs intended? Do you think that his original recommendations have been watered down too far?

**5**   Explain the ways in which the Tyson Report has added to Higgs' findings and should lead to a broadening of the gene pool for the recruitment of non-executive directors. In your view, does such a broadening help to develop confidence and trust among stakeholders?

**6**   From reading the literature, do you agree with our 'Recipe for a good board'. Would you prefer a different set of 'ingredients'? Compile your own list, explaining which 'ingredients' you consider to be the most important.

**7**   To what extent has the empirical research been useful in providing clarity regarding the structure of the board of directors and the firm's financial performance?

# Chapter 5

# The role of institutional investors in corporate governance

## Aim and objectives

This chapter explores the role of institutional investors in corporate governance, mainly from a UK perspective. The specific objectives of this chapter are to enable readers to:

- highlight the important monitoring role that institutional investors play in UK corporate governance;

- discuss the complex web of ownership that arises from institutional investment;

- consider ways in which institutional investors are becoming more active in corporate governance;

- assess the evidence on the impact of shareholder activism on corporate performance and company value.

## Introduction

In the previous chapter we investigated the role of boards in corporate governance. However, boards of directors are not the only people with responsibility for ensuring effective corporate governance. Shareholders, especially institutional investors, also have an important role to play. In the UK the four main types of institutional investor are pension funds, life insurance companies, unit trusts and investment trusts. The position of institutional investors in corporate governance, from a theoretical perspective, is complicated. From one viewpoint, institutional investors represent another powerful corporate governance mechanism that can monitor company management, as their influence on company management can be substantial and can be used to align management interests with those of the shareholder group. The ways in which shareholders can monitor management in an agency theory framework were introduced briefly in Chapter 1. The monitoring role of institutional investors is increasingly important as they have grown so large and influential, at the same time gaining significant ownership concentration. Indeed, ownership concentration has been acknowledged in the literature as an important mechanism which controls agency problems and improves investor protection (Shleifer and Vishny, 1997). Such concentration can however have negative effects, such as their access to privileged information, which creates an information asymmetry between themselves and smaller shareholders. Institutional investors can also worsen agency conflicts by their existence as a significant principal who mitigates the problem due to the dispersion of ownership and control, although the growing concentration of ownership is resolving this problem.

Nevertheless, the importance of the corporate governance role that institutional investors can play in monitoring company management has been stressed in the academic literature. For example, Agrawal and Knoeber (1996) emphasized that the involvement of institutional investors can have a positive effect on corporate financial performance:

> ...concentrated shareholding by institutions...can increase managerial monitoring and so improve firm performance.
>
> (Agrawal and Knoeber, 1996, p. 377)

Further, Stapledon (1996) commented that:

> ...monitoring by institutional shareholders fits within a broad tapestry of devices and market forces which operate to reduce the divergence between the interests of managers and shareholders.
>
> (Stapledon, 1996, p. 17)

Indeed, a large intermediary, such as an institutional investor, can solve agency problems because of their ability to take advantage of economies of scale and diversification (Diamond, 1984). From the above discussion, it seems that institutional investors, as shareholders in companies, represent both the cause and the solution of the agency problem. Their presence as shareholders creates a divorce of ownership and control, whereas their increasing involvement in companies and concentration of ownership provides a means of monitoring management and actually solving agency problems. We now consider in depth the growth of institutional investment in the UK which has resulted in a transformation of the ownership structure of UK listed companies. This growth has led to a transformation from dispersed ownership to ownership concentrated in the hands of a small number of large institutional shareholders. We then consider the implications of this ownership transformation for corporate monitoring and corporate governance.

## The transformation of UK institutional ownership

Ownership structure, once characterized by Berle and Means (1932) as 'dispersed', has in recent times become more concentrated. Indeed, the growing concentration of shareholding by a relatively small number of institutional investors is resulting in the evolution of a capitalist system in the UK and in the USA that bears little resemblance to the fragmented and dispersed stock market of Berle and Means (Hill and Jones, 1992;

Monks, 2001). Mainly, this is a result of the gradual transference of ownership from individuals to investment institutions. Institutional investors are organizations with millions of pounds invested in the shares of listed UK and foreign companies, as well as in other forms of financial asset. As already mentioned, they include pension funds, life insurance companies, unit trusts and investment trusts.

We can see this pattern clearly in the changes in ownership structure in the UK over the past 40 years. The proportion of institutional shareholding in UK listed companies has grown gradually to the point where they now represent the dominant shareholder class (see, e.g., Briston and Dobbins, 1978; Dobson, 1994). At the end of 1992 insurance companies and pension funds accounted for 51.8 % of share ownership of the UK stock market. Unit and investment trusts held 8.5 % and banks held 0.2 %. Individual shareholders held only 20 % of UK listed company shares, while overseas investors accounted for 12.8 % (International Investment Management Directory, 1993/94). Indeed, individual ownership of shares in UK listed companies has declined from 54 % in 1963 to less than 18 % in 1993. By 1993 institutional ownership had risen to 62 % of ordinary shares (Stapledon, 1996). The stake held by institutional investors in the UK stock market has continued to grow, and the Hampel Report (1998) stated that:

> 60 % of shares in listed UK companies are held by UK institutions – pension funds, insurance companies, unit and investment trusts. Of the remaining 40 %, about half are owned by individuals and half by overseas owners, mainly institutions. It is clear from this that a discussion of the role of shareholders in corporate governance will mainly concern the institutions, particularly UK institutions.
>
> (The Hampel Report, 1998, p. 40, para. 5.1)

However, it is not just the growth of institutional ownership that has characterized the transformation of ownership structure, and consequently corporate governance, in the UK. It is also the increase in ownership concentration. Listed companies are increasingly owned by a small number of large institutions. The UK pension fund industry is now highly concentrated and represents the most significant group of institutional investors in the country. For example, in 1994 the largest five pension funds managed almost £ 66 billion of all occupational pension fund assets. Further, the largest 68 pension funds accounted for approximately 57 % of the assets of all occupational pension funds (Faccio and Lasfer, 2000).

The power of the institutional investors started to grow in the UK with the formation of the Institutional Shareholders Committee (ISC) in April 1973. When this class of dominant, large-scale investors first began to emerge, Briston and Dobbins (1978) studied their growth and predicted the impact of this growth on share ownership and influences on decision making within firms:

> We suggest that the persistent growth in the ownership of industry by institutional shareholders will inevitably involve those institutions in managerial decision-making.
>
> (Briston and Dobbins, 1978, p. 54)

This increase in ownership concentration and the transferral of ownership from individuals to institutions has had important repercussions for corporate governance in the USA and the UK. Institutional investors have moved away from being a cause, as shareholders, of the agency problem to being a means of solving the agency problem. They are now in a prime position to monitor company management and help to align the interests of management with those of their shareholders. Indeed, institutional investors today are far more involved in all areas of corporate decision making and have been encouraged to take on a more active role by the recommendations in corporate governance codes of practice and policy documents. Instead of creating an agency problem via dispersed, detached ownership, this new, dominant breed of shareholder is presenting a solution to agency problems, as they are providing a means of monitoring company management. Nevertheless, there have been warnings to avoid excessive 'interference' by institutions in the day-today running of businesses (e.g., the Hampel Report, 1998). If they are not managing, they are definitely monitoring company management, which is a form of pseudo-management. Similarly, in the USA Smith (1996a) stated that institutional ownership of domestic equities surpassed 50 % in 1992. He suggested that their influence had grown to such a degree that monitoring by these institutions was becoming known as shareholder activism – a term with which we are now far more familiar than we were at that time.

## A complex web of ownership

One problem with institutional investors as monitors of company management is that they are not actually the shareholders! Their relationship with companies and with the true shareholders involves a complicated web of ownership and accountability. The real shareholders are the clients of the institutional investment organizations. For example, most company employees are members of an occupational pension scheme. The pension scheme is run by a fund manager. The pension fund manager selects companies for the portfolio and purchases the shares, using the pooled funds entrusted to him by all the employees in the company. The employee is the ultimate 'owner' of the companies in which the pension fund manager invests. It is the employee who will be the ultimate beneficiary of the investment (via eventual pension payments). If the pension fund manager does not ensure that the various investee companies pursue shareholder wealth maximization, pension payments will not be maximized. Therefore, from an agency theory perspective there is an added agency problem. Not only does the shareholder (the individual pension fund member) have to worry about the possibly divergent objectives of investee company management but they also have to worry about the activities of the pension fund manager. The same analysis applies for people who invest in a unit trust, or who hold life insurance or endowment policies. It is because of this complex web of ownership that institutional investors' responsibilities of ownership are so pronounced. They are not responsible for themselves but for others, their clients. The pension fund manager is in fact the agent of the pension fund member. Pooling (also referred to as 'collectivization', or 'institutionalization') of investment funds adds another layer of complexity to the issue of monitoring company management.

In pension fund management (as opposed to other forms of instituti/
there is a further layer of complexity in the web of ownership and ac
only is the pension fund manager an intermediary, operating be
shareholder and the investee company, but there is also a pension fund trustee.
trustee, according to pension fund law, is entrusted with ultimate responsibility over the
pension fund assets. It is the pension fund trustee who has a fiduciary responsibility to
ensure that the eventual pension is maximized and that the funds of pension fund
members are invested as effectively as possible. This complex web of ownership and
control, resulting from the structure of pension fund investment, is alluded to in the
Hampel Report as follows,

> Pension funds are the largest group of institutional investors. The trustees of the fund
> are the owners of the shares; but in many cases they delegate the management of the
> investments, including relations with companies, to a fund management group. In
> these cases the actions of the trustees and their relations with the fund manager have
> an important bearing on corporate governance.
>
> (The Hampel Report, 1998, p. 41, para. 5.6)

From this we can see that the existence of intermediaries, such as trustees in institutional
investment, can obscure the corporate governance monitoring function. One of the
problems arising from this complex ownership structure is that there tends to be an
emphasis on short-termism in investment. Institutional investors are notoriously interested in short-term profit maximization in order to make their returns look as healthy as
possible in the short run. They therefore pressure companies to focus on short-term profits
rather than long-term profits. This can be detrimental to long-term company survival, as
companies need to invest in long-term projects in order to ensure they grow and prosper
in the long run. Such short-termism has been thought to have plagued British industry in
the latter half of the 20th century. As early as the 1930s, the short-term attitudes of
institutional investors were acknowledged by John Maynard Keynes, who stipulated in
the following lengthy discourse that:

> It might have been supposed that competition between expert professionals, posses-
> sing judgement and knowledge beyond that of the average private investor, would
> correct the vagaries of the ignorant individual left to himself. It happens, however, that
> the energies and skill of the professional investor and speculator are mainly occupied
> otherwise. For most of these persons are, in fact, largely concerned, *not with making
> superior long-term forecasts of the probable yield of an investment over its whole life,
> but with foreseeing changes in the conventional basis of valuation a short time ahead of
> the general public*. They are concerned, not with what an investment is really worth to a
> man who buys it 'for keeps', but with what the market will value it at, under the
> influence of mass psychology, three months or a year hence...Thus the professional
> investor is forced to concern himself with the anticipation of impending changes, in the
> news or in the atmosphere...The actual, private objective of the most skilled

investment today is 'to beat the gun', as the Americans so well express it, to outwit the
crowd, and to pass the bad or depreciating, half-crown to the other fellow.

(Keynes, 1936, pp. 154–155, emphasis added)

One of the main pressures for such short-term corporate behaviour is the insistence of the
increasingly powerful institutional investors. In particular, pension funds may be seen as
the chief culprits. The fiduciary duties of pension fund trustees emphasize such short-term
profitability. As stated in Hampel:

> It is often said that trustees put fund managers under undue pressure to maximise
> short-term investment returns, or to maximise dividend income at the expense of
> retained earnings; and that the fund manager will in turn be reluctant to support board
> proposals which do not immediately enhance the share price of the dividend rate.
> Evidence to support this view is limited...but we urge trustees to encourage invest-
> ment managers to take a long view.

(The Hampel Report, 1998, p. 41, para. 5.6)

We can see from this section of the Hampel Report that an emphasis for long-termism
rather than short-termism is another important aspect of the agenda for corporate
governance reform in the UK. Indeed, agency problems arising from the relationship
between institutional fund managers and their clients (the ultimate beneficiaries of the
institutional funds) may lead to a great emphasis being placed on short-term profits at the
expense of longer-term issues of corporate governance (Short and Keasey, 1997). There
is, however, little evidence from the academic literature to support ongoing short-termism
among institutional investors. Myopic institutions theory, which suggested that institutional shareholders were more short-sighted in their investment decisions than individual
investors, has gained little support. The theory was based on the idea that fund managers
competed for clients and that their performance, in terms of return to investment, was
used as a competitive indicator (Hansen and Hill, 1991). Indeed, institutional investors
have now become so influential that their ability to divest from companies has been
marred, such that they have been forced to become more long term (Graves and Waddock,
1994). This is because an 'exit' policy is far more expensive, as they have to accept
substantial discounts in order to liquidate their holdings (Faccio and Lasfer, 2000). The
complexity of pension fund share ownership may be simply represented as in Figure 5.1,
where the arrows signify the chain of ownership.

| Owners (pension fund members) | → | Trustees of the pensions fund Fiduciary duty is to maximize investment returns | → | Pension fund managers Duty is to pursue an investment strategy indicated by the trustees | → | Investee company management |
|---|---|---|---|---|---|---|

**Figure [5.1]**   Chain of share ownership in pension funds

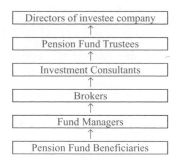

**Figure [5.2]**   Sources of Conflict in Pension Fund Investment*

In a presentation at a recent conference examining emerging issues in shareholder and stakeholder relations,[1] Colin Melvin (the director of corporate governance at Hermes) talked of a similar, but slightly more refined, version of this diagram to demonstrate the element of conflict in institutional investment. His ideas have been summarised in Figure 5.2.

As discussed earlier, the conflict arises because although the true owners of company shares are the pension fund beneficiaries, there are a whole host of intermediaries in between the true owners and the company directors. Their involvement creates frictional transaction costs (see also Myners, 2001) and result in the dissolution of genuine accountability. It is damaging to have the interests of the owner diluted by those inter-mediaries who profit from their involvement but who are not involved in the investee company. Shareholders' views are not being heard by companies because of these ownership conflicts and value is lost.

According to Melvin (2006), it is this complicated ownership structure which has contributed to a complete breakdown in trust between companies and their shareholders. Institutional investors now need to examine their own governance structures in order to actively rebuild trust among their beneficiaries. As mentioned in Chapter 3, a discussion paper issued by the NAPF (NAPF, 2005) examined pension scheme governance, concluding that there was no effective mechanism in place to represent the collective interests of the millions of pension scheme members. The report showed there to be a 'governance vacuum' in pensions governance.

Melvin (2006) also offers practical solutions, which are currently being explored by Hermes and other global investment institutions. The primary suggested solution is to create a raft of institutional investors at an international level who will collaborate in order to improve accountability in institutional investment and restore trust. This will remove what may currently be termed 'irresponsible activism'. In order to collaborate, this raft of investment institutions should share resources, taking advantage of economies

---

\*   This diagram is similar to the figure outlining 'web of ownership' in Solomon and Solomon, 2003.

[1]   Solomon (2006) summarizes the day's proceedings.

of scale. Melvin (2006) also noted that regulation was a threat to institutional shareholder collaboration. He supported the ISC guidelines which committed institutional investors to understanding company objectives and intervening appropriately, engaging with companies. It is essential that institutional investors hold meetings with their investee company directors if they stand any chance of gaining a genuine understanding of companies from the inside.

Investment institutions, according to Melvin (2006) are engaging actively with their investee companies. However, he questions their genuine commitment to the level of engagement and dialogue they actually practise. The resources that are actually being dedicated to active engagement policies are inadequate and belie any genuine commitment to this essential activity. MacKenzie (2004) stated that too few institutional fund managers have invested sufficiently in the area of shareholder activism to secure the experienced staff necessary. He emphasizes that talented and experienced staff are essential in order to achieve value-creating governance activism. The staff need to have a genuine understanding of what creates shareholder value. They also need to have the ability to exercise judgement and flexibility in decision making. MacKenzie endorses Melvin's concerns by stating that fund managers often delegate their engagement programmes to one person who has to take responsibility for activism with hundreds of companies. This individual is often inexperienced in fund management, which leads to a box-ticking approach.

If institutional investor engagement programmes are to be run and managed effectively, it is essential that they are supported both by the owners and their clients. Substantial resources need to be channelled into these programmes. In Hermes, Melvin (2006) stated that there are 50 people dedicated to corporate governance, which is four to five times more than any other investment institution. Another suggestion is, as stressed by Mallin (2006), the possibility of promoting cross-border voting by institutional investors and electronic voting. This is being debated at present by the ICGN. Electronic voting, as we see later in this chapter, has been the focus of recent corporate governance initiatives in the UK (Myners, 2004; 2005).

## Conflict and pension fund trustees

As we have seen from the above discussion, trustees are in an influential position in their pension funds. They have a fiduciary duty to maximize the investment returns for the members of the pension fund. They are responsible for the asset allocation decision and for the pension fund's investment policy. However, they are traditionally undertrained and unprepared for their hefty responsibilities. From his own research, Myners (2001) found that:

- 62 % of trustees had no professional qualification in finance or investment;

- 77 % of trustees had no in-house investment professionals to assist them;

- over half the population of trustees had received less than three days' training when they assumed their responsibilities;

- 44 % of trustees had not attended any course since their initial 12 months of trusteeship;

- 49 % of trustees spent 3 hours or less preparing for pension investment matters (implying that, given 4 meetings a year, trustees spent less than 12 hours a year on investment matters!).

Concerned by his findings, Myners commented that:

> The review ... does ... view the lack of investment understanding among trustees in general as a serious problem.
>
> (Myners, 2001, p. 43, para. 2.27)

Indeed, one of the primary conclusions of the Myners Review was that trustees required far more preparation in order to take on their important role. One means of improving the trustee function and encouraging trustees to take a more active interest in their role may be to pay them. At present, few trustees are paid (except for items such as travel expenses to/from trustee meetings). Indeed, a survey by the *Financial Times* found that more than half of a poll of 50 from the top 100 UK listed companies did not pay their trustees (Targett and Gimbel, 2003). The implications and potential impact of increasing trustee compensation have been explored in Solomon and Solomon (2003b). Further, trustee board effectiveness has been the focus of a recent review by the NAPF (NAPF, 2005). The report concluded that trustees and quasi trustee bodies should adopt a voluntary governance code which would ensure that they have a clear idea of what constitutes good governance. This would help to solve the problems associated with trustees' lack of training and expertise in institutional investment and governance issues.

We now consider a significant trend in institutional investment, namely the growth of shareholder activism, which has accompanied the growth of institutional investment in the UK and has affected corporate governance significantly.

## The growth of institutional investor activism

The role of institutional investors in corporate governance received significant attention in the Cadbury Report (1992) in a section devoted to shareholders' rights and responsibilities. Perhaps the most 'radical' aspect of the Cadbury Committee's work was its success in refocusing corporate governance not only on companies and the effectiveness of their boards of directors but also on the role that should be played by responsible shareholders, especially institutional investors. Specifically, the Cadbury Report stated:

> Given the weight of their votes, *the way in which institutional shareholders use their power to influence the standards of corporate governance is of fundamental importance*. Their readiness to do this turns on the degree to which they see it as their responsibility as owners, and in the interest of those whose money they are investing,

to bring about changes in companies when necessary, rather than selling their shares.

(The Cadbury Report, 1992, p. 50, emphasis added)

As a result of the Cadbury recommendations and successive corporate governance policy documents, ownership of shares can no longer be viewed as a passive activity, with institutional shareholders buying and selling shares as if they were gamblers in a casino, considering solely the financial benefit of the holdings (Keynes, 1936). Instead, institutional shareholders are now encouraged to play an active role in the companies they manage. They are no longer traders but *responsible* owners, taking an interest in their investment and maintaining it over time. In this respect it seems that Cadbury and its successors have initiated a paradigm shift in the City of London, which is having repercussions in stock exchanges across the world. Institutional investors, as well as the companies in which they invest, are recognizing the importance of their relationship with investee companies. My own research, involving interviews with a large number of fund managers, has revealed a deep-rooted shift in approach toward institutional investment over the last decade, with institutional investors embracing an active, rather than passive, approach to investment. Further, the research has indicated that this transformation is unlikely to halt and should continue to grow in the future. In terms of specific recommendations on shareholder activism, the Cadbury Report suggested that institutional investors:

- should encourage regular one-to-one meetings with directors of their investee companies (a process referred to as 'engagement and dialogue');

- should make positive use of their voting rights; and

- should pay attention to the composition of the board of directors in their investee companies.

Institutional shareholders can also form representative groups and present resolutions to company management. This, however, is an extreme form of shareholder activism that is used in the USA but rarely in the UK. One of the only examples of a shareholder resolution in the UK occurred on an environmental issue, where shareholders compiled a resolution for BP-Amoco concerning their environmental practices. This is a rare and isolated event and in this country is usually inspired by a strong lobby on a social, ethical or environmental issue. This is considered in some detail in Chapter 10 (see Illustration 10.2). The forms of shareholder activism that institutional investors can employ to monitor company management and resolve agency problems are summarized in Figure 5.3.

Following Cadbury, the Myners Report (1995) emphasized the importance of developing a 'winning partnership' between institutional investors and their investee companies. Further, Monks (1994) emphasized the need for institutional investors to practise what he termed 'relationship investing' with their investee companies. Another important initiative in the area of shareholder activism has been the publication, in October 2002, of *The*

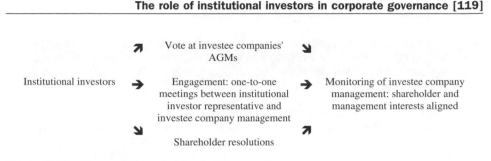

**Figure [5.3]**   Forms of Shareholder Activism

*Responsibilities of Institutional Shareholders and Agents: Statement of Principles* for institutional investors by the ISC (2002).[2] The Higgs Report (2003) expressed support for this 'Code of Activism', requesting that it should be endorsed by the revised Combined Code (2003). The ISC Code established a benchmark for institutional investor practice in the areas of engagement and voting. The aim was principally to provide a reference point for institutional investors, such that activism would become more organized and less *ad hoc*. An interesting aspect of the Code was its recommendation that the process of shareholder activism should become dynamic in nature. In other words, it suggested that activism *per se* was inadequate and that institutional investors should monitor the effectiveness of their intervention in companies and their monitoring activities, in order to improve and refine their engagement, voting and related practices. Not only does such shareholder involvement benefit shareholders but it can also have a positive impact on other stakeholder groups. Illustration 5.1 provides a more philosophical perspective on shareholder activism, exploring sociological reasons why increased activism may contribute to society, in a broader context, by restoring the trust that has been lost in institutions, mainly as a result of scandals in the financial community.

Clearly, shareholder activism is an important means of monitoring company management and of restoring trust in financial institutions. We now discuss the role of voting by institutional investors.

## Illustration 5.1

### Restoring trust

Reading the sociological literature in recent years provides a rather jaundiced view on the way in which British society is evolving. For example, the literature discusses a breakdown in 'social cohesion'. One of the main characteristics of this move to 'High Modernity' has been a breakdown in the level of trust in society. People seem to have lost the trust that they once had in institutions. This breakdown in trust is having serious implications for investment institutions. Trust in financial institutions has

---

[2]  The members of this Committee are: the Association of British Insurers (ABI); the Association of Investment Trust Companies; the British Merchant Banking and Securities Houses Association; the National Association of Pension Funds (NAPF); and the Investment Management Association.

reached a low point. The publication of the Sarbanes–Oxley Act (2002) and the Higgs Report (2003) and Smith Report (2003) in the UK may be interpreted as attempts to salvage public trust: 'We do know what we're doing – honest! We are trying to put things right.' As Myners commented:

> . . . the decline of trust is one of the greatest issues to affect not only the financial services industry but also the traditional professions. Lawyers, doctors, teachers, the clergy, they all have suffered from the loss of trust in them and their work. Where does this come from? There are individual reasons in each profession – but the combination of transparency, scandal and bellicose consumers means that trust is the first casualty of the new social order.
>
> (Myners, 2003, p. 6)

Myners went on to explain that there are two sorts of trust in the financial markets that have collapsed. One is the personal trust held in a fund manager, to perform as well as possible for a client. The second type is the confidence once enjoyed by pension funds and other institutional investors. This confidence was based on the abilities of professional investors and fund managers to handle money safely and prudently. The main cause for decline of trust in this area is linked to the ongoing pensions crisis in the UK. It is becoming increasingly evident that vast numbers of people will not receive the pension they had hoped for when they retire. Maxwell did little to inspire confidence in pensions. A recent survey conducted by MORI, the UK national polling agency, revealed that one in four people did not consider that company pension schemes were worth joining. Further, the survey found that almost two-thirds of workers interviewed did not believe that companies could be trusted to honour pension commitments to their staff (Blitz, 2003). As we discussed in Chapter 1, unethical behaviour can only be checked by regulations and policy documents, it cannot be cured. Trust within the financial sector can only arise from self-regulation and ethical behaviour. So what is the answer? More regulation is one way of recapturing society's trust in financial institutions, but it is not a panacea *per se*. Myners suggests that greater accountability and transparency by financial institutions, concerning their fund management activities, provides the best way forward. As he states:

> We will trust again those institutions that make their internal and commercial processes as pellucid as possible. This means that transparent business – and through it, good governance and accountable relationships – is the key to rebuilding trust.
>
> (Myners, 2003, p. 6)

It is essential that, for investment institutions, pension funds and indeed the traditional capitalist system in the UK to be maintained, trust is restored. This can only be done by the institutions themselves. From this perspective, increased activism and participation by institutional shareholders, accompanied by communication of their activities to their clients and other stakeholders, provides an important means of regaining and recapturing trust. The philosophical aspects of institutional investment have been explored in some depth in McCann et al. (2003). Solomon (2005) provides empirical evidence from company interviews to show that they are using social and environmental reporting to restore trust among their shareholders and other stakeholders. This paper will be discussed in more depth in chapter nine.

## Institutional investor voting

Until the 1990s the level of voting by institutional investors remained fairly low (Stapledon, 1995). However, the use of voting rights by institutional investors has increased significantly in recent years (Mallin, 1999). The NAPF has encouraged members to vote (NAPF, 1995), yet overall voting levels remain below 40 % (Hampel Report, 1998). The Hampel Report featured an extensive discussion of the voting rights of institutional investors. Voting rights, as we discussed in Chapter 1, constitute an important component of a shareholder's financial asset. However, prior to the Cadbury recommendations, institutional investors had been neglecting to use their voting rights. The importance of the voting right as part of the institutional fund manager's responsibility was acknowledged in the Hampel Report as follows:

> The right to vote is an important part of the asset represented by a share, and in our view an institution *has a responsibility to the client to make considered use of it*...We therefore strongly recommend institutional investors of all kinds, wherever practicable, to vote all the shares under their control, according to their own best judgement...
>
> (Hampel Report, 1998, pp. 41–42, para. 5.7, emphasis added)

The accompanying Combined Code specified that:

> Institutional shareholders have a responsibility to make considered use of their votes.
>
> (Combined Code, 1998, para. E1)

In 1995 the NAPF produced a report entitled *The Powerful Vote* encouraging their members to exercise their voting rights. This was likely to have a significant impact on institutional investors' voting policies because most pension funds in the UK are members of the NAPF and most institutional investors are pension funds.

Overall, since the Cadbury Report (1992) there has been a transformation in the institutions' attitudes toward their voting rights, to such an extent that many institutional investors have established their own voting policies. However the impact of such policies on corporate governance in their investee companies is unclear, as:

> Several institutions have recently announced a policy of voting on all resolutions at company meetings. This has yet to be reflected in a significant increase in the proportion of shares voted, which has risen only marginally in the last five years.
>
> (Hampel Report, 1998, p. 41, para. 5.7, emphasis added)

Given the strength of the recommendations for institutional investor voting, there has been an ongoing debate concerning whether or not voting by institutions should be made mandatory. However, Hampel emphasized the importance of keeping the use of voting rights voluntary and not moving toward regulation:

But we do not favour a legal obligation to vote. No law could compel proper consideration. The result could well be *unthinking votes* in favour of the board by institutions unwilling or unable to take an active interest in the company.

(Hampel Report, 1998, p. 42, para. 5.7, emphasis added)

In relation to the question of whether or not voting by institutional investors should be made mandatory, one academic paper concluded that such regulation should be avoided as it would result in institutions 'paying lip service to votes' (Short and Keasey, 1997). Further, Stapledon (1996) argued that compulsory voting for institutional investors in the UK would not be a 'worthwhile reform' (p. 287). He arrived at this conclusion by examining the impact of a compulsory voting requirement for the equity investments of non-public pension plans in the USA. Despite the more rules-oriented approach in the USA (discussed in Chapters 1 and 2) this mandatory voting policy resulted in fund managers creating formalized procedures and voting guidelines that were basically 'window dressing'. Stapledon also stipulated that disclosure of the direction of institutional investor voting should not be made mandatory (as had been deliberated by the UK Government in the mid-1990s) as he believed that institutional fund managers are principally accountable to their clients and not to other shareholders in the investee company, or other stakeholder groups. This perspective has been emphasized by the Code of Activism produced by the ISC, who stated that the duty of institutional shareholders is in the end to beneficiaries and not to the wider public (ISC, 2002). However, I feel that this argument does not fit comfortably within a broader, stakeholder approach to corporate governance. Not only do institutional investors have a responsibility to their clients but also, given the immense size of their collectivized assets, to society at large (see, e.g., Solomon et al., 2002, for discussion of this issue). We consider this viewpoint more fully in Chapter 10.

In 1999 the Newbold Committee was established by the NAPF to investigate the means by which votes were exercised by institutional investors in the UK. The Committee had to report its findings to the NAPF's Investment Committee and to make recommendations that would lead to improvements (where necessary) in the system of voting by institutional investors. This was targeted principally at pension funds but contained useful advice and recommendations for all types of institutional investor. Further, the recommendations were aimed at raising the level of institutional voting in the UK. Recently, there has been an intensification in shareholder activism, especially in the area of voting on remuneration policy. Early in 2003 the NAPF decided to form a joint venture with Institutional Shareholder Services, the influential US-based shareholder voting agency. The joint venture has been labelled Research, Recommendations and Electronic Voting. It provides detailed information on more than 22,000 companies in 80 markets around the world, with the aim of providing a basis for more active shareholding, through voting. Furthermore, there have been moves to encourage greater shareholder activism, or 'shareholder democracy', at a pan-European level, with the European Commission establishing a corporate governance action plan. The plan, linked to plans to improve company law within the European Union, aims to bolster shareholder rights, so that shareholders can use their voting rights more effectively. One initiative involves ensuring that shareholders throughout the European Union can participate in AGMs electronically and vote by proxy (Dombey, 2003).

### Reviewing the impediments to voting shares

Two reports have recently been published which have reviewed the impediments in the UK financial system to voting shares, making recommendations for improvements to the system (Myners, 2004; 2005). The review was conducted because of concerns that votes were being 'lost' because the voting system was not as effective as it should be. The main problems seem to arise from the complexity of the voting process. Myners' personal view of the problems was that,

> ...there is not one structural weakness that needs to be addressed. Rather, it is like old pipework which could have been more effectively maintained over the years, and is now leaking at various points. It does not need to be ripped out and replaced, but instead the points of weakness need to be overhauled and upgraded.
>
> (Myners, 2004, p. 2)

From a wide array of recommendations, the principal area where Myners (2004) felt improvements should be made was in the use of electronic voting systems. CRESTCo was one such system which had been introduced in 2003, but which had not been adopted widely. Myners argued that electronic voting represented the key to improving voting of UK shares. The second report (Myners, 2005) revisited the issue of voting, focusing on the extent to which recommendations of the previous year had impacted on the shareholder community. Myners (2005) found that significant progress had been made. He reported that there had been a significant increase in the number of share issuers who had facilitated electronic voting. However, he comments that there was still not the 100 % take up by institutional investors that he was hoping for. Myners (2004; 2005) also emphasized the role of the pension fund trustees to discharge their responsibilities to beneficiaries by ensuring efficient voting of shares.

### Voting on remuneration policy

In Chapter 4, we discussed the introduction of voting on executive remuneration from the point of view of the board of directors. Here, we revisit this important new development from the perspective of shareholder activism and accountability. Since 2001, investors have been allowed to vote on remuneration policies in a growing number of companies. This does not mean they can now vote on the levels of pay of individual directors but rather on the policy designed for setting that remuneration. This is an area which is likely to witness increasing levels of activism and which demonstrates much greater accountability, both on the part of companies to their shareholders and on the part of institutional shareholders to their clients. From a wider perspective, interest in directors' pay and proactive involvement by powerful financial institutions, are likely to result in improved accountability of companies and shareholders to other corporate stakeholders, such as employees and society. A flavour of the intense shareholder activism on remuneration that has been taking place is provided in Illustration 5.2.

## Illustration 5.2

### Fat Cat Slim

One of the most interesting and notable trends in UK business in 2002 and 2003 was the intensity of shareholder activism in relation to executive remuneration policies. In October 2001 the Government announced proposals for listed companies to produce an annual directors' remuneration report to be approved by shareholders. Since that time there has been a steady increase in companies allowing shareholders to vote on their remuneration policy. This has ushered in a spate of shareholder activism, with shareholders voting at AGMs in order to effect changes in these policies. The ABI and NAPF are two of the largest shareholder lobby groups in the UK, and much of the recent shareholder activism has been channelled through these two organizations. Another organization that is active in lobbying for shareholder 'voice' is Pirc, the corporate governance consultants.

There are a number of issues that shareholders have expressed views on. One has been to encourage companies to link remuneration more closely to performance. Shareholders and indeed the general public have been dismayed at companies who have rewarded failure. There have been numerous cases of executives receiving excessive remuneration packages in poorly performing companies (*Financial Times*, 4 June 2003). Another issue that has sparked shareholder action has been an encroachment of US-style remuneration packages crossing the Atlantic, as they are considered excessive. There are fears of contamination, as where one company chooses to go, the rest are likely to follow.

Let's take a snapshot of activism in the two months, May and June 2003. In May 2003 Kingfisher was targeted by the ABI and NAPF over its remuneration policy, as they condemned some aspects of the company's directors' remuneration packages as excessive and encouraged the company's shareholders to vote against them. The action was successful, as Kingfisher reacted by introducing tougher share option performance targets for the chief executive. They also lowered some of their directors' compensation for potential loss of office (Wendlandt, 2003). In the same month, HSBC staved off a shareholder rebellion concerning a controversial $37.5 million three-year remuneration package for Mr Aldinger, the bank's new director of operations in the USA. There was a shareholder outcry over his remuneration, with about 15 % of shareholders abstaining or opposing his re-election to the board of directors. His remuneration package included, for example, a lifetime of free dental care and use of a company jet for personal holidays (Croft, 24 July 2003). One of the most tantalizing tales involved GlaxoSmithKline. According to Michelle Edkins, director of institutional relations at Hermes, the company had failed to appreciate that it had pushed its shareholders to the boundaries of their tolerance (Skapinker, 2003). Whereas institutional shareholders in the UK tend to have a preference for confidential discussions with investee company management, in this case they used their last resort, public shaming of the company. Shareholder dissatisfaction manifested itself in 63 % of the company's shareholders voting against the company's remuneration policy, or abstaining, at the AGM.

In June 2003 Telewest bent over backward to avoid a disaster in its investor relations arising from their dissatisfaction with the company's remuneration policy. Specifically, shareholders criticized the board for deciding to pay the outgoing chief executive, Adam Singer, £ 1.4 million in severance (Kirchgaessner, 2003). Also in June 40 % of Tesco's shareholders voted against the company's remuneration policy, or abstained. This was the third largest protest by shareholders at a large company AGM since the beginning of the year (Voyle and Tassell, 2003). Northern Foods was under fire in June for granting pay rises of more than 16 % to two executive directors, even though the company's underlying profits had fallen significantly and its share price had seen a substantial drop in January. However, the company's remuneration committee retaliated to criticisms by stating that they intended to make an increasing proportion of their remuneration and incentive packages performance-related. Also in June almost a third of shareholders in Whitbread either abstained or voted against the company's remuneration report, due to their dissatisfaction with the continuation of two-year contracts for the company's executive directors. The NAPF was instrumental in firing up the shareholders before the company's AGM. Whitbread reacted by stating an intention to offer only one-year contracts to new executive directors (Boxell, 18 June 2003). Yet another case in the same month – 46 % of the shareholders of WPP Group opposed the company's remuneration report, or abstained their vote. The main problem was that Sir Martin Sorrell, the chief executive, had a three-year contract, whereas most companies are now turning to one-year contracts, as a result of shareholder concern. Further, Mr Sorrell was paid almost £1.6 million in 2002. Pirc estimated that his total remuneration package amounted to £65 million, if valued at the company's market share price (Harris, 2003).

It is clear that such public displays of shareholder dissatisfaction with executive remuneration policies and packages are having a deep impact on public attitudes, as a recent MORI poll found that almost 80 % of those surveyed agreed that directors of large companies were overpaid. By July 2003 it was clear that such activism by the institutional shareholder community was having a substantial impact. Leading companies have been forced to increase the proportion of their executives' pay linked to performance, according to a survey. The survey indicated that two-thirds of chairmen in the FTSE 350 companies expected to increase the proportion of performance-related pay. Further, half of the chairmen surveyed stated that shareholder activism had forced them to review their remuneration policies (Tassell, 9 July 2003).

## Research Into voting by institutional investors

The corporate governance literature has burgeoned in recent years, and the evolving role of institutional investors in corporate governance has not been ignored by academic researchers. In relation to voting, Stapledon (1995) shed light on the practical difficulties that can inhibit the exercise of voting rights by institutional investors. The paper also provided empirical evidence on the extent of voting by institutional investors prior to 1993. Stapledon emphasized that little evidence was available at that time on the voting practices of institutional investors. This was probably a reflection of the fact that institutional investors (*inter alia*) were not interested in voting their shares. He provided a summary of the empirical evidence on institutional investor voting in the UK as follows:

(i) Midgley (1974) surveyed an extensive sample of UK companies and found that only about 11 % of votes were exercised. However, this included all types of investor (not just institutions).

(ii) Minns (1980) stated that in the 1970s institutional investors did not generally exercise their voting rights.

**(iii)** The ISC performed a study in 1990 and found that on average the total votes received by companies amounted to about 20 % (including institutional and other investors). This was similar to, but a little higher than, the findings of Midgley's study from the 1970s. This report was not published and did not appear to break down the voting for institutions.

**(iv)** A second survey was conducted by the ISC in 1993. This was published (ISC, 1993), and the findings indicated that 24 % of votes were exercised in a sample of top UK companies. Again, this indicated a rise in the exercise of voting rights over time.

Stapledon performed a series of interviews in order to gather evidence on institutional investors' voting practices. He found that voting practices among UK fund managers were diverse. Some institutional fund managers had always voted all of their shares. Others had only just started to vote on all issues since Cadbury in the early 1990s. Others were continuing to vote on major, contentious issues. The paper presented solid evidence that before Cadbury, voting was sparse and disorganized, whereas by 1995 (three years after Cadbury) institutions were beginning to improve and formalize their voting policies.

An interesting point raised in Stapledon's (1995) paper was whether or not pension fund trustees had a duty to vote. He argued that under the contemporaneous legal framework, trustees and fund managers did not have any obligation to vote. However, whether they should be obliged through regulation, or a moral responsibility, to employ their voting rights was, he considered, an altogether different issue. Interestingly, a change to pension fund law has since stipulated that pension fund trustees have to (as from July 2000) disclose the extent to which (if at all) their fund managers exercise their voting rights in investee companies. Although this only forces trustees to disclose whether or not they instruct their fund managers to vote and does not make them vote, such disclosure *per se* can have an effect on voting practices.

Mallin (1996) compared the voting practices of UK institutional investors with those of US institutions. She carried out an extensive number of personal interviews with institutional fund managers, with the aim of canvassing their attitudes toward voting and discussing whether or not they had voting policies. Three categories of institutional voting policy emerged from the interview data:

 **(i)** fund managers voted on all issues (routine and non-routine);

 **(ii)** fund managers voted only on non-routine issues;

**(iii)** fund managers did not vote at all.

It appeared from the interviews that the first category was the most popular. However, fund managers who voted on all issues were not necessarily acting responsibly. It appeared that there were two types of fund manager who voted on all issues: 'box tickers' and those who actually considered their votes. The first group voted with the incumbent management on all issues without considering the issues carefully and perhaps voting against the management. In this case, the use of voting rights could hardly be considered effective from a corporate governance perspective. They are called box tickers because they are simply voting for the sake of voting and not reflecting on the impact of their votes. This is the sort of approach the Hampel Report warned could result from mandatory voting. Perhaps it is a negative result of recommendations of the Cadbury Committee. The second group did consider their votes carefully and decided in each case whether or not to vote with the incumbent management. This is a more responsible approach from a corporate governance perspective and is likely to result in far more effective monitoring of company management.

A later paper (Mallin, 2001) compared the voting practices of institutional investors across four countries. This study focused on the issue of whether or not voting was a fiduciary duty for institutional investors. Whereas Stapledon (1995) suggested that institutions were not bound to vote as part of their legal and fiduciary responsibilities, Mallin considered that they were. Indeed, she provided evidence that in the USA the right to vote was considered to be a fiduciary duty of institutional investors. The paper discussed the focus on encouraging institutional investors to exercise their voting rights since the early 1990s, as we have shown in the above discussion. On this issue the Newbold Committee had stated that voting was a fiduciary duty of institutional investors. Indeed, this Committee concluded that regular voting should be one of the first principles of proper conduct by the trustees of pension funds. Mallin concluded that, although the concept of voting as a fiduciary duty had long been accepted in the US, it had only been introduced in the UK relatively recently.

The author's research addressed voting via a questionnaire survey to UK unit trusts (Solomon and Solomon, 1999). The paper tested the hypothesis that UK unit trust managers were activist, were developing voting policies vis-à-vis their investee companies and were disclosing them to their clients and investee company directors. The questionnaire results showed that 72 % of the respondents' institutions had a written voting policy for their investee companies. In relation to whether the unit trust managers had ever attempted to influence the decision-making process within their investee companies through private meetings, 84 % responded that they had. A similarly strong indication of shareholder activism was whether the institutional investors had ever formed coalitions with other institutional investors, if an investee company was in crisis: a clear indication of relationship investing. Again, 84 % indicated that they had. Interestingly, one respondent, in a telephone discussion, expressed surprise at this question, saying that it tended to act well in advance of an imminent crisis. In Table 5.1 we can see how the respondents ranked a series of statements relating to shareholder activism.[3]

The institutional investors demonstrated strongest agreement with suggestions that they should disclose their voting policy to their clients, probably because this was the main

---

[3] They were asked to indicate the extent of their agreement/disagreement with four statements relating to shareholder activism, by selecting a score from 1 (strongly disagree) to 7 (strongly agree), with 4 indicating neutral.

**Table [5.1]**   Evidence on institutional investors and shareholder activism

| Rank | | Average response |
|---|---|---|
| 1 | Institutional investors should disclose their voting policy to their clients | Strong agreement |
| 2 | Companies should disclose, in a published form, the level of voting on each resolution at the last AGM | Strong agreement |
| 3 | Institutional investors should disclose their level of voting in their investee companies to their clients | Agreement |
| 4 | Institutional investors should be more actively involved in the management structure of their investee companies | Slight disagreement |

Reproduced by permission of Blackwell Publishers Journals

group to whom they are accountable (as suggested by Stapledon, 1996). However, the same level of accountability did not extend to disclosure of their level of voting, as this received weaker agreement (statement 3 as ranked in Table 5.1). These findings also supported Hampel's concerns that institutional investors should not become involved in the day-to-day running of businesses in which they invest, as statement 4 was met by general disagreement.

There has, however, been some level of resistance to increasing shareholder activism. As we can see from Illustration 5.3, institutional investors are not seen by all as responsible shareholders, improving corporate behaviour and performance.

---

### Illustration 5.3

### Hypocrisy Among Investment Institutions: Corporate Governance Activists Should Carry a Wealth Warning!

Not everyone sees the rising shareholder activism by the institutional investment community in a favourable light. Sir John Banham, chairman of Whitbread and former director general of the UK's Confederation of British Industry (the CBI) has spoken out against the institutional investment community (Targett, 2004; MacKenzie, 2004).

> I think the fund management industry really has to smarten up its act. Otherwise, it is heading for the door marked 'exit'.

Sir John stated that the fund management industry had been responsible for destroying a huge amount of investors' assets over the past five years, because they could not discriminate between which companies to invest in and which to avoid. He emphasized that there was no link between good corporate governance and good investment return. Indeed, he stated that companies with the worst corporate governance had actually delivered the best returns! He went further, by attacking the growing trend towards institutional investor activism and saying that such activists should carry a wealth warning because they damage investors' wealth!

Sir John also raised awareness of hypocrisy among institutional investors. Although they were actively attacking corporate directors' remuneration packages they were guilty of attracting high payouts for themselves. Standard Life, a flagship among active investment institutions, had been criticized for their directors' excessive remuneration packages. As Sir John said,

> They have been whingeing on about corporate governance, yet guess who has been paid huge amounts?

Transparency and accountability within the institutional investment community have also been attacked by John Sunderland, chairman of Cadbury Schweppes and president of the CBI. He proposed a new code of conduct for institutional investors. Amateurism in the pension fund industry is on its way out and this can only be an improvement (Myners, 2005). He suggested, for example, that investment consultants should develop fund manager engagement rankings. Sir John Banham has in the past caused controversy with the institutional investment community when he called fund managers 'incompetent lemmings'. He did however, qualify his remarks, by asserting that there were some exceptionally good fund managers. So all is not lost!

Indeed, as MacKenzie (2004) argues, this one-man view contrasts strikingly with the general emerging consensus. There is, as we see throughout this text, a steadily growing body of evidence to suggest that good corporate governance is associated with long-term shareholder value creation and bad corporate governance is associated with weak performance and corporate failure. Notably,

> . . . one reason why the UK's governance is so good, is that companies have benefited from a couple of decades of shareholder activism conducted by a band of governance specialists in the handful of fund management houses that have taken the issue seriously.
>
> (MacKenzie, 2004)

## Institutional investors: engagement and dialogue

The Cadbury Report and the Myners Report (1995) stressed the importance of institutional investors holding regular meetings with executives of investee companies. The Hampel Report (1998) developed the recommendations made by the Cadbury Committee in this area. Hampel stated that earlier recommendations had been 'broadly welcomed' by companies and investors, although the Report did not provide any solid evidence of this. The accompanying Combined Code stipulated that:

> Institutional shareholders *should be ready, where practicable, to enter into a dialogue* with companies based on the mutual understanding of objectives.
>
> (Combined Code, 1998, p. 24, para. E2, emphasis added)

The most recent corporate governance policy document, the Higgs Report, reemphasized the important role that institutional investors can play in corporate governance through investor relations by commenting that:

> I endorse the Government's approach to more active engagement by shareholders.
>
> (Higgs Report, 2003, p. 70)

Further, the Higgs Report recommended a revision to paragraph E2 from the Combined Code (cited above) to the following, stronger version:

> Institutional investors *should enter into a dialogue* with companies based on the mutual understanding of objectives.
>
> (Higgs Report, 2003, Annex A, Suggested Revised Code, emphasis added)

The importance of active engagement between institutional investors and their investee companies was also stressed by the institutional shareholders' Code of Activism (ISC, 2002). This Code of practice stipulated that institutions had a responsibility to intervene in investee companies 'when necessary' in order to discharge their accountability to their own clients. Indeed, the Code highlighted several instances when institutional shareholders might wish to intervene in their investee companies, namely, when they had concerns about: the company's strategy; the company's operational performance; the company's acquisition/disposal strategy; non-executive directors failing to hold executive management properly to account; internal controls failing; inadequate succession planning; an unjustifiable failure to comply with the Combined Code; inappropriate remuneration levels (and related packages); and the company's approach to corporate social responsibility (ISC, 2002, p. 3). The Higgs Report also added another dimension to the debate over the corporate governance role and responsibilities of institutional investors. It drew attention to the lack of involvement that non-executive directors had in relationships between their companies and institutional investors as:

> ... only rarely do non-executive directors hear at first hand the views of major shareholders. The majority of non-executive directors ... never discuss company business with their investors.
>
> (Higgs Report, 2003, p. 67)

This was an issue which had not been raised by previous corporate governance recommendations and reports and which represented an area for significant improvement in the corporate governance monitoring mechanism.

As we saw in the discussion in Chapter 4, a chief recommendation of Higgs was for non-executive directors to attend some of the regular meetings that executive directors and the chairman hold with key shareholders, in their process of engagement and dialogue. However, the idea of improving links between institutional investors and investee companies' non-executive directors was not entirely new. Stapledon (1996) had pointed out that non-executive directors could not be truly independent unless they were connected to a powerful group outside the company which could counterbalance company management, such as institutional investors. Indeed, Stapledon considered a more far-reaching recommendation than that later proposed in the Higgs

Report, as he suggested that UK institutional investors should appoint non-executive directors on boards and that these non-executives would monitor management more effectively.[4] He concluded that the Cadbury Report had not gone far enough in bringing two powerful monitoring mechanisms together, institutional investors and non-executive directors. However, Stapledon also explained that there were significant economic disincentives making such radical proposals unrealistic for Cadbury. One disincentive included the notorious freerider effect, whereby institutional investors do not want to monitor management effectively for the benefit of their competitors. Perhaps the reason that Higgs was able to make more progress in this area was that the free-rider problem had diminished, with the growth of engagement and dialogue.

Almost all major institutional investors are now engaging actively with investee companies. They are now more interested in competing with each other by winning clients, as a result of having the best and most effective engagement strategies, rather than worrying about other institutions benefiting from their efforts. Engagement and dialogue have become an area for competitive advantage for institutions, as well as a means of monitoring management and improving corporate (and therefore portfolio) performance. Indeed, the Code of Activism (ISC, 2002) stressed that monitoring by institutional investors may require the sharing of information with other shareholders in order to agree a common course of action. The revised Combined Code, published in July 2003, has also led the way for greater shareholder activism, with a clearly defined role for institutional investors in promoting corporate governance reform. See Illustration 5.4 for a discussion of the impact of the revised Code.

---

### Illustration 5.4

### The revised Code: a clear mandate for institutional investor activism

Despite the initial unfavourable reactions to Higgs' recommendations in January 2003 (see Illustration 4.2), by July 2003 both the institutional investment community and the corporate community had softened and decided on the whole to endorse a revised version of the Combined Code. The redrafted Code embraced the Higgs Report, changing the original language to appease business but not the spirit of his recommendations (see Chapter 3). The new Code encompassed all 50 of Higgs' recommendations, comprising 21 supporting principles, as opposed to 14 in the original Combined Code. Following the approval of the revised code by the Financial Reporting Council, Higgs commented that, 'The new code will encourage professionalism and objectivity in the boardroom. Shareholders will benefit from greater transparency and understanding of how boards work. The code will raise boardroom standards, drive company performance and help restore confidence in the listed company sector' (Tassell, 24 July 2003).

The revised Code received the endorsement of the UK business community, as Digby Jones, Director-General of the Confederation of British Industry (CBI), said the revised Code represented a 'Victory for common sense' that should strengthen boards and

---

[4] Similar recommendations for institutional investors in the USA were also made by Gilson and Kraakman (1991).

bolster the reputation of business, concluding that, 'The Financial Reporting Council has delivered a code that will encourage better corporate governance but not have damaging unintended consequences' (Tassell, 24 July 2003).

The institutional investment community, represented by its powerful lobby groups (the NAPF and the ABI) also supported the revised Code. Despite initial concerns among the institutional shareholders that Higgs' recommendations were too prescriptive, the final outcome was welcomed. The revised Code, expressed in softer language than the original report, was felt to have retained the essence, while avoiding the 'straitjacket of excessive prescription', according to Mary Francis the Director-General of the ABI. The role of institutional investors in endorsing the revised Code and pushing forward corporate governance reform is unquestionable. The new Code places the onus on shareholders to push forward corporate governance reform. More active shareholders should, with the support of the revised Code, be able to make deep-seated changes to their investee companies and to boardroom behaviour. Christine Farnish, chief executive of the NAPF, commented that, 'UK investors are increasingly ready to make their voices heard in Britain's boardrooms. We have already seen a number of high profile shareholder moves in some companies in order to encourage them to follow best practice. The new code establishes best practice firmly in the mainstream' (Fitzpatrick, 2003).

However, all has not been entirely rosy. Following the approval of the revised Code, there were widespread concerns that it might result in a massive increase in companies' disclosure burden (Tassell, 25 July 2003). This would be a result of the increased requirements for companies to disclose their level of compliance with the revised Code and explain any case of non-compliance.

There are also legal constraints on the engagement process. The Hampel Report raised potential problems with increased dialogue, such as risks of price-sensitive information being given to institutional investors. From a legal perspective, there are restrictions on the manner in which companies should disclose private information, especially risk-related information, to their core shareholders, as the process could be construed as insider dealing (Holland and Stoner, 1996; Solomon et al., 2000b). There have been various attempts to agree a legal definition of insider dealing, where the exploitation of price-sensitive information is the essential component (e.g., LSE, 1994). Further, there have been several attempts during the last decade to construct a statutory framework that could apply to the centuries-old phenomenon of insider dealing. The several specific statutory provisions that have emerged in this field seem to share the following generalized characteristics, when determining the parameters of legally (as opposed to ethically) unacceptable insider dealing. These characteristics can be encapsulated as follows:

- inside information relates to particular securities or to a particular issuer of securities, and not to securities generally or to issuers of securities generally;

- inside information is specific or precise;

- inside information has not been made public, which therefore covers information provided to institutional investors in one-to-one meetings with the managers of investee companies; and

■ if inside information were made public, it would be likely to have a significant effect on the price of any securities.

As we can see, this draws a fine line for companies that enter into detailed dialogue with their core shareholders. Information can be passed to the shareholder that is not in the public domain, but the offence occurs if the information is 'price-sensitive' (i.e., if the information would affect share prices as soon as it became public). An early statutory attempt to deal with insider dealing was the Financial Services Act 1986, which stipulated that the user of the information does not need to make a profit to be considered for an offence. Therefore, the problem is how do companies know whether information is price-sensitive? It is very difficult for individuals to make the distinction between information that is price-sensitive and information that is not. The complexity of the area and the difficulty of defining price-sensitive information is perhaps best evident in the extremely small number of successful prosecutions that have taken place during the past decade. Having looked at the encouragements for increased engagement and dialogue, as well as constraints on the process, we turn to considering the academic research into the engagement process.

## Research into engagement with institutional investors

Charkham and Simpson (1999) confirmed the emerging importance of the role of institutional investors in corporate governance. An extensive series of research interviews with companies and investment institutions has shown that the public disclosure of financial reporting information has been viewed as inadequate by institutional investors, who have therefore turned to private disclosure channels in many areas of financial reporting (Holland, 1998). This has led to the development of sophisticated systems of engagement between institutional investors and their investee companies, which cover many areas of financial reporting and corporate strategy. The author collaborated in research which addressed engagement and dialogue via a questionnaire survey to UK unit trusts (Solomon and Solomon, 1999). We tested the hypothesis that UK unit trust managers were encouraging relationship investing, supporting moves to encourage long-termism rather than short-termism in the UK system of corporate governance. Table 5.2 presents responses to a question in which unit trust managers were asked to rank their attitudes toward statements on relationship investing.[5]

The results in Table 5.2 indicate clearly that institutional investors support longer and stronger communication and decision links with their investee companies. The respondents agreed unequivocally that corporate activities that promoted long-term relationships should be encouraged. This is a clear endorsement of the recent UK policy promoting institutional shareholder activism. As we saw from the results presented in Table 3.2, the

---

[5] Investment institutions were asked to select a score from 1 (strongly disagree) to 7 (strongly agree).

**Table [5.2]**   Evidence on institutional investors and relationship investing

| Rank | | Average response |
|------|---|------|
| 1 | I believe that corporate activities that promote long-term relationship investing should be encouraged | Strong agreement |
| 2 | I believe that institutional investors should be more involved with the long-term strategic management of their investee companies | Agreement |
| 3 | I believe that the directors of our investee companies consider that the representatives from institutional investors change frequently and that they therefore have to educate them in the running of the business at each meeting | Agreement |
| 4 | I believe that the legal rights and responsibilities of institutional investors are sufficient to encourage and facilitate long-term relationship investment | Agreement |
| 5 | I believe that the directors of our investee companies resent the increasing time spent in meetings with institutional investors, as it detracts from their duties | Agreement |
| 6 | I believe that reforms in corporate governance lead to relationship investing | Agreement |
| 7 | I believe that stronger legal disclosure obligations placed on companies would encourage longer-term investment commitment | Strong disagreement |

institutional investors displayed a preference for a continued voluntary, rather than a regulated, corporate governance environment in the UK. This attitude is again reflected in the findings in Table 5.2.

From my interview research into institutional investors and corporate governance reform, fund managers appeared to be engaging with their investee companies on a regular basis and were holding dialogue on a diverse range of corporate governance issues. Interviewees indicated that this level of engagement has been operating for several years and was continuing to grow. Further, the research showed that dialogue was developing into an interactive, two-way process. Not only were institutional fund managers asking companies questions about their strategy and performance but also companies were initiating discussion and asking for advice from corporate governance specialists in investment houses (Solomon and Solomon, 2003a). Our research interviews also re-emphasized concerns raised in the Hampel Report that institutional investors were not business managers and should not assume the role of managing companies. On this issue, one of the interviewees, a corporate governance executive in a large investment institution, commented that:

> Investors don't want to run companies, they don't want to tell managers how to run companies, but they do like discovering what their clients are thinking.

Although quite a lot of literature has appeared on voting practices, less research has been conducted into the development of dialogue between institutional investors and their investee companies. This is partly due to the confidential nature of such information and partly due to the difficulties in obtaining data, but interviewing is really the only means of data collection for research in this area, as questionnaires cannot gain rich enough data, but interviewing is expensive and time-consuming. However, it is increasingly clear that institutional investors prefer the engagement route to the voting route as a means of influencing investee company management. Institutional investors prefer to discuss sensitive issues with companies behind closed doors, rather than embarrass companies by raising issues in public. Recent shareholder activism at AGMs on remuneration policy represents an exception rather than a rule and demonstrates the depth of dissatisfaction on this issue. Generally, fund managers consider that turning to voting rather than engagement is a last resort. As one of the institutional fund managers interviewed commented, voting is equivalent to 'major heart surgery' in his view, as it is used only when other channels of engagement and dialogue have failed. As well as the established areas where institutional investors have conducted activist strategies, there are now a host of new issues grabbing their attention. Some of these are discussed in Illustration 5.5.

---

### Illustration 5.5

### Shareholder Activism: Emerging Issues

The agenda for corporate governance reform in recent years has focused principally on board membership, director remuneration and audit independence issues. However, recently there has been a growing interest in a number of new issues.

*Business Continuity Issues*

Investors are starting to concern themselves with companies' attempts to address business continuity planning. Terrorist attacks have had substantial impacts on companies (such as bombs exploding in the Marriott Hotel in Jakarta or bank headquarters in Istanbul). Any type of plans ensuring business continuity such as office evacuation procedures, are now being incorporated into the corporate governance remit. Company value is clearly at risk if companies are affected substantially by such incidents and struggle to recover financially in the aftermath (Murray, 2005). Shareholder pressure has brought business continuity issues to the attention of the board of directors, as a corporate governance matter. Companies are appointing chief security officers as mechanisms to deal with issues relating to business continuity planning.

*Boardroom Appraisals and Succession Planning*

The shareholder activist group, Pensions Investment Research Consultants (PIRC), the London-based governance voting service, is starting to refocus corporate governance activism on issues such as boardroom appraisals and succession planning (Tucker, 2005). This change in strategy was disclosed by PIRC as part of its 2005 shareholder voting guidelines. This is partly because the activist group feels the worst excesses associated with bad corporate governance have now been alleviated.

## Factors affecting shareholder activism

A number of organizational factors seem to influence the extent to which institutional investors are active shareholders. For example, as with most issues in accounting and finance, size matters. Larger investment institutions have more resources available to allow them to focus on corporate governance issues, such as voting. My own collaborative research involving interviews with investment institutions have shown that fund managers in larger institutions are more proactive in corporate governance affairs than those in smaller institutions.

Some institutional fund managers operate index-tracking funds whereas others can select the investee companies more freely in their portfolios. An index-tracking fund is one that invests in companies in a fixed proportion relative to their position and size on the stock exchange. They cannot vary their investment allocation unless the index that they are tracking is changed. For example, some funds will track the FTSE 100 and therefore will have to hold the companies included in that index in their portfolios. The aim is to achieve a return on investment at least equivalent to the index itself. Index-tracking investors are called passive investors as they do not choose the companies in the portfolio. Active institutional investors manage non-index-tracking funds. Intuitively, one may anticipate that passive investors would be less interested in corporate governance and would be less interested in the activities of their investee companies than active investors. However, the reverse seems to be the case. Indeed, passive investors are 'stuck with' their investee companies and cannot divest if they are dissatisfied with management. Therefore, it is in their interests to employ their voting rights and active dialogue to influence company management. In the literature, shareholder activism is considered to be particularly important for passive, index-tracking fund managers as they cannot divest their shares and therefore need to improve companies through direct activism (Monks, 2001). However, even funds that are not passive but have very large holdings cannot divest because of the potential impact of such action on the stock market. It is also possible, theoretically, that different types of investment institution display different attitudes toward corporate governance. In other words, it is likely that institutional investors are not a homogeneous group with respect to corporate governance. Faccio and Lasfer (2000), for example, argued that pension funds had more incentive to monitor companies in which they held large stakes than other types of institutional investor, suggesting that they might be more activist. However, this was not borne out by their research findings, which instead indicated that pension fund activism was having little or no impact on companies.

## Shareholder activism and financial performance

An essential issue in the whole debate about shareholder activism and the role of institutional investors in corporate governance is whether or not such intervention results in higher financial performance in investee companies. There are many studies that have attempted to address this issue, but the evidence is inconclusive, as we see from the following discussion. Also, most of the studies are on US data and have not focused on the UK. This issue needs to be addressed in order to vindicate the increasing involvement of institutional investors in corporate governance. It is clearly an implicit assumption of the Hampel Committee and other proponents of shareholder activism that institutional investors' intervention in investee companies produces higher financial returns. There is certainly a perception among the institutional investment community that activism brings financial rewards, as more efficient monitoring of company management aligns shareholder and manager interests and therefore helps to maximize shareholder wealth.

Academic research has produced mixed evidence on the impact of shareholder activism on corporate performance and company value. Some academic studies have found that institutional investors have a significant impact on top management turnover, which is interpreted as positive for corporate governance, as this tends to result in improved financial performance. Franks and Mayer (1994) showed this link for Germany, while similar evidence was presented for Japan by Kaplan and Minton (1994) and Kang and Shivdasani (1995). Further, some research has shown that block purchases of shares by institutional investors tended to result in an increase in company value, top management turnover, financial performance and asset sales (e.g., Mikkelson and Ruback, 1985; Shome and Singh, 1995; Bethel et al., 1998). Also, Strickland et al. (1996) showed that shareholder monitoring led to increases in company value. Nesbitt (1994) and Smith (1996a) found that pension fund activism had a significant positive impact on the financial performance of companies targeted by the funds.

There is also evidence to the contrary, as several studies have found only weak evidence of a relationship between holdings by institutional investors and corporate financial performance (Agrawal and Knoeber, 1985). Further, one study found that shareholder activism in the form of shareholder proposals did not seem to lead to an increase in company value and seemed to have no influence on corporate policy (Karpoff et al., 1996). Indeed, Faccio and Lasfer (2000) poured cold water on the perceived benefits of UK pension fund activism. They found no evidence that blockholding of listed company shares by occupational pension funds in the UK was positively related to profitability and company value. The paper employed a correlation matrix to discover whether there was a positive relationship between firm value and ownership structure. They found, in most cases, a weak, negative relationship and concluded that:

> We report that pension funds do not add value to the companies in which they hold large stakes. Our results cast doubt on the monitoring role of pension funds which are considered theoretically, on the one hand, to be the main promoters of corporate

governance in the UK and, on the other hand, to be short-termist and dictate their rules to companies.

(Faccio and Lasfer, 2000, p. 105)

The possible reasons they proffered for their results were, first, that occupational pension funds may not have a material effect on investee companies, because the blocks of shares that they held tended to represent relatively small fractions of the total values of the funds' assets. Second, they suggested that pension funds did not monitor because monitoring was costly, as this activity was not likely to result in a modification in the company's pay-off structure and did not therefore lead to net gains. Third, the authors suggested that perhaps pension funds avoided intervention because they did not wish to draw public attention to the investee company's problems. However, their overall conclusion was that pension funds were essentially passive and that this was the reason their holdings did not influence company value. Yet, their results used data from the mid-1990s. As we have seen from the discussion earlier in this chapter (p. 115), institutional changes, such as the change to trustee law, as well as successive corporate governance policy documents have exhorted pension fund activism. It is therefore likely that they have become less passive. Clearly, more research is required to establish the extent to which the situation has changed and the extent to which pension funds have become more active, influencing the performance and value of their investee companies. This finding does cause us to question the genuine contribution that pension funds can make as a corporate governance mechanism for monitoring company management. Indeed, the agency problems prevalent within pension funds, resulting from their complex web of ownership, as we saw earlier, have been considered to hinder pension funds' ability to monitor investee companies effectively.

It does need to be borne in mind that, despite the positive monitoring potential of institutional investors, their relative power in the stock market also bears some costs. One of the important principles of 'good' corporate governance, according to the Organization for Economic Co-operation and Development (OECD, 1999; 2004) Principles, is for all shareholders to be treated equally. As institutional investors in the UK, and elsewhere, gain larger stakes in companies and become more influential over company management through engagement and dialogue, their treatment by company management is likely to be preferential. This problem was debated in Shleifer and Vishny (1997), who emphasized that large investors, such as financial institutions, represented their own interests rather than the interests of the whole group of shareholders. This type of problem has been exemplified by cases such as British Gas, where there was a clear division between the views of the institutional shareholders and the individual shareholders (see Illustration 3.2). In some countries, by using their control rights, large shareholders can redistribute wealth from other shareholders, resulting in a significant cost to shareholders as a whole. Indeed, Shleifer and Vishny (1997) discussed a number of potential costs associated with the presence of large investors, such as institutions, namely: expropriation of other investors, managers and employees; inefficient expropriation through pursuit of personal (non-profit-maximizing) objectives; and incentive effects of expropriation on other stakeholders.

However, these cases are more applicable to countries where large shareholders are related to founding families than to such countries as the UK where large shareholders tend to be financial institutions that follow ethical codes of practice and undergo substantial financial market regulation. We revisit these issues in Part II. There has been some dissent among the corporate community, with high profile figures decrying shareholder activism and querying any positive relationship between activism and performance. This development was discussed in Illustration 5.3.

## Chapter summary

In this chapter we have examined an important corporate governance mechanism, the role of institutional investors. More active shareholding can lead to better monitoring of company management and therefore to a lessening of the agency problem. Specifically, we have discussed the recommendations made by policy documents and codes of best practice in the UK on the issues of voting and engagement by institutional investors. We have also examined some of the empirical research, which suggests, generally, that there has been an increase in institutional shareholder activism and that this has had a positive effect on UK corporate governance and company value. The chapter has introduced the idea that institutional investors have a responsibility as majority owners of companies to influence company management and take an active interest in their investment, rather than remain passive observers.

The remit of institutional investor activism is broadening such that the areas of corporate management and business strategy affected by active shareholders are constantly expanding. Risks, especially reputation risk, are driving institutional investor dialogue with investee companies. See, for example, Illustration 5.6 for a discussion relating to the risks of an unhealthy diet and the impact of changing consumer tastes on business and the investment community.

---

### Illustration 5.6

### Fizz and Fat

Bacon and eggs for breakfast this weekend? Trim the fat off and go easy on the salt – especially for the kids. The trend towards healthier eating looks unstoppable and anyone who peddles unhealthy food or drink to children faces public condemnation.

(*Financial Times*, 4 March 2006, p. 8)

As we have seen from our discussion of corporate governance so far, the quest for 'good' corporate governance is being driven in part, by risk and especially reputation risk. The negative relationship between reputation risk and financial performance is now well established and forms the basis of the corporate governance agenda for reform, as factors associated with bad corporate governance affect financial performance negatively over the medium to long term.

A relatively new risk issue which has arisen and which institutional investors are incorporating into their corporate governance agenda is that of obesity. Society's fears about health risks and obesity are affecting the food and drinks industry. The big drives by champions such as Jamie Oliver to persuade schools to provide healthier school dinners and by campaigners trying to discourage people from piling down fast foods, are having a deep impact on society. The British Government, despite accusations of creating a 'nanny state', has focused on advertising healthy eating, with the NHS promoting 'five-a-day' for fruit and vegetables. The Government has also been addressing the issue of childhood obesity by establishing the School Food Trust which has, for example, now recommended a complete ban on sweets and soft drinks being sold in school.

Although the institutional investment community have generally believed that changes in consumer patterns resulting from health concerns would have only marginal effects on the performance of the food and drinks sector, their views are altering rapidly (Maitland, 2006). Institutional investors are rapidly repositioning their investment portfolios in response to the dramatic and sudden change in consumer behaviour. Similarly, companies are rapidly adjusting their product portfolios, so as to recapture market share in a new, healthy eating, healthy drinking world.

### Britvic

Paul Moody took over Britvic in 2005 and assured shareholders he would focus over the long term on existing brands – recent events have shaken this decision (Wiggins, 2006). The experiences of the soft drinks company, Britvic, have taken the markets by surprise. The share price of Britvic fell by almost a quarter (*Financial Times*, 4 March 2006) as a result of significant falls in fizzy drink sales, due to concerns about their relationship with obesity. Almost half of Britvic's business is in fizzy drinks and the change in consumer demand has had an immense effect on the company's sales. Although Britvic are responding by focusing on still, 'healthy' drinks, institutional investors are worried that the change will not happen quickly enough to offset the losses arising from the abrupt decline in fizzy drink sales. For example, Britvic still has only a minor position in the area of bottled waters and is struggling with low sugar products such as 7UP Free and Tango Clear. It remains to be seen whether Britvic's new products such as 'Drench' for teenagers and 'Fruit Shoot' water based drinks for children will compensate for carbonated drinks losses.

### Managing the Risk

A recent report for fund managers by EIRIS analysed six food and drink companies and concluded that Unilever and McDonald's had limited systems in place to deal with the social, ethical and environmental risks associated with obesity, whereas Coca-Cola, Kraft, PepsiCo and Cadbury Schweppes were doing moderately in this respect. Indeed, McDonald's has been singled out as the only company in the sector which has responded to the obesity issue. The company offers a wide range of low-fat meals and promotes healthy snacks such as fruit and salad, as well as water and orange juice. Despite its efforts, McDonald's intends to close 25 outlets in the UK following 5 years of falling sales due mainly to consumer concerns about fatty foods (*Financial Times*, 4 March 2006).

Nestlé is responding to the new risk by making nutrition an essential ingredient of all its food products and is pouring investment into research and development programmes (Wiggins, 2006). Small companies are also responding to the new health-conscious consumers, developing new, innovative healthy eating products. Innocent Drinks have started to produce 'smoothies', whereas large companies such as Pepsi are taking the easy route of buying small producers, such as PJ Smoothies, to keep their place in the market.

As well as highlighting the importance of risk to institutional investment and to corporate governance, this illustration also shows how dynamic corporate governance is. Institutional investors' dialogue with their investee companies is constantly changing and being refocused by external, uncontrollable factors such as consumer tastes. Codes of practice and guidelines are necessary but cannot substitute for sensitivity, flexibility and communication. Improvements in the communication and engagement between companies and their institutional investors are essential in our changeable environment. Now that companies are establishing better links with their principal shareholders and the institutions have closer relationships with the companies, the mechanisms are in place to respond to changes such as these more quickly and more effectively, thus avoiding financial losses and even corporate failure.

# Questions for reflection and discussion

1  Assess the extent to which you consider UK institutional investors are active shareholders. In your discussion comment on whether or not they are developing longer and stronger communication and decision links with their investee companies.

2  Read Illustration 5.1. Do you believe that trust in financial institutions can be rebuilt through legislation? Do you have any suggestions as to the ways in which institutional investors might inspire greater confidence in society, following recent scandals?

3  Read Illustration 5.2. To what extent do you think that shareholder activism on remuneration policies is a positive step? Do you think the trend will continue? Have a look in the newspapers for the most recent examples of such activity. Do you consider that sharcholder activism has a positive impact on corporate policy?

# Chapter 6

# The role of transparency in corporate governance

## Aim and objectives

This chapter discusses the ways in which corporate transparency contributes to corporate governance and the mechanisms by which companies may become more transparent. The specific objectives of this chapter are to:

- emphasize the essential role played by corporate disclosure and financial accounting information in corporate governance;

- define internal control, risk and risk management, and emphasize their role in effective corporate governance;

- appreciate the importance of the audit function in relation to corporate governance;

- introduce the emerging areas of governance reporting and forward-looking narrative reporting.

## Introduction

Transparency is an essential element of a well-functioning system of corporate governance. Corporate disclosure to stakeholders is the principal means by which companies can become transparent. This chapter examines the role of disclosure in corporate governance and considers the importance of a company's system of internal control and the audit function in relation to corporate governance. Specifically, the initiatives recommended in UK corporate governance policy documents and codes of best practice that relate to these areas are discussed. The Enron debacle drew acute attention to the need for well-functioning audit committees and internal control systems, as we saw from the case study in Chapter 2. Weaknesses in these areas can easily lead to corporate failure, as they provide central monitoring mechanisms in corporate governance. Therefore, we examine the contribution that the audit function makes to corporate governance.

## Disclosure and corporate governance

Disclosure is critical to the functioning of an efficient capital market. The term 'disclosure' refers to a whole array of different forms of information produced by companies, such as the annual report which includes the director's statement, the Operating and Financial Review (OFR),[1] the profit and loss account, balance sheet, cash flow statement and other mandatory items. It also includes all forms of voluntary corporate communications, such as management forecasts, analysts' presentations, the AGM, press releases, information placed on corporate websites and other corporate reports, such as stand-alone environmental or social reports (Healy and Palepu, 2001). Voluntary disclosure is defined as any disclosure above the mandated minimum (Core, 2001). Improvements in disclosure result in improvements in transparency, which is one of the most important aims of corporate governance reform worldwide (see, e.g., OECD, 1999, as discussed in Chapter 7). Increasing corporate transparency is a major initiative of corporate governance reform in the UK and elsewhere, as emphasized in the Cadbury Report:

> The *lifeblood of markets is information* and barriers to the flow of relevant information represent imperfections in the market ... The more the activities of companies are *transparent*, the more accurately will their securities be valued.
>
> (Cadbury Report, 1992, p. 33, emphasis added)

Increased and improved disclosure is likely to reduce agency costs as better information flows from the company to the shareholder, which in turn reduces information asymmetry. Indeed:

> Disclosure has long been recognised as the dominant philosophy of most modern systems. It is a *sine qua non* [essential aspect] of corporate accountability.
>
> (Farrar and Hannigan, 1998, p. 11)

From an agency theory perspective (see Chapter 1) the existence of information asymmetry results in managers being far more knowledgeable about the company's activities and financial situation than current or potential investors. This applies equally to stakeholder theory, as inadequate information places all stakeholders, not just shareholders, at a disadvantage. Without a structured system of disclosure, and in particular financial reporting, it would be very difficult for shareholders to obtain appropriate and reliable information on their investee companies.[2] Such information asymmetry leads to

---

[1]  The equivalent of the OFR in the USA is the Management Discussion and Analysis (MDA) section of the annual report.

[2]  The ways in which financial reporting addresses the problems of information asymmetry are analysed in Beaver (1989).

moral hazard and adverse selection problems.[3] By ensuring frequent and relevant corporate disclosure, shareholders are in a better position to monitor company management. The accounting function is an essential aspect of a well-functioning corporate governance system. However, financial reporting *per se* is not the subject of this textbook.

Accounting has long been acknowledged as a necessary means of monitoring the shareholder–manager relationship according to the stewardship concept. From a historical viewpoint a widely held hypothesis stipulates that both accounting and auditing developed as a monitoring mechanism and that accounts have always been demanded by investors for decision-making purposes. Watts and Zimmerman (1986), in particular, highlighted the importance of financial reporting as a means of reducing information asymmetry. They discussed the agency theory approach of Jensen and Meckling (1976), *inter alia*, and showed that accounting plays a contracting role, as accounting is used in the nexus of contracts aimed at monitoring managers. Inefficiencies in the market for information have resulted in the need for mandatory disclosure by companies. One reason in the literature for disclosure regulation is that accounting information may be regarded as a public good, because existing shareholders implicitly pay for its production but have no means of exacting a share of this payment from new shareholders (Leftwich, 1980; Watts and Zimmerman, 1986; Beaver, 1989). This implies that potential investors and stakeholders are free riders on information, paid for by existing shareholders. This in turn leads to underproduction of information, which represents a form of market failure (Healy and Palepu, 2001).

Bushman and Smith (2001) described the role of financial accounting information in corporate governance, arguing that the use of externally reported financial accounting data in control mechanisms promotes the efficient governance of companies. However, we need to stress that this relates to the quality of the information disclosed, as in accounting terms it needs to be relevant and reliable. For the sake of clarity, a clear distinction needs to be drawn between corporate disclosure (defined earlier) and financial accounting information. Financial accounting information represents one aspect of corporate disclosure, which has been defined as:

> ...the product of corporate accounting and external reporting systems that measure and publicly disclose audited, quantitative data concerning the financial position and performance of publicly held firms.
>
> (Bushman and Smith, 2001, p. 238)

They couched their analysis in the finance paradigm of agency theory (see Chapter 1). They perceived financial accounting information as a control mechanism that aids outside

---

[3] Adverse selection has been defined as an aspect of information asymmetry whereby those offering securities for sale practise self-selection, implying that securities of different 'quality' sell for the same price. Moral hazard, another product of information asymmetry, implies that the agent will attempt to benefit from the principal's inferior information set (see Beaver, 1989).

investors in their quest to discipline investee company management, encouraging them to act in the interests of their shareholders. However, often in the real world, financial accounting information is manipulated by management, as we saw on p. 36 from Enron's use of off-balance-sheet vehicles. In such cases, financial accounting information can increase rather than reduce agency problems, as creative accounting deliberately clouds the image of the company. Nevertheless, disclosure that is 'honest' should lead to a more transparent organization, thereby reducing agency costs.

At this point it is useful to consider the legal aspects of corporate disclosure. Chapter 3 emphasized that the UK has adopted traditionally a comply and explain approach to corporate governance. Although financial reporting is a legal requirement for companies, the sanctions for companies that fail to disclose, or misrepresent information, are civil rather than criminal. A firmer environment, such as that introduced in the USA with the Sarbanes–Oxley Act (2002), would make directors more personally liable for the disclosure they produce. However, within the current UK legislative environment, companies that fail to disclose information adequately would find it difficult to maintain listing on the stock market or to attract investors. This should deter many directors from irregular accounting practices. We now turn to the findings of academic research in the area of disclosure and corporate governance.

## Research into disclosure and corporate governance

Academic research indicates that investors perceive a value to corporate disclosure. There is a theoretical prediction that relevant and reliable disclosure by companies attracts institutional investors (Diamond and Verrecchia, 1991; Kim and Verrecchia, 1994). Indeed, increases in corporate disclosure have been shown to be associated with increases in ownership by institutional investors (Healy et al., 1999). Further, research in accounting has shown that regulated disclosure provides new and relevant information for investors (Kothari, 2001).

In relation to monitoring company management in an agency theory setting, how does financial accounting information help shareholders to monitor and control company management in an agency theory framework? One example of how accounting information is used to control management is through their remuneration, as the principal–agent model predicts that there is a direct link between company performance and managerial remuneration. As we saw in Chapter 1, one way of reducing agency problems is to establish explicit (and implicit) contracts between company management and their providers of finance. Such contracts require management to disclose relevant information that enables shareholders to monitor their compliance with these contractual agreements, so as to evaluate the extent to which management has utilized the company's resources in the interests of its shareholders (Healy and Palepu, 2001). A large body of academic research has investigated the extent to which financial accounting information is used to determine management remuneration packages. This text does not attempt to provide exhaustive coverage of the literature in this area, as an extensive review has been published (Bushman and Smith, 2001). However, it is worth noting, for example, that half of managerial bonuses were found to be determined by corporate performance, as reported in the financial accounts (Bushman et al., 1995). Further, research has shown that corporate performance measures have been used in evaluating managerial performance and that remuneration contracts depended significantly more on disclosed accounting measures than on share price (Keating, 1997).

As can be seen from these findings, if publicly disclosed financial accounting information is used to determine management remuneration contracts, then it serves as a means of controlling company management and reducing the agency problem. However, as agency theory states that managers should maximize shareholder value, then surely managerial remuneration should more logically be determined by share price, not financial accounting information. This is the case to some extent, but research has shown that share price is only one of many factors found to influence remuneration contracts. This area of theory and research provides an insight into the current transformation of corporate governance in the UK, with respect to shareholder activism on executive remuneration. Principal–agent models imply that the shareholders should design a remuneration contract that is based on performance as disclosed in financial accounts, in order to align managerial incentives to their own (Bushman and Smith, 2001). Therefore, increasing shareholder activism on remuneration policy is likely to help shareholders to align managerial interests with their own. For the first time, in recent years, shareholders in UK listed companies have been able to implement a core corporate governance mechanism (i.e., their voting rights) to make the link between remuneration and performance (see Chapters 4 and 5).

The example we have used here is the most obvious means of using accounting information to reduce agency problems. Accounting information generally provides similar benefits (e.g., studying the profit and loss account and the balance sheet gives an insight into the stewardship of a company over a period of time). We now turn to a relatively new development in the pursuit of greater transparency, that of improving governance reporting.

## Developments in governance reporting

One area of corporate disclosure which has, until now, been largely neglected, and which has lagged significantly behind the agenda for corporate governance reform in the UK, is that of governance reporting. A new initiative, arising from collaboration between Independent Audit Limited[4] and the ACCA, has been established to tackle this area of reporting, with the aim of highlighting the issues companies should take into account when disclosing governance-related information. The report (Independent Audit Limited, 2006) falls into two sections. Firstly, it provides empirical evidence on users' attitudes towards the current state of governance reporting. Second, the report provides a practical framework for corporate governance disclosure.

---

[4] This independent organization specializes in helping boards strengthen their leadership and control.

The empirical survey underlying the report involved consultation with companies, institutional investors, investor representative bodies, the Financial Reporting Council, and a variety of other users of governance information. The report's main finding was that there is a substantial expectations gap between the corporate governance information provided by companies and the information required by users and interested parties. Although some institutional investors do not use corporate governance disclosure its usefulness in decision-making is rising. Further, if the information were available, investment institutions would use it. Clearly, governance reporting is important for rating agencies, which provide information for institutional investors, as a risk-based attitude towards corporate governance is beginning to dominate (see the discussion in Chapter 3). The report is generally cautious about the usefulness of governance disclosures to the institutional investment community, but does acknowledge that,

> ...Most long-term investors do think seriously about governance. They are increasingly recognizing that good governance is about good leadership, direction and control, and should be taken into account in the assessment of management performance...
>
> (Independent Audit limited, 2006, p. 2)

Specifically, the report found that investors unanimously require:

- less boilerplate disclosures, with the focus on quality not quantity;

- inclusion of illustrative examples to provide insight;

- governance reporting that reflects each individual company's approach to corporate governance, reflecting its strategy and culture;

- a focus on current, relevant issues to avoid year-on-year repetition of themes;

- a focus on the role boards play and a link with performance rather than a description of what it does;

- discussion of how board membership contributes to corporate strategy;

- information about the effectiveness of the non-executive directors' role in challenging executive management and complementing the skills of the executives.

The report also highlighted the potential for better governance reporting to contribute to the growing dialogue between companies and their investors. Many of the issues upon which investors are asked to vote are governance-related and improved disclosure of corporate governance information will help to inform investors in making their voting decisions. Overall, investors seem to want companies to disclose discussions of their approach to the key aspects of 'good' corporate governance.

The corporate governance reporting framework recommended by the report moulds itself around a series of questions which boards of directors can use to evaluate their approach to corporate governance. The aim of governance reporting should be to communicate the nature and quality of the strategic leadership and control exercised by the board. The recommended questions are (Independent Audit Limited, 2006, p. 6):

■ What is the board's role and what did it do?

■ What gives the board confidence it has the right people?

■ How did the board work together?

■ How did management support the workings of the board?

■ How did the board ensure it was fully effective?

■ How did dialogue with investors help the board to meet its objectives?

The report emphasizes the need for boards to consider these questions as a means of integrating governance reporting into the annual report, without making it a separate, disconnected component. The recent review of the Turnbull guidance on internal control (Financial Reporting Council, 2005) has stressed the importance to shareholders of the internal control statement in the annual report, highlighting the need for companies to disclose information about risk and control issues in order to demonstrate the effectiveness of the company's internal control system to report users. Overall, the report stresses the need for greater self-evaluation and reflexivity in the board's reporting of their own effectiveness. This type of introspective and evaluative reporting is starting to emerge, for example BP's (2005) annual report comments that,

> The board continued its ongoing evaluation processes to assess its performance and identified areas in which its effectiveness, policies or processes might be enhanced. A formal evaluation of board process and effectiveness was undertaken, drawing on internal resources, individual questionnaires and interviews were completed; no individual performance problems were identified. The results showed an improvement from the previous evaluation, particularly in board committee process and activities, while also identifying areas for further improvement. Regular evaluation of board effectiveness underpins our confidence in BP's governance policies and processes and affords opportunity for their development.
>
> (BP, 2005, p. 161)

This represents an admirable attempt to disclose the board's self-evaluation of their performance and effectiveness in the governance area. The BP (2005) annual report also states that in order to discharge its corporate governance function in the most effective manner the board has developed a series of policies: a governance process policy; a board executive linkage policy; a board goals policy; and an executive limitations policy.

A similar, positive view of board self-evaluation of its effectiveness can be found in Tesco's (2005) annual report which states that,

> With the full support of the Board, the Chairman led a formal evaluation of the performance of the Board and its key committees ... The review concluded that the Tesco Board is highly effective and that there have been significant improvements in the Board's culture, dynamics and administrative processes during the year.
>
> (Tesco, 2005, p. 12)

It is notable that although self-evaluation of board effectiveness is taking place and the results are now being disclosed by leading UK companies, the disclosures tend to be self-congratulatory. Whether it is simply the case that boards are becoming more effective or whether only evaluations with positive outcomes are being reported requires research.

It is interesting that despite extensive rhetoric concerning stakeholder inclusion in investor dialogue and in the corporate governance agenda, not only in the UK but throughout the world, this report (Independent Audit Limited, 2006) into governance reporting makes no reference to stakeholders at any point. The report seems to assume that the only important stakeholder in the governance reporting process is the sophisticated investor. There is absolutely no consideration at any point in the report or in its proposed reporting framework of stakeholder needs in relation to corporate governance disclosures. This attitude is also reflected in governance reporting by listed companies. Although the BP (2005) report makes significant inroads into a more self-evaluative style of governance reporting, the primacy of shareholders is established from the outset,

> Our board is accountable to shareholders for the performance and activities of the entire BP group. It embeds shareholder interest in the goals established for the company.
>
> (BP, 2005, p. 158)

However, in the narrative, the company does explain that the pursuit of promoting long-term shareholder interest can include gaining an understanding of the environmental and social consequences of the company's actions. Although this is further qualified by the statement that it remains a matter of business judgement as to how these consequences are properly taken into account in maximizing shareholder value. The conflicts of interest in reconciling shareholder and non-shareholding stakeholder concerns are evident in the report.

## Internal control and corporate governance

A company's system of internal control represents from an agency theory perspective another corporate governance mechanism that can be used to align the interests of managers and shareholders. Internal control has been defined as:

> The whole system of controls, financial and otherwise, established in order to provide *reasonable* assurance of: effective and efficient operations; internal financial control; and compliance with laws and regulations.
>
> (Rutteman Working Group, 1994, p. 1, emphasis added)

Note the use of the word '*reasonable*' in this quotation rather than a term such as 'absolute', as this definition implies that it is impossible to have complete insurance against risks. The Turnbull Report (1999) represented the culmination of several years' debate concerning companies' systems of internal control. The report was accompanied by a code of practice and recommendations for listed companies. Again, the recommendations are voluntary, but as with the Combined Code (2003, see Appendix), if companies do not comply with any aspect of the Turnbull recommendations, they have to state where the lack of compliance arises and explain why they have not complied in their annual reports. As with earlier corporate governance codes of practice, the Turnbull Report aimed not to transform companies' systems of internal control but to make explicit the systems of internal control, which many of the top-performing companies had developed, in order to standardize internal control and achieve best practice. The revised guidance on internal control (FRC, 2005) issued from two consultation exercises, which confirmed and consolidated the flexible, principles-based approach to internal control adopted by the original Turnbull Report.

Without an effective system of internal control, companies can undergo substantial financial losses as a result of unanticipated disasters. The recent collapse of Enron has been attributed in part to a failure of the company's system of internal control (see Chapter 2). Similarly, the earlier cases of Maxwell (see Illustration 3.1) and Barings (see Illustration 3.3) involved weaknesses in internal control systems. Smith (1996b) discussed a number of cases of corporate failure and explained how inadequate systems of internal control, as well as investors' inadequate analysis of disclosed information, contributed to collapses such as Coloroll and Polly Peck. Companies need to establish a system for internal control so that they can manage risk effectively, thereby increasing transparency. But how may we define risk?

### Risk and risk prioritization

Risk has been defined as the possibility of loss as a result of the combination of uncertainty and exposure flowing from an investment decision or a commitment (Boritz, 1990). Uncertainty can however result in gain as well as loss. Unless companies and investors take risks they cannot expand. For example, foreign direct investment is essential for companies if they are to expand internationally but it involves significant risks. Although risk needs to be managed by organizations, it should not be eliminated. There are many different types of risk that face companies including financial risks (such as interest rate and exchange rate risk), environmental and social risks, and the risks arising from non-compliance with regulation. However, each company faces a different risk profile, and their prioritization of these risks is likely to vary. For example, a toy manufacturer will be faced with such risks as seasonal variation in consumer demand whereas an oil company will be concerned about the risks of oil tankers sinking and polluting areas of outstanding natural beauty, such as protected coastlines. The need for companies to prioritize risks was emphasized in a report by the Institute of Chartered Accountants in England and Wales (ICAEW, 1998).

As outlined in Chapter 3 the Combined Code (1998) dealt with internal control in Provisions D.2.1 and D.2.2, where it stated that company directors should conduct a review of the effectiveness of their internal control systems and should report this information to shareholders (Combined Code, 1998). The Turnbull Committee was established specifically to address the issue of internal control and to respond to these provisions in the Combined Code. Company management use the operating and financial review to disclose risk information and ways in which they are assessing and reducing risk. Such disclosure increases corporate transparency, thereby reducing agency problems.

*An existing implicit framework for internal control*
Despite practitioners' increasing interest in internal control, academic research has made little attempt to conceptualize a system of internal control that accommodates the issues associated with corporate governance. Individual companies have developed their own approaches to internal control and risk management. The risk management approach of British Aerospace has been documented in terms of corporate governance (see Meyrick-Jones, 1999). This approach involved: providing the main board with information on the risks within the group; facilitating internal control as well as providing the disclosure required for reporting; safeguarding the group's assets; and providing a set of rules that the companies within the group could use to assess risk. These, in turn, were expected to safeguard shareholder value (see also Groves, 1999; Thomas, 1999). Thus, although there may be generic categories for implementing risk control mechanisms, companies appear to have developed their own systems in order to meet their specific needs. Before the publication of the Turnbull Report, listed companies had been focusing generally on developing complex and detailed systems of internal control. However, as each company produced an individual system there had been concern that these different systems may not have been addressing internal control effectively. Although the general consensus was that standardization of internal control would be impossible as companies' risks varied so diversely, some common recommendations were deemed necessary. This was the aim of the Turnbull Report (1999). A need for formalizing the sets of procedures implemented across individual listed companies had arisen and the Turnbull Report represented an attempt to create an explicit framework for companies to refer to as a benchmark, when developing their own internal control strategies. For an excellent discussion of internal control see Blackburn (1999).

*The Turnbull framework for internal control*
The stated objectives of the Turnbull Report appeared to represent a conceptual framework that attempted to make the existing implicit corporate risk disclosure framework explicit. The aim of the framework was to:

...reflect sound business practice whereby internal control is embedded in the business process...

(Turnbull Report, 1999, para. 8)

My own research summarized the chief components of the Turnbull framework for internal control in a diagram that represented the Turnbull framework (see Figure 6.1, adapted from Solomon et al., 2000b). The diagram showed that a company's system for internal control, according to Turnbull, included several stages. The first stage of the framework was *identification* which involved both the identification and prioritization of relevant risks. The recommendation from Turnbull corresponding to this stage of the framework was that in determining a company's internal control policies the board of directors should consider:

...the nature and extent of the risks facing the company.

As well as:

...the extent and categories of risk which it regards as acceptable for the company to bear.

(Turnbull Report, 1999, para. 17)

The specific types of risk that should be identified explicitly were not specified in Turnbull, so it would be up to the company to identify the sources of risk that were relevant to them. The *estimation stage* of the conceptual framework depicted the assessment of the potential impacts of identifiable sources of risk. This was described explicitly as a consideration of:

...the likelihood of the risks concerned materialising.

(Turnbull Report, 1999, para. 17)

At the *developmental stage* the company should develop its specific risk management strategy, tailored to match specific risks. Thus, the board should consider the:

...company's ability to reduce the incidence and impact on the business of risks that do materialise.

(Turnbull Report, 1999, para. 17)

This stage should also involve an evaluation of:

...costs of operating particular controls relative to the benefit thereby obtained in managing the related risks.

(Turnbull Report, 1999, para. 17)

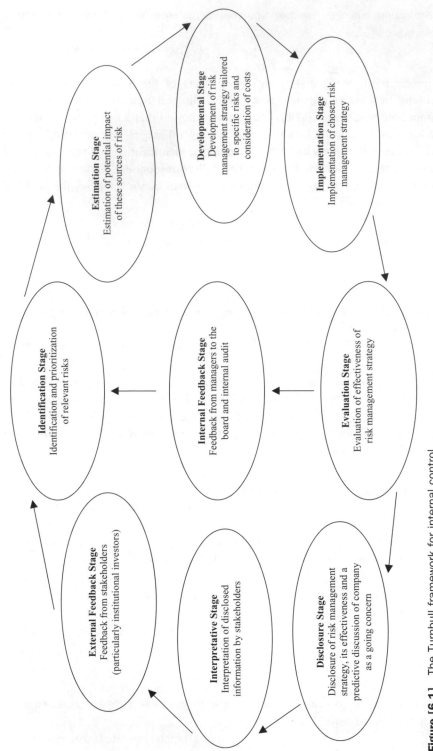

**Figure [6.1]** The Turnbull framework for internal control
Adapted from Solomon et al., 2000b, reproduced by permission of Academic Press

The development of a risk management strategy led naturally to the next stage of *implementation*, where the board put their chosen risk management strategy into operation. Following implementation, the internal control system was shown to involve an *evaluation stage* where the effectiveness of the implemented strategy was evaluated. This stage involved:

> ...effective monitoring on a continuous basis.
>
> (Turnbull Report, 1999, para. 27)

So as to ensure a dynamic and effective system of internal control, the evaluation stage flowed directly into an *internal feedback stage*, as frequent feedback in the form of reports from managers to the board, as well as (in some cases) an internal audit, to link evaluation to internal disclosure. Indeed, where companies do not operate an internal audit they should review the need for one at frequent intervals (Combined Code, 1998, D.2.2).

An outlet for the company's risk management strategy involves formal public disclosure to its stakeholders. This *disclosure stage* involves reporting information relating to the company's risk management strategy, its effects and success, as well as some predictive discussion of the company as a going concern. Despite the explicit guidance for an internal control framework, Turnbull provided remarkably little detail concerning the format of disclosure within the system of internal control. However, Turnbull provided detailed guidance concerning what should be discussed in an annual assessment preceding the company's public statement on internal control (Turnbull Report, 1999, paras 33 and 34). Indeed, the only explicit guidance on what should be disclosed stated that in their narrative statements companies should:

> ...as a minimum, disclose that there is an ongoing process for identifying, evaluating and managing the significant risks faced by the company.
>
> (Turnbull Report, 1999, para. 35)

This was followed by a suggestion that the company could choose:

> ...to provide additional information in the annual report and accounts to assist understanding of the company's risk management processes and system of internal control.
>
> (Turnbull Report, 1999, para. 36)

There was also a recommendation for some disclosure of the process that the company used to review the effectiveness of its internal control system, as well as information relating to the process it had applied to deal with *material* control aspects of any significant problems disclosed in the annual report and accounts. Of course, this left the decision on materiality to company managers, and it is this materiality decision that therefore governs the disclosure.

The last stage of the framework for internal control was one of *interpretation* of the disclosed material by stakeholders, which was intended to facilitate *external feedback* and control. This feedback should be incorporated in the first identification stage of the framework as a crucial aspect of the company's overall risk management strategy and system of internal control. The strengthening of communication and decision links between shareholders and investee companies, for example, is one sign that this feedback process is evolving (see Solomon and Solomon, 1999).

Although the main emphasis of the Turnbull Report was on the assessment, estimation, management and disclosure of financial risks, there was also an implication that companies should take account of non-financial risks in their systems of internal control. This broader agenda for internal control is discussed in Illustration 6.1.

## Illustration 6.1

### Broadening the Turnbull agenda

In 2000 the Association of Chartered Certified Accountants produced a report that considered the relevance of risks other than solely financial risks from a Turnbull perspective (ACCA, 2000). This report is extremely interesting as it combines the importance of stakeholder issues with financial issues and extends the Turnbull remit to a broader community of stakeholders. The aim of the report is stated in a short introduction that says: 'This short report seeks to illustrate some of the wider implications of the Turnbull Report – especially as it relates to social, environmental and sustainable development risk issues.' A number of involved practitioners set out their views on what Boards of Directors really do need to know about Turnbull – but probably won't be told by their finance director. There are a number of short articles included in the report and we shall deal with them in turn.

*Accountability, transparency, corporate social responsibility:*
*a new mantra for a new millennium*

This article represents the introduction to the report. It emphasizes that Turnbull is based on the '. . . adoption of a risk-based approach to establishing a sound system of internal control and on reviewing its effectiveness.' This should not be an additional 'extracurricular' activity for company management but should instead be incorporated in normal, everyday management and corporate governance. The review highlights the fact that Turnbull is not intended to deal solely with financial controls but also with social and environmental issues. The way that such concerns are incorporated in a risk-based corporate framework is by the back door of 'reputation risk' issues. In other words, the reason why environmental and social issues are important for companies is because they can pose serious reputational risk by damaging corporate image. As a result of such reputational concerns, pension funds are now required to disclose the extent to which they invest according to social, ethical and environmental criteria. This is something we will be dealing with specifically in Chapter 10. The important point is that Turnbull requires a company board of directors to consider environmental, ethical and social issues as part of their compliance. Indeed, the authors state that, 'In our joint view, disclosure of broader risk-related issues is fundamental to the principles of accountability and transparency. Companies that hide behind a narrow definition of risk will be doing themselves a disservice, as the ability of stakeholders to penetrate that shield increases. As both Shell and Nike have found, openness is definitely the best policy when it comes to developing sustainable long-term relationships with stakeholders'.

### Corporate governance in a CNN world (John Elkington and Peter Zollinger from SustainAbility)

CNN as an international news network is one media form that implies that reputational risk has a broader impact than ever before. The make-up and activities of corporate boards are in the spotlight more than ever before. Companies are now required to address such issues as health, the environment and ethics as part of their daily business decision-making process. Business leaders and boards are going to have to be able to pick up 'weak signals' in order to be globally competitive.

### Turnbull and reputational risks: an investment view (Craig Mackenzie from Friends & Ivory Sime, now ISIS)

This article emphasizes that Turnbull is a corporate governance issue. They comment that for a while institutional investors have been encouraged to influence companies by means of their voting rights as a part of their good corporate governance practice. Social, environmental and ethical issues have in the past been considered only for specialized investors. However, the new pension fund disclosure requirement has brought these issues to the forefront for mainstream investors.

### Risk analysis and management: the role of dialogue (Simon Zadek from AccountAbility)

For Zadek, the author of this short article, the key to the Turnbull recommendations is stakeholder dialogue. It is vitally important for a company to know what its stakeholders require, what their concerns are and the issues that affect the business that are utmost in their minds.

### Environmental and reputational risk in the annual report and accounts (Roger Adams from ACCA)

Adams is a strong advocate of companies providing environmental information and is the accounting representative on many committees, such as the Global Reporting Initiative (GRI). Adams believes that it is important for companies to disclose environmental information in their annual reports. Being an accountant, he is particularly interested in the financial impacts. However, more qualitative-type disclosures such as poor ethical, environmental and employment practices, are also important for him. In particular, he advocates the disclosure of forward-looking reporting, in that financial reporting as we know is retrospective. Adams advocates disclosure that includes information on provisions for contaminated land, decommissioning of long-lived assets and contingent environmental liabilities.

### The implications of Turnbull: a corporate view (Chris Tuppen from British Telecom)

Tuppen has been at the forefront of environmental disclosure at BT for many years. It is his view that social and environmental reports can be useful in the identification of risk. Also he considers that they should be included in the appropriate internal control mechanisms as suggested by Turnbull. For Tuppen there are two main risks to companies in the environmental and social sphere. The first includes liabilities resulting from past pollution, and the second concerns the company's reputation. For example, when BT was owned by the Government, people did not own their own telephones. They could only be hired from BT (which was part of the Post Office). An innovation in the 1970s was to produce a (by 1970s standards) 'trimphone' that was turquoise in colour (pathbreaking stuff at the time). The major innovation was that it was not only 'slim' but it had a neon dial. When these phones reached the end of their useful life BT found that they were radioactive. They dismantled them and the radioactive dials were stored in a warehouse somewhere, as BT did not know what to do with them. If this isn't an environmental/ethical/social risk what is?

*Managing reputational risk (John Browne from PricewaterhouseCoopers)*

Browne discusses the importance of managing reputational risk. In Browne's experience as a director of PricewaterhouseCoopers boards are as concerned about reputational risks as with financial loss *per se*. Browne considers at some length how it is important for companies to 'engage' with their stakeholders. To some extent this supports Zadek's views. In the Brent Spar incident in the early 1990s Shell wanted to dismantle an oil platform that had come to the end of its useful life. Shell wanted to dispose of it at sea. Greenpeace wanted it disposed of on land. A boycott of Shell products ensued. National governments became involved. Shell's reputation suffered badly. The scientific advice was to dispose of the platform at sea (!) implying that Greenpeace were misguided in their views. For Shell the main lesson was that it must manage its reputation and that stakeholder dialogue was essential. For further details check the Shell website which documents this fiasco in some detail.

*Managing risk: a case study in the National Health Service (Nigel Woodcock)*

Woodcock discusses the implications of Turnbull for the public sector. It is interesting to note that over the last 15 or so years the public sector has taken on many of the characteristics of the private sector. Corporate governance is no exception. This is in part due to an extensive privatization programme and the view by various governments that the market model is superior to the state model. Of particular interest here is that the direction of influence is not just private to public sector but also public sector to private sector, as non-financial indicators have been used for evaluating performance. For example, the railways should really be disclosing how many people have died on the railways each year! Indeed, this is now being considered. It is the ultimate in benchmarking performance. In a different paper, Belcher (2002) discussed the issue of 'corporate killing' as a corporate governance issue. Indeed, she stated that Turnbull opened the way for discussion on many more risk-related issues than the purely financial! To some extent, parts of the National Health Service have been privatized, with each hospital now in command of its own budget. There is no board of directors as such or shareholders, rather an NHS Trust exists in order to undertake a similar monitoring role. The Trust Board now has a statutory duty to certify that management has covered all risks in the management of the Trust and has systems in place to deal with these risks.

*Turnbull and your company: identifying and managing the risks*
*(Rachel Jackson from ACCA and Chris Tuppen from British Telecom)*

In the final section of this interesting report, Jackson and Tuppen provide a three stage model for identifying and managing risks. Stage 1 identifies the sources of risk. These risks may include:

- *Supply chain risks.* These are suppliers based in countries that have:
  - human rights abuses;
  - child and forced labour concerns;
  - living wage issues.

Suppliers that are:
  - high pollutants;
  - using unsustainable production technologies (e.g., forestry, fisheries, etc.);
  - involved with GMOs.

If this is an area that you are interested in, B&Q DIY provide examples of how they have tried to overcome some of these problems (see their website or visit a store).

- *Operational risks*. Companies operating in countries with:
  - o human rights abuses;
  - o child and forced labour concerns;
  - o living wage issues.

Also:

  - o unsatisfactory employee satisfaction levels;
  - o potential to contaminate land;
  - o involvement with dangerous activities;
  - o level of noise/visual pollution (e.g., brightly coloured outdoor clothing!);
  - o compliance with environmentally and socially regulated processes;
  - o location of sites (urban/rural).

- *Product risks*
  - o the use of unsustainable or hazardous raw material in product composition;
  - o quantity and type of waste produced during production;
  - o end-of-life disposal methods;
  - o health and safety concerns related to product use;
  - o environmental effects from product use.

- *General societal expectation*
  - o disclosure of environmental and social performance via a report;
  - o certification to environmental and social standards;
  - o statement of business principles.

Stage 2 of the model evaluates the significance of these risks and Stage 3 considers how these risks may be managed.

Overall, we can see how this report brings stakeholder accountability and a much wider perspective on risk management and internal control into the corporate governance debate. This approach embodies stakeholder theory and inclusivity, as discussed in Chapter 1. We pick up on the broader agenda for corporate governance and the importance of an inclusive approach in Part III.

## The revised guidance on internal control

In 2005, the Financial Reporting Council published an updated version of 'Internal Control: Guidance for Directors on the Combined Code' which contained only limited

**Table [6.1]**   Summary of the Main Revisions to the Turnbull Guidance in 2005

1.   A new preface was added to encourage boards to review on a continuing basis their application of the guidance and consider the internal control statement as an opportunity to communicate to their shareholders how they manage risk and internal control.

2.   The introduction was reorganized to reinforce the message that the guidance aims to reflect sound business practice as well as to aid companies in complying with the internal control requirements of the Combined Code.

3.   Changes to the Combined Code and Listing Rules since 1999 were incorporated.

4.   The new guidance emphasized the need for directors to apply the same standard of care when reviewing the effectiveness of internal control as when exercising their general duties.

5.   The section of the guidance relating to the Code provision on internal audit was removed and incorporated into the Smith guidance on audit committees.

6.   The revised guidance requires boards to confirm in their annual report that they have taken the action necessary to remedy any significant failings or weaknesses identified from their review of the effectiveness of the internal control system. They are also required to include in the annual report information considered necessary to aid shareholders in understanding the main features of the company's risk management processes and system of internal control.

changes, as shown in Table 6.1.[5] One of the main aims of the consultation process was to evaluate the impact of the original Turnbull Report on improving internal control in UK listed companies. The Financial Reporting Council concluded that,

> In reviewing the impact of the guidance, our consultations revealed that it has very successfully gone a long way to meeting its original objectives. Boards and investors alike indicated that the guidance has contributed to a marked improvement in the overall standard of risk management and internal control since 1999.
>
> (Financial Reporting Council, 2005, preface, p. 1)

Although the review endorsed the flexible, comply or explain approach of the original Turnbull Report, the Financial Reporting Council stressed the need for companies to review constantly their systems of internal control. They emphasized the need for companies' internal control systems to be dynamic and to take into account new and emerging risks, failure of internal control, changes in market expectations, business objectives and company circumstances.

The last point made in the review was that boards should disclose in their annual reports how they have dealt with any weaknesses or failings identified from their review of the internal control system. The lack of attention to this particular point in the first

---

[5]   The material in this table has been adapted from the Financial Reporting Council Press Notice, 2005.

Turnbull guidance was highlighted as a weakness of the Turnbull framework, as it showed that reporting of risk-related information was considered inadequate and that the Turnbull guidance did not go far enough in encouraging companies to be self-evaluative in the assessment of their internal control systems (see Solomon et al., 2000b).

We see from the following section, ways in which the disclosure stage of the internal control system should evolve.

## Risk disclosure and corporate governance

Corporate risk disclosure represents an important, specific category of corporate disclosure. One of the main developments in the area of corporate disclosure for UK companies, linked to the general agenda for corporate governance reform, has been an increasing emphasis on corporate risk disclosure. This was highlighted by the publication of the Turnbull Report, which focused attention on this crucial aspect of the Turnbull framework for internal control. Emphasis on the reporting stage of the internal control system is essential, both for corporate accountability and for the future success of the business. Indeed, the USA and Canada recognized the need to improve corporate risk disclosure before the publication of the UK Turnbull Report (see Treadway Commission, 1987; Boritz, 1990; Courtis, 1993), and this need was also acknowledged a little later by interested parties in the UK (e.g., see Arthur Andersen, 1996). The Cadbury Report (1992) also highlighted the relevance of risk disclosure to the corporate governance agenda by suggesting that validating the company as a going concern and improving the disclosure of internal control should lead to improvements in the communication links between investors and their investee companies. Further, if the aim of company management is to reduce the cost of capital by raising confidence in the market, then the communication of risk management policies must be a significant factor. Improving information flows between companies and their shareholders represents one effective way of reducing information asymmetry, thereby lessening the agency problem inherent in UK corporate governance, as discussed in Chapter 1.

### An 'ideal' framework for corporate risk disclosure

As can be seen from the earlier discussion of the Turnbull Report, the section of the report relating specifically to corporate risk disclosure was unspecific and short. Therefore, Solomon et al. (2000b) developed a diagrammatic framework for corporate risk disclosure that presented several possible alternatives for an 'ideal' framework. The paper attempted to provide companies with a little more in the way of structure for their risk disclosure process. It is from Solomon et al. (2002b) that the possible ingredients of an ideal corporate risk disclosure framework are reproduced in Figure 6.2. The diagram incorporates six variable elements that interrelate to create the extant framework for corporate risk disclosure. One important element is whether corporate risk disclosure should remain in a voluntary environment or whether it should be made mandatory. Another element is the appropriate level of risk disclosure: Is the current level of information that is disclosed adequate or would increased corporate risk disclosure facilitate investment decision

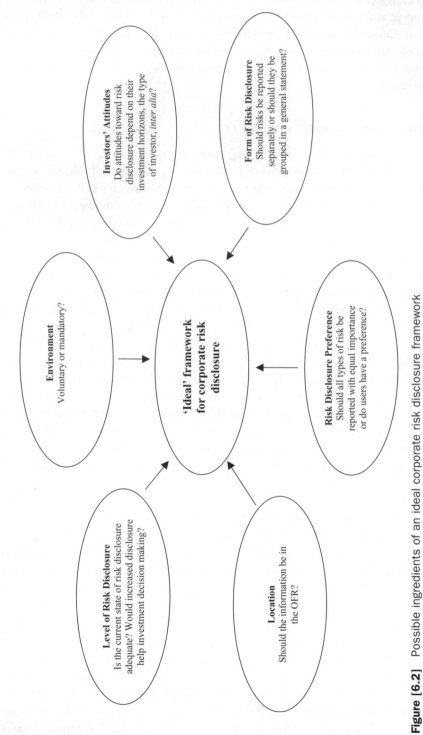

**Figure [6.2]** Possible ingredients of an ideal corporate risk disclosure framework
OFR = Operating and Financial Review. Adapted from Solomon et al., 2000b, reproduced by permission of Academic Press

making? The most desirable location for risk disclosure within the annual report is also an important element of the risk disclosure framework. Is the OFR, for example, the most appropriate vehicle for risk disclosure? The review of modern company law pushed for this sort of information to be contained within an augmented OFR (see Modernising Company Law, 2002). However, as we see later, a mandatory OFR has been rejected by the Government. The framework also presents different possibilities for investors' risk disclosure preferences and the form of disclosure that certain risks should take. Should all types of risk be reported with equal importance? Should every risk be reported individually or should all risk information be grouped in a general statement for external reporting purposes? Is there a distinct preference for some types of risk information? Whether future developments in the risk disclosure framework will involve explicit guidance on specific risks remains to be seen. At present, it is unclear whether users of financial reports have strong preferences for the disclosure of particular types of risk. This issue requires clarification to inform future policy recommendations. Lastly, the framework considers whether investors' attitudes are influenced by specific factors. For example, are institutional investors' attitudes toward corporate risk disclosure influenced by their general attitudes toward corporate governance? Are their perceptions of corporate governance related to their requirements for risk information? Indeed, it is likely that there is a strong link between these issues, since internal control has recently become a central aspect of the UK agenda for corporate governance reform.

Having developed a framework that considered the possible ingredients of an ideal corporate risk disclosure system, it seemed important to gather some empirical evidence in order to establish the most desirable ingredients of an ideal framework. By obtaining empirical evidence, Solomon et al. (2000b) were able to determine which of the possible ingredients constituted 'the' ideal corporate risk disclosure framework – at least from the perspective of one group of people. Some work had already been done on this area in the USA, as evidence indicated that there was a demand from institutional investors for disclosure of internal control information and that this type of information was considered useful to external decision makers (Hermanson, 2000). However, relatively little evidence has been collected in the UK. Therefore, the research canvassed the views of an extensive sample of UK institutional investors in order to find out what their preferred or ideal framework was for corporate risk disclosure. Their views are important and influential given that the size of their stake in UK listed companies has grown substantially (recall the discussion in Chapter 5). To conduct the questionnaire survey, a sample of 552 institutional investors was drawn randomly from four sources. The sample comprised the four main types of investment institution: pension funds, investment trusts, unit trusts and insurance companies. The questionnaire was distributed between January and April 1999. Of the responses received, 97 (17.6 %) were satisfactorily completed. The majority of respondents were from pension funds and insurance funds. Table 6.2 presents the responses to a question asking the investors to indicate the extent to which they agreed with a number of statements.[6] The table ranks the statements in order of mean average response, with the statement receiving the highest response at the top of the table.

---

[6] They were asked to select a score from 1 (strongly disagree) to 7 (strongly agree).

**Table [6.2]**   Institutional investors' attitudes toward corporate risk disclosure

| Rank | Statements | Average response |
|---|---|---|
| 1 | I believe that increased corporate risk disclosure would help institutional investors in their portfolio investment decisions | Strong agreement |
| 2 | I believe that the best way of improving risk disclosure would be to report exposure to and management of different types of risk separately | Agreement |
| 3 | I believe that increased risk disclosure would improve the corporate governance of our investee companies | Agreement |
| 4 | I believe that financial risk information is more relevant to institutional investors than other risk information (e.g., product/service, compliance and environmental risks) | Agreement |
| 5 | I believe that the current state of risk disclosure by our UK investee companies is inadequate | Agreement |
| 6 | I believe that improvements in risk disclosure are essential to a company's reporting as a going concern | Agreement |
| 7 | I believe that the Operating and Financial Review (OFR) is the most appropriate vehicle for increased risk disclosure | Agreement |
| 8 | I believe that all types of risk affecting an investee company should be reported with equal importance | Some agreement |
| 9 | I believe that the best way for companies to improve risk disclosure would be to publish a general statement of business risk | Some agreement |
| 10 | I believe that increased risk disclosure would encourage the development of long-term relationships between institutional investors and their investee companies | Some agreement |
| 11 | I believe that corporate risk disclosure should be voluntary | Some agreement |
| 12 | I believe that corporate disclosure of risk information should be regulated through Government legislation | Disagreement |

Reproduced by permission of Academic Press

One important finding from this survey was that institutional investors endorsed the improvement in corporate risk disclosure and viewed such disclosure as decision useful. The statement that received the highest mean average response concerned the relevance of risk disclosure to investors' portfolio investment decisions. The investors evidently felt that better risk disclosure improved their investment decisions. This provides a mandate for further improvements in corporate risk disclosure and is encouraging to policy makers. Further, the statement suggesting that the current state of risk disclosure by UK companies is inadequate also received support from the respondents, indicating that attention needed to be paid to this area. The results also indicated that the current voluntary framework of disclosure should be maintained. The institutional investors clearly preferred a voluntary, to a regulated, framework, as indicated in Table 3.2. Indeed, one questionnaire respondent remarked:

> ...these [corporate governance] reforms are generally acceptable, though the most important point to emphasize is the maintenance of self-regulation.

Another interesting finding was that, despite some published recommendations, the institutional investors appeared to prefer different risks to be reported and managed separately. They did not seem to favour an overall business risk report. Clearly, financial risks were shown to be of most relevance to the institutional investors. There was also some evidence to support the OFR as being the most appropriate vehicle for risk disclosure. This is an especially poignant finding given the Government's abolition of the mandatory OFR, as discussed on p. 169. It seems that on a practical level the Turnbull Report has had a far-reaching impact on corporate risk disclosure, as companies have been encouraged to comply with its recommendations by producing detailed reporting of their risks. Some examples of risk disclosure following Turnbull are presented in Illustration 6.2.

## Illustration 6.2

### The state of corporate risk disclosure

In the BP Annual Report (2000, p. 78) there was an illustration of disclosure relating to risk and the Turnbull Report, as follows:

> The Board Governance Policies include a process for the board to review regularly the effectiveness of the systems of internal control as required by Code Provision D.2.1. As part of this process, executive management presented a report to the November meetings of the Audit Committee, Ethics and Environment Assurance Committee and the Board about their system of internal control during 2000. The Report identified and evaluated seven significant risk categories, summarised the state of internal control and described the executive management's assurance process ... The Report also described enhancements implemented by executive management to their internal control systems during 2000. The Committees and Board reviewed this Report. In the Board's view, the information it received was sufficient to enable it to review the effectiveness of the company's system of internal control in accordance with the Guidance for Directors on Internal Control (Turnbull).

The Shell Transport and Trading Company Annual Report (2000) disclosed the following information:

> The approach in the Group to risk management and internal control ... which demonstrates that risk and control reporting was enhanced to provide from the beginning of 2000 a process designed to involve management in regular reviews of the risks that are significant to the fulfilment of the objectives of the business. These enhancements were designed to formalise the mechanisms for ongoing identification, evaluation, management and review of significant

risks and the Directors consider that these internal control arrangements are compatible with the guidance for directors published in September 1999 (known as the Turnbull Report) in relation to the internal control provisions of the Combined Code.

The company was having a quarterly boardroom meeting to discuss risk. In contrast to this, Kingfisher (2001, p. 31) stated that they reviewed and assessed the Group's risks 'at least annually'. The reason for this may have been that Kingfisher operated in a more stable environment, showing that the Turnbull framework is a dynamic framework that is especially applicable to companies that are not stable. This type of review is a result of the Turnbull Report in that it was not happening before! Indeed, the company stated that since Turnbull:

...efforts to fully embed the risk-based approach to internal control are now being cascaded within the business.

This implied that Shell (a top company) was only establishing this type of internal control system as a result of Turnbull and that they had not been doing it before! In the Diageo Annual Report (2001) the company stated that:

Internal control: The directors acknowledge that they are responsible for the Group's systems of internal control and reviewing their effectiveness ... An ongoing process, in accordance with the guidance of the Turnbull Committee on internal control, has been established for identifying, evaluating and managing risks faced by the Group. This process has been in place for the full financial year and up to the date the financial statements were approved. The risk management process and systems of internal control are designed to manage rather than eliminate the risk of failure to achieve the Group's strategic objectives. It should be recognised that such systems can only provide reasonable, not absolute, assurance against material misstatement or loss.

The statement went on to describe the main parts of the control system for each business. The auditors for Diageo were KPMG at the time.
The Corus Annual Report and Accounts (2000, p. 26) stated that:

Internal control: The directors are responsible for the Group's system of internal control and reviewing its effectiveness ... The Board has designed the Group's system of internal control in order to provide the directors with reasonable assurance that its assets are safeguarded, that transactions are authorised and properly recorded and that material errors are either prevented or would be detected within a timely period. However, no system of internal control can eliminate the risk of failure to achieve business objectives or provide absolute assurance against material misstatement or loss [note that this is very similar to the statement in Diageo's report].

The statement went on to describe the main parts of the control system for each business. The auditors were PricewaterhouseCoopers. These examples provide evidence that the Turnbull Report had an immediate and significant impact on corporate disclosure.

Recent research has investigated factors which may influence the level of corporate risk disclosure. Abraham and Cox (2006) found that corporate risk disclosure appears to be related to institutional ownership. They found that companies with a higher proportion of ownership by in-house managed pension funds were characterized by lower levels of risk disclosure. This may be explained by the fact that this group of institutional investors participates in less fluid trading. Conversely, companies with more fluid investors tended to disclose more risk information. Abraham and Cox (2006) also found that the higher the number of independent directors present on a board, the greater the amount of financial risk information disclosed. Lastly, the researchers showed that companies with a listing on the US stock exchange disclosed more risk information.

## The revised guidelines and corporate risk disclosure

The revised guidance on internal control has placed far more emphasis than the original Turnbull Report on the disclosure of risk management information. As stated earlier, one of the weaknesses of the original Turnbull guidance on internal control was that very little detail was provided concerning the format of the disclosure. The disclosure stage of the explicit framework for internal control was weak in the first Turnbull guidance. Apart from suggesting that companies should disclose the process that they used to review the effectiveness of their internal control systems, the materiality issue rendered the recommendation impotent. The revised guidance (FRC, 2005) places far more emphasis on the need for companies to disclose narrative information on the effectiveness of their internal control systems. The revised guidance states that companies should, as a minimum, disclose that there is an ongoing process for identifying, evaluating and managing the significant risks faced by the company and that it is regularly reviewed by the board. Not only should companies disclose what actions have been taken to resolve significant failings or weaknesses identified by the review, but also they should disclose the process they have applied to deal with material internal control aspects of any significant problems disclosed in the annual report. If the company's board has not conducted a review of the effectiveness of its internal control system, it has to disclose the reasons why.

## Sarbanes–Oxley and internal control

The Sarbanes–Oxley Act ('Sarbox' as it is affectionately referred to) was published in 2002. Since the start of 2004, all US companies have been forced to submit an annual assessment of the effectiveness of their internal control systems to the Security Exchange Council (SEC). Further, the Sarbanes–Oxley Act has forced companies' independent auditors to audit and report on the internal control reports produced by management, in the same way as they audit the financial statements.

The Sarbanes–Oxley Act, as mentioned in earlier chapters, represented the USA's equivalent of the UK's Smith Report. It was the American reaction to Enron. The main difference between the two was in the nature of the reviews. As mentioned throughout this text, unlike the UK, the USA adopts a rules-based approach to corporate governance and to accounting in general. This means that the changes to companies' internal control systems did not take the form of principles-based recommendations, as in the UK case, but constituted an amendment to US company law.

As outlined in Ramos (2004), the Sarbanes–Oxley Act (2002) made substantial changes to the financial reporting process. As with the revised Turnbull guidance (2005) the Act specified that management had to report on the effectiveness of their company's system of internal control over financial reporting. Specifically, the legislation defined internal control over financial reporting as:

> ...a process designed by, or under the supervision of, the issuer's principal executive and principal financial officers, or persons performing similar functions, and effected by the issuer's board of directors, management and other personnel, to provide reasonable assurance regarding the reliability of financial reporting and the preparation of financial statements for external purposes in accordance with generally accepted accounting principles and includes those policies and procedures that:
>
> (1) Pertain to the maintenance of records that in reasonable detail accurately and fairly reflect the transactions and dispositions of the assets of the issuer;
>
> (2) Provide reasonable assurance that transactions are recorded as necessary to permit preparation of financial statements in accordance with generally accepted accounting principles, and that receipts and expenditures of the issuer are being made only in accordance with authorizations of management and directors of the issuer, and;
>
> (3) Provide reasonable assurance regarding prevention or timely detection of unauthorized acquisition, use or disposition of the issuer's assets that could have a material effect on the financial statements.

In this sense, Sarbanes–Oxley focused attention on the financial reporting aspects of internal control. In other words, the new legislation considered that internal control was principally concerned with the preparation of financial reports. Sarbanes–Oxley also required that all listed companies must have a disclosure committee with the remit of overseeing the process by which disclosures are created and reviewed. Further, the new legislation required the company's principal executive officer and principal financial officer to sign two certifications, making them personally responsible for the correctness of the financial reporting. Also, the company's external auditors are now required to audit the companies' report on the effectiveness of internal control systems. This means that, in effect, the internal control system is assessed twice: first, by management, second by the independent auditors. As with the Smith Report, Sarbanes–Oxley also emphasized the need for auditor independence to be assured.

The Sarbanes–Oxley Act has had a significant impact on audit fees. The big four accounting firms have doubled their audit fees with US clients because of the additional work arising from Sarbanes–Oxley legislation (Parker, 2005a). Research anticipated that European companies listed on US stock exchanges would face a 35 % increase in audit fees as a result of Sarbanes–Oxley compliance (Corporate Governance Update, April 2004). The main area where the audit function has been augmented as a result of

Sarbanes–Oxley is in the area of internal control, as audits have broader responsibility for ensuring good accounting and blowing the whistle on fraud (section 404 of the Sarbanes–Oxley Act). Auditors are now expected to report their opinions on the effectiveness of their clients' internal controls in the annual report (Parker, 2005b).

It is important to reflect on the impact of the US Sarbanes–Oxley Act in considering the effectiveness of the Smith Report in the UK. The two initiatives represent a prime illustration of the difference between the US and UK approaches to corporate governance and accounting generally. The hard-line US approach of harnessing company law and forcing companies to act differently contrasts sharply with the softly, softly approach of the UK. Which is actually more effective in practice remains to be seen over the long term, but the UK continues to shy away from any attempt to introduce mandatory corporate governance. There is a persisting belief that genuine changes in corporate ethicality and attitude can only be achieved through a voluntary framework, which allows individuals to think about the issues at hand and decide at what level they feel willing and able to comply with corporate governance recommendations. Whether a little additional regulation could push them more effectively in the right direction is still unclear and up for debate.

We now consider a specific area of reporting in the UK which has been at the centre of recent debate about transparency.

## The Operating and Financial Review Fiasco

An Operating and Financial Review (OFR) is a detailed report within the annual report, on the company and its financial position, written in non-financial language. It focuses on narrative disclosure, rather than financial and is intended to include forward-looking rather than solely historic information. The OFR plays an important role in corporate governance, as it helps to make a company's activities transparent, by ensuring the information is accessible to a broad range of report users, not just sophisticated investors. The recent developments relating to the OFR make an interesting story in the regulation of financial reporting in the UK. Instead of a logical progression towards a mandatory narrative statement, the process has turned into a fiasco, with the UK Government reversing the company law decision to make the OFR mandatory, several months after the new law had already come into place. There was strong support for the mandatory OFR from many quarters, rendering the Government's change of mind even less comprehensible. For example, the NAPF (2005) review of internal control guidance highlighted the usefulness of the OFR,

> Taken together with the Operating and Financial Review, the internal control statement provides an opportunity for the board to help shareholders understand the risk and control issues facing the company, and to explain how the company maintains a framework of internal controls to address these issues and how the board has reviewed the effectiveness of that framework.
>
> (NAPF, 2005, p. 2)

The same point was made by the Turnbull Review Group's preface to the revised guidance on internal control (FRC, 2005). As we saw earlier in this chapter, Solomon et al. (2000b) found that institutional investors viewed the OFR as an important and appropriate vehicle for risk disclosure. High hopes had also been attached to the mandatory OFR as a vehicle for social and environmental reporting. Company management from top UK listed companies viewed the mandatory nature of the OFR as an essential step towards making social and environmental disclosure mandatory (Solomon and Edgley, 2005). Such support for the mandatory OFR, from both the corporate and institutional investor communities, hardly forms the basis for scrapping it! Although the government has supported a 'Business Review' instead of the OFR, what message do their actions give to shareholders and other users about the whole consultation process? What message do their actions portray in terms of a democratic system? Were the six years involved in the process of rewriting UK company law, with a mandatory OFR as one of its principal outcomes, simply empty rhetoric? Indeed, the general view is that all confidence has been lost in the Government's consultation process, following their backtracking on the OFR (Grant, 2006). The reaction of Friends of the Earth was monumental, with a court case being raised against the Government for their change of policy, when so many stakeholder groups had placed their trust and hopes in the new mandatory OFR as a means of enhancing corporate accountability. The move by the Government to review the scrapping of the OFR ended the Friends of the Earth's legal action. However it has not quelled concerns about the about-turn on policy.[7]

The European Accounts Directive for member-wide adoption of a Business Review has provided an escape route for the turnaround on the OFR. On 3 May 2006, the Department of Trade and Industry (DTI) announced a new draft of the Company Law Reform Bill relating to narrative reporting, inter alia. This followed a consultation process completed in March 2006 (Allen and Overy, 2006).

However, the Business Review could be seen as falling short of the OFR in a number of ways as a vehicle for meaningful narrative disclosures of a forward-looking nature. The Business Review is to be included in the director's report and not in any other section of the annual report and accounts. The Business Review requirements, deriving from the EU Accounts Modernisation Directive, include

- a fair review of the business;

- a description of principal risks and uncertainties facing the company;

- a balanced and comprehensive analysis of the development and performance of the business during the financial year and the position of the business at the end of the year;

---

[7] When this text went to press, there were a significant number of Members of Parliament supporting Friends of the Earth in their anticipated call to the Government to reinstate the mandatory OFR.

■ a requirement (to the extent necessary)[8] to include financial key performance indicators and (where appropriate) non-financial key performance indicators.

Further, the Business Review still applies to all UK companies except those subject to the small companies guidelines. Also, auditors are still required to report on consistency of the Business Review.

There are however, some deep concerns relating to the new Business Review, and its replacement of the mandatory OFR (Allen and Overy, 2006). There is a dearth of guidance on what is required in order to satisfy the contents requirements and there is no proposed reporting standard. There are also issues relating to directors' liabilities and safe harbours.

## The role of audit in corporate governance

Within a company's system of internal control, the external audit represents one of the most indispensable corporate governance checks and balances that help to monitor company management's activities, thereby increasing transparency. The Cadbury Report emphasized that:

> The annual audit is one of the cornerstones of corporate governance ... The audit provides an external and objective check on the way in which the financial statements have been prepared and presented.
>
> (Cadbury Report, 1992, p. 36, para. 5.1)

From an agency theory perspective, the audit function represents another important corporate governance mechanism that helps shareholders in their monitoring and control of company management. The audit of a company's financial statements makes disclosure more credible, thereby instilling confidence in the company's transparency. Indeed, auditing has been considered to play a role in contract monitoring, as a company's auditors contract with debtholders to report any observed breaches of restrictive covenants and audited earnings numbers are used in bonus plans (Watts and Zimmerman, 1986). As we saw from reading the case of Enron in Chapter 2, failure of the audit function was one of the principal factors that contributed to the company's downfall. A recent scandal relating to the Japanese arm of PricewaterhouseCoopers is discussed in Illustration 6.3. However, the existence of an 'audit expectations gap' needs to be acknowledged, as the audit function can only do so much where fraud is rife.[9] According to the Cadbury Report, it is important to bear in mind that the auditor's role is not to

---

[8] This phrase was the replacement for materiality in the company law review's discussions and guidance on the 'new' mandatory OFR.

[9] The problem of the audit expectations gap is discussed in the Cadbury Report (1992, p. 37, para. 5.4) in relation to the Caparo Judgment.

prepare the financial statements, nor to provide absolute assurance that the figures in the financial statements are correct, nor to provide a guarantee that the company will continue as a going concern, but the auditors have to state in the annual report that the financial statements show 'a' true and fair view rather than 'the' true and fair view. The Cadbury Report stressed that there was no question as to whether or not there should be an audit but rather how its effectiveness and objectivity could be ensured. We consider ways in which these may be ensured below.

---

### Illustration 6.3

### Scandal for Japanese Arm of PricewaterhouseCoopers

In May 2006, Chuo Aoyama PwC, the Japanese arm of PricewaterhouseCoopers (PwC) were ordered to suspend their auditing services for its largest clients for a two month period. Given the difficulties involved in finding a temporary auditor, PwC in Japan is likely to lose a significant number of clientele, potentially a maximum of 2,300! The reason for their suspicion was lax internal controls which contributed to accounting fraud at Kanebo, a Japanese cosmetics company (Jopson and Nakamoto, 2006).

In 2004, Kanebo was a conglomerate producing food, textiles and cosmetics and was heavily laden with debt. Kao, a Japanese company specializing in home products, was planning to take over Kanebo for 400 billion Yen but Kanebo decided to go to the Industrial Revitalization Corporation of Japan for help. The organization took Kenebo's cosmetics division and made it into a separate company, while recapitalizing the company and waiving its debt. However, it was found later that former executives had massaged the shareholder equity figures and produced fraudulent accounts (Sanchanta, 2006a). This resulted in the company being delisted and three of its former executives being arrested for creative accounting. PwC was implicated because it emerged that four accountants at Chuo Aoyama PwC aided Kanebo executives in falsifying accounting reports. There was clear evidence of collaboration between the accounting body and the company's executives. Three Chuo Aoyama PwC partners were arrested for knowingly certifying the falsified reports of Kanebo over a five year period (Sanchanta, 2006b). The case is clearly reminiscent of Arthur Andersen's fate following Enron's collapse.

---

### Auditor independence

The Cadbury Report pointed out that auditor independence could be compromised due to the close relationship that is inevitable between auditors and company managers and due to the auditor's wish to develop a constructive relationship with their clients. Indeed, the Cadbury Report stated that:

> The central issue is to ensure that an appropriate relationship exists between the auditors and the management whose financial statements they are auditing.
>
> (Cadbury Report, 1992, p. 38, para. 5.7)

The Cadbury Report stressed that a balance needed to be attained, such that auditors worked with, not against, company management, but in doing so they needed to serve shareholders. This is a difficult path to tread and one that is clearly bedecked with obstacles. Establishing audit committees and developing effective accounting standards were suggested as the most apt means of ensuring this balance is attained. We now look at a number of other issues relating to auditor independence.

*Provision of non-audit services*

Another problem raised in the Cadbury Report regarding the independence and effectiveness of the audit function involves the multiple services offered by auditors to their clients. Cadbury asserted that auditing tended to comprise only a part of auditors' business with their client companies. The desire for auditors to compete on price in offering a number of services, as well as their desire to satisfy their client's wishes, can lead to shareholder interests being sidelined. Auditing companies offer consultancy services and IT services to the companies that they audit. The immediate response to this is to prohibit auditors from offering other services, in order to prevent their objectivity from being compromised through inevitable conflicts of interest. However, as the Cadbury Report comments, such a prohibition could increase corporate costs significantly, as their freedom of choice in the market would be restricted. Consequently, a weaker recommendation was made in the Cadbury Report that companies should disclose full details of fees paid to audit firms for non-audit work, such as consultancy. Despite fears arising from the Enron case, the Smith Report (2003) was reluctant to deal with the issue in a proactive manner. The report stated that:

> .. ฺwe do not believe it would be right to seek to impose specific restrictions on the auditor's supply of non-audit services through the vehicle of Code guidance. We are sceptical of a prescriptive approach, since we believe that there are no clear-cut, universal answers ... there may be genuine benefits to efficiency and effectiveness from auditors doing non-audit work. )
>
> (Smith Report, 2003, p. 27, para. 35)

This statement begs the question: Are the benefits of allowing auditors to provide non-audit services to their audit clients really greater than the possibly dire consequences that could arise from resulting conflicts of interest? The Enron case study highlighted the problems of restricted auditor independence. Research is needed in this area and plenty is currently under way. Rather than making specific recommendations on auditing practice the Smith Report seems to pass the buck on to the audit committee. The Smith recommendations centre around passing responsibility for auditor independence and objectivity on to the audit committee function.

*Rotation of auditors*

The Cadbury Report also discussed the possibility of establishing compulsory rotation of auditors, as this could be a means of avoiding cosy auditor–client relationships. However, the report concluded that the costs of such an initiative would outweigh the benefits, as it would result in a loss of confidence and trust between the auditor and their client company. The potentially negative attributes of a close relationship may be outweighed by the benefits, such as auditor's in-depth knowledge of the company's affairs. Again, since Enron, this has become a more important initiative worldwide.

*Audit committees*

( The Cadbury Report recommended that all companies should establish audit committees. Despite wide adoption of the audit committee concept, corporate failures have continued to occur, which have been attributable in part to failure of the internal audit function (see Chapter 2). Therefore, recent initiatives such as the Smith Report (2003) have focused on improving the effectiveness of mechanisms such as the audit committee. The Smith Report emphasized the essential role the audit committee should play in ensuring the independence and objectivity of the external auditor, as well as in monitoring company management. The Report provided detailed guidance on the role of the audit function and stipulated that the main role and responsibilities of audit committees should be to: monitor the integrity of companies' financial statements; review companies' internal financial control systems; monitor and review the effectiveness of companies' internal audit functions; make recommendations to the board in relation to the appointment of the external auditor and approve the remuneration and terms of engagement of the external auditor; monitor and review the independence, effectiveness and objectivity of the external auditor; and develop and implement policy on the engagement of the external auditor to supply non-audit services (Smith Report, 2003, p. 6, para. 2.1). Most significantly, the Smith Report highlighted the need for the audit committee to be proactive, raising issues of concern with directors rather than brushing them under the carpet. Further, the Smith Report stressed that all members of the audit committee should be independent, non-executive directors. Companies' annual reports should disclose detailed information on the role and responsibilities of their audit committee and action taken by the audit committee in discharging those responsibilities (Smith Report, 2003, p. 17, para. 6.1). )

Recent research has shown that there is convergence in corporate governance within Europe in the area of audit committees. Collier and Zaman (2005) analysed the most up-to-date codes of best corporate governance practice issued by 20 countries in Europe. They found from a review of the existing literature that audit committees were not present throughout Europe, except in the UK, before the 1990s. Collier and Zaman (2005) show that there has been wide adoption by European countries of the audit committee concept in the most recent codes of practice and principles. This adoption has not precisely mirrored the Cadbury recommendations, but has rather represented a widespread move to incorporate recommendations on some form of audit committee.

There is however, less harmonization in the detailed form of the audit committees in each country studied. Although the importance of the independence of audit committee members is acknowledged in most European codes and guidelines, the acknowledgement varies in emphasis. Similarly, they found some lack of consistency across European countries in their approach towards frequency of meetings and the role of the audit committee in financial reporting, external auditor selection and internal control and risk assessment.

As the audit committee was a salient recommendation of the Cadbury Report (1992), this is an indication that countries with diverse systems of corporate governance (such as two-tier as well as unitary boards) are gradually adopting Anglo-Saxon style corporate governance, which is indicative of a convergence in corporate governance towards the Anglo-Saxon model. This leads us on to a full discussion of international differences in corporate governance systems and structures and the notion of corporate governance convergence in the following chapter. It is also an illustration of how corporate governance reform has diffused from the UK around the world.

## Research into the effectiveness of the audit function

The academic literature has provided mixed evidence on the effectiveness of the audit function, with respect to whether the audit adds value for investors and whether auditors' actions are independent of client interest (Healy and Palepu, 2001). There is evidence that shareholders consider audited accounting information to be credible because academic research has shown that share prices react to earnings announcements (Kothari, 2001). Further endorsement of the effectiveness of the audit function comes from research that has shown that providers of finance require companies to appoint an independent auditor before they will provide funds, even without regulation. One example comes from Leftwich (1983), who found that banks required companies to present audited financial information, again indicating that shareholders and other capital providers consider that the audit enhances credibility.

Our own research into the views of the UK institutional investment community toward corporate governance has provided less encouraging evidence on the usefulness and effectiveness of the audit function. Indeed, we found that there was general scepticism surrounding the role of the audit.[10] The institutional fund managers and fund directors we interviewed considered that auditors were not as informed as they should have been and that the audit was often more of a formality, having relatively little value for investors. For example, one head of corporate governance in a major investment institution commented that:

> We do have – not officially, not publicly – concerns about their independence overall ... you would be amazed at how, when you speak to auditors, from big firms as well as little firms, at drinks parties, at non-official events, and when they are in isolation (you would never get this if you had an audit conference), they often say that they are amazed that more does not come to light or that they often get their arm

---

[10] Our research has involved 25 interviews of members of the institutional investment community. However, these views on auditing have, to date, not been published anywhere else in the academic literature.

twisted by management – not from their own practice but of the companies they are auditing – to not worry about it, it is under control. I do find that quite alarming. What do you do about it? You cannot go out and say, 'Investment management believes that the auditing profession is completely corrupt!'.

If anything ever brought the credibility of the audit into question, this statement does! And coming from a major institution in the City of London! Furthermore, it was by no means an isolated view. If nothing else, this sort of view, so prevalent from my own interview research, begs urgent research in the area. Not necessarily the type of abstracted empiricism that is so evident in the market-based accounting literature, but qualitative, interview evidence that provides an insight into how the institutional investment community really views the value of audit. Fortunately, my research also provided a ray of hope, which to some extent explained why audits continue to be supported by the investment community, as another interviewee commented that:

> ...*something is better than nothing* and one hopes that by going through the process most companies will say, 'Oh, my God, we didn't realise that we had that exposure or that we weren't doing this properly, or whatever. We will try and remedy it.'
> (Head of corporate governance at a leading investment institution,
> emphasis added)

As with any criticism of the accounting framework, there needs to be a consideration of what could take its place. There is a lot of academic literature in accounting that exposes serious flaws in our current system but offers no serious alternative. Overthrowing the status quo requires a viable system to replace it and a lot of support to impose the alternative.

## Chapter summary

This chapter has reviewed the importance of transparency to the efficient workings of the corporate governance system. We have looked at the essential role that corporate disclosure, and specifically financial accounting information, plays in corporate govern-ance and the ways in which these forms of information can help to solve the agency problem. We have also considered a specialized area of corporate transparency, that of internal control. The impact of the Sarbanes–Oxley Act on internal control and audit has been discussed. Also, there has been an evaluation of the recommendations of the latest Turnbull review and its suggestions for improving risk disclosure. Lastly, the role of the audit function in corporate governance was discussed and the ways in which these essential functions help to resolve agency problems. Such corporate failures as Maxwell, Barings and Enron have highlighted the need to improve the effectiveness of these functions. Indeed, qualitative evidence from my own research shows that there is a genuine lack of credibility regarding the usefulness of the audit function within the institutional investment community, which begs further research. The chapter has also debated emerging issues in transparency including the growing importance of improving governance disclosures and the OFR fiasco.

## Questions for reflection and discussion

1  Discuss the importance to shareholders of the conceptual framework for corporate risk disclosure that is made explicit in the Turnbull Report.

2  Evaluate the extent to which you consider UK listed companies are complying with the recommendations of the Turnbull Report in spirit. In your answer make reference to the information disclosed in annual reports that you have examined as well as to academic papers and other published sources that you have read.

3  To what extent do you think that the Smith Report has produced recommendations that will improve the objectivity and independence of the external auditors?

4  Choose a company listed on the London Stock Exchange (preferably one in the Top 350). Download the latest annual report for this company from the Internet. Examine the information provided in the report on internal control, risk management and compliance with Turnbull. Evaluate the extent to which you consider the recommendations of Turnbull are being complied with in substance as well as in form.

5  Do you think there are real reasons why institutional investors should be concerned about the independence and genuine effectiveness of the audit function? Search newspapers and the Internet for cases supporting your view.

6  Debate the abolition of the mandatory OFR. What impact on the introduction of more forward-looking narrative disclosure do you think its replacement with the Business Review will have?

7  Do you think that current governance disclosures in UK company annual reports are lacking? Look at a selection of such disclosures from current annual reports as evidence to support your arguments.

# Part II

# Global corporate governance

# Chapter 7

# An introduction to corporate governance systems worldwide

## Aim and objectives

This chapter extends our discussion of corporate governance by introducing different types of corporate governance system prevalent throughout the world, highlighting the difficulties of categorizing such a diversity of systems. The specific objectives of this chapter are to:

- appreciate the diversity of corporate governance systems worldwide and consider the difficulties of forcing idiosyncratic systems into discrete categories;

- discuss the characteristics of the insider-oriented versus the outsider oriented categorization for corporate governance systems at an international level;

- consider the influence of legal systems and other factors on the evolution of corporate governance systems;

- discuss the concept of a global convergence in corporate governance.

## Introduction

Earlier chapters focused on the UK system of corporate governance. Now we turn to considering systems of corporate governance in other countries around the world. Every country exhibits a unique system of corporate governance: there are as many corporate governance systems as there are countries. The system of corporate governance presiding in any country is determined by a wide array of internal (domestic) factors, including corporate ownership structure, the state of the economy, the legal system, government policies, culture and history. There are also a host of external influences, such as the extent of capital inflows from abroad, the global economic climate and cross-border institutional investment. The main determinants of a company's corporate governance system are ownership structure and legal frameworks. However, cultural and other influences are discussed where relevant and are highlighted in relation to specific countries' corporate governance systems.

## Categorizing corporate governance: the Cinderella problem

The ways in which companies finance themselves and the structure of corporate ownership within an economy are considered to be principal determinants of a country's corporate governance system. We have seen from the discussion in Chapter 5 that in the UK institutional investors hold the majority of shares in listed companies. Since the 1970s there has been a reversal of share ownership, with individual shareholders becoming less important and institutional investors taking on a larger and larger proportion of UK equity in their investment portfolios. However, this pattern of ownership is by no means common to all countries around the world. The transformation of UK ownership structure has, as we have seen, had a substantial impact on corporate governance in the UK, as the change from dispersed to concentrated ownership has had implications for the way shareholders interact with their investee companies. Other countries are experiencing transformation of corporate governance but in many different ways, as we shall see in this and the following chapter.

Attempts have been made to categorize countries' corporate governance systems. However, such categorization is at best loose, and at worst incorrect, as it represents in some cases, oversimplification of extremely complicated financial systems. Trying to force a country's corporate governance framework into a neat category is reminiscent of the ugly sisters' attempts to squeeze their unshapely feet into Cinderella's shoe! Nevertheless, some broad categorization of corporate governance systems can be extremely useful for analytic purposes and allows analysis of the way in which countries interact with each other. Such categorization can be helpful in providing researchers with a hinge, on which they can rest their analyses and empirical work. As with any theorizing, practice may differ, but at least a useful framework is provided as a basis for discussion and further research.

One well-known and generally accepted means of categorizing corporate governance systems is the 'insider/outsider' model. Franks and Mayer (1994) and Short et al. (1998) discussed this categorization. The terms 'insider' and 'outsider' represent attempts to loosely describe two extreme forms of corporate governance. In reality, most systems of corporate governance fall somewhere in between these two, sharing some characteristics of both extremes. The polarization of corporate governance may have arisen from differences that exist between cultures and legal systems. However, as we shall see later in our discussion, countries are attempting to reduce the differences and there is a possibility that corporate governance will converge at a global level.

### Insider-dominated systems

An insider-dominated system of corporate governance is one in which a country's publicly listed companies are owned and controlled by a small number of major or commercial law frameworks. Nevertheless, UK corporate governance reform is, as we have seen in earlier chapters, quasi-mandatory, due to listing rules. Compliance is a necessary condition of listing on the London Stock Exchange.

## Global convergence in corporate governance

International harmonization is now common in all areas of business. For example, in recent years we have observed strong moves toward international harmonization in the area of accounting and financial reporting, with the International Accounting Standards Board driving toward a comprehensive set of internationally acceptable standards for accounting. As a result of rising international trade and transnational business links, the development of internationally comparable business practices and standards is becoming increasingly necessary. The need for a global convergence in corporate governance derives from the existence of forces leading to international harmonization in financial markets, with increasing international investment, foreign subsidiaries and integration of the international capital markets. Companies are no longer relying on domestic sources of finance but are attempting to persuade foreign investors to lend capital. Corporate governance standardization is one way of building confidence in a country's financial markets and of enticing investors to risk funds.

The last decade has witnessed a proliferation of corporate governance codes of practice and policy guidelines across the globe. Since the publication of the Cadbury Report in 1992, there has been a gradual diffusion of policy documentation and initiatives aimed at corporate governance reform worldwide. Figure 7.1 shows in a timeline the publication of the first corporate governance code of practice in each country. The Anglo-Saxon economies appear to have taken the initial lead, but corporate governance reforms in countries with very diverse systems of corporate governance have quickly followed by publishing guidelines and policy documents.

We now look at several initiatives aimed at standardizing corporate governance at a global level.

### The OECD principles

One of the most significant influences on corporate governance reform at a global level has been the introduction of several international corporate governance codes of practice. The first set of internationally acceptable standards of corporate governance were produced by the Organization for Economic Co-operation and Development (OECD, 1999). The OECD is an international organization, based in Paris. Its membership comprises 29 countries from all around the world. These principles represented a lowest common denominator of principles for 'good' corporate governance. Many of the principles displayed similarities to the Cadbury Code (1992) and covered such issues as equitable treatment of shareholders, shareholder responsibilities, transparency and disclosure in terms of corporate reporting and audit, the role and responsibilities of company boards of directors, and the importance of non-executive directors. For the purposes of the OECD Principles, corporate governance was defined as, 'that structure of

**Figure [7.1]** Corporate Governance Diffusion: First Codes of Practice or Policy Documents

| 1992 | 1993 | 1994 | 1995 | 1996 | 1997 | 1998 | 1999 | 2000 | 2001 | 2002 | 2003 | 2004 | 2005 |
|---|---|---|---|---|---|---|---|---|---|---|---|---|---|
| UK | | Canada | Australia | Spain | Japan | Belgium | Brazil | Denmark | China | Austria | Finland | Bangladesh | Jamaica |
| | | South Africa | France | | The Netherlands | Germany | Greece | Indonesia | Czech Republic | Cyprus | Lithuania | Iceland | ICGN |
| | | | | | USA | India | Hong Kong | Kenya | Malta | Hungary | Macedonia | Norway | |
| | | | | | | Italy | Ireland | Malaysia | Peru | Pakistan | New Zealand | Slovenia | |
| | | | | | | Thailand | Mexico | Romania | Singapore | Poland | Turkey | OECD | |
| | | | | | | | Portugal | The Philippines | Sweden | Russia | Ukraine | | |
| | | | | | | | South Korea | | | Slovakia | Latin America | | |
| | | | | | | | OECD | | | Switzerland | | | |
| | | | | | | | ICGN | | | Taiwan | | | |
| | | | | | | | Commonwealth | | | | | | |

relationships and corresponding responsibilities among a core group consisting of shareholders, board members and managers designed to best foster the competitive performance required to achieve the corporation's primary objective' (IMF, 2001). As we can see from this definition, the OECD attempted to describe corporate governance in the broadest terms, in order to embrace as many different forms of corporate governance system as possible. However, one of the problems with the OECD Principles and code of practice was their impotence, as they have no legislative power. Nevertheless, their impact has been substantial. Countries have used them as a reference point for self-assessment and for developing their own codes of best practice in corporate governance. In 1999 ministers representing the 29 countries in the OECD voted unanimously to endorse the OECD Principles (Monks and Minow, 2001). The World Bank has researched many countries around the world to assess the extent to which they have complied with the OECD principles, and all of these country assessments are available on the Internet.

### The ICGN statement on the OECD principles
The International Corporate Governance Network (ICGN) is an international organization comprising many groups interested in corporate governance reform. The organization represents the interests of investors, financial intermediaries and companies, inter alia. The organization promotes discussion on corporate governance issues and holds an annual conference for members, policy makers and academics, which acts as a forum for debate. The ICGN has been instrumental in promoting the OECD Principles and produced a statement to this effect in 1999. The statement confirmed the OECD Principles as the foundation stone of good corporate governance. However, they provided guidance for companies on how to put the Principles into practice, by presenting the essence of the Principles in a 'working kit' statement of corporate governance criteria. The ICGN approach to the OECD Principles was reproduced in Monks and Minow (2001).

### The revised OECD principles 2004
In 2004, the OECD issued a revised set of principles on Corporate Governance. The OECD has expanded to include 30 members, with the accession of the Slovak Republic in December 2000. The OECD Principles (2004) stated that the 1999 principles provided specific guidance for legislative and regulatory initiatives in OECD member countries but also in non-member states. The 1999 principles have been thoroughly reviewed in order to take account of recent developments and experiences in both OECD member and non-member countries. In reviewing the 1999 principles, the OECD drew on the findings of a comprehensive survey of how member countries addressed a variety of corporate governance challenges. The revised principles have maintained the spirit of a non-binding and principles-based approach, which recognised the need to adapt implementation to varying economic, legal and cultural situations. The need for sound corporate governance systems at a global level is reinforced in the preamble to the revised principles,

> If countries are to reap the full benefits of the global capital market, and if they are
> to attract long-term 'patient' capital, corporate governance arrangements must be

e, well understood across borders and adhere to internationally accepted
ples.

(OECD, 2004, p. 13)

revised principles cover the following areas: (i) Ensuring the basis for an effective
ate governance framework; (ii) The rights of shareholders and key ownership
ons; (iii) The equitable treatment of shareholders; (iv) The role of stakeholders;
isclosure and transparency; and (vi) The responsibilities of the board. It seems that
eholders have been given greater weight in the redrafted version of the principles. The
le principles are as follows:

(i) The corporate governance framework should promote transparent and efficient markets, be consistent with the rule of law and clearly articulate the division of responsibilities among different supervisory, regulatory and enforcement authorities.

(ii) The corporate governance framework should protect and facilitate the exercise of shareholders' rights.

(iii) The corporate governance framework should ensure the equitable treatment of all shareholders, including minority and foreign shareholders. All shareholders should have the opportunity to obtain effective redress for violation of their rights.

(iv) The corporate governance framework should recognize the rights of stakeholders established by law or through mutual agreements and encourage active co-operation between corporations and stakeholders in creating wealth, jobs, and the sustainability of financially sound enterprises.

(v) The corporate governance framework should ensure that timely and accurate disclosure is made on all material matters regarding the corporation, including the financial situation, performance, ownership, and governance of the company.

(vi) The corporate governance framework should ensure the strategic guidance of the company, the effective monitoring of management by the board, and the board's accountability to the company and the shareholders.

The OECD has collaborated with the World Bank Group to create the Global Corporate Governance Forum. This is a multi-donor trust aimed at promoting global, regional and local initiatives for improving the institutional framework and practices of corporate governance. The Forum also focuses on promoting sustainable development and global reduction in poverty. See Appendix B for the 2004 Principles.

### The CalPERS principles

Another significant step to harmonize standards of corporate governance was taken by CalPERS, the California Public Employees' Retirement System, in the USA. CalPERS established a set of principles that they considered were the minimum standards with which all markets throughout the world should strive to comply (see CalPERS, 1999). The aim of these standards was to allow markets across the world to function freely and equitably for all investors. A global compromise in corporate governance was clearly a remit of these principles with the aim of creating a free, efficient and globally competitive market in all countries. A main characteristic of the principles was to attain increased and comparable levels of accountability (by companies to stakeholders) between countries. One primary emphasis of seeking to establish global convergence in corporate govern- ance standards was to achieve 'long-term vision'. This would involve company managers in companies across the world creating long-term strategies.

### The European Union

The European Commission of the European Union has spent a number of years deliberating about the ways in which it could provide guidance on corporate governance to its members. The report from the Centre for European Policy Studies (CEPS, 1995) documented the substantial reforms that have taken place in recent years in Western European countries' corporate governance systems. Within the European Union there has been, to date, no attempt to develop an overarching code of corporate governance best practice for member states. A detailed comparative study of existing corporate govern- ance codes within European Union member states has been carried out that found substantial commonalities between the codes (Weil, Gotshal and Manges LLP, 2002). There are at present 42 corporate governance codes of practice existing in European Union member countries. However, differences that were found to exist were attributed to differences between the countries themselves. It has traditionally been considered inadvisable by the European Union to force member states to harmonize as a result of regulation. The consensus has tended to be that harmonization should take place at a natural pace rather than through the imposition of a European Union-wide code of practice. Nevertheless, the European Commission introduced the first set of European Union standards for corporate governance best practice in 2004. These standards have focused on disclosure of directors' remuneration and non-executive directors (Corporate Governance Update, January, 2005).

In June 2003 Frits Bolkestein, EU Commissioner for the Internal Market and Taxation, outlined the top regulatory priorities for the Financial Services Action Plan and corporate governance. He stated that the approach of the EU Commission was to provide essential measures at a pan-European level, at the same time encouraging better co-ordination among members' codes of conduct. The Commission is focusing on increasing transpar- ency and disclosure, as well as improving the effective exercise of shareholder rights. The Commission requires listed companies in all EU member states to publish an annual statement of their structures and practices for corporate governance, which should as a minimum cover: the operation and powers of the shareholder meeting; the composition and function of the board and relevant committees; the national codes of conduct to which the company subscribes; and the steps taken for compliance along with an explanation for any failure to do so (European Financial Services Regulation, 2003). The Commission also requires institutional investors to disclose their policies for investment and the exercise of voting rights. European Union Finance Ministers have produced a new directive on harmonization of transparency requirements for member states (Corporate Governance Update, April, 2004; Corporate Governance Update, March, 2005). There has also been a relatively new initiative, from the European Commission, aimed at consulting on director remuneration in European member states (Corporate Governance Update, July, 2004).

There is also evidence of collaboration between the European Union and the United States, in order to create a dialogue on 'good' corporate governance. In July 2004, the European Corporate Governance Institute has created a partnership with the American Law Institute in order to nurture Transatlantic Corporate Governance Dialogue (Corporate Governance Update, October, 2004). This is clear evidence of efforts to achieve global corporate governance harmonization. A survey by Deminor in 2003 showed that corporate governance and awareness of corporate governance are improving dramatically in European companies (Corporate Governance Update, July, 2004).

### The Commonwealth Guidelines

The corporate governance guidelines produced by the Commonwealth have focused attention in the last couple of years on the evolution of corporate governance systems in a number of developing African economies. However, there are relatively few studies that focus on African countries' corporate governance systems. Full details of the Commonwealth initiatives in promoting corporate governance harmonization are available on the Internet, on the Commonwealth website (http://www.thecommonwealth.org).

### The United Nations Conference on Governance

The United Nations Conference on Trade and Development's (UNCTAD) group dedicated to International Standards of Accounting and Reporting have decided to publish guidance on corporate governance disclosure (Corporate Governance Update, 2004). This represents yet another global initiative pushing for corporate governance harmonization.

## The outcome of corporate governance convergence

The ability of any international code of best practice to be applied successfully depends on the extent to which such varied systems of corporate governance can comply in practice with the recommendations. Each country has a system of corporate governance characterized by extremely different legal structures, financial systems and structures of corporate ownership, culture and economic factors. South Korea, for example, entered the OECD in 1996. The country has been characterized traditionally by corporate bodies with strong family control (the *chaebol* groups) and state influence. In addition, South Korea's legal protection of investors was, until the last few years, relatively low. Taiwan, although similar with respect to the extent of family ownership and control, is characterized by companies with extremely different board structures. Taiwanese companies have a supervisory system as well as a main board of directors. Such different existing corporate governance frameworks make the application of blanket codes of practice extremely problematic. Principles, such as those produced by the OECD, that are to be applied to countries with such different systems need to be flexible and not too prescriptive. Such differences as a unitary or a dual-board structure are not flexible and need to be accommodated in any initiative aimed at international standardization of corporate governance. Therefore, corporate governance reform at the global level needs to be effected with sensitivity for such international differences. It is important that countries can retain their individuality, while trying to harmonize their corporate governance standards to reflect good practice. Indeed, it is widely acknowledged that a 'one size fits all' approach is unrealistic, as 'alien practices cannot be transplanted or imposed' (Monks and Minow, 2001, p. 252). A problem for many policy makers and politicians is the potential for countries to be forced into Anglo-American style capitalism and corporate governance, when this is not the best route for them to take, given the characteristics of the economy. This is a sensitive political issue and one that requires careful treatment in all attempts to reform corporate governance. Nevertheless, investors can only be attracted to buy shares in foreign stock markets if they feel that basic standards of corporate governance, understandable at an international level, are being adhered to. In this sense the OECD has helped to further the development of stock markets around the world and is aiding capital market integration. There is however a body of academic research that has presented a case against corporate governance convergence. Mayer (2000) argued vehemently against corporate governance convergence suggesting that systems should remain inherently different so as to promote competition and take advantage of comparative advantage.

As we have seen from our earlier discussion (p. 185), both the insider and outsider systems possess advantages and disadvantages, and as both have proved successful it is difficult to argue relative superiority or inferiority. However, in recent years there have been moves toward some level of convergence. Countries with traditionally outsider-dominated systems have made significant efforts to reduce the main problem associated with outsider systems (namely, that of agency). We have seen from our detailed discussion of corporate governance reform in the UK that the agency problem has been dealt with via a broad range of initiatives, such as improving the effectiveness of non-executive directors, of the audit function, of the relationship between institutional investors and their investee companies. We have seen how ownership structure has been transformed by the increasing concentration of ownership in large financial institutions and the impact of this on control in companies. This agenda for corporate governance reform is not unique to the UK but has also been instigated in other outsider-dominated economies, such as the USA and Australia. Similarly, countries with traditionally insider-dominated systems of corporate governance have been attempting to alleviate some of the problems associated with their type of system. Many countries in East Asia have focused on improving the legal protection of minority shareholders. They have concentrated on improving corporate accountability by, for example, forcing companies to produce consolidated accounts. Further, traditionally insider-dominated systems have been encouraging greater dispersion of equity ownership. This has helped to cultivate a broader shareholder base and to encourage greater shareholder democracy.

The notion of a global convergence in corporate governance has been discussed in the literature in a number of ways. Overall, there seems to be a general rapprochement of corporate governance structures, with perhaps a trend toward a global compromise that may eventually lead to a worldwide system lying somewhere in between the traditional insider/outsider extremes. Theoretically speaking then, what would this global compromise involve? What characteristics would such a compromise adopt? Solomon et al. (1999) considered how an eventual global corporate governance compromise would look. They considered that, theoretically, a global convergence in corporate governance would be likely to take the most effective and successful characteristics from the existing systems around the world. Countries would eventually adopt those characteristics that would lead to the optimum balance between efficient business operations and an ethical, stakeholder-oriented society. They suggested that, from the direction of current trends and forces in international investment and current reforms in systems of corporate governance, an eventual global compromise would involve economies being mainly outsider-dominated but displaying characteristics of long-termism rather than short-termism. This would be an attempt to merge the competitive market forces of the traditional Anglo-American systems of finance and control with the more long-term styles of management and investment prevalent in the traditional insider systems of corporate governance. Figure 7.1 illustrates this view of global convergence in corporate governance by depicting a move from the extreme forms of the insider and outsider systems toward a similar and internationally accepted system of finance, investment and management.

The consensus in the literature appears to be that there is a global move towards convergence in national systems of corporate governance and in corporate governance codes of practice and principles (for example, Cuervo, 2002; Mallin, 2002). The emerging literature seems to suggest that a global convergence in corporate governance will involve a wide adoption of many characteristics of best practice in the Anglo-Saxon systems of corporate governance, but that this would involve principally fringe aspects of the framework. For example, as discussed in the previous chapter, there has been some level of convergence among European countries towards adoption of an Anglo-Saxon style audit committee (Collier and Zaman, 2005). Although there is some variation in the way in which the audit committee concept is being recommended in European codes of practice, the overall notion of an audit committee is being taken on board universally. This suggests that,

... there will be convergence at the margins but that embedded interests in Europe will prevent convergence to one corporate governance model.

(Collier and Zaman, 2005, p. 764)

## Country studies

As academic and professional research into corporate governance has grown progressively in recent years, academics and practitioners have started to study corporate governance systems across the globe. There has been a proliferation of country studies, investigating the process of corporate governance reform for individual countries. The aims of these studies are varied but tend to focus on:

- defining the traditional system of corporate governance within a country and analysing the factors that have led to that system;

- comparing the country's system with other systems around the world and attempting to categorize the country as 'insider-dominated' or 'outsider-dominated';

- considering recent changes within the country's financial system and its relationship with other economies;

- evaluating the impact of recent changes on the country's corporate governance system;

- discussing the corporate governance system that will arise from recent developments and whether or not the country will comply with a general trend toward global convergence in corporate governance;

- suggesting the characteristics of a 'converged' system of corporate governance;

- using empirical evidence (econometric evidence, questionnaire evidence, interview evidence) to support the author's arguments.

The next chapter considers corporate governance in a sample of countries around the world, in the form of a 'reference dictionary'. The discussion focuses specifically on research into each country's corporate governance system. The intention is not to provide an exhaustive coverage of all the countries, as this would be beyond the scope of the current text. It is not possible to do justice to corporate governance in every country in one chapter of a general corporate governance text. However, the following chapter attempts to give a flavour of different systems of corporate governance around the world by illustrating the main forms of corporate governance system with selected examples.

## Chapter summary

This chapter has introduced some of the international initiatives aimed at reforming and harmonizing corporate governance at a global level. There has been a discussion of internationally acceptable standards for corporate governance. The OECD produced one of the first sets of international corporate governance standards which were intended to represent a lowest common denominator of corporate governance standards for companies around the world. The chapter has summarized the principal characteristics of the 'insider' and 'outsider' extreme forms of corporate governance and shown that, despite the 'Cinderella problem', categorization can be a useful tool to enable further analysis and research. Further, there has been a discussion of the literature relating to international corporate governance comparisons as well as a sample of the research that examines the factors that influence a country's system of corporate governance. Specifically, the importance of a country's legal system and corporate ownership structure in determining its corporate governance has been highlighted. Further, the extent to which a global convergence in corporate governance is possible and the type of system to which countries will aspire have been considered.

## Questions for reflection and discussion

1   To what extent do you consider that the research into factors determining a country's corporate governance system is useful? Are you persuaded that corporate ownership structure and countries' legal systems have been more relevant to the evolution of corporate governance in countries around the world than factors such as culture and politics?

2   Do you think that the insider–outsider framework is a useful basis for analysing and discussing corporate governance systems in an international context?

3   *A global convergence in corporate governance is under way. In a few years there will be one internationally acceptable model of corporate governance that will be based on the US market-based, outsider-type system.* Do you agree with the above statement? Support your view with a discussion and refer to appropriate academic work and other published sources that you have read.

## Chapter 8

# A reference dictionary of corporate governance systems

## Aim and objectives

This chapter illustrates the ongoing process of global corporate governance reform, using a wide sample of countries from around the world. The specific objectives of this chapter are to:

- illustrate the broad diversity of corporate governance systems worldwide by outlining the main characteristics of the systems in a selection of countries;

- outline the specific codes of practice and policy documents that have been developed in a sample of countries around the world and evaluate their impact, with reference to academic studies.

### Argentina

A paper by Apreda (2001) provided evidence on two issues. First, it supported the allusion that there has been a marked shift in ownership and control in Argentina from large, family-owned domestic companies toward foreign groups and investment funds. Second, the paper provided evidence that while coping with corporate governance issues, Argentina has followed the common law countries' tradition, fostering a capital market-based financial system and swapping its corporate governance practices outright. The paper discussed the historical system of corporate governance in Argentina and its process of reform in recent years. The country was characterized by substantial family control and state ownership of companies, inefficient corporate operations and a closed economy. In the 1990s this situation changed dramatically with Argentina opening its borders to trade and investment and attempting to improve its system of corporate governance. Reform has included a privatization programme and a series of reforms of company law.

### Australia

Stapledon (1996) compared the role of institutional investors in Australia with that of institutional investors in the UK. He explained that Australia has been characterized traditionally as having an outsider system of corporate governance, possessing the same basic characteristics as the UK. Despite this general similarity, there are significant differences between the two countries with respect to ownership structure and level of shareholder involvement in companies. The quoted corporate sector is not as significant in Australia as it is in the UK. Further, there is a higher incidence of founding family and intercompany ownership in Australia than in the UK. As in the UK, the two largest categories of institutional investor are the occupational pension funds and insurance companies (Stapledon, 1996). The early 1990s witnessed a growth in shareholder activism in Australia, with the introduction of the Australian Investment Managers' Group (AIMG), which provides a mechanism for collective shareholder action. Stapledon (1996) compared the level of institutional investor involvement in Australian companies with that in the UK, concluding that until the mid-1990s Australian shareholder activism was far less evident. He considered this was because Australian companies were effectively immune from intervention by institutional investors, as they tended to have a significantly large non-institutional shareholder base that controlled the company. Australia has its own code of corporate governance practice deriving from the Bosch Report (1995). Bosch (1993) described the development of the Bosch Report. From his discussion it seems that the Bosch Report followed the UK Cadbury Report (1992) closely.

## Bahrain

Although Bahrain does not have a code of best practice for corporate governance, companies are established according to the Commercial Companies Law 2001 (Hussain and Mallin, 2002). This law requires that companies have a board of directors that acts in a responsible manner and that shareholders exercise their voting rights. In 2001 Hussain and Mallin conducted a questionnaire survey to investigate the status of corporate governance in Bahrain. They sent the questionnaire to all companies listed on the Bahrain Stock Exchange Market, finding that listed companies in Bahrain have in place some of the features of international corporate governance 'best practice'. However, they did question the effectiveness of the nomination committees and felt that company directors tended to be entrenched in their attitudes.

## Belgium

In a paper examining corporate governance in Belgium, Wymeersch (1994) explained that Belgian companies were generally secretive and unaccountable to the outside world until a process of reform in 1991, when a series of amendments to Belgian company law focused on minority shareholder protection and rights. Also, corporate disclosure has been improved substantially. This is another example of an insider-type system becoming more market-oriented. Institutional investors in Belgium constitute about 20 % of shareholding, with shareholder activism on the increase. However, the market for corporate control through takeover has been viewed as relatively undeveloped. There is a Belgian code of corporate governance, the Cardon Report (1998).

## Brazil

Traditionally an insider-oriented system, Brazil has focused attention on corporate governance, issuing its third version of the Brazilian Code of Best Practice in 2003 (Corporate Governance Update, April 2004). The Code was expanded to include recommendations on audit, risk management and training of boards. In 2004, the National Association of Capital Market Investors in Brazil issued a 22-point handbook that should add value of the shares of listed companies in Brazil, according to minority shareholders. The handbook specifies that there is a disparity between words and action and that companies need corporate governance to be imposed, and that simply adopting transparency and rules is not enough (Corporate Governance Update, January 2004).

## Canada

Daniels and Waitzer (1993) described the Canadian system in detail, emphasizing the importance of improving corporate governance in order to remain globally competitive and to attract foreign investment. An in-depth review of corporate governance was performed by Daniels and Morck (1996), which considered various policy options for the future development of Canadian corporate governance. Their study showed that there was an element of outsider-type corporate governance in Canada, as some of Canada's largest companies and all its major chartered banks were widely held by a large number of small shareholders, each of whom had little effective control over managerial decision making. However, they also showed that this type of ownership structure was not common, quoting evidence that only 16 % of the 550 largest Canadian companies were placed in this mould (Morck and Stangeland, 1994). Indeed, research has shown that most large Canadian companies were not widely held by investors. Rao and Lee-Sing (1995) found that in more than three-quarters of the Canadian companies they studied, one large shareholder controlled at least 20 % or more of the voting shares. Corporate ownership was found to be concentrated significantly in the hands of company management, leading to management control over director appointments and corporate decision making. Although this situation removes the traditional agency problem to some extent, other problems are introduced, as managerial control can lead to the appointment of board members for reasons of friendship rather than merit. Indeed, Morck and Stangeland (1994) showed that Canadian companies whose dominant shareholders were their founders performed significantly worse than other companies of comparable age and size. Daniels and Morck (1996) stressed that improving corporate governance in Canada was essential, arguing that its absence would erode public confidence in Canada's financial markets and depress company share prices. This would result in Canadian companies experiencing difficulties in raising equity capital. These arguments may be applied to countries around the world in an attempt to support corporate governance reform. One way of improving corporate governance is to encourage monitoring of company management by institutional investors, as discussed in Chapter 5. Institutional investors controlled over 38 % of Canadian companies in the mid-1990s (Rao and

Lee-Sing, 1995), and that proportion has increased gradually. Their influence on corporate governance is likely to increase commensurately, as it has in the UK, Australia and other countries. Corporate governance reform in Canada was encouraged by the publication of the Dey Report (1994) and by the publication of a series of corporate governance standards by the institutional shareholder representative group, Pensions Investment Association of Canada (PIAC, 1998).

## Chile

Following an upgrade of the legislative and regulatory framework dealing with corporate governance, Chile has become a standard setter for the entire Latin American region (Frémond and Capaul, 2003). Chile's system of corporate governance fits into the traditional insider model, with concentrated corporate ownership and pyramidal owner- ship structures. The stock market is quite large, with 249 companies listed on the Santiago Stock Exchange at the end of 2001. Frémond and Capaul concluded that Chile complied reasonably well with the OECD Principles for good corporate governance. Seven pension funds and insurance companies held 30 % of total assets at the end of 2001. The evidence suggests that pension funds have influenced corporate governance in Chile, urging better disclosure of information by companies, as well as lobbying for the protection of minority shareholder rights. The country's legal system is based on French law, which is typical of insider-type corporate governance systems. However, a complete overhaul of company law in 2000 has strengthened the corporate governance framework, focusing on improv- ing shareholder protection. However, in relation to corporate accountability to a broad group of stakeholders, Chile seems to be falling short as:

Although the legal framework protecting stakeholders is fairly well developed, Chilean corporations still too often relate to their stakeholders in a confrontational manner, perpetrating the idea that entrepreneurs and stakeholders are rent-seeking indivi- duals. Anecdotal evidence indicates that this approach often leads to corporate shortsightedness, which may jeopardize important opportunities for future economic development in Chile.

(Frémond and Capaul, 2003, p. 9)

This suggests an acknowledged link between corporate social responsibility and corporate/economic performance, which we explore in Chapter 9.

## China

As China is still a communist state, progress in the capital markets and in the area of corporate governance has been slower than in several other East Asian countries. However, as in many of the Central and Eastern European economies there has been a significant move toward a more liberal market system and a more transparent and 'Western' corporate governance system. In China, until recently, companies were owned chiefly by the Government. Consequently, China fits into the insider mould, with little separation of ownership and control. The Government owned Chinese companies and ran them. Recent reforms have initiated extensive privatization of these State Owned Enterprises (SOEs). Tam (2000) discussed the state of corporate governance reform in China and explained how SOEs have been privatized in some detail. SOEs were restructured into shareholding companies whose shares could then be traded on one of the two Chinese stock markets, the Shanghai and Shenzhen, which only opened in 1990 and 1991, respectively. One of the main corporate governance problems for Chinese companies has been to create a separation between company management and government, because the Government, as the principal owner of Chinese companies, has traditionally had a substantial influence over company activities and decision making. The notorious agency problems associated with outsider-type systems are now emerging in China, as they are in all countries with nascent equity markets and whose companies' capital structures are undergoing transformation. At face value it seems that corporate governance is improving considerably in Chinese companies. Company law in China specifies three levels of control over company activities: the shareholders' general meeting; the board of directors and supervisors; and company management. However, despite corporate governance reform progressing quickly there are evident weaknesses (Shi and Weisert, 2002). The shareholders' AGM has been considered impotent as managers tend to rubber-stamp decisions they made earlier, thus gaining control over the meetings. There is in practice a negligible amount of shareholder democracy. Further, insiders tend to gain positions on the boards of directors and supervisory board and simply become puppets for the controlling parties. Minority shareholders have few rights and their concerns are usually ignored by majority shareholders. As in all the countries we are studying, reform involves a long and difficult process that takes many years, even when the systems and structures are in place.

## The Czech Republic

Mallin and Jelic (2000) summarized corporate governance changes in three countries in Central and Eastern Europe, making comparisons between the programmes of reform of the countries involved. They highlighted the commonalities and differences between the processes of change in the countries involved. For the Czech Republic they explained that during the communist regime Czechoslovakia was more tightly controlled than other Central and Eastern European countries. An agenda for corporate governance reform was instigated in 1991 that needed to be extremely ambitious in order to achieve privatization and an active market for corporate control. Shops and small business units were the initial focus of the privatization programme, with large-scale businesses being included over time. Despite reform, the state has retained substantial control over privatized Czech companies. In 1991, 400 Investment Privatization Funds (IPFs) were created that were intended to mimic Western mutual funds. Coffee (1996) found that IPFs and individual investors were mainly involved in the privatization programme. According to Mallin and

Jelic (2000) it was unclear whether IPFs or banks will evolve as the dominant forces in Czech corporate governance.

An assessment of corporate governance in the Czech Republic was carried out by the World Bank and the International Monetary Fund (IMF, 2001). They explained that a major package of legislation affecting corporate governance was approved by Parliament for January 2001. This package included extensive changes to the country's Commercial Code, the Securities Act and the Auditing Act. As with most countries we are considering, changes to the legal framework are one of the main ways in which corporate governance reform is orchestrated, as a country's legal system is one of the most important factors influencing corporate governance. The assessment (IMF, 2001) stated that the changes to the Commercial Code were extensive, improving significantly the internal corporate governance mechanisms in the Czech Republic. However, they also suggested that, despite such changes, a number of institutional deficiencies implied that genuine improvements in corporate governance would take time. Such institutional deficiencies included a slow and inefficient court system. The report ended on a positive note:

> When implementation and enforcement of the new laws and regulations are strengthened, the Czech Republic will observe most of the principles on corporate governance.
>
> (IMF, 2001, p. 72)

## Denmark

Rose and Mejer (2003) described the traditional system of corporate governance in Denmark. They explained that the Danish system was originally oriented towards protecting the rights of a broad group of stakeholders rather than just the shareholder group. These included employees, creditors, the community as well as shareholders. However, the pressures of increasingly integrated international capital markets have forced Denmark to adopt a more Anglo-Saxon style of corporate governance which focuses on shareholder value. The principal characteristic of the Danish system of corporate governance is foundation ownership. From the 100 largest companies, 19 are controlled by foundations. The two types of foundation existing under Danish law are industrial foundations and family foundations. Rose and Mejer (2003) defined a foundation as a legal entity without owners, created in many cases to administer a large ownership stake in a specific company, often donated by the company's founder or the founder's family. The foundations are run on a non-profit basis and are intended usually to serve some social purpose, such as using excess profits to support charitable causes. The Copenhagen Stock Exchange included about 13 % of foundation ownership in 1999. Although foundation-owned companies are intended to be non-profit companies, it is still likely that such companies pursue profit maximization because of management's interest in securing their jobs. Empirical research has found that foundation-controlled companies have not underperformed other forms of company in Denmark (Thomsen and Rose, 2002).

Further, about 35 % of companies listed on the Copenhagen Stock Exchange are owned by institutional investors, implying that these large shareholders have a significant role to play in monitoring corporate activities. They do have close ties with management. However, the power of institutional investors is curbed in Denmark due to the existence of shares with dual class voting rights. Danish law, embodied in the Danish Corporate Act 1973 protects not only shareholder rights but also the rights of other groups of stakeholders. Also, similar to the German system, Danish companies have a supervisory board. Recent attempts to reform Danish corporate governance have focused on the role of this supervisory board. Employees, according to Danish law, have the right to elect a third of the supervisory board members in larger companies.

In 2002, the Danish Corporate Governance Network was founded. This is an independent body consisting chiefly of academics with backgrounds in finance, law and management, which aims to provide a forum for corporate governance research. Recommendations for reforming corporate governance in Denmark were encapsulated in the Norby Committee Report 2001. These recommendations derived mainly from the Anglo-Saxon corporate governance model and therefore encouraged changes to the Danish company law and corporate ownership structure in Denmark.

To summarize, the Danish system of corporate governance falls somewhere between an insider and an outsider system, with ownership concentrated to some extent and share-holders' rights being somewhat curbed due to the existence of different classes of share, with varying degrees of voting rights. The Danish system has therefore not been characterized by hostile take-over activity, as in the Anglo-Saxon model. Take-over activity has also been constrained by the predominance of foundation ownership. Further, non-shareholder stakeholders have traditionally played a greater role in Danish corporate governance. However, recent attempts to reform corporate governance in Denmark have pushed the system further towards the outsider-oriented model. These have been chiefly motivated by the increasing integration of international capital markets and globally competitive market forces. Illustration 8.1 considers corporate governance and stake-holder accountability in one Danish company.

## Illustration 8.1

### Novo Nordisk: One of the Top Three Environmental Sustainability Reporters in Europe

The organization SustainAbility, the UNEP and Standard & Poor's joined forces to conduct the sixth international review of corporate environmental and sustainability reports in 2004. The report concluded that boards were failing to disclose to financial investors how environmental and social issues posed strategic risks and opportunities for their businesses (Joint UNEP, SustainAbility and Standard & Poor's Internet Press Release, March 2005).[1] In this report into best practice in non-financial reporting only three from the top 50 reports were considered to assess the balance sheet implications of key environmental and social risks, despite the information gathering growing

[1] The website for this press release is: http://www.unep.org.

importance among the investment community and other stakeholder groups. These three companies were Novo Nordisk (Denmark), Co-operative Financial Services (UK) and BP (UK). However, the report did find an overall and significant rise in the quality of sustainability reporting since the previous survey carried out in 2002.

*Ownership and Corporate Governance Issues:* Novo Nordisk is primarily listed on the Copenhagen Stock Exchange and is characterized by foundation ownership (see the section on Danish corporate governance for a definition of foundation ownership in Denmark). The company is run on a non-profit basis as a foundation, with the aim of providing a stable basis for the company's operations as well as contributing to scientific, humanitarian and social progress. The A class shares (which hold ten times the voting power of B shares) are owned by the foundation and cannot be traded, whereas the B shares are traded on the Copenhagen Stock Exchange, the London Stock Exchange and the New York Stock Exchange). The company has a two-tier board structure, common to Danish companies, with a board of directors and the executive management. The board of directors supervises the performance of the company, its management and organization. The Executive Management has responsibility for day-to-day operations. No person serves on both. Half of the members of the board are elected by the company's employees in line with Danish company law. The company complies with the three codes of corporate governance relevant to it, due to its listing. Namely: the Norby Committee Recommendations (2001, Denmark), Corporate Governance Standards (2004, New York), and the Combined Code (2003, UK).

*Sustainability Issues:* The company states on its website that, 'Sustainable Development is about preserving the planet while improving the quality of life for its current and future inhabitants ... In all our work we strive to be economically viable, socially responsible and environmentally sound. Balancing the Triple Bottom Line is about considering each of these elements when making business decisions. Thereby, we do not only manage a sound business – we also demonstrate our commitment to being a driver towards sustainable development – globally and locally'.

## Finland

The first code of best corporate governance practice was published in Finland in 1997, and arose from a collaboration between the Central Chamber of Commerce of Finland, the Confederation of Finnish Industry and Employers, and Hex plc. In July 2004, a revised Finnish Corporate Governance Code was issued, and mirrors internationally acceptable standards of corporate governance (Corporate Governance Update, July, 2004).

## France

The control of French companies tends to be divided between the state, company management and families. There is little dispersion of ownership and the system is clearly closer to the insider, rather than the outsider, model of corporate governance. The state has a powerful role in French companies, termed *dirigisme*, partly due to their necessary involvement in the redevelopment of industry following World War II (Monks and Minow, 2001). State control has included restructuring state-owned industries for policy purposes and ensuring that key industries remained under state control. Even listed companies are under state influence, as French financial institutions, such as banks and insurance companies, are state owned and/or controlled, and represent the major capital providers to private companies in France. An estimated two-thirds of French listed company shares are characterized by cross-company shareholdings, termed the *verrouillage* system. French boards are strong and control decision making in companies. They also interlock to a high degree. Monks and Minow (2001) provided statistics to show that, in 1989, 57 people accounted for one-quarter of all the board seats of the largest 100 listed companies in France. This is clear indication of director control. According to company law, French companies can choose either a unitary board (as in the UK) or a two-tier board structure (as in Germany), although most opt for a unitary board.

France initially produced two codes of best practice in order to promote corporate governance reform (Viénot, 1995, 1999). The evidence suggests that companies have embraced the recommendations of the first report, as 92 % of companies were applying the recommendations by 1999. Also, 30 % of directors were classified as independent and 90 % of boards had audit, remuneration and nomination committees (Monks and Minow, 2001). More recently, France has published the Bouton Code (2002). However, a research report has indicated that non-compliance with this new code is high with only 16 % of the top 120 companies appointing predominantly independent boards. Further, only 20 % of the 40 companies in the CAC index have one share one vote rights for their shareholders (Corporate Governance Update, May, 2005).

### Germany

German corporate governance has attracted significant interest from academics, as the German economy was extremely successful following World War II. Many attributed this success to the inherent differences between the German system of corporate governance and the Anglo-American system. The merits of the relationship-based, insider corporate governance system that has traditionally characterized German corporate governance have been heralded by many authors. The notorious short-termism problem, blamed for constraining British industry, was less evident in Germany, where long-term relationships between companies and their providers of finance led to long-term investment. This allowed companies to invest in long-term projects and enjoy a more secure financial environment. However, Edwards and Fischer (1994) questioned the extent to which superior economic performance was related to corporate governance in Germany.

In more recent times, such 'advantages' have become disadvantages for German companies, as they have not been able to attract capital from institutional investors in global markets, due to 'parochial governance practices that have obstructed shareholder rights' (Monks and Minow, 2001, p. 275). One initiative aimed at improving German corporate governance through better corporate transparency was the publication of a report by the *Deutsche Bundestag* (1998). Further, Germany produced a corporate governance code of best practice in January 2000, followed by an updated version in September 2001 (Government Commission, 2001). The code's stated aims were to present essential statutory regulations for the management and governance of German listed companies, as well as to contain internationally and nationally recognized standards for good and responsible governance. Clearly, achieving harmonization with internationally acceptable standards was a main driver of reform in Germany, as in most countries.

The German system of corporate governance is significantly different from the Anglo-American model in a number of respects. German companies are characterized by a two-tier board and significant employee ownership. The supervisory board, in theory, is intended to provide a monitoring role. However, the appointment of supervisory board members has not been a transparent process and has therefore led to inefficient monitoring and governance in many cases (Monks and Minow, 2001). Further, German corporate governance has been characterized traditionally by pyramidal ownership structures, with companies owning each other through a series of cross-shareholdings. There has also been a strong tendency toward employee representation, as a result of the Co-Determination Act of 1976, which stipulated that employees should be involved in the corporate governance mechanisms by being represented on supervisory boards. However, companies have rallied against the idea of co-determination since the 1970s, considering it infringed ownership rights (Alkhafaji, 1989). Employee representation at the heart of companies derives from an extremely different cultural attitude toward corporate governance from that operating in Anglo-Saxon economies. It is far more in keeping with a stakeholder, than a pure shareholder, approach to corporate governance.

Schilling (2001) discussed changes in corporate governance in Germany, concluding that there are strong market forces pressuring for change in Germany. International institutional investment and increasingly open economies are forcing countries such as Germany to become more market-oriented. She suggested that there were moves toward a more equity-based system, with shareholders' involvement becoming increasingly important.

In 2004, the Cromme Commission voted to upgrade its call for disclosure of individual's remuneration to full scale best practice, on a comply or explain basis (Corporate Governance Update, January, 2004). Further, June 2005 saw an updating of the German Corporate Governance Code, which focused principally on the function of the supervisory board (Corporate Governance Update, September, 2005).

## Greece

Corporate governance in Greece is characterized by family ownership patterns and therefore traditionally falls into the insider-oriented model. The Greek stock exchange published an introductory paper on corporate governance issues in the mid-1990s and since then a voluntary Code of Conduct, the Blue Book, has been produced. Corporate governance developments in Greece have accompanied rapid growth of the country's stock market, with 350 companies being listed in 2002 (Tsipouri and Xanthakis, 2004) and the Greek stock market was upgraded to that of a developed market. However, since 1999, the Athens stock exchange (ASE) has suffered substantial losses creating a need for initiatives to restore investor confidence. Improving corporate governance is one means of achieving this aim (Tsipouri and Xanthakis, 2004; Mertzanis, 2001). Tsipouri and

Xanthakis (2004) developed a rating system to assess the compliance of Greek companies with the Blue Book. A questionnaire, structured around the five chapters of the Blue Book (which mirror those of the OECD Principles) was distributed to Greek listed companies. From the results, the authors found that Greek companies demonstrated a high level of compliance in the areas of shareholders' rights, transparency and executive management. Medium compliance was found in the area of boards. Only a weak level of compliance was found regarding issues of corporate social responsibility and stakeholder relations. Interestingly, Tsipouri and Xanthakis (2004) considered that the rating exercise per se had helped companies to evaluate their corporate governance performance, as respondents had been afforded the opportunity of discussing corporate governance issues with the researchers in face-to-face interviews. This was a positive outcome of the study, as it allowed managers to assess their own level of compliance and consider ways of improving the corporate governance culture within their organization.

## Hong Kong

Brewer (1997) discussed the evolution of Hong Kong's corporate governance system. This paper was written just before the handover of Hong Kong to China in June 1997. It is a professional rather than an academic paper and the author's discussion arises from his professional experience rather than from research. Brewer stated that, although Hong Kong appears to have an outsider system of corporate governance, it really has an insider system. He explained that in terms of company law, Hong Kong companies have imitated the UK model of a joint stock company. They have a broad base of owners, who delegate management of the business to a small number of company directors. However, the reality is very different. Ownership is not by a diverse range of outsiders who dominate control over the companies. Rather, in all companies, shareholding is concentrated and a small group of shareholders, or even a single shareholder, dominates the investee company management. Indeed, he states that up to 75 % of a company's shares can be owned by management and friends of the management. There is therefore very little true separation of ownership and control, despite appearances. Two sets of corporate governance guidelines have been published in Hong Kong to promote corporate governance reform in the area of audit committee formation (HKSA, 1997) and boards of directors (SEHK, 1997).

Cheng and Firth (2005) investigated the relationship between executive remuneration and corporate governance characteristics such as ownership structure and board composition. They found that directors' shareholdings were negatively related to remuneration. They suggested that this was because directors who own shares take lower remuneration because their dividend income satisfies them.

## Hungary

The evolving system of Hungarian corporate governance was discussed in Mallin and Jelic (2000). They explained that Hungary was more liberal than other economies in Central and Eastern Europe. A series of banking and accounting reforms took place in

1991 (see Pistor and Turkewitz, 1996). A privatization programme was initiated by the communist Hungarian Government in the early 1990s, and this programme of reform increased in pace as communism was dispensed with. As a result of the reforms the number of limited liabilities rose from 450 in 1988 to 79,395 in 1994. In the newly evolving Hungarian corporate governance system, banks appear to be taking on a major role.

## Iceland

A recent study examined boards in Icelandic companies to discover whether the role of Icelandic boards differed between companies (Jonsson, 2005). The study involved a questionnaire survey with some interviews. Icelandic listed companies generally have small unitary boards of directors, with an average of five members, all non-executive, with a split role of CEO and chairman (Jonsson, 2004). Corporate ownership tends to be concentrated with shares held in blocks, implying that Iceland fits most neatly into the insider-oriented model of corporate governance. Jonsson (2005) concluded that the boards studied carried out very different roles and that the role of the board could change, usually as a result of new management or a shift in ownership structure.

## India

India's Bombay Stock Exchange has the largest number of listed companies in the world. Yet, despite the size of the stock market in India, ownership remains concentrated in families and an insider-dominated structure seems to persist. However, Sarkar and Sarkar (2000) described the Indian system of corporate governance as a 'hybrid' of the outsider and insider model, as small shareholders participate in corporate governance. There is also significant institutional investor involvement in listed companies. Indeed, Sarkar and Sarkar (2000) found some evidence of a positive relationship between block shareholding by institutional investors and company value. They also provided evidence that the principal shareholders of Indian listed companies were: directors and their relatives, corporate bodies, foreign investors, Government-controlled financial institutions and the public. Their statistics indicated that about 43 % of all sample companies had equity ownership by corporate bodies in excess of 25 %. Directors and their relatives held about 21 % of shares in private companies. This pattern of ownership results from the predominance of family ownership in listed companies.

India is following the global trend in reforming its corporate governance system. As in other countries a series of corporate scandals focused keen attention on corporate governance weaknesses (see Illustration 8.2). However, as a former colony of Britain, India has a UK-style legal system that offers a reasonable level of protection to minority shareholders in comparison with other East Asian countries. Since the second half of the 19th century, Indian industry has generally followed an English common law framework of joint stock limited liability (Goswami, 2000). The Confederation of Indian Industry (CII, 1998) have produced a code of practice aimed at reforming corporate governance. The adoption of a structural adjustment and globalization programme by the Indian

Government in 1991 forced policy attention on corporate governance issues. A survey of company directors in India showed that they were keen on reforming corporate governance in the wake of the Asian crisis and were focusing on improving the board of directors and investor relations (Solomon et al., 2003).

### Illustration 8.2

### Scandal in India

A major fraud in the securities markets was uncovered in April 1992 in India. Harshad Mehta illegally led a cartel of bull players in the stock market to use liquidity provided by interbank credit and debit receipts to drive up the prices of certain company shares. The cartel succeeded in driving up the Bombay Stock Exchange Sensex index by almost 150 %, due to the lack of depth and width of the Indian stock market as well as to the herding mentality of investors in the market (see Goswami, 2000). Specifically, he had diverted funds from the public sector firm Maruti Udyog Limited (MUL) to his own accounts, provoking a record fall in the index. In April 1992 the State Bank of India asked Mehta to return Rs 500 crores (1 crore = 10 million) that he had illegally put into the stock market (*Frontline*, 2002). As soon as Harshad's activities became public knowledge, the markets crashed. However, it was not until 1997 that a joint parliamentary committee could produce adequate evidence to link him to events. This affair demonstrated an urgent need to address transparency and the regulation of financial markets in India. The effects of Harshad's unethical activities have spilled over into the 21st century. In 1999 he was given a four-year jail sentence for defrauding MUL, but continued to appeal. However, he was arrested in 2001 for fresh fraud charges, the alleged misappropriation of 27 lakh (1 lakh = 100,000) shares of 80 companies (*The Hindu*, 12 January 2002). Do leopards change their spots? See the Maxwell case in Illustration 3.1 for further discussion of this issue. On New Year's Eve 2001, Harshad died from a massive heart attack, but still left questions relating to the scandal a decade earlier (*The Hindu*, 12 January 2002). At the time of his death he was still in judicial custody. His death has left many unanswered questions. Why did it take 10 years to bring him to justice? What weaknesses in the financial markets allowed such abuse to succeed? As in the UK and other countries, such examples of unethical behaviour set a clear agenda for corporate governance reform.

## Indonesia

Indonesia represents a corporate governance system in East Asia with an emerging stock market. Most companies are family-owned and controlled. Indonesia's corporate governance fits neatly into the insider-dominated model and demonstrated severe cases of minority shareholder wealth expropriation following the Asian financial crisis. For example, managers diverted funds in order to finance a political party in the Indonesian PT Bank Bali, between 1997 and 1998. Further, group managers transferred currency losses from a manufacturing company to a group-controlled bank in Sinar Mas Group between 1997 and 1998, which effectively represented expropriation of wealth from the bank's minority shareholders and creditors (see Johnson et al., 2000). These cases present a clear mandate for corporate governance reform, as in many other countries. In September 2004, the Asia Asset Management Event emphasized the need for Indonesia to improve corporate governance. The underlying motivation for this recommendation was the desire to attract foreign investors (Corporate Governance Update, January, 2005).

## Italy

Italian corporate governance fits well into the insider mould, with companies being predominantly family-owned, or owned through a structure of cross-company share-holdings. Further, the shareholdings are extremely concentrated. The main shareholder in Italian companies (termed a blockholder) exerts control over the company's management. Melis (2000) described the insider system as 'relationship-based' and discussed the possibility that Italian law has favoured family control rather than shareholder protection. This has deterred small shareholders from investing in Italian companies. Indeed, Italian corporate governance mechanisms have been found to be so underdeveloped that they significantly retard the flow of external capital to firms (see Shleifer and Vishny, 1997). The process of corporate governance reform in Italy has been called the Draghi Reform, a new corporate law produced in 1998 (Draghi, 1998). The Draghi Reform was aimed at regulating financial markets and corporate governance in listed companies and should lead to better investor protection. It is not a code of practice like Cadbury but is rather a legally binding series of amendments to company law. This is interesting as it seems that countries with less developed market systems (which are categorized as strongly insider in nature) have had to develop mandatory, regulated corporate governance reforms, rather than the voluntary codes that have been applied in more market-based, developed economies. In this way the nature of codes of practice reveal much about the character of countries' traditional systems and state of their financial markets. It is evident that emerging markets are reforming corporate governance by means of changes to their company law. Overall, Italy has been characterized by an almost non-existent market for corporate control and poor capital market orientation.

## Japan

Japan fell traditionally into the insider-dominated group (Hoshi et al., 1991) and had a 'credit-based' financial system (Zysman, 1983), as the economy was characterized by intercompany shareholdings, intercompany directorships and frequently substantial bank involvement. Japan's economy, despite the reorganization following World War II is still to some extent characterized by the *zaibatsu*, a group of family-run businesses that emerged as early as the 17th century (Bison, 1954). These business enterprises have since evolved into the *keiretsu*, which are related closely through share ownership to one or more banks. In this type of system, there is little takeover activity and shares are not traded as frequently in market-based economies. More recently, the trend has been toward a more market-dominated Japanese system of corporate governance (Cooke and Sawa, 1998), perhaps as a result of pressures arising from recent economic problems. However, Japan and other East Asian economies still retain a different attitude toward business from Anglo-American-style economies, as expressed in the following:

> East Asian and particularly Japanese capitalist structures emphasise trust, continuity, reputation and co-operation in economic relationships. Competition is ferocious, but co-operation is extensive; the juxtaposition of apparently inconsistent forms of behaviour may strike those schooled in Anglo-American capitalism as irrational, but for the Japanese the tension actually enhances the strength of each. There is even a widely quoted phrase for it – *kyoryoku shi nagara kyosa* – *literally* 'co-operating while competing', so that out of the subsequent chaos comes harmony.
>
> (Hutton, 1995, p. 269)

Indeed, the differences between the corporate governance systems in Japan, the USA, the UK and continental European models have been summarized recently as follows:

> The continental European and Japanese model of corporate enterprises are somewhat similar, in that a sense of corporate solidarity with social harmony is expected and actually exists. The Anglo-American model, by contrast, is based on a respect for individuality as the societal norm; a key factor defining the structure of corporate enterprise is the notion of a contractual relationship between equal individuals. In this Anglo-American model, the governance of the corporation is based on the notion that shareholders are entitled contractually to claim the residual profit as the ultimate risk-takers of the corporation. In the continental European and Japanese models however, management and employees are recognised as institutionally cooperative in the context of corporate governance.
>
> (Corporate Governance Forum of Japan, 1999, pp. 210–211)

Hoshi and Kashyap (2001) considered corporate governance, finance and investment in Japan from a historic viewpoint and made predictions about the way in which corporate governance and the Japanese economy would evolve in the future. The authors presented substantial empirical evidence (from gathering financial data over long periods of time) to support their arguments. Before World War II Japan's corporate system was dominated by huge family-owned businesses (the *zaibatsu*). However, the Americans broke these companies up and reduced their powers over the economy and the Japanese market after the war ended. After the war and until the 1970s Japan's system of corporate governance still fitted well into the 'insider-dominated' mould. Companies in Japan were mainly financed by bank loans and as already mentioned the *zaibatsu* evolved into the *keiretsu* (literally 'relationship investing'). The banks that owned companies also sat on company boards and played an important role in monitoring company management. Companies were strongly influenced by their bank managers. There was little separation of ownership and control, and companies were disciplined by their banks. Many have suggested that this system of corporate governance was superior to the UK and US systems.

A pattern is emerging in Japan that is being repeated in many countries around the world. The system of corporate governance traditionally dominated by 'banks and bureaucrats' is being replaced gradually by a market-oriented system. A decade ago, when the *keiretsu* system of complicated intercompany shareholdings was still flourishing, companies were protected from shareholder influence. A series of aggressive liquidations of banks holdings in Japanese companies is breaking the close ties that banks and companies have traditionally enjoyed in Japan. There has also been a transformation of corporate ownership structures. Institutional investors are now estimated to own almost three-quarters of the equity market in Japan, reflecting the ownership structure in the UK. Further, Japanese institutional investors are beginning to recognize the financial benefits that may be gained from improved corporate governance. For example, Sparx Asset Management, Japan's only listed independent fund manager, has launched a $ 200 million fund. The fund's management is based on actively improving the corporate governance of investee companies and has been inspired by the involvement of CalPERS,[1] the activist US pension fund (Tassell, 28 July 2003). Therefore, the Japanese system of corporate governance is gradually moving much further toward a market-based, outsider-dominated system of ownership and control.

Despite recent changes, the empirical evidence indicates that Japan continues to fit more closely within an insider than an outsider system, if we consider the empirical evidence. Significant concentration of ownership in Japanese companies has been found by a number of studies. Although the corporate governance system is increasingly dominated by financial institutions, it is also characterized by concentration of ownership rather than wide dispersion, which implies that the agency problems associated with the market-based model are less prominent. For example, Prowse (1992) found that for a sample of Japanese firms in the mid-1980s ownership was highly concentrated with financial institutions being the dominant class of large shareholders. Indeed, they found that ownership concentration in Japanese companies was significantly greater than in US companies, which is consistent with Japanese companies fitting into the insider-dominated model of corporate governance. Berglof and Perotti (1994) also found Japanese companies to be characterized by significant concentration of ownership. It seems that the Japanese model is resembling the UK model as they are both being transformed into market-based systems, with a high proportion of ownership by financial institutions, which is concentrated rather than dispersed. Japan has issued guidelines on exercising voting rights (Pension Fund Corporate Governance Research Committee, 1998) and a series of corporate governance principles (Corporate Governance Committee, 1998).

## Jordan

Jordan's system of corporate governance is insider-oriented with most companies on the Amman stock exchange being owned predominantly by founding families. Accountability and transparency are almost non-existent with minority shareholders'

---

[1]  This comment was made by Mr Shuhei Abe, founder and chief executive of Sparx Asset Management (see Tassell, 28 July 2003).

rights being insignificant. There is currently no code of practice for corporate governance in Jordan. However, corporate governance reform is high on the agenda in Jordan. The newly formed Arab Business Council is likely to focus attention on corporate governance issues, as reform will help to boost investor confidence in the Middle East (Alrawi, 2003).

## Malaysia

Traditionally, Malaysia typifies the insider-based model of corporate governance, with most companies owned and controlled by founding families. Corporate governance problems have been blamed in part for the way in which Malaysia (and other East Asian economies such as South Korea) succumbed to the financial crisis of 1997. This realization has inspired corporate governance reform throughout East Asia. A policy document aimed at improving corporate governance practice in Malaysian companies was produced in 1999 (High Level Finance Committee Report on Corporate Governance, 1999). Ow-Yong and Kooi Guan (2000) discussed the potential impact of the first code of practice for Malaysian corporate governance, published in the same year. The most salient characteristic of the Malaysian code was its mandatory nature. Recall that the Combined Code (2003) in the UK is essentially voluntary, following the spirit of 'comply and explain' (see Chapter 3). Regulation appears to have been more necessary in Malaysia, as in the past minority shareholders have had few rights. It seems that the efforts taken by Malaysian regulators and market participants to improve the country's corporate governance framework have improved Malaysia's standing in the region, according to the results of a survey carried out by the Kuala Lumpur Stock Exchange (KLSE) and PricewaterhouseCoopers (KLSE, 2002). Further, the survey provided strong evidence that Malaysia's corporate governance practices have improved since the code's publication. Specifically, institutional respondents to the survey suggested that a greater separation of company management and ownership had been achieved, as well as clearer definition of the roles and responsibilities of managers and directors, greater focus on internal control and increased disclosure of corporate non-financial information.

Attention has also been paid to encouraging growth in shareholder activism, with the establishment of the Minority Shareholder Watchdog Group by some large institutional investors.

## The Netherlands

The Dutch system of corporate governance is characterized by a two-tier board. This is common to a number of countries worldwide. Under this structure, overall management is carried out by the executive board. This board is responsible for day-to-day running of the business and general corporate operations. There is then a supervisory board that acts like a watchdog. It supervises the conduct of the executive board and provides advice when necessary. The supervisory board, known as the *Struktuurvennootschap*, is compulsory for large companies but optional for smaller companies. A report on corporate governance in the Netherlands was printed in the journal *Corporate Governance: An International Review.* The report summarized the recommendations for corporate governance reform arising from the Committee on Corporate Governance in October 1996. This Committee produced a report that dealt with: the profile, constitution, duties, appointments and remuneration of the supervisory board; procedures of the supervisory board; the work of the board of directors; the functioning of the AGM and investors' role in the organization; compliance with the Committee's recommendations; the function of the auditors; and corporate disclosure. The report is commonly referred to as the Peters Report (Peters Committee, 1997).

Recently, research surveyed Dutch non-executive directors in order to establish how they perceive their roles and whether they consider they can perform their role effectively. An overriding conclusion of the study was that Dutch non-executive directors felt that blowing the whistle on the misuse of funds by executive directors was an important element of their work but that they did not feel they were able to perform this role effectively (Hoohiemstra and Van Manen, 2004). One of the main reasons why non-executive directors felt that they could not perform this role as effectively as they would wish was information asymmetry between the management and supervisory board. In this case, we can see that the dual board structure may create frictional effects which impede 'good' corporate governance. Further, a study by the Netherlands Corporate Governance Foundation found that most Dutch companies were making progress in their compliance with the Netherlands' Corporate Governance Code (Corporate Governance Update, January, 2005).

## Nigeria

Yasaki (2001) discussed the evolution of corporate governance in Nigeria. The author explained that, before Nigeria became independent, company management was not controlled or monitored by external agents but that in recent years this has changed. Nigerian companies are being increasingly called on to increase accountability. Yasaki (2001) focused specifically on the Nigerian banking industry. The Commonwealth initiatives aimed at improving corporate governance, embodied in their *Principles for Corporate Governance in the Commonwealth: Towards Global and Economic Accountability*, are having a substantial impact on corporate Nigeria and other Commonwealth countries.

## Oman

The stock market in Oman, the Muscat Securities Market, began trading in 1989, and is presided over by the Capital Market Authority. The Capital Market Authority produced a detailed Code of Corporate Governance in January 2003 (Al-Busaidi, 2005). Oman has an insider-dominated system of corporate governance, with most companies having ownership concentrated in one or two family shareholders. Interviews with a small sample of company directors in Oman found a reasonable level of compliance with the Code (Al-Busaidi, 2005). However, the interviewees expressed concerns about the difficulties of finding independent non-executive directors. They expressed concerns about allowing outsiders into the boardroom, which perhaps reflected the majority family ownership structure in Omani listed companies.

## Poland

Lawniczak (1997) described the process of stock market creation that has occurred as a result of a government policy to liberalize the Polish economy. Lawniczak explained that the Polish model of mass privatization was characterized by the development of National Investment Funds (NIFs). The introduction of this process was the 30 April 1993 Law on National Investment Funds and their Privatization. This assigned over 500 small and medium-sized companies to 15 NIFs that control 60 % of the companies overall. The state retained 25 % corporate ownership and corporate employees were given the remaining 15 %. The role of the NIFs has been to invest in companies created by restructuring state-owned enterprises and in other Polish companies. The mass-privatized companies were not sold but transferred free of charge to the NIFs. The eventual aim is for the ownership of shares under the NIFs to be transferred to the general public (individual investors). Shares should eventually be traded freely on the Warsaw Stock Exchange. However, the road toward a free market in Poland has been rocky. There have been severe problems of conflicts arising between management firms and companies' supervisory boards. Indeed, the evolving corporate governance system has been termed a 'Bermuda Triangle', which describes the problems involved in the complicated NIF governance relationship.

Koladkiewicz (2001) discussed the most recent developments in the process of corporate governance reform in Poland. She concluded that in the past 10 years the basic skeleton of a new corporate governance system has been constructed. She showed that Polish banks have been prepared to provide companies with necessary capital but have not wanted to take on an active ownership role. She also considered that there are still problems arising from the close relationship between companies' supervisory boards and the political environment. She indicated that there should be less control of corporations' activities by the state.

## Portugal

The first corporate governance recommendations for best practice for Portuguese companies were published in 1999 (The Portuguese Securities Market Commission (CMVM), 1999). This code of best practice was based on the OECD (1999) guidelines. Alves and Mendes (2004) tested whether there was a significant relationship between compliance with corporate governance codes of practice and financial return and found some evidence of one. This is another example of progress toward better corporate governance in a traditionally insider-oriented country.

## Russia

Since the end of the Cold War, Russia has been opening up its financial markets and the Russian stock market has been developing. In a way, the changes in Russia have probably been too fast and furious for the economy to keep up with. The legal framework has been trying to catch up with the pace at which a market economy has been developing in Russia. In 1996, Yeltsin, the President of the Russian Federation, produced a document aimed at enforcing greater shareholder rights (Yeltsin, 1996). Jesover (2001) discussed corporate governance reform in Russia, explaining that the collapse of the communist state led to rapid embrace of a decentralized, free economy. However, businesses are struggling to adapt to the fast pace of change. The 1990s witnessed wide-scale privatization in Russia. Although a large proportion of Russian companies were transferred from the public to the private sector, the upheaval created many problems. Instability in ownership rights ensued. Most companies are characterized by an insider system whereby the company is controlled by a controlling shareholder. Monitoring of company activities by outsiders, such as institutional investors, has been weak. Jesover (2001) argued that, unless Russia improved corporate governance substantially, Russian companies would not be able to attract finance from abroad. Foreign investment is essential for the development of the Russian economy in the long term and its accession to global competitiveness. The author also went through the OECD Principles for 'good' corporate governance and considered how they matched up with the situation in Russia. The paper suggested that there had been wide abuse of power by Russian companies and many examples of corporate misconduct, which have had a devastating impact on the country's international reputation. The conclusion of the paper was that the reforms would take a long time because they involve not just institutional and corporate reform but also deep change in the society's culture. It appears from the paper that Russia has been taking significant steps toward reforming corporate governance. The Supreme Arbitrazh Court and the Federal Commission for the Securities Market have focused their attention on the need for corporate governance reform, which signifies a move in the 'right' direction.

Judge and Naoumova (2004) ascertained that the institutionalization of 'good' corporate governance practices is widely viewed as the next crucial step for Russia, in its path towards fully embracing capitalism. They explain that following the privatization of Russian companies, shareholders' essential rights have been frequently disregarded through the self-dealing transactions of management and/or majority shareholders. The types of techniques used by Russian companies over the last decade include (Judge and Naoumova, 2004; Sprenger, 2002):

- asset stripping/transfer pricing used to skim off profits;

- new share issues where the new shares have preferential rights for insider shareholders in order to dilute minority shareholders' rights;

- delaying payment of dividends;

- provision of fraudulent information to minority, outside shareholders;

- redistribution of property from bankruptcy protection accompanying weak legal recourse.

Judge and Naoumova (2004) argue that Russian corporate governance is at a crossroads with a choice between adopting Anglo-Saxon style corporate governance or that of Western European corporate governance, through banks. This latter choice involves Russian privatization materializing through bank-led financial-industrial groups (termed FIGs). They suggest that 'This approach is more aligned with Russian culture and history, which combine paternalistic and hierarchical control with participative decision-making' (p. 306).

In addition to these cultural factors evidence is emerging that the bank-led financial-industrial groups are outperforming other companies (Perotti and Gelfer, 1998; 2001). Russia's initial choice of Anglo-Saxon style governance is now likely to be replaced by a move toward this form of bank-driven reform, given its cultural characteristics. However, a middle road may be possible with Russia taking some elements of both frameworks. Alternately, Russia may adopt a unique style of corporate governance (McCarthy and Puffer, 2002). Indeed,

> It is currently unknown what model of governance that Russia will choose in its efforts to enter and flourish within the global economy, but it will be fascinating and potentially lucrative to those who predict the future and its pacing accurately.
>
> (Judge and Naoumova, 2004, p. 312)

## Saudi Arabia

Traditionally the Saudi Arabian framework for corporate governance falls neatly into the insider mould, with companies being owned predominantly by founding family members and the government. To date there is no published code of practice for corporate governance in Saudi Arabia, although the development of one is under way. The only comprehensive study of corporate governance in Saudi Arabia has been carried out by Al-Harkan (2005) who investigated the emergence of a framework for corporate governance in the Kingdom. From extensive questionnaire and interview research involving members of the corporate, academic and accounting communities in Saudi Arabia, Al-Harkan (2005) found that there was general support for developing a code of corporate governance best practice and that good corporate governance was viewed as important. The research found that the corporate governance system was viewed as a useful mechanism for protecting shareholder and stakeholder rights and for determining the responsibilities of the board of directors in Saudi companies. Indeed, the research found that most companies and organizations in Saudi seemed to be applying the OECD corporate governance principles, despite the lack of a Saudi code. With the entry of Saudi Arabia into the World Trade Organisation in 2005, convergence with international standards of corporate governance was considered to be of importance by all sectors of the economy. Illustration 8.3 examines the emerging corporate governance framework in Saudi Arabia in more depth. In Illustration 8.4 we examine the findings of recent interview research into the views of Saudi company management on corporate governance issues.

## Illustration 8.3

### The Emerging Corporate Governance Framework in Saudi Arabia

*Ownership Structure in Saudi Arabia*

The Saudi Arabian stock market, which began trading in the 1930s, is dominated by family block holdings. Growth of the Saudi stock market has been slow but steady with only five companies listed by 1954 and 14 by 1975. With the introduction of automated clearing and settlement in 1989, and Tadawul, a more evolved form of security trading in 2001, the Saudi stock market has grown substantially, with a dramatic rise in market capitalization in recent years and over 80 companies listed on the Saudi stock exchange (Al-Harkan, 2005). On average, 75% of companies are owned chiefly by founding families with the rest being owned by the Government (AlTonsi, 2003). Family firms have gone through public initial offerings to obtain listing but families have entrenched themselves by maintaining the bulk of the shares, thereby maintaining control (Al-Harkan, 2005). The Saudi stock market was closed to foreign investment in its early years. This factor, combined with the family and state control of companies, has rendered the Saudi stock market quite illiquid.

The newly-formed Capital Market Authority is an agency responsible for issuing rules and directives, with the main tasks of: regulating and developing the stock market; regulating the issue and trading of securities; protecting shareholders from unfair practices; seeking to achieve fairness, efficiency and transparency in security transactions; and, regulating and monitoring disclosures by companies. The creation of this agency should encourage the growth of the Saudi stock market, raising investor confidence and encouraging corporate governance improvement.

*Three Factors Constraining Saudi Corporate Governance*

Three factors appear to be constraining the speed and effectiveness of corporate governance reform in Saudi companies (Al-Harkan, 2005). These are family ownership, government ownership and religion. As discussed above, the Saudi ownership structure is dominated by family and to a lesser extent, Government, holdings. Family and Government ownership represent a constraining influence on the extent to which corporate governance initiatives can be implemented effectively. Founding family block shareholders are reluctant to relinquish control to minority shareholders and discharge accountability to other stakeholders. However, corporate governance reform is taking place effectively in other countries with insider-oriented frameworks of corporate governance, indicating that although family and government ownership may be constraining factors they are by no means insurmountable.

Religion may also be viewed as a factor inhibiting corporate governance reform in the Kingdom. However, Al-Harkan (2005) argues that there is little genuine difference between the ethical and altruistic foundation of Islamic (Shariah) law and the ethical principles of good corporate governance. Saudi companies which are founded on the basis of Shariah law have a Shariah Committee responsible for protecting shareholder/ stakeholder rights and reviewing financial and non-financial disclosures. This is entirely consistent with the OECD principles of good corporate governance, indicating little genuine conflict between religion and corporate governance reform in Saudi Arabia. However, one element which is at variance is that Shariah law generally prohibits interest whereas corporate governance principles do not. As with all countries, religion and culture need to be taken into account when moulding internationally accepted corporate governance principles to an individual country: there is no blanket code which could apply to all countries, because they are so diverse. Hence, we see the development of individual codes of practice in countries throughout the world.

## Illustration 8.4

### Attitudes of Saudi Company Management towards Corporate Governance Reform

A recent study investigated the attitudes of Saudi companies towards corporate governance reform in Saudi Arabia (Al-Harkan, 2005). The study involved interviewing 23 financial managers from companies spanning six industry sectors.

*Introduction of Corporate Governance Principles in Saudi Arabia*

The interviewees were asked whether they felt it was worthwhile introducing corporate governance principles for Saudi companies. Only one out of 23 interviewees did not consider it worthwhile. The consensus view is summarized in this quote:

> It is very important to introduce an effective corporate governance framework for Saudi companies, in order to protect the rights of shareholders and stakeholders, and to promote the company to a higher level in the financial markets.

*Equitable Treatment of Shareholders*

Under Saudi company law, shareholders have the right to attend annual general meetings and have one share, one vote. They have the right to appoint the board of directors. In relation to the protection of shareholder rights, all interviewees felt that although in principle Saudi company law protected shareholders' rights, in practice treatment varied between companies:

> Shareholders' rights in Saudi companies are, to a certain extent, theoretically protected and maintained, but in practice, we find that shareholders do not view their rights as seriously as they should. This, in my view, is due to the misconduct of the company as well as to shareholders. Shareholders do not participate in, or appear at the annual general assembly. More awareness is required on the part of shareholders, which will lead to better performance by the company.

*Responsibilities of the Board of Directors*

Saudi company law specifies the duties and responsibilities of Saudi company boards. The specified goal of boards is to protect shareholder wealth and the interests of stakeholders. Boards are now required to appoint audit committees from non-executive directors. As with shareholder rights, some interviewees indicated that there was a gap between what was prescribed by Saudi company law and what was happening in practice:

> In reality, boards of directors act outside the guidelines and responsibilities set down by Saudi company law, to which they should closely adhere. For example, sometimes they make decisions to increase the company's capital without consulting shareholders or other stakeholders or they appoint a new finance manager without observing the company's employment rules.

*Disclosure by Saudi Companies*

As stipulated by the OECD (2004), transparency is a cornerstone of good corporate governance. Before the 1990s, Saudi disclosure requirements were low, with companies only required to provide a balance sheet, a profit and loss account, a directors' report and an auditor's report. In 1986, a statement of concepts and objectives of financial accounting and a disclosure standard were issued, and in 1992 the Saudi Organization for Certified Accountants (SOCPA) was established which raised the profile of financial reporting and disclosure by Saudi companies (Al-Mulhem, 1997). However, most interviewees indicated that disclosure needed to be improved and increased, for example:

> the current system is deficient in many ways, in terms of the disclosure of financial and non-financial data and information on the company. For example, the methods followed in appointing the board of directors and the external auditor of the company are generally kept secret and are not disclosed.

The overall impression from the interviews was that corporate governance in Saudi Arabia was improving but that there were still gaps between company law and corporate practice. Furthermore, interviewees tended to support the introduction of corporate governance principles in Saudi companies as a means of encouraging further corporate governance reform.

## South Africa

The first King Report (1994) was published in South Africa in order to formalize an ongoing process of corporate governance reform. It was a code of corporate practice and conduct that was based on a broad consensus of the South African business community. One of the most distinguishing aspects of South African corporate governance reform has been its focus on a more stakeholder-oriented approach. The first King Report (1994) included a code of business ethics for companies and their stakeholders, representing one of the most forward-looking codes of corporate governance practice. However, 2002 saw the publication of an updated report, again taking the title the King Report (2002) from the chair of the Corporate Governance Committee, Mervyn E. King. The 2002 King Report continued in the same vein, by focusing on a stakeholder approach to corporate governance. In Illustration 8.5 we discuss the South African approach to accountability and responsibility as defined in the King Report (2002) in more detail.

### Illustration 8.5

#### Differentiating between accountability and responsibility

In Chapter 1 we discussed the differences between an agency approach to corporate governance that focuses on corporate accountability to shareholders and stakeholder theory. Stakeholder theory suggests that companies should discharge an accountability to other groups of stakeholders, rather than shareholders alone. The Corporate Governance committee in South Africa has thought long and hard about these issues and has adopted a form of stakeholder approach to corporate governance, but one that draws an extremely important and interesting distinction between accountability and responsibility, as follows:

> One is liable to render an account when one is accountable and one is liable to be called to account when one is responsible. In governance terms, one is accountable

at common law and by statute to the company if a director and one is responsible to the stakeholders identified as relevant to the business of the company. The stakeholder concept of being accountable to all legitimate stakeholders must be rejected for the simple reason that to ask boards to be accountable to everyone would result in their being accountable to no one. The modern approach is for a board to identify the company's stakeholders, including its shareowners, and to agree policies as to how the relationship with those stakeholders should be advanced and managed in the interests of the company.

(King Report, 2002, p. 5)

The Committee was clearly emphasizing the need to satisfy shareholders, as long as it is not to the detriment of other stakeholders. However, this approach toward stakeholders may be seen by some as a backward step away from a broader corporate social responsibility agenda. The quote above begs many questions, such as: What is this 'modern approach'? What evidence is there that such a modern approach is successful? Does it not seem that such an approach to corporate governance is focusing on the 'interests of the company', whereas corporate governance is more about running companies in the interests of at least the shareholders and then possibly other groups of stakeholders? The King Report (2002) states that it takes an inclusive approach to corporate governance.

## South Korea

From a corporate governance perspective, the case of South Korea is intriguing, as reform has been speedy and has engendered massive changes. Since the 1980s the Korean political environment has been liberalized. A recent President of the Republic of South Korea, Kim Dae Jung, has made efforts to attract foreign funds to Korea, to make Korean business more transparent, to improve corporate governance and to make Korea a globally competitive economy. He initiated a policy of reform called *segyhewa*, or 'globalization'. Until well after World War II, Korea was occupied by Japan. This meant that Korean business was influenced substantially by the Japanese structure of business. As in Japan, the corporate ownership structure has been characterized by founding family ownership concentration. The Korean *chaebol*, or conglomerate business groups, have arisen from small family-run companies and are now global players (e.g., Hyundai and LG). Until very recently, the corporate governance structure in Korea has kept its traditional 'insider' character. There has been little separation of ownership and control in Korean companies as the owners and managers have tended to be the same people at the highest level. Indeed, outdated hierarchical business strategies have been blamed in part for the way in which South Korea succumbed to the Asian crisis in 1997. As the following quote suggests:

...anachronistic activities by chaebol were part of what caused Korea's economic crisis and the government has the responsibility to protect the rights of the people. Lee Yong-keun, Chairman of the Financial Supervisory Commission

(*Digital Korea Herald*, 27 April 2000)

However, in more recent times efforts have been made to create more equity financing for business and therefore to extend share ownership to a wider community of shareholders – institutional investors and the general public. The Government has forced companies to reduce debt in their financial structures and to take on equity finance to a greater extent. The proportion of institutional investor ownership in Korea is now about 35 % – a lot lower than in the UK but a lot higher than it was before. Another important aspect of Korean corporate governance is the historic influence of factors such as the state, culture and the legal system. We explore the influence of culture in more depth in Illustration 8.6. Until relatively recently, company law in Korea gave hardly any rights to minority shareholders (such as institutional investors). This is changing dramatically now. The Asian crisis in 1997 hit South Korea heavily and resulted in significant expropriation of minority shareholder wealth by majority shareholders in such companies as Samsung Electronics and SK Telecom (see Johnson et al., 2000). Such transfers of wealth highlighted a need for tightening of company law. The Government has had a substantial impact on company activities as state-owned banks have provided finance and the Government has instructed Korean companies on the strategic direction they wish them to take. Links with the state are now being lessened.

## Illustration 8.6

### The influence of culture on corporate governance

From a cultural point of view, Confucianism has had an important role to play in the conduct of Korean business. This religious tradition still dominates the Korean people, although the process of Westernization that is ongoing in East Asian countries is reducing Confucian influence. A hierarchical structure has always been characteristic of Confucianism, with family structures dominated by the 'father' of the household and women playing minor roles. This is changing but remains in existence. Solomon et al. (2002a) discussed the traditional, historic framework of corporate governance that prevailed in South Korea before the recent reforms in some detail. They explained that Confucianism emphasizes the importance of the family and provides moral guidance on how human relationships should be conducted (Song, 1997). Reflecting Confucian family structures, within the traditional Korean *chaebol*, power filters down from the chairman (the head of the *chaebol* owner family) to the most junior employees, through a top-down, hierarchical structure. Indeed, the hierarchical structure of the chaebol has been interpreted as military in nature (Song, 1997). As well as the writings of Confucius, Korean folklore, influenced by the Confucian tradition, has had a strong impact on business. The three values emphasized by Koreans are commitment, seniority and humility (Choi and Wright, 1994). In relation to corporate ethics, Ungson et al. (1997) explained that Daewoo, for example, emphasized 'co-prosperity', which involved companies shouldering responsibility to give equal benefits to workers, suppliers, customers, partners and the Government – a true stakeholder approach. Solomon et al. (2002a) also explained the diverse range of initiatives that have been instigated in order to improve and develop the country's corporate governance system. The paper attempted to evaluate the success of the agenda for corporate governance reform. A conceptual framework was proposed to aid analysis of the reforms. A further paper (Solomon et al., 2002b) provided empirical evidence from a postal questionnaire and personal interviews conducted in Korea. The results indicated that institutional investors in South Korea were becoming far more active in corporate governance and were taking more interest in corporate governance issues. The paper also documented in some detail the recent amendments to Korean company law in terms of specific changes to the Korean Commercial Code (see also Hemmings and Solomon, 1998; Solomon et al., 1999). Overall, it appears that the pace of reform has been heightened since the Asian crisis. The Korean culture is changing, embracing a less hierarchical attitude to company management and encouraging companies to become more transparent and accountable. In a way it is sad to see a country's traditions being watered down. However, corporate governance, like society, is dynamic in nature. It is quite clear that if Korea wants to keep its status as a global business player, corporate governance reform is an essential tool to success.

## Sweden

The Swedish Association of Exchange Listed Companies and the Stockholm Stock Exchange produced a new Swedish Code of Corporate Governance in May 2005. This has been incorporated into the country's stock exchange listing rules, but is being adopted on a comply or explain basis, as in the UK (Corporate Governance Update, September, 2005).

## Taiwan

Taiwan's system of corporate governance fits neatly into the insider mould, with the majority of companies characterized by family control and concentrated share ownership. The legal system in Taiwan derives from the German mould and therefore places the Taiwanese system somewhere between the Anglo-Saxon type system and the French law-based systems of stock markets and corporate governance (see, e.g., La Porta et al., 1997). However, the system of corporate governance in Taiwan is individualistic, with a board of directors accompanied by a group of supervisors, whose role is to provide an independent view to executive directors. On 15 October 2002, the Security and Futures Commission (SFC) of the Taiwan Stock Exchange (TSE) produced the first code of best practice on corporate governance, entitled *Practical Guidance on Corporate Governance for Listed and OTC* [Over The Counter] *Companies*. We examine some of the recent problems in Taiwanese corporate governance and the anticipated reaction to the recent code of practice in Illustration 8.7.

### Illustration 8.7

#### Corporate governance reform in Taiwan

Taiwanese companies have been branded with many of the negative characteristics associated with insider corporate governance systems. Crony capitalism, lack of corporate transparency, minority shareholder wealth expropriation and managerial abuse of power are all problems traditionally occurring in East Asian countries' systems of corporate governance. However, the notorious agency problem associated with outsider-dominated systems of corporate governance has, until relatively recently, been insignificant in Taiwan. As the TSE expands and shareholding gradually becomes more dispersed, agency problems are beginning to encroach on Taiwanese companies. It is therefore necessary for Taiwan to improve corporate governance standards in order to tackle these emerging problems of separation of ownership and control. Also in order to attract foreign capital, Taiwanese companies need to improve internal corporate governance standards, as international investment institutions require a minimum level of corporate governance and accountability before they are prepared to lend funds to foreign companies. Indeed, corporate governance has now become one of the main factors determining investment in Asian stocks, according to the latest research (McBride, 2002). As a result of the corporate governance reform process, in October 2002 Taiwan produced its first code of corporate governance best practice entitled *Practical Guidance on Corporate Governance for Listed and OTC Companies*. This document is voluntary in nature, although companies listed on the TSE are required to state whether or not they are complying with the guidance. The details of the document are very similar to those of the OECD and to the original UK Cadbury Code (1992). As a result of this new initiative, local Taiwanese newspapers have been full of commentary and discussion on corporate governance issues. One article enumerated all the reasons why corporate governance reform in Taiwan was likely to be difficult (Zun, 2002). Excessive control by founding family members was highlighted as probably the most significant problem. Systematic lack of transparency in Taiwanese companies arising from a desire to produce annual reports that provide an overly positive view for company analysts and shareholders has also been pinpointed as an obstacle to corporate governance reform. Indeed, Taiwanese companies have been widely associated with creative accounting and lack of transparency in their operations, as well as notorious and frequent cases of fraud by company management (*Taipei Times*, 15 July 2000, 18 July 2002). One of the principal problems with Taiwanese company accounts, according to foreign institutional investors, has been an unwillingness to disclose information relating to the companies' investments in mainland China (McBride, 2002).

Nevertheless, reform is progressing at a steady pace. In July 2002 TSMC (Taiwan Semiconductor Manufacturing Company) was the first Taiwanese company to establish a formal audit committee in the style of the Cadbury Report (Chang and Chan, 2002). Recently amended Company Law (2001) and the new guidance on corporate governance recommended that half of a company's board of directors should comprise independent directors. There are, however, concerns that there will be an inadequate supply of appropriate people to fill the role of independent director in all Taiwanese listed and OTC companies. Further, there are concerns that the presence of independent directors on boards will stifle creative and innovative activities: a common response to corporate governance checks and balances (Guan, 2002). In the wake of the corporate accounting scandals in the USA, the SFC in Taiwan has charged the TSE with tightening its scrutiny of financial reports of companies applying for a listing on the TSE or the OTC market. Further, the Accounting Research and Development Foundation in Taiwan is reviewing the current corporate accounting system in order to detect and correct any weaknesses. Further, many shareholders have been filing lawsuits against a number of noted accounting firms on suspicions that they may have collaborated with local companies in concealing financial losses and producing false annual reports.

Another initiative that has aided wider shareholder dispersion and encouraged foreign investment institutions to invest in Taiwanese companies is Taiwan's Qualified Foreign Institutional Investor (QFII) scheme. This scheme has been in place since the early 1990s, but is currently being disbanded. It allows all types of institutional investor to apply for a licence which, after giving a relatively small deposit to the Taiwan central bank, lets the institution trade freely in local shares up to an established limit. This scheme has been successful, attracting significant foreign investment. However, the investment process can be fraught with difficulties, as retrieving funds from Taiwan is not always easy, with foreign institutional investors faced frequently by long waits (*South China Morning Post*, 19 April 2002). Taiwan has been so serious about corporate governance reform that in December 2002 the government (the Executive Yuan) made improving corporate governance a national policy. The government has set up a new commission and task force under the Cabinet to supervise progress. Their initial aim is to produce a White Paper on government policy that will detail government policies designed to promote improvements in corporate transparency and governance (*Taiwan Business News*, 3 December 2002). A recent study investigated the attitudes of Taiwanese company directors toward corporate governance reform and found that they were strongly in favour of reform and wanted to see Taiwanese companies adopt internationally accepted standards of corporate governance, mainly with an aim of attracting international funds (Solomon et al., 2003b). Further, the paper indicated that Taiwanese directors were uncomfortable with the level of family control in Taiwanese companies and concluded that crony capitalism and managerial abuse of power needed to be curbed in order to make Taiwan internationally competitive. There are, however, many other factors influencing the speed of corporate governance reform in Taiwan and the country's ability to attract institutional investment from abroad. The political situation in Taiwan is extremely sensitive and the cultural roots are not necessarily conducive to an Anglo-American-style system of corporate governance. Indeed, the American Chamber of Commerce in Taipei has emphasized the need for Taiwan to pursue political stability and subordinate partisan politics to improving corporate governance, reducing corporate fraud and focusing on attracting foreign investment (Namgyal, 2001).

## Thailand

Thailand represents an insider-dominated system of corporate governance with an emerging stock market. Again, Thailand's economy was affected severely by the Asian crisis, and this has been attributed to corporate governance weaknesses, among other factors. Indeed, the whole crisis emanated from Thailand. In summer 1997 there was a devaluation of the Thai baht, following a collapse of the property market. Following the crisis there was, as in many of the other Asian economies, significant expropriation of minority shareholder wealth. In the case of Thailand, managers in the Bangkok Bank of Commerce transferred huge funds offshore to companies under their control (Johnson et al., 2000). Since the Asian financial crisis, Thailand has been one of many countries to produce a code of best practice for the directors of listed companies (SET, 1998). Indeed, corporate governance weaknesses have been used partly as a scapegoat by the authorities in many countries since 1997.

A survey by the Thai Institute of Directors, conducted in 2004, found that governance progress was being made. There had been substantial improvements specifically in the areas of board independence and the reduction of crony capitalism. The report did, however, criticize companies for low levels of transparency, when compared to other East Asian countries (Corporate Governance Update, October, 2004).

## United States

Corporate governance has been a hot topic in the USA. No one can think about corporate governance without turning immediately to the problems of Enron and WorldCom. If the

USA has not got things right, being such an economically prosperous nation, what chance do smaller, poorer countries stand? Countries around the world have become introspective in their reaction to the problems in the USA, checking their own systems and corporate governance controls for similar Enron-type weaknesses. 'Enronitis' has spread across the world like a rampant virus. However, interest in US corporate governance is by no means new. The weight of literature and research in the corporate governance domain centres around the US system, or at least draws comparisons of countries' systems with that of the USA. Berle and Means' (1932) work was based on the US system of corporate governance. The first papers on agency theory (e.g., Jensen and Meckling, 1976) focused on the US corporate governance system. Similarly, much of the path-breaking work on boards of directors and corporate performance, the impact of outside directors on performance and the impact of mergers and takeovers came initially from US academics, as we saw in Chapter 4. Although the UK and the USA have outsider, market-based systems of corporate governance, these systems display many differences. Shareholder activism is different between the two countries, with US investment institutions presenting shareholder resolutions to companies far more frequently. As discussed in Chapter 4, the notion of splitting the chairman and chief executive roles in the USA has not been viewed favourably, as board culture is extremely different from the UK, although things are gradually changing in this respect. Another difference that we have already discussed is in remuneration. Executive remuneration in the USA has been traditionally far more excessive than in other countries, such as the UK. Monks and Minow (2001) provided a detailed insight into US corporate governance. The literature in this area will not be covered in detail here as much of it has been mentioned in comparisons with the UK system in earlier chapters. Table 8.1 summarizes a selection of the many corporate governance codes of practice and policy documents that have been published in recent

**Table [8.1]**   Corporate governance policy documents in the USA

| Title | Organization | Year |
|---|---|---|
| Corporate Governance Market Principles | CalPERS | 1998 |
| Report of the NACD Blue Ribbon Commission on Improving the Effectiveness of Audit Committees | NYSE and NACD | 1998 |
| Report of the NACD Blue Ribbon Committee on CEO succession | NACD | 1998 |
| Core Policies | CII | 1998 |
| Statement on Corporate Governance | Business Roundtable | 1997 |
| GM Board of Directors Corporate Governance Guidelines on Significant Governance Issues | GM | 1997 |
| TIAA-CREF Policy Statement on Corporate Governance | TIAA-CREF | 1997 |
| Report of the NACD Blue Ribbon Commission on Director Professionalism | NACD | 1996 |

years. Recently, however, corporate governance in the USA has come under sharp criticism. Monks (2005) states that there is almost universal agreement that corporate governance in America is failing and that despite much energy being applied to corporate governance reform in the 1990s, no 'real' reform seems to have occurred. Monks attributes this failure to a general loss of confidence in stock market investment, as he asserts that corporate governance is principally about the creation of wealth. Indeed, he considers that business leaders are experiencing 'governance fatigue', which is leading to apathy in the governance area. Monks suggests that real corporate governance reform in the USA is not happening, as there is little evidence of shareholder involvement in issues such as the nomination of directors. Other areas where he considers corporate governance reform is simply not happening are in non-executive director independence, long-term shareholding, institutional investors as 'responsible owners', the independence of auditors, and executive remuneration, which he terms the 'smoking gun' of governance failure! Indeed, he states that,

> Persons having power are reluctant to give it up. This is the problem, and this is the challenge. Governance is stuck in the mode of confrontation between owners and managers and the managers have won. The informing energy of business is greed ... Reform proposals will be credible only to the extent they make desired action profitable.
>
> (Monks, 2005, p. 109)

## Chapter summary

This chapter has provided a 'reference dictionary' of corporate governance in a selection of countries around the world. This dictionary has attempted to provide a flavour of the rich diversity of corporate governance systems internationally and the attempts that have been made in these countries to reform corporate governance. Clearly, there is a vast diversity of different systems, with many factors combining to determine a country's corporate governance environment, including legal framework, corporate ownership structure, culture and economic factors.

## Questions for reflection and discussion

1   Select two countries from the 'reference dictionary' in this chapter and compare and contrast their systems of corporate governance. Research these countries' systems of corporate governance using newspapers, academic articles and the Internet. Consider the corporate governance reforms that have taken place there. To what extent do you feel these have been successful?

2   Read the OECD Principles on Corporate Governance (OECD, 1999). Choose two countries listed in the 'reference dictionary' and evaluate the extent to which you

think they are adopting these principles? To assist you, there is a selection of country assessments on the World Bank website (http:// www.worldbank.org). These assess each country's success in complying with the principles.

3  Choose a country that is not covered in the 'reference dictionary'. Search for information relating to corporate governance in the country of your choice, using the Internet and academic journals. Is this country reforming its system of corporate governance? If so, describe the ways in which this is occurring and the extent to which you think the country's evolving system of corporate governance is converging with other systems around the world.

4  Look at a selection of corporate governance codes of practice (using the Internet). Consider the different ways in which the codes deal with stakeholders. To what extent do you think corporate governance reform around the world is taking a genuine interest in stakeholder concerns?

# Part III

# Broadening the corporate governance agenda

## Chapter 9

# Discharging a broader corporate accountability

## Aim and objectives

This chapter considers a broader agenda for corporate governance by extending the theoretical paradigm from a narrow agency theory perspective to encompass a stakeholder theory perspective. The specific objectives of this chapter are to enable readers to:

- consider the growth of corporate social responsibility in a broad philosophical and historical context, highlighting the potentially strong impact of corporate behaviour on a wide range of stakeholders;

- emphasize the importance of establishing a positive relationship between corporate social responsibility and corporate financial performance;

- discuss social, ethical, environmental and sustainability disclosure as one of the main ways in which companies can discharge their accountability to a wide range of stakeholders, with an emphasis on environmental reporting;

- discuss the use of stakeholder engagement to discharge broader corporate accountability.

## Introduction

The preceding chapters have focused on corporate governance from a rather narrow, finance-dominated, agency theory perspective. Part I examined the ways in which corporate governance mechanisms, such as the board of directors, play a role in aligning the interests of shareholders and company management. However, recent years have witnessed a growing interest in corporate social responsibility. Growing fears of such high-consequence risks as global environmental disaster, terrorism and nuclear war have focused people's attention on environmental and social issues.[1] Companies have become

---

[1] Giddens (1991) discussed the rise of what he termed 'high consequence risks', which include such potentially catastrophic events as nuclear war and global warming.

so large and pervasive, extending their operations on a global scale, that their account-ability to society is becoming an urgent issue.

> Corporations dominate all aspects of our lives. Their power affects the quality of life, food, water, gas, electricity, seas, rivers, environment, schools, hospitals, medicine, news, entertainment, transport, communications and even the lives of unborn babies ... Unaccountable corporate power is damaging the fabric of society, the structure of families, the quality of life and even the very future of the planet.
>
> (Mitchell and Sikka, 2005, p. 2)

Policies and corporate governance initiatives have highlighted the importance of broad-ening the corporate governance agenda to incorporate a more 'inclusive' approach (i.e., an approach to corporate governance that focuses not only on the needs of shareholders but also on the needs and requirements of all corporate stakeholders). As discussed in Chapter 1, stakeholder theory has attracted increasing attention in recent years and the needs of stakeholders are being taken more seriously by businesses. Indeed, there is an emerging perception that shareholder and stakeholder theories are not dichotomous, as traditionally thought, but display many similarities and commonalities.

In the UK there has been a complete overhaul of company law in recent years, based on a belief that the existing documents had become outdated and less relevant for modern companies. The first drafts of the Modern Company Law Review appeared to be refocusing company law on social, ethical and environmental issues (frequently referred to as SEE issues) and emphasized the broadening responsibilities of company directors in the UK (see Modern Company Law, 2000; Modernising Company Law, 2002). Indeed, the text of the accompanying White Paper reflected a paradigm shift in the way directors perceive their role in companies and in society. There were many references to company stakeholders included in the White Paper, representing an attempt to demonstrate a broadening corporate agenda, for example:

> The Review considered to whom directors should owe duties ... the basic goal for directors should be the success of the company in the collective best interests of shareholders, but that the *directors should also recognise, as the circumstances require, the company's need to foster relationships with its employees, customers and suppliers, its need to maintain its business reputation, and its need to consider the company's impact on the community and the working environment.*
>
> (Modernising Company Law, 2002, Section 3.3, emphasis added)

However, the extent to which this shift in emphasis within the new versions of UK company law may really be viewed as a genuine change, in the discourse of company directors, is debatable. The final draft of the review inspired far less optimism for those wishing to pursue a stakeholder perspective, as any reference to stakeholder account-ability was surrendered to a materiality constraint. Any suggestion within the law document stating that directors were responsible for managing and disclosing information pertaining to social and environmental issues was rendered important only if they were to prove material. In other words, directors were considered liable for social and environmental risks and were encouraged to disclose social and environmental information only when such issues were considered material, as:

> It will, of course, be for directors to decide precisely what information is material to their particular business.
>
> (Modernising Company Law, 2002, Section 4.33)

This means that if company directors consider a social and environmental issue is not material, then they are not liable and do not have to disclose information pertaining to it. Materiality is such an intangible, abstract notion that it would in practice be extremely difficult to prosecute a director on a point of social and environmental materiality. This problem, especially in relation to the proposed (and abandoned) mandatory OFR and social and environmental disclosure, is discussed in Solomon and Edgley (2005). A series of interviews with institutional investors and lawyers in the City of London revealed a deep scepticism over the potential impact of the review of company law in the area of social and environmental accountability. Indeed, one of the lawyers I interviewed commented that the new legislation was unenforceable in this area and was, in her opinion, simply a 'marketing ploy'. Certainly, institutional investors regard the social responsibility aspect of the Modern Company Law Review to be related to public relations rather than to financial return or genuine interest in social and environmental issues. Its eventual impact on corporate behaviour is certainly in question.

One initiative that has focused corporate attention on social responsibility and especially on social and environmental concerns within companies in the UK has been the guidelines on social and environmental disclosure published by the Association of British Insurers (ABI). The emphasis of these guidelines was on the responsibilities of directors for considering social and environmental issues in their general decision making within the company. Such emphasis on the social and environmental responsibilities of company boards was not new but picked up from writers and practitioners, such as Garratt (1996), who emphasized the importance of social and environmental issues to board effectiveness. More recently, Cadbury (2002) has highlighted the way in which companies are assimilating a socially responsible role.

As mentioned in Chapter 6, another outcome of the Company Law Review was a mandatory Operating and Financial Review (OFR). The fiasco relating to the introduction of the mandatory OFR was discussed on p. 169 in relation to transparency. Many groups of stakeholders had attached high hopes to the new mandatory OFR as an appropriate vehicle for social and environmental reporting. Its abolition and demise has raised deep concerns about the genuine accountability of corporate Britain. The replacement, Business Review, may do the job, but the signal sent out by the Government's back-tracking can only be negative. Solomon and Edgley (2005) evaluated the potential for the new mandatory OFR to act as an appropriate vehicle for social and environmental disclosure and concluded that company directors would use materiality as an escape route to help them avoid uncomfortable social and environmental information being included in the public reporting process. Indeed, they conclude that the materiality issue renders the OFR impotent as a means of encouraging and increasing social and environmental reporting. Perhaps this is why it was disbanded, as it had no real power to change anyway?

We now consider the emergence of corporate social responsibility, from a UK perspective, and its ensuing influence on business. We begin by delving into the historical roots of corporate social responsibility.

## Early roots of corporate social responsibility in the UK

Corporate social responsibility (often referred to as CSR in the literature) has existed for some time. Indeed, ever since the Industrial Revolution in Britain in the 18th century there has been a growing consciousness of the harm that irresponsible corporate behaviour can bring. The terrible living and working conditions of people involved in early industrialization moved many members of the 'higher classes' to write extensively on the evils of industry. The blast furnaces developed by Abraham Darby in Ironbridge and the cotton and woollen mills in the North of England were seen by visitors as inhuman environments for people to work in. Some writers described Abraham Darby's Coalbrookdale as the 'mouth of hell'. The poverty and appalling living conditions that millworkers suffered in Manchester horrified visiting academics and novelists. For example, Thomas Carlyle (1795–1881) passionately bewailed the suffering of the industrialized working class in the 1840s and was one of the first writers to produce novels encouraging a social consciousness (e.g., *Past and Present*). Other contemporary writers with similar intentions were Elizabeth Gaskell (1810–1865) and Benjamin Disraeli (1804–1881). Gaskell encouraged social reconciliation and a better under-standing between employers and workers as well as between different classes of society. She observed the pitiful living conditions of the industrial workers in Manchester and was deeply affected by what she saw.

By Victorian times social-oriented movements were being established based on philanthropic and Christian values. There was a slow realization among certain circles of society that unethical corporate behaviour could have a detrimental influence on society. The founding of the Christian Socialist movement by philosophers, political economists, philanthropists and novelists was a step in the direction of corporate social responsibility. The early Christian Socialists were mainly middle-class intellectuals, writing between 1850 and 1870. Charles Kingsley (famous for writing *The Water-Babies*) and John Ruskin (an artist and architectural writer as well as an early political economist) were founders of the Christian Socialist movement. They were deeply affected by the working class misery they encountered on their travels. They were deeply concerned that the massive wealth arising from industrial activities was not necessarily generated by socially responsible business practices as:

Any given accumulation of commercial wealth may be indicative, on the one hand, of faithful industries, progressive energies, and productive ingenuities ... or, on the other, it may be indicative of mortal luxury, merciless tyranny, ruinous chicane. Some treasures are heavy with human tears...

(Ruskin, 1862, p. 180)

These writers and philosophers tended to be unimpressed by industrialization and dreamed of returning to a peaceful, rural England without mechanization. As well as being early socialists in the political sense, their philosophy was deeply rooted in Christian principles. Their belief was that Christianity was the only foundation of Socialism and that a true Socialism was the necessary result of a sound Christianity. The writing that they produced reached a far wider public than purely social political literature in contemporary society because of the close relationship between the population and their church. Even though many may feel that such Christian-based ideologies are irrelevant in our predominantly multifaith society, the continuing influence of Christian Socialism is surprising. Today, the relevance of Christian Socialism is demonstrated by leading politicians such as Tony Blair and Stephen Timms belonging to the movement.

There were also individuals who championed environmental issues. William Morris, a famous Pre-Raphaelite painter and poet, devoted his life to raising environmental awareness in Victorian Britain, as well as bringing attention to workers' rights and architectural preservation. Morris lectured and wrote widely about environmental issues such as pollution and the pitiful conditions of Britain's working classes. He also paid £500 (a substantial sum in the 1880s) for lawyers to oppose the tapping of a Surrey river, on aesthetic and environmental grounds. This is one of the earliest cases of environmental lobbying through the courts (Solomon and Thomson, 2006b).

According to Boatright (1999) corporate social responsibility as a discipline in its own right (and the terminology surrounding it) originated in the 1950s. The consciousness of corporate social responsibility has grown continuously since the first roots of industrialization in England to the gradual growth of business around the world. However, it is increasingly clear from the emerging literature that awareness for environmental accountability, for example in the area of pollution, was an important issue in early 19th century Britain (Solomon and Thomson, 2006a). The larger that companies have become, the greater their potential impact (good or bad) on society and, therefore, the greater the need for them to act in a socially responsible way.

One of the problems with discussing corporate social responsibility is in deciding whether we can treat a company in a similar way to a person: Can a company be attributed with ethics and morals? Is a company an entity, equivalent to a 'person', capable of behaving in a socially responsible or irresponsible manner? The problem is: How can a company, which is a collection of different people – employees and managers – be treated as a 'person' in its own right? There is an interesting discussion of the corporation as a moral subject in Lozano (2000), which shows the difficulties of making such an assumption and describes the way in which the debate has gone round in circles over time. Strong supporters of the idea of a company as a moral person are French (1979, 1984) and Goodpaster (1982, 1987).

The sole aim of companies to maximize profitability and maximize shareholder wealth has come seriously into question in more recent times. Pursuing profit at the expense of damage to the environment, local communities, employees and other stakeholders is not a route many people support any longer. The pure ethics case for business to act in a socially responsible manner was outlined in Chapter 1, which showed that some writers consider that company management cannot subordinate basic moral obligations to shareholder obligations (Quinn and Jones, 1995). However, as we see from the following section, other writers disagree.

## Friedman and corporate social responsibility

One person who has been demonized by proponents of corporate social responsibility is Milton Friedman. A free market economist, he believed that the *only* responsibility a company had to society was to maximize returns to its shareholders. He adopted a purely agency theory perspective of the company, believing that any attempts by companies to spend money on charitable donations, or attempt to satisfy stakeholders other than shareholders, were at best misguided (Friedman, 1962, 1970). A full discussion of Friedman's viewpoints *inter alia* may be found in Lozano (2000). Similarly, the work of Sternberg (1998) derided corporate social responsibility and echoed Friedman's sentiments. It is however hard to see that if corporate social responsibility makes companies more successful in the long term, as well as making companies more sustainable and accountable to society, this would not be in the long-term interests of shareholders as well as stakeholders. The crunch is whether or not corporate social responsibility engenders profits. As we emphasized in Chapter 1, it is unrealistic to assume that business managers will act in a socially responsible manner if this reduces profits. However, there is a growing body of literature that shows a positive relationship between corporate social/ environmental performance and financial performance. We consider some of this literature in the following section.

## Does corporate social responsibility improve financial performance?

There is a growing perception within the corporate and shareholder communities that companies that perform well in the social, ethical and environmental arena also perform well financially. Innovest Strategic Value Advisors, an organization that rates companies in more than 50 industries according to a wide spectrum of social, environmental and corporate governance issues, have provided evidence that companies with superior social and environmental ratings, as well as better corporate governance, also have the best performing shares (*Pensions Week*, 2003). In the academic literature there are a number of reasons given for a possible positive relationship between corporate social responsibility and corporate financial performance. One reason that corporate financial performance may be positively related to corporate social and environmental performance derives from the view that if company management act in a socially responsible manner they are more likely to possess the skills to run a company well, improving its financial performance and making it an attractive investment (Alexander and Buchholz, 1978). My own research, based on extensive interview and questionnaire evidence, has certainly shown that the UK institutional investment community view social and environmental management as an important indicator of management quality more generally (Solomon and Solomon, 2002). Illustration 9.1 returns to the unfortunate case of Enron by using Enron's unethical activities to illustrate the possible link between management quality and management's behaviour in the SEE social and environmental domain.

## Illustration 9.1

### Enron and ethics

We studied Enron's downfall in Chapter 2, analysing the various corporate governance weaknesses abounding in Enron and considered their contribution to its collapse. However, we did not consider the relevance of social and environmental accountability to Enron. There is a growing perception in the financial markets that social and environmental corporate performance is a good indicator of financial performance. Furthermore, there is a growing feeling that a company's management of social and environmental issues is indicative of the quality of the company's management in other areas. Enron was plagued with accusations of human rights abuse in India in the mid-1990s. Their handling of the situation raises several questions about the company's ethics and ability to manage risks effectively. In 1995 Enron's power project in Maharashtra in India encountered a long and bitter dispute with nationalist politicians. A change in the country's government after Enron's initial negotiations regarding foreign direct investment in India resulted in more nationalist leadership. The company was accused of corruption, lack of transparency, insensitivity to local citizenry and complicity in human rights abuses by police (*The Economist*, 1 June 2000). Protestors demonstrating against the company's new site were allegedly beaten by security guards hired by Enron. By 1998 controversy over the Indian project seemed to have been quelled (*The Economist*, 26 February 1998), which was a relief for the company. But did it leave a scar on the company's ethical profile? Perhaps more attention to this detail would have provided an important insight into the character of the senior management at Enron. Their handling of the situation left much to be desired and was perhaps indicative of things to come. Certainly, if companies' handling of social and environmental issues is indicative of their general management quality, this was not a positive sign for Enron.

Another reason that company management would wish to concern themselves with social and environmental issues is in the case where their financial performance could be negatively affected by socially irresponsible behaviour. This view had underpinned initiatives aimed at improving internal control in the areas of social and environmental risk management (as endorsed by ACCA, 2000, see Illustration 6.1). It is however possible that a positive link may be found, simply because companies that have performed better financially may be better able to afford to act in a socially responsible manner, as suggested by McGuire et al. (1988) as they found that prior financial performance was a better predictor of corporate social responsibility than subsequent performance, again using US data. Academic research has found some support for a positive link between corporate social performance and financial performance. For example, Moskowitz (1972) found that the share returns of a small sample of US listed companies which he deemed were socially responsible had increased at a higher rate than major market indices.[2] Another study, which improved on earlier methodological approaches by including a variable in the analysis to take account of asset age, found weak evidence of a positive correlation between corporate social responsibility and financial performance for a sample of 61 US listed companies (Cochran and Wood, 1984). It is not our intention to attempt a comprehensive review of the literature in this area, but there are many more studies from the last 30 years that have found evidence of a positive relationship, including Bowman and Haire (1975), Belkaoui (1976) and Johnson and Greening (1994).

There are also numerous empirical studies that have found no evidence of a positive or a negative link. Such a result could be interpreted as positive evidence by those supporting corporate social responsibility: if acting in a socially responsible manner is costless in terms of financial performance, then surely from a pure ethics perspective it is better to pursue social responsibility. One reason proffered for an insignificant positive or negative relationship between corporate social responsibility and financial performance is couched in market efficiency arguments. If stock markets are efficient (in the sense of Fama, 1970) all new information relevant to the earnings outlook of a company is rapidly and accurately incorporated in share prices. Therefore, either information relating to social and environmental performance is not relevant to earnings, having no effect on financial performance, or the information is immediately impacted into share prices and reflects a trade-off between risk and return (Alexander and Buchholz, 1978). Indeed, Alexander and Buchholz (1978) found no significant relationship between social responsibility and stock market performance, using a set of rankings of social responsibility derived from the opinions of businessmen and students. An early review of some of the first empirical studies examining this issue concluded that economic performance was not directly linked in either a positive or a negative way to social responsiveness (Arlow and Gannon, 1982).

There are also a number of reasons given in the academic literature for a negative relationship between corporate social responsibility and corporate financial performance. One view is that socially responsible companies may be at a competitive disadvantage due to the added expense incurred by socially responsible behaviour. Vance (1975) used students' rankings of companies according to social responsibility criteria to demonstrate a negative link between socially responsible behaviour and financial performance, as those companies perceived as the most socially responsible were the worst financial performers. Again, we are not going to attempt a comprehensive view of the literature that provides empirical evidence of a negative relationship, but some papers worth reading are

[2] Moskowitz (1972) was the first to develop reputational indexes that list companies exhibiting remarkably 'good' or 'bad' social performance. Their usefulness has however been criticized as they measure perceived social performance rather than social performance per se (Ullman, 1985).

Shane and Spicer (1983) and Strachan et al. (1983). The implication for companies of a negative link would be that investors would avoid including socially responsible companies in their portfolio if they felt this would reduce their investment return. We return to this important issue in Chapter 10 when we discuss socially responsible investment and the extant evidence concerning the relationship between this type of investment and financial return. However, at this point it is worth mentioning that several studies have found evidence to conclude that improving a company's social performance does not discourage institutional investors from buying shares (Graves and Waddock, 1994). One of the problems in comparing the results of the wide range of studies is the diversity of techniques used by the researchers. In short, all empirical research has limitations and there is no 'perfect' technique or methodology that can be applied. Whatever approach is adopted, there are always people who will doubt the findings. Nevertheless, the weight of evidence in the literature seems to point to a positive relationship between corporate social responsibility and corporate financial performance (e.g., as concluded by Griffin and Mahon, 1997). Furthermore, general perceptions concerning the relationship between corporate social responsibility and financial performance are important. It is clear from my own research that the most influential group of corporate stakeholders in the UK, the institutional investors, consider corporate social responsibility to have a significant positive effect on corporate financial performance. As one pension fund director pointed out:

> You can make a fast buck by ignoring corporate social responsibility but you can't run a long-term sustainable business without it!
>
> (Quoted in Solomon and Solomon, 2002)

Having discussed corporate social responsibility in a broad sense, we now discuss ways in which companies may discharge this social responsibility, focusing specifically on the finance and accounting arena. A wealth of academic literature has burgeoned in the areas of environmental, ethical, social and, more recently, sustainability reporting. There are a number of textbooks dedicated to these areas (e.g., Gray et al., 1993, 1996). This text does not intend to cover all of these issues in exhaustive detail. Instead, environmental reporting is used to illustrate the way in which companies discharge their accountability in the social and environmental area. This seems a reasonable approach, as many of the theoretical arguments for and against environmental reporting can be applied equally well to social reporting. Further, environmental reporting was the first non-financial area of reporting to receive significant attention and is therefore the most developed.

## Corporate environmental reporting

One of the first areas where companies have been encouraged to discharge a wider accountability has been the environment. Although corporate environmental reporting is a relatively recent phenomenon, there is evidence of 'shadow' environmental reporting dating back to the early 19th century. Solomon and Thomson (2006a) show that as early as the 1850s, detailed disclosures of environmental pollution were published. Their paper examines a survey documenting pollution of the River Wandle in Surrey (UK). The disclosures were not produced by the mills, the industrial polluters in this case, but rather by a surveyor from the Institution of Civil Engineers. Nevertheless, the disclosure was inspired by human health considerations as well as by an aesthetic desire to clear up the rivers of England at that time. The environmental disclosure included detailed quantitative and qualitative reporting of the pollution and has been interpreted as an early 'shadow' account (Solomon and Thomson, 2006a).

In recent years environmental issues have attracted increasing attention from many sectors of society worldwide. The seeds of corporate environmental reporting were sown by organizations such as the Coalition for Environmentally Responsible Economies (usually abbreviated to CERES), who provided the first guiding principles for companies wishing to discharge accountability to the environment. See Illustration 9.2 for an outline of the history of CERES.

## Illustration 9.2

### CERES – the seeds of corporate environmental reporting

CERES was one of the early pioneers of environmental reporting, encouraging companies worldwide to discharge their accountability to the environment through the accounting framework. The organization took its name from the Roman goddess of fertility and agriculture. In 1988 the board of the US-based Social Investment Forum formed an alliance with environmental lobby groups in order to consider ways in which investment may lead to improvements in, rather than depletion of, the environment. Since that time CERES has become a worldwide leader in standardized CER and the promotion of transformed environmental management in companies. The CERES agenda was pushed forward by a number of corporate disasters. First, there was the case of *Exxon Valdez*, where a tanker poured thousands of gallons of oil into the ocean, destroying natural habitats and killing wildlife. Second, there was the disaster in Bhopal (India), where the Union Carbide plant suffered an explosion that resulted in poisonous gases entering the atmosphere and had terrible consequences for the local population. Both these cases horrified people worldwide and focused attention on corporate activities in relation to the environment and local communities. In 1989 CERES produced the 'Valdez Principles' (later renamed the 'CERES Principles'). These Principles comprised a 10-point code of corporate environmental conduct, to be endorsed publicly by companies as an environmental mission statement or ethic. The code carried the expectation for companies to report environmentally at regular intervals. Despite initial negative reactions from the corporate community, the 1990s witnessed an increase in CER and a deep change in corporate attitudes toward environmental, as well as social, issues. Companies began to recognize that their reputation depended on the way that they managed their impacts on the environment and on their stakeholders. Indeed, society as a whole began to be characterized by an 'environmental ethos', becoming more concerned about environmental issues and the future of the planet (Solomon, 2000). See the CERES website http://www.ceres.org/about/history.htm, for a detailed account of the development and impact of CERES.

Society's increasing awareness of environmental issues has encouraged companies to consider their interaction with the natural environment. This has led to increased calls for corporate environmental reporting by such organizations as the European Federation of Accountants (FEE, 2000) and the Global Reporting Initiative (GRI, 2000). This growing demand is not a recent phenomenon. Earlier studies suggested that groups of users demanded and required environmental performance information in corporate annual reports (e.g., Deegan and Rankin, 1996).

Despite growing demand, it appears that the quality and quantity of corporate environmental reporting has been considered insufficient to meet users' needs (see, e.g., Harte and Owen, 1992; Deegan and Rankin, 1996; Adams et al., 1995). Indeed, the United Nations Environment Programme concluded that:

> ...report-makers still have a long way to go before they can fully meet the emerging information needs of their key target audiences – and those of the rapidly growing ranks of report-users.
>
> (UNEP, 1996a, p. 43)

Significantly, most companies are still not reporting any environmental information, and where there is reporting it is mixed and inconsistent (KPMG, 2002). Not only is there an inadequate level of environmental reporting but some studies have found that most corporate environmental reporting is of a descriptive, self-congratulatory nature, alluding more to good intentions than actual environmental programmes and rarely reporting any bad news about a company's relationship with the environment (Harte and Owen, 1992; Deegan and Rankin, 1996; Gray et al., 1996; Adams et al., 1998). We now consider a number of incentives and disincentives underlying corporate environmental reporting arising from the literature, as well as a number of factors characterizing corporate environmental reporting.

### Incentives for corporate environmental reporting

Solomon and Lewis (2002) suggested that incentives for corporate environmental reporting fell loosely within four categories (namely, markets, social, political and accountability incentives). These arise from different perspectives held by different sectors of society, who require information for decision making.

From a free market perspective, demand for corporate environmental reporting can be met through the market mechanism. Indeed, pressure from the marketplace is seen by some as one of the main incentives for corporate environmental reporting (Macve and Carey, 1992). The existence of voluntary corporate environmental reporting per se provides some support for a market motive, as where there is no legal requirement the production of information is likely to be in response to market demand. More substantially, a growth in socially responsible investment is creating an increasing demand for social and environmental disclosure by companies, as we discuss in the following chapter (Friedman and Miles, 2001). Indeed, the author's collaborative research has shown that institutional investors are demanding improvements in social and environmental disclosure generally

(Solomon and Solomon, 2002). However, if demand for corporate environmental reporting is not being met, then market failures are likely to exist. We discussed the problems of market failure and information asymmetry in Chapter 6, in relation to corporate disclosure generally. Information asymmetry represents a serious form of market failure in corporate environmental reporting, as in other areas of disclosure, as information that is voluntarily disclosed tends to have major inadequacies, often appearing to market the company rather than reveal problems relating to environmental issues. An issue as sensitive as the commercial use of the environment is likely to encourage secrecy, rather than transparency (Gray, 1992).

Stakeholder, legitimacy and political economy theory can be grouped under the category of social incentives for voluntary corporate environmental reporting, according to Solomon and Lewis (2002). As we saw in Chapter 1, stakeholder theory involves recognizing and identifying the relationship between a company's behaviour and the impact on its stakeholders. The difficulties of balancing the needs of a diverse range of stakeholders has implications for corporate environmental reporting, as companies struggle to provide appropriate and adequate information for these different groups. Nevertheless, the need to provide information to these stakeholder groups represents an incentive for corporate environmental reporting.

Legitimacy theory also establishes an incentive for corporate environmental reporting, stemming from the existence of a theoretical social contract between companies and society (Mathews, 1993). Companies need to demonstrate that they have a licence to operate. They need to legitimize their existence not just to their shareholders but also to society as a whole. From this perspective, voluntary corporate environmental reporting represents a way in which companies can legitimize their existence to society (Lehman, 1983; RSA, 1995). Indeed, a company's licence to operate has been acknowledged as an important incentive for corporate environmental reporting (RSA, 1995). Legitimacy theory has also been used to explain why companies may voluntarily disclose only positive aspects of their performance (Harte and Owen, 1992; Deegan and Rankin, 1996).

A third social incentive for corporate environmental reporting arises from political economy theory, which centres around the social, political and economic framework within which human life takes place (Gray et al., 1996). From a corporate environmental reporting perspective, political economy theory focuses on power and conflict in society, the specific historical/institutional environment of the society in which it operates and the acknowledgement that corporate environmental reporting can reflect different views and concerns.

As well as the social and market categorizations of incentives for corporate environmental reporting, there appears to be a political incentive, underlying the voluntary production of environmental information by companies. In other words, companies are encouraged to report environmentally due to political pressure. Political interest in environmental issues has been reflected in the creation over time of the Conservative Ecology Group, the Green Alliance, the Green Party, the Socialist Environmental and Resources Association, the Tory Green Initiative and the Environment Agency. Large-scale integration of environmental issues into the political spectrum has led to the integration of environmental issues into all aspects of mainstream politics. Incentives for corporate environmental reporting may be summarized as follows:

- to improve the company's corporate image;
- to market the company;
- to market company products;
- peer pressure from companies in the same industry;
- to comply with regulations;
- pressure from customers/consumers;
- to attract investment;
- as an acceptance of a change in society's ethics;
- to acknowledge social responsibility;
- as a result of company ethics;
- as a form of political lobbying;
- to meet the demand for environmental information.

A questionnaire survey of a large sample of organizations revealed that, from the above list, acknowledging social responsibility and marketing the company were viewed as the main reasons why companies produce corporate environmental information voluntarily (see Solomon and Lewis, 2002).[3] This is interesting as it shows that companies are believed to use corporate environmental reporting to legitimize their existence, as discussed above. However, the results also suggest that companies are seen as being socially responsible in their disclosure.

### Disincentives for corporate environmental reporting

As discussed above, the growth in corporate environmental reporting has fallen short of satisfying users' requirements. Both the quality and quantity of the corporate environmental information disclosed by companies are considered to be inadequate on the whole. There is, however, a countervailing view in the literature that, if financial markets were genuinely interested in corporate environmental information, then more voluntary disclosure would take place and mandatory disclosure would be avoided (Perks, 1993). There must be reasons why corporate environmental reporting continues to be viewed as inadequate. Why are companies not increasing the quantity and quality of their corporate environmental reporting? Gray et al. (1993) gave a number of explanations for inadequate

---

[3] The total sample consisted of 635 organizations, which was broken down into three groups (namely, an interested party group, a normative group and a company group).

corporate environmental reporting: absence of any demand for information, absence of a legal requirement, the problem that the cost would outweigh the benefits, and the possibility that the organization had never considered it. Further, several reasons why companies do not disclose certain information publicly were given by the World Industry Council for the Environment (WICE, 1984), including: the possibility of the information costing too much, companies wishing to report not possessing adequate information systems, and legal or customer confidentiality issues, or security implications. In practice, secrecy relating to environmental pollution has been considered to be significant and has been endemic to environmental legislation, as many statutes contain specific sections forbidding corporate environmental reporting (Ball and Bell, 1995).

The role of the financial community has also been substantial in discouraging corporate environmental reporting, as, until relatively recently, soft information in the area of social and environmental issues was awarded less status by institutional investors than it is today. Unless the financial community perceive a need for corporate environmental reporting, reporting is less likely to be forthcoming (see, e.g., ACBE, 1996). Given recent developments in which social responsibility is being encouraged, the financial community's attitudes, particularly in the form of institutional investors, may change. Another possible disincentive for companies not addressing environmental issues may be inefficient management, because managers consider that environmental issues do not apply to the company and view environmental reporting as expensive. Further, management may be stuck in their ways and unable to accept a broader, more socially responsible agenda. Another reason, arising from a common sense view of companies, is that it would be irrational for corporations to disclose any information detrimental to them (Benston, 1982).

Given this discussion we can see that it is not surprising that companies have been unwilling to produce environmental information (Owen, 1992). The voluntary reporting framework also causes company management to feel exposed if they disclose more than their competitors. The possible disincentives for corporate environmental reporting may be summarized as follows:

- reluctance to report sensitive information;

- general lack of awareness of environmental issues;

- there is no legal obligation for companies to report environmentally;

- possible damage to companies' reputation;

- to avoid providing information to competitors;

- cost of disclosure;

- to avoid providing incriminating information to regulators;

- inability to gather the information;

- lack of awareness of competitive advantage;

- insufficient response feedback from stakeholders;

- companies generally believe they do not have an impact on the environment;

- users may not understand the information.

From their questionnaire survey, Solomon and Lewis (2002) found that a reluctance to report sensitive information was considered to be one of the most significant disincentives for corporate environmental reporting. This is not surprising, especially if companies view social and environmental disclosure as a marketing tool. They are unlikely to market themselves by producing unfavourable information on their treatment of environmental issues, preferring instead to focus on the positive aspects.

*A risk society theory of social and environmental reporting*
Recent developments in sociology have sought to explain deep-rooted changes in society's attitudes toward environmental and social issues. A German sociologist, Beck (1992, 1993) developed a theoretical framework known as risk society theory. According to the framework, we live in an era known as modernity which is characterized by the proliferation of 'high consequence risks', such as global warming and the risk of nuclear accidents. These risks affect all sectors of society at a global level. They are the direct result of human and corporate behaviour and are to some extent unmanageable. Further, they are difficult to quantify and it is hard to attribute them to any specific cause. In other words, identifying who is ultimately accountable for their creation is extremely difficult. Associated with risk society theory is a decline in trust, especially trust in institutions and organizations.[4] This decline in trust was discussed in Chapter 5 in relation to institutional investment. Risk society theory is now being used to explain the growth of voluntary environmental and social reporting. Unerman and O'Dwyer (2004) explored the possibility of using risk society theory in the context of experts and counter-experts in the NGO sector. According to the risk society framework, lack of trust in institutions has led to the creation of counter-experts who put forward their views, competing with traditional 'experts'. Further, risk society theory is being used to explain the growth in voluntary social and environmental reporting by companies. In a society where people have lost faith in the genuine ethical motivation of business, social and environmental reporting may be a conduit for re-establishing trust. Companies may be using social and environmental disclosures as a means of communicating with their shareholders and other stakeholders, so as to restore trust. Indeed, my own research interviews with UK listed companies have found evidence that companies are disclosing social and environmental information with the primary aim of rebuilding trust, through the management of reputation risk. For example, when asked why his company published a sustainability report, one corporate social responsibility manager from a FTSE 100 company said,

---

[4]   See also Giddens (1990, 1991) for a full theoretical discussion of the decline of trust as a consequence of the era of modernity.

Wanting to *maintain a reputation*, wanting to show the City and shareholders that we are operating in an *environmentally friendly way and in a sustainable way*. It's really demonstrating to everybody that we have the proper systems in place and that they are effective.

(quoted in Solomon, 2005, p. 17, emphasis added)

A director of social responsibility from another FTSE 100 company reaffirmed this view as follows:

It's the *reputational issue* rather than any other and more importantly, it is about the *image of the business*, you know, not just in the UK, but more broadly. If you ask consumers in the UK 'Which companies *do you trust, do you respect*? Which companies produce quality products? Which companies look after employees, are good neighbours in the community?' ... So there's a long heritage of being a well-respected business and seen to be so in the eyes of consumers generally. What's the value of that? Well! Probably incalculable

(quoted in Solomon, 2005, p. 18, emphasis added)

Having considered theoretical frameworks used to explain voluntary environmental (and social) reporting we now turn to a consideration of the content and characteristics of environmental reports.

*Users of corporate environmental reporting*
A fundamental aspect of corporate environmental reporting, as with financial reporting, is the identification of users. Although there is no consensus on the possible users of corporate environmental reporting, the United Nations Environment Programme (UNEP, 1996) identified the following corporate environmental reporting user groups: employees, legislators and regulators, local communities, investors, suppliers, customers and consumers, industry associations, environment groups, science and education, and the media. A number of other similar corporate environmental reporting user groups were suggested by Gray et al. (1996): management, trade unions, potential employees, communities, pressure groups, national governments, local government, competitors, peers, industry groups and society in general. These groups overlap to a greater or lesser extent those user groups suggested by other organizations such as the Canadian Institute of Chartered Accountants (CICA, 1994), the World Industry Council for the Environment (WICE, 1994), the Confederation of British Industry (CBI, 1995) and Deloitte, Touche, Tohmatsu International (DTTI, 1993). A selection of possible users suggested in the literature is summarized below:

■ legislators and regulators;

■ local communities;

■ employees;

- shareholders;

- customers;

- insurance companies;

- ethical investors;

- environmental groups;

- quangos;

- local government;

- potential investors;

- banks;

- media;

- suppliers;

- stock market;

- central government;

- industry associations.

From the findings of a questionnaire survey, Solomon (2000) showed that legislators and regulators, employees, local communities and ethical investors were considered to be the main recipients of corporate environmental information from companies.

## Qualitative characteristics of corporate environmental reporting

In financial reporting, qualitative characteristics are essential for the production of decision-useful information (ASB, 1996). It is reasonable to suggest that the qualitative characteristics for financial reporting are also applicable to corporate environmental reporting. Strong recommendations have been made for the qualitative characteristics that are established in financial reporting to be modified and applied in a structured way to corporate environmental reporting (FEE, 2000). The application of qualitative characteristics from financial reporting to environmental reporting has been discussed in the literature (see, e.g., Gray et al., 1987; Macve and Carey, 1992; Gray et al., 1996). However, the usefulness for corporate environmental reporting of those qualitative characteristics applied in financial reporting is debatable. Certainly, the characteristic of transparency is essential to all areas of corporate disclosure if it is to be useful. The importance of transparency for effective corporate governance was stressed in Chapter 6. This characteristic is no less important in the area of environmental information than in the area of internal control of financial reporting. Certainly, the academic literature acknowledges that transparency represented one of the first qualitative characteristics to be applied to environmental reporting (see Gray, 1992; Gray et al., 1993). Possible qualitative characteristics for corporate environmental reporting may be summarized as follows:

- a true and fair view;
- understandability;
- relevance;
- faithful representation;
- reliability;
- freedom from error;
- consistency;
- valid description;
- substance over form;
- neutrality;
- completeness;
- corresponding information for the previous period;
- confirmation of information;
- timeliness;
- comparability;
- materiality;
- predictive value;
- prudence.

Solomon (2000) found from his survey evidence that the most important qualitative characteristics for corporate environmental reporting were considered to be understandability, relevance, reliability, faithful representation, freedom from error, and a true and fair view. The paper used this to show a distinct similarity between the evolving framework for corporate environmental reporting and the existing financial reporting framework.

*Elements of corporate environmental reporting*
It is unlikely that corporate environmental reporting could bear similarity to financial reporting in the area of recognition and measurement, as the elements have to be different. Within the current financial reporting framework, a company has legally to own/control the assets on which it reports. Clearly, the natural environment cannot be

owned or controlled in the same way as financial assets. Therefore, reporting on society's natural assets represents a completely different paradigm from that of financial reporting. Recognition and measurement in corporate environmental reporting are probably most appropriately based on the elements of air, land, water and sound. However, an alternative view was proposed by CICA (1994), who considered that recognition and measurement should be based on the consumption of resources (processing, transportation and distribution) and the use and disposal of products. Other approaches to recognition and measurement criteria focus on actual environmental problems, such as global warming, ozone depletion, smog, acidification, neutrification potential, toxicology (both human and ecotoxicology), waste problems, biodiversity and others (odour, noise, light) (Muller et al., 1994). Jones (1996) suggested an inventory approach to accounting for biodiversity, advocating the use of wildlife habitats (land or water, flora and fauna). Cowe (1992) advocated a hybrid approach combining natural elements and environmental problems, suggesting, for example: total energy used in heating, lighting and power; total fuel used for transport; total water used; volume of physical waste materials produced; and volume of waste output discharged into the atmosphere and waterways. Evidently, no consensus approach exists. Air, water, land and sound seem to represent the most sensible elements for corporate environmental reporting. Indeed, Solomon (2000) proposed these four elements in his questionnaire survey, finding that the respondents considered all the elements were important, but that water was the most significant element for environmental reporting purposes.

*Bearing the cost of corporate environmental reporting*
Corporate environmental information tends to be provided free of charge to interested parties, with companies absorbing the full cost of disclosure. In financial reporting the company bears the cost of disclosure in return for its standing in law as a separate legal entity. Financial disclosure at no cost to the end-user was established in the Companies' Acts (see Mayson et al., 1998), applying principally to shareholders but usually to anyone requesting a report. However, this argument does not necessarily apply to environmental reporting. The costs of environmental disclosure may be substantial and are indeed 'material' for both compliance with legislation and for voluntary disclosure. Indeed, why would companies choose to pay for disclosure that is not mandatory and, worse, may have a negative impact on their reputation (Perks, 1993)? Companies that endorse the Ceres Principles support open environmental reporting and corporate accountability, which would imply that they should bear the entire cost. Solomon's (2000) survey demonstrated a consensus on companies bearing the full cost of environmental reporting.

*Time period and communication of corporate environmental reporting*
Corporate environmental information is usually disclosed via the annual report or a separate environmental report (usually annual), with the use of the media for any interim reporting (see Zéghal and Ahmed, 1990; Roberts, 1992; Mathews, 1993). The majority of environmental disclosure tends to appear in annual reports, and a number of companies have produced separate annual environmental reports for several years. In relation to time

period, CERES (1992), DTTI (1993) and the CBI (1994) recommended that corporate environmental reporting should be on an annual basis. The consensus view from Solomon's (2000) findings supported environmental disclosure in the annual report as presenting the most useful form of corporate environmental reporting in terms of time period and communication.

*The suggested content of corporate environmental reports*
There have been a host of suggestions concerning the most desirable contents of corporate environmental reporting. The possible basic contents of an environmental report may be summarized as follows: environmental statement by company chairman; environmental policy statement; environmental strategy statement; environmental management system; management responsibilities for the environment; environmental audit; independently verified environmental disclosure; legal environmental compliance; research and development and the environment; company environmental initiatives; context of company environmental disclosure; product life cycle design; environmental reporting policy; product packaging; product impacts.

In addition to the characteristics of corporate environmental reporting and its contents discussed above, there has been an increasing focus on risk-related aspects of corporate environmental reporting, following the Turnbull Report (1999), as suggested in Chapter 6 (see Illustration 6.1). Social and environmental risks are an increasingly important aspect of a company's system of internal control, as sudden events in these areas can turn latent environmental risks into material financial losses. The sinking of an oil tanker is a notable example. Having considered the ways in which companies may discharge their accountability for the environment to their shareholders and other stakeholders, we now consider the emerging importance of the sustainability agenda and its impact on corporate disclosure.

# Sustainability and a stakeholder perspective

A stakeholder perspective is perceived as more consistent than other theoretical frameworks such as agency theory, with notions of corporate social responsibility. As discussed in Chapter 1, there have been many attempts in recent years to show that stakeholder and shareholder theories may be more compatible than theorists once believed. The concept of sustainability arises naturally from stakeholder theory. Sustainability and the concept of sustainable development are terms that have evolved over the last 20 years. There is at present no commonly accepted definition. Nevertheless, the Brundtland Commission (WCED, 1987) explained that sustainable development implies development that meets the needs of the present without compromising the ability of future generations to meet their own needs. An obvious interpretation of this is in relation to the environment, as where contemporary society chooses to meet its needs by depleting a natural resource, that same resource will be consequently unavailable to future generations. A preferred and more intuitively pragmatic definition has been provided stating that sustainability is value creation in three dimensions: economic, social and environmental (Wheeler et al., 2002). From an accounting and finance viewpoint, the novel notion of a triple bottom line was coined by Elkington (1998), which implied the inclusion in financial reports of social and environmental impacts. Similarly, the 'balanced scorecard' was an appealing term developed under the guise of sustainability (Kaplan and Norton, 1996). So, what impact have notions of sustainability had on companies and the information they disclose to their stakeholders? We consider this question in the next section.

## Sustainability reporting

Interest in sustainability has encouraged companies to orient their disclosure toward a sustainability objective. There is as yet no clear definition as to what sustainability reporting is. However, the Global Reporting Initiative (GRI) has produced sustainability reporting guidelines, and the suggestion is that, for the GRI at least, sustainability reporting centres around economic, environmental and social performance: the so-called triple bottom line. This type of reporting is not new. There are examples of early joint stock companies reporting on their environmental and social activities for one reason or another. In relatively recent times (1970s) the accounting profession produced the Corporate Report (ASSC, 1975) which advocated a wider remit for accountants, as we discussed in Chapter 1. This included social and environmental disclosure. However, by the late 1980s and early 1990s companies were beginning voluntarily to disclose environmental information, even though this was mostly in environmentally unfriendly industries. Events such as *Exxon Valdez* and Bhopal *inter alia* gave social/environmental lobby groups the opportunity to encourage companies to disclose a range of information voluntarily. This in turn led to a need for some type of reporting guidelines, and to a certain extent the culmination of this increased reporting by companies can be seen in the GRI.

Every three years KPMG produce a survey of environmental reporting patterns. This began in 1973 with environmental reporting and in 1999 it began to look at sustainability reporting. The survey looks at reporting practices from the Top 100 companies in 11 countries. Table 9.1 summarizes its findings since 1993, indicating the proportion of

**Table [9.1]**  A summary of results from the KPMG surveys

| Year | Companies producing a separate corporate environmental report (%) |
|---|---|
| 1993 | 13 |
| 1996 | 17 |
| 1999 | 24 |
| 2002 | 28 |

Anglo American (2004) explain at the beginning of their report all the ways in which they are responding to the sustainability challenge,

> By their very size, scope and global distribution, Anglo American's activities have an impact on the human, economic and natural environments in which we operate. We are committed to working to extract and transform the natural resource capital wisely: creating jobs, building skills, contributing to social and physical infrastructure. We continue to work to conserve biodiversity and minimize pollution, waste and resource consumption for the benefit of our shareholders, our employees and the communities and countries in which we operate.
>
> (Anglo American, 2004, p. 5)

This statement demonstrates a stakeholder rather than purely shareholder-oriented perspective. It also shows that the company acknowledges its own contribution to environmental and social impacts.

*Health and safety disclosures*
Health and safety is one of the main areas of social reporting. The sustainable development report produced by Rio Tinto (2004) provides a range of information including the company's performance against targets. For example, the company shows that there has been a significant improvement in relation to 'fatalities', in other words the number of employees dying in accidents at work. Rio Tinto's stated target is, understandably, 'zero fatalities'. There was one fatality in 2004 compared with six in 2003, suggesting an improvement in safety. Clearly, with business activity as dangerous as mining, health and safety of employees is of paramount importance. Xstrata (2004) reported that the total recordable injury rate had been reduced by 30 %. However, they also disclosed the tragic loss of six employees from workplace incidents in 2004. Addressing this urgently was one of the company's priorities for the future. In the case of Anglo American (2004), the chief executive opened the report with,

> I must, however, report with deep regret the deaths of 49 people (21 employees and 28 contractors) in our operations last year. This is particularly distressing because we have been making steady progress in reducing the frequency of deaths and injuries over the last few years.
>
> (Anglo American, 2004, p. 2)

This type of disclosure helps to dispel a wide-held belief that social and environmental reporting exclusively involves cherry-picking, with companies not disclosing bad news in their reports. Not only have the incidents been reported, up-front, but also the company has reflected on how these figures represent a backward, not forward, step.

Xstrata provides details of the health risks which employees are exposed to. These include exposure to: high levels of dust, carcinogenic chemicals, asthma-creating fungus, lead. There are also problems of employees suffering from degenerative musculoskeletal conditions from manual labour, and heat stress.

Companies also report on the extent to which they involve themselves in local communities. Working closely with local communities is increasingly important for multinational businesses. Rio Tinto, for example, works hard to relate to indigenous people in Australia, where their primary business operations are located. Anglo American (2004) describe their stakeholder engagement programme and their principles for community engagement in detail.

*Environmental disclosures*

Companies are bound by law to comply with environmental legislation and many implement environmental management systems such as ISO 14001. Where companies choose to report on environmental issues, they tend to refer to their level of compliance and the system they have adopted. For example, Rio Tinto (2004) comment that,

> By the end of 2004, 84 per cent of operations had implemented ISO 14001 or an equivalent environmental management system and 72 per cent of the total number of operations were already certified.
>
> (Rio Tinto, 2004, p. 20)

The extractive industry has a substantial impact on the environment, as it directly affects land, water and air, the basic elements relevant to corporate environmental reporting.

Xstrata is the world's largest producer of export thermal coal. The company is dedicated to climate change management and has devised a detailed approach which includes reducing greenhouse gas emissions per unit of production by 10 % on 2003 data over five years (Xstrata, 2004). Anglo American (2004) have set up complex environmental management systems, for example programmes to improve air quality by reducing emissions, improve energy efficiency and reduce water discharges.

*Biodiversity and animal species*

Companies are making efforts to monitor the effect of their business activity on biodiversity in the vicinity of their operations. They include information on biodiversity in their social, environmental and sustainability reports. Legitimacy theory seems to underpin companies' desire to protect biodiversity, for example,

> Loss of biodiversity due to competing land use is a significant risk for native ecosystems around the world. To obtain and retain a licence to operate, mining and metal production companies must exceed community and legislative expectations for environmental stewardship.
>
> (Xstrata, 2004, p. 48)

Strategies employed to protect biodiversity include the establishment of offset areas for wildlife and the rehabilitation of disturbed land as well as surveys of flora and fauna (Xstrata, 2004).

*Sustainability and economic contributions*
As well as disclosures on social and environmental issues, sustainability reporting includes discussion of the company's economic contribution. This is due to a general acknowledgement that for a company to be sustainable it has to contribute to economic growth as well as to the protection of the environment and social welfare. For example, Rio Tinto (2004) stated that in 2004 they had a gross turnover of US$ 14.1 billion, a 20 % increase on its 2003 figure. They emphasize that,

> A contribution to sustainable development is not possible without viable economic activity to underpin it.
>
> (Rio Tinto, 2004, p. 25)

Xstrata highlights its economic contribution to social and economic development by explaining that its direct foreign investment in countries in which it operates amounted to approximately $ 645 million in 2004, with a total since the Group's creation in 2002 of about $ 7.2 billion. Anglo American (2004) stated that during 2004, value added increased 39 % from $ 7,783 million to $ 10,833 million. The company emphasized that its operations add value mainly in the developing world.

*Photographic images*
It is notable that companies employ a vast array of photographic images in their social, environmental and sustainability reports. A cynical view would be that such images are simply a way for the company to market itself, by demonstrating a commitment to the environment and society. Indeed, glossy social and environmental reports are clearly a very efficient means for the company to 'sell itself'. However, it is not necessarily the case that by taking advantage of the opportunity to use images to portray a positive 'green' image of the company, this marketing is not founded in a genuine accountability to society and the environment. Images promoting environmental, 'green' issues, used in the three reports included: crocodiles, indigenous trees and their seeds, lakes, forests, mountains, grasses, kangaroos, elephants, rivers, rhinos, puppies and deer. In the social responsibility domain, reports are packed with photographic images of employees. They tend to be either concentrating on their work or smiling and laughing. They also tend to represent wide ethnic diversity. We now turn to the important issue of verification.

# Verification of social, environmental and sustainability reporting

As discussed in Chapter 6, auditing plays an important role in transparency and therefore in corporate governance. Information needs to be verified in order to make it credible and therefore useful to interested parties. Verification is so important in financial reporting that it is compulsory. The growth in environmental audit has been commensurate with the growth of social and environmental reporting per se (Maltby, 1995). Indeed, Owen et al. (2000) found that environmental audit has become more firmly established over time than social audit.[5] Solomon (2000) suggested that there are two fundamental questions that arise in relation to the verification of corporate environmental reporting. These are, first, 'should voluntary corporate environmental disclosure be verified?' and, second, 'who are the most appropriate agents for verification?'

In relation to the first question, there has been support for verification of environmental and social disclosure in the academic literature (Gray et al., 1987; Buck, 1992; Owen, 1992). It is unlikely that corporate environmental reporting will be credible to the user unless the information is externally audited (Adams, 1992). In contrast, CERES (1992) advocated annual self-evaluation and the timely creation of generally accepted environmental audit procedures. Maltby (1995) suggests that it is likely that companies which are prepared to go to the trouble and expense of publishing environmental reports would prefer them to be accompanied by an audit opinion. The European Commission emphasized that external assurance of social and environmental reporting was necessary to deter criticism that it was simply a public relations exercise without substance (Commission of the European Communities, 2001). Adams and Evans (2004) also stated that external verification was important to the credibility of social and environmental reporting. Indeed, O'Dwyer and Owen (2005) went as far as saying that the whole objective of social and environmental reporting would be undermined unless robust assurance processes are introduced. From a legitimacy theory viewpoint, if companies desire to maintain their license to operate, then verification of voluntary social and environmental reporting represents an important element in this legitimization process.

In relation to the second question, 'who should provide the verification', Perks (1993) suggested that the existence of a qualified independent body of auditors would add to the credibility of corporate environmental reporting. He also suggested that financial audit arrangements could be used but qualifies this by considering that financial auditors lack independence and the appropriate expertise to deal with environmental disclosure. Welford and Gouldson (1993) suggested that accountants were appropriate agents for verification. Perks (1993) also emphasized the need to consider the expectations gap, discussed in Chapter 6, where society expects more from auditors than they provide in practice (Humphrey et al., 1992). However, Power (1991) proposed that accountants may not be the most appropriate professional body to undertake environmental audit and verification, as they may not have the appropriate experience and may be subject to pressures from company management. A selection of possible alternatives for verification are summarized below:

- environmental consultants within their existing framework;

- a registered auditor of the Environmental Auditors Registration Association;

---

[5] The literature relating to the verification of social, environmental and sustainability reports has been reviewed by Jones and Solomon (2006).

- scientists within their existing framework;

- internal management team;

- a new professional body that includes accountants, scientists and environmental consultants;

- accountants within their existing framework;

- verification is not necessary.

From his questionnaire survey on corporate environmental reporting, Solomon (2000) found that existing frameworks for verification were generally preferred to a new body designed for the specific purpose. Specifically, respondents to the survey preferred the following verifiers: registered auditors of the Environmental Auditors Registration Association, environmental consultants within their existing framework and an internal management team.

The literature has, however, highlighted conflicting objectives in social and environmental audit. Power (1991) describes a dichotomy within environmental audit by suggesting it is being driven by professionalism, rather than 'protest'. He views environmental audit as a management tool which is employed to evaluate environment business risk and develop controls. This professional bias in environmental audit is seen as capturing any genuine, pure-ethics, environmental discourse. The translation of environmental audit into financial audit language by the audit profession has watered down the genuine accountability potential of the verification process. Indeed, Power (1991, 1994, 1996, 1997a, 1997b) also theorized that social and environmental verification statements were not adding value from the perspective of external stakeholders. Verifiers seemed to be more involved with assessing the quality of the company's environmental management control system rather than the company's actual environmental performance. The AccountAbility AA1000 Assurance Standard (AccountAbility, 2003) commented that assurance standards focus heavily on robustness of accounting systems and accuracy of quantitative data rather than on approaching the verification in a way that would materially help stakeholders.

There has been substantial criticism of verification statements in the literature. Kamp-Roelands (1996) found limited assurance from an analysis of 47 verification statements from environmental reports across 13 European countries. Ball et al. (2000) used content analysis to evaluate the extent to which verification statements of 72 'leading edge' corporate environmental reports promoted organizational transparency and the empowerment of external stakeholders. They found that although the environmental reports were mainly addressed to external stakeholders there was confusion over the extent to which companies were really carrying out the exercise for internal constituencies.

Ball et al. (2000) also considered the independence of the verifiers, finding that half of the verifications in their sample did not appear to be independent. They also found that there was a managerial bias evident, with the verification focusing on the company's environmental management system rather than the quality of the environmental report *per se.* The paper concluded that little value was being added by the verification statement to stakeholders.

Whereas Power (1991) was concerned with professional capture of the environmental audit process (i.e. by the auditing profession), Ball et al. (2000) and Owen et al. (2000) were more concerned with managerial capture of environmental verification. Owen et al. (2000) define 'managerial capture' in this context as,

> ... the concept that sees management take control of the whole process (including the degree of stakeholder inclusion) by strategically collecting and disseminating only the information it deems appropriate to advance the corporate image, rather than being truly transparent and accountable to the society it serves.
>
> (p. 85)

The literature has also focused on a 'huge' (Adams and Evans, 2004) expectations gap in the verification of social and environmental reporting, with the verification not satisfying users' expectations. Adams and Evans (2004) argued that in order to close the expectations gap, the assurance provider should ensure that social and environmental reports are complete and that processes are inclusive.

Jones and Solomon (2006) canvassed the views of corporate social responsibility managers in FTSE 100 listed companies on the verification of social and environmental reports. They found a reluctance by companies to wholeheartedly endorse external verification of social and environmental reports for a variety of reasons. These included the interviewees' belief that social and environmental reporting was relatively unimportant and complex. Further, the cost in money and managerial resources of verification was considered an obstacle, as was the apparent lack of independence of the audit. Jones and Solomon's (2006) findings supported the view from earlier literature that there was managerial and professional capture of the social and environmental audit process. Interviewees confirmed that the verification process was dominated more by internal control concerns than by a genuine desire to discharge accountability to stakeholders. Indeed, in one of the interviews, the interviewee demonstrated the company's preoccupation with verification as a management tool within the internal control system by arguing for internal rather than external social and environmental audit, stating that,

> I think companies should be given the opportunity to *regulate themselves* as much as possible. If that doesn't work, then you can use regulations and imposition of external audits. Because there's nothing to stop a company carrying *out internal audits with its own internal audit function* and stipulating that it has been audited by its own internal auditors and the report has been reviewed by the *Audit Committee*, which, if that's rejected by the shareholders, goes to the core of the company, i.e. it's a vote of no confidence for the Audit Committee.
>
> (Quoted in Jones and Solomon, 2006, p. 18, emphasis added)

Returning to the three companies from the extractive industry used earlier to illustrate social, environmental and sustainability reporting, what were their verification statements like? The assurance statement provided by Environmental Resources Management for Rio Tinto's (2004) report on sustainable development gives an overall assessment as follows:

> We believe that the 2004 Sustainable development review is a fair and balanced representation of Rio Tinto's programmes and performance. Subject to the comments set out below, we believe that it covers the key issues that interested parties need to know to inform decision making (i.e. is relevant), does not avoid major issues (i.e. is complete), fairly reflects programmes and performance on the ground (i.e. is accurate), and that Rio Tinto has taken on views from outside the Group (i.e. is responsive).
>
> (Rio Tinto, 2004, p. 36)

Xstrata's (2004) verification statement was provided by URS Verification Ltd (URSVL), which commented that they welcomed the report as demonstrating the company's commitment to sustainability. Anglo American's (2004) report was verified by KPMG, rather than by a specialist sustainability verifier. KPMG explain the work they carried out and conclude that the company's sustainable development criteria are fairly stated.

Reporting and verification are, however, not the only way that companies can discharge a broader accountability to a range of stakeholders. They can also involve themselves more directly with stakeholder groups through a process of active engagement and dialogue. We now turn to consider the ways in which this process is evolving.

## Stakeholder engagement

An emerging trend in UK business is the growth of stakeholder engagement. Engagement with non-shareholding stakeholders has become the focus of recent research, with stakeholder engagement being described as:

> . . . a range of diverse, qualitative information gathering methods.
>
> (Thomson and Bebbington, 2002, p. 20)

These information-gathering methods include questionnaire surveys, interviews, focus groups and public meetings (Owen, 2003). An acknowledged accountability requirement of the developing social and environmental engagement process between companies and stakeholders, and especially the process of social and environmental disclosure, is the emergence of dialogic[6] engagement (Owen et al., 2001; Thomson and Bebbington, 2002). Thomson and Bebbington (2002) built their theory on Freire's (1996) pedagogic concept, which emphasized the need for education to be dialogic rather than didactic, such that the teacher and the student learn from each other. He considered a dialogic education process

---

[6] The term 'dialogic' has been defined as pertaining to a discussion, especially one between representatives of two political groups (The Concise Oxford Dictionary, 1995).

as one that brings about liberation, transforming the world through a praxis. Thomson and Bebbington (2002) extended this concept to shed light on the potentially dialogic relationship between companies and their stakeholders in social and environmental disclosure via the process of stakeholder engagement but found little evidence of such dialogue. If the process is to lead to improved corporate accountability and greater corporate social responsibility, then it needs to become dialogic in nature. Indeed, the emerging literature that focuses on the role of stakeholder engagement in the social and environmental field tends to be sceptical of the accountability benefits of stakeholder engagement and considers the process to be undeveloped and sporadic (Owen et al., 2001; Adams, 2002). There is scepticism concerning the true value of the engagement process to the stakeholders themselves. Companies seem to be gaining considerable information from stakeholder engagement and are probably using the process to their advantage by gaining information for public relations and marketing (Owen, 2003). However, stakeholders seem to be gaining relatively little. The extent to which stakeholder engagement could enhance corporate accountability has been seriously questioned (Owen et al., 2001). It may be that the focus on stakeholder engagement is misplaced, as its impact is limited and companies have captured the process and turned it to their own advantage, as:

> Within the engagement processes we have been involved in, the scope of engagement was largely controlled by the organisation ... Whilst there was scope for active participation by stakeholders the dialogue was in the direction of stakeholders to the organisation. They appear to be a way for the organisation to learn about those outside, not for the stakeholders to learn about the organisation. These were not mutual learning exchanges and they did not develop meaningful dialogic exchanges.
>
> (Thomson and Bebbington, 2002, p. 29)

One of the most vigorous attempts to satisfy stakeholders through the engagement process has been conducted by Camelot, the Lottery operating company. Illustration 9.3 discusses their stakeholder engagement programme in detail.

## Illustration 9.3

### Stakeholder engagement at Camelot

Camelot operates the National Lottery Company. The Company aims to raise money for good causes and their mission statement is 'To serve the nation's dreams through The National Lottery'. Camelot's primary business objective is to embed corporate social responsibility in order to meet its prime business objective, 'To deliver the target returns to good causes in a socially responsible way'. Camelot produced its first social report in 2002. It was the first company in the UK to apply the AA1000 standard.

The company has focused on developing and maintaining interstakeholder engagement. Camelot specifies its stakeholders as: the public, its employees, the community, its retailers, its suppliers, pressure groups, the environment and its shareholders. It is interesting that Camelot includes the shareholders at the end of its list in the social report – a striking difference from a traditional agency theory approach. For effective stakeholder engagement the company: arranges meetings between stakeholders; produces publications; organizes focus groups and events, such as seminars, conferences and receptions. The dialogue Camelot has nurtured between retailers and social lobby groups is a shining example of its work in this area. Retailers (typically small corner shops) have been confronted with children attempting to purchase tickets. The law does not allow anyone under 18 years old to participate in gambling, and buying lottery tickets falls into this category. This is a severe problem for retailers. How do they check younger people's age without appearing officious and potentially losing custom? Further, they could attract intimidating behaviour from some groups of young people by not allowing them to buy tickets. These sorts of difficulties are not always appreciated by social lobby groups who are attempting to prevent children becoming involved in gambling. Bringing these two important groups together helps to nurture more mutual understanding of the issues of concern. Camelot has arranged a series of meetings between representatives from retailers and lobby groups that have fostered better appreciation between the two parties. Further, Camelot has investigated ways in which it can curb the spread of gambling to children. For example, the company is introducing Lottery games for players on the Internet. This opens up greater potential for children to become involved in gambling as many have their own PCs at home. Therefore, Camelot has invested substantial funds in setting up an electronic age verification system, preventing children from playing the interactive games. Further, in relation to the broader ethical issue of tempting people of any age to spend excessive amounts on gambling, Camelot has invested in a countrywide electronic system that prevents people from spending more than a fixed amount at any one time.

On face value Camelot is making great strides in the area of corporate social responsibility. Its efforts are impressive and the structures are in place to deliver a high level of accountability to society. For a company whose very essence may be viewed by some as unethical, it is making massive efforts to alter public perceptions. However, balancing commercial objectives with such a self-acclaimed social responsibility aim is a hefty challenge to undertake. Further, there has been controversy from the start of the National Lottery about the organizations that have been selected to distribute funds to. The term 'good cause' is unspecific and extremely subjective. There has been a perception among some sectors of society that the Lottery may be seen as a silent tax, 'taking money from the poor and distributing it to the rich' in the form of more attractive arts, which only the rich can afford to participate in. This jaundiced view may have been dispelled by the company's recent efforts.

In the stakeholder engagement literature the extent of social and environmental engagement between the (arguably) primary stakeholder group, the institutional investment community and their investee companies is often dismissed in favour of examining the involvement of other stakeholder groups.[7] However, unless the primary shareholders, the institutional investors, are involved in social and environmental issues and are encouraging social and environmental disclosure because of their perception of a 'business case', significant developments in the social and environmental area will be hindered. The overemphasis on the 'ethics case' is likely to result in weaker lobbying of companies and a lack of genuine progress and commitment by the business community. This important

---

[7]  We suggest that this dismissal of the primary shareholder group is due to a belief among some that the business case for SEE disclosure and SEE engagement is misplaced and that the ethics case, which focuses more strongly on the inclusion of other stakeholders in corporate social responsibility, is more important.

change in attitude among the academic community, previously committed to the ethics case as a means of furthering the stakeholder and corporate social responsibility agenda, has been recognized in the recent literature as:

> At the present time we simply appear to be drowning in a sea of stakeholder rhetoric which, in the current political and economic climate, leads us up a blind alley as far as extending corporate accountability is concerned ... Given the absolute primacy awarded to the interests of financial capital by European legislatures it can be argued that, for those seeking to promote the cause of corporate accountability, *focussing attention on the operations of the capital markets, in particular the unaccountable power wielded by institutional fund managers, offers more hope of success than engaging in corporate controlled stakeholder dialogue processes.*
>
> (Owen, 2003, p. 27, emphasis added)

Perhaps another route to greater corporate accountability and social responsibility, such as institutional investor engagement, needs to be harnessed. As we saw in Chapter 5, institutional investors in the UK are arguably the most influential and therefore most relevant group of corporate stakeholders. Engagement between institutional investors and their investee companies is therefore likely to be representative of the most evolved form of stakeholder engagement in UK companies on social and environmental issues. Indeed, my own research has shown that there is a sophisticated process of private disclosure on social and environmental issues that is already taking place between institutional investors and their investee companies (Solomon and Solomon, 2006). The involvement of the institutional investment community is discussed in more detail in Chapter 10.

## Chapter summary

This chapter has considered the growth in importance of corporate social responsibility from a historical perspective, especially the early roots of social and environmental awareness. There has also been a discussion of how this growth of interest has influenced companies and encouraged them to discharge a broader accountability to diverse stakeholders in the social and environmental arena. One of the main ways in which this accountability may be discharged is through social, environmental and now, sustainability reporting, as shareholders and other corporate stakeholders require such information for decision making and for pure accountability purposes. Corporate environmental reporting has been used to illustrate the characteristics of disclosure in these areas. The chapter has also outlined the growth of social and environmental audit, reviewing the academic literature in this area and focusing on whether the verification process is satisfying the accountability needs of stakeholders. Generally, the UK Government is pushing companies to disclose more social and environmental and ultimately sustainability information. There is, as discussed throughout the chapter, a growing perception that good management of social and environmental issues is a reflection of good general management, which is helping to drive the sustainability agenda. Lastly, the evolving process of stakeholder engagement and the academic debate surrounding its genuine success in promoting corporate accountability to stakeholders has been considered.

## Questions for reflection and discussion

**1** Discuss the reasons why some companies undertake CER and others do not. What are the wider implications of companies not undertaking CER?

**2** Download a corporate environmental report from the Internet from those shortlisted by ACCA. Summarize the content of the report, focusing on the areas discussed in this chapter, highlighting both positive and negative aspects of the reporting.

**3** Look at any company's latest social report on the Internet. Consider all the different stakeholder engagement techniques and strategies that the company is employing. Critically evaluate the usefulness of these techniques and strategies. What is your personal view of the company's success in discharging accountability to society and behaving as a socially responsible company?

**4** Do you think that sustainability is achievable by companies in the UK?

# Chapter 10

# Environmental, social and governance considerations in institutional investment

## Aim and objectives

This chapter considers the important role that institutional investors are playing in broadening the corporate governance agenda and in driving corporate social responsibility, by increasingly taking account of environmental, social and governance (ESG) factors in their investment decisions. The specific objectives of this chapter are to enable readers to:

- highlight the important role that institutional investors are playing in progressing corporate social responsibility and encouraging greater accountability to a broad range of stakeholders;

- consider the growth of socially responsible investment in the UK and elsewhere, highlighting the ways in which socially responsible investment has moved from a marginal to a mainstream area of institutional investment;

- discuss the potential implications of the socially responsible investment movement for companies, their stakeholders and ultimately for society;

- evaluate new evidence on the integration of environmental, social and governance factors into institutional investment.

## Introduction

The last chapter considered a broader agenda for corporate governance by discussing the development of corporate social responsibility. The ways in which companies can discharge accountability to a broad range of stakeholders through social, ethical, environmental and ultimately sustainability reporting and stakeholder engagement were discussed. This chapter looks at another very important aspect of this wider accountability and broader corporate governance. We now consider ways in which institutional investors can contribute to corporate social responsibility and to a greater accountability to stakeholders through their investment policies. Indeed, institutional investors are playing an important role in progressing corporate social responsibility and have an important role to play in promoting more responsible business behaviour. The UK Government has recently endorsed the important role institutional investors have to play in integrating corporate social responsibility into business by their recognition of the impacts of social and environmental factors on long-term business performance (Government Update, 2004).

From a stakeholder theory perspective, companies are accountable to all stakeholders, not just their shareholders, as portrayed in the definition of corporate governance presented in Chapter 1, designed specifically for this text. As discussed in Chapter 9, corporate environmental and social reporting represent ways in which corporate accountability to stakeholders may be discharged. There has been a growing awareness, or consciousness, in society that unless companies take account of the social and environmental issues in their business decisions, then future social welfare may be in question. Serious repercussions from socially irresponsible behaviour have highlighted the need to pay attention to and influence companies' actions. Exxon Valdez, Brent Spar, Nike and Huntingdon Life Sciences present just a handful of notorious examples that have shown companies in a negative light and have resulted in significant shareholder reactions. Illustration 10.1 provides a detailed discussion of the case of Huntingdon Life Sciences and its implications for socially responsible investment and corporate social responsibility. However, Illustration 10.2 shows how extremists can produce the opposite to their desired effect. Corporate social responsibility has been encouraged by lobbyists who have pressured companies to improve their performance in the areas of the environment and human rights. They have also put pressure on shareholders, especially institutional investors, to become more involved in the social and environmental-related behaviour of their investees. However, it is not just outside pressure that has led companies to adopt a more stakeholder-oriented attitude. Experience has shown companies that they can suffer substantial financial losses as a result of social and environmental problems and incidents. The reputation risk attached to social and environmental incidents is tremendous, with share prices falling almost instantaneously in reaction to bad social and environmental news. As shown in Chapter 6, the Turnbull Report (1999) encapsulated an agenda to improve internal control in the area of non-financial as well as financial risks. Turnbull's recommendations have focused attention on a risk-driven approach to social and environmental management. Institutional investors are adopting a socially responsible investment mandate because of their perceptions of the importance of reputation risk arising from social and environmental misbehaviour. Indeed, CalPERS (California Public Employees' Retirement System), the largest and most influential investment institution in the USA, has opted to apply social criteria to all its investment decision making, stating that:

> ...equity in corporations with poor social and ethical records *could represent an excessive fiduciary risk* because such firms court boycotts, lawsuits, or labor activity.
>
> (Quoted in Monks, 2001, p. 134, emphasis added)

**Illustration 10.1**

**Shareholder activism on animal rights: the case of Huntingdon Life Sciences**

The British have always been viewed as a nation of pet lovers. Nowhere could this be more obvious than in the case of Huntingdon Life Sciences (HLS). The company's failure to treat animals in its care with adequate respect has turned it overnight from a successful market leader in the biotechnology industry to a pauper, struggling to gain funding. The case is controversial and has inspired a broad range of emotional responses. A study of the problems experienced by HLS demonstrates unequivocally that lack of attention by a company to social and environmental matters can impact significantly on financial performance. In 1997 HLS was a company with a great future. The company was at the forefront of biotechnology, specializing in testing new chemicals, often on animals. The practice of vivisection is common in the production of chemicals and drugs. The term 'vivisection' means 'physical experimentation on a living animal...especially if considered to cause distress to the subject' (*Longman Dictionary*, 1984). Vivisection has aroused an emotional response from the British public for many years, who continue to be dismayed by information relating to animal tests. For example, in 2001 the European Commission's plans to test thousands of chemicals for toxicity, resulting in the death of at least 50 million animals, resulted in an uproar from animal rights groups (Osborn, 2001). The animals that are used in tests include monkeys, rabbits, guinea pigs, mice, dogs, rats, hamsters, birds and fish. Generally, tests involve administering increasingly large doses of the chemical under test in order to observe the side effects. Such force-feeding causes bleeding from the eyes and nose, convulsions, vomiting, and a slow and painful death. All for the sake of scientific advancement and public protection.

In 1997 a documentary on Channel 4 entitled *It's A Dog's Life* provided video evidence that animals kept at the company's laboratories for testing purposes were undergoing terrible cruelty. For example, footage was shown of an HLS employee hitting a beagle. As soon as this information became public, the government threatened to revoke its licence to conduct animal experiments. All major pharmaceutical clients suspended contracts. In 1997 HLS's share price reached 117p, but by August 2000 this had fallen to 9p (Oakey, 2000). Given the dire financial situation that HLS found itself in, the company suspended trading in its shares in August 1998 in order to gain refinancing. The company called an extraordinary meeting and was successful in gaining approval for a £20.2 million refinancing package. Even this attempt to save the company was met by intense protests and lobbying (*Financial Times*, 2 September 1998). Five shareholders were thrown out of the meeting for persistent unruly behaviour. Animal rights lobbyists exerted terrific pressure on institutional shareholders and succeeded in 'persuading' major institutions to sell their shares in the company. Phillips & Drew, for example, sold its 11% stake in HLS in 2000, following a bomb threat, three years after the company's exposure (Skapinker, 2000). In December 2000 animal rights campaigners forced HSBC, the world's second largest bank, to sell its stake of almost 1% in HLS (Firn and Guerrera, 2000). Indeed, animal rights activism has been forceful to say the least, with activists from the British Union for the Abolition of Vivisection Reform Group threatening to protest outside the homes of HLS investors unless they sold their shares (Guerrera, 2000a). Pressure on UK investment institutions and banks was so intense that HLS repaid financing from UK financial institutions, such as the National Westminster, in order to release them from the embarrassment of association with the company. Instead, HLS turned to US institutions for financial backing in 2000 (Guerrera, 2000b). However, this did not deter lobbyists from the group Stop Huntingdon Animal Cruelty (commonly referred to as SHAC), who vowed to pursue the company and its new shareholders across the Atlantic. In December 2000 HLS lost its listing on the New York

Stock Exchange (Firn, 2000) but gained approval to switch its stock market listing from the London Stock Exchange to the US NASD over-the-counter bulletin board market in January 2001 (Jenkins, 2001). In 2002, five years after the Channel 4 programme was broadcast, the US bank Stephens ended its backing of HLS (Firn, 2002). Animal rights activists pursued the world's largest insurance broker in the USA, Marsh, by attacking offices with smoke bombs and vandalizing a golf course (Bolger and Jenkins, 2002). They have even followed customers of HLS as far as Japan (Firn and Jenkins, 2003).

The problem is that however honourable the intentions of the activists may have been, they have certainly damaged their own cause, probably irrevocably. In the wake of scientific advances, animal rights activists may be viewed by some as reminiscent of the activities of the Luddites in an earlier era. Threats on employees and shareholders were enough to enrage supporters of animal research and scientist lobbies, but when these threats crystallized into action it was far easier for them to build defences. For example, six cars belonging to HLS employees were set on fire in August 2000. This type of activity clearly represented criminal behaviour, with the managing director of HLS commenting, 'How can people with such callous disregard for the safety of people purport to be campaigning for the welfare of animals' (*The Guardian*, 29 August 2000). The activists have clearly gone far too far. A professor of physiology at Oxford University has suffered two bombs being delivered to his home and his daughter being threatened with kidnap. In December 2000 a manager from the animal research centre at HLS was attacked outside his home. Chemicals were sprayed into his eyes and he was struck on the back (Eagle, 2000). It is hard for any reasonable person to be sympathetic to the cause of activists who inflict harm in this way. Not only has the company lost support from financial institutions in the UK but also pharmaceutical companies from foreign countries have been discouraged from investing directly in the UK. This could have serious repercussions in the long-term on the British economy. For some, the activities of animal rights groups range from the sublime to the ridiculous. A prime example of behaviour that was likely to remove rather than establish the credibility of such lobby groups as the Animal Liberation Front was the laying of a wreath for the guinea pigs bred for testing purposes at a farm in Newchurch (Griffin, 2000). This case is particularly interesting from the point of view of ethical relativism. Everyone has a slightly different opinion on what is 'right' and 'wrong', 'good' and 'bad'. Whereas some people feel strongly enough about animal rights and cruelty to animals to risk a prison sentence, others consider that any testing on animals is worthwhile and acceptable if it leads to improvements in the quality of human life. Animal rights activists have been referred to frequently as 'urban terrorists' in the press and by senior members of Government. The gulf between these extreme positions is hard to bridge, as there is no real meeting place. Nevertheless, the views of animal rights activists have been enforced in the market place, as even the largest institutional investors in the UK and USA have given in to pressure from lobby groups and divested their shares in HLS.

There has been a distinct backlash against animal rights activists as a result of their at times violent outbursts. For example, in 2000 all laboratories performing experiments on animals were granted official exemption, allowing them to keep the details of their work secret (*The Independent*, 16 September 2000). This decision arose from concerns for the safety of employees working in laboratories. In November 2000 Tony Blair attacked animal rights lobby groups, accusing them of 'anti-science attitudes' and warning that the Government would not allow 'blackmail' and physical assault to stand in the way of research (*The Independent*, 18 November 2000). Nevertheless, the latest reports into the use of monkeys in experiments have concluded that they are a 'regrettable necessity' but demonstrate concerns that there are ethical problems involved in using primates and suggest that such tests should be reduced wherever possible (Brown, 2003).

## Illustration 10.2

### Backlash Against Animal Rights Extremists

Despite the way in which the financial markets dropped Huntingdon Life Sciences like a lead balloon, the industry lobby has spent a couple of years building its case against what it considers to be unacceptable, violent behaviour by extreme animal rights activists.

In May 2006, Tony Blair, the UK Prime Minister, committed the Government to protecting employees and shareholders in companies involved in animal testing with the maximum possible police and legal backing. The chief executive of the most significant pharmaceutical companies in the UK, GlaxosmithKline, Jean Pierre Gautier, has explained in detail the reasons why companies should not accept such unreasonable behaviour and why financial investors should not be blackmailed into relinquishing their investment in pharmaceutical companies. The type of behaviour includes, for example, disinterring the body of a relative of an animal testing company's employee from its grave. Fortunately, the remains were found by the police, but the distress caused to the family was substantial. Another example of threatening and intimidating behaviour is the posting of addresses of family members of the pharmaceutical companies on the world wide web. Employees involved in animal testing are frequently threatened and harassed. Similarly, shareholders, including large financial institutions, have been targeted by extremists for investing in companies involved in animal testing.

There are serious financial and economic implications of this extremist activity. The UK needs to attract investment in 'new' industries such as pharmaceuticals to replace 'old' industrial activity such as mining and steel. Already, small drugs companies are choosing to locate production and testing facilities in other parts of Europe rather than the UK because of fears relating to animal rights activists. This is having a detrimental effect on UK inward foreign direct investment and is therefore of great concern to the British Government.

Overall, it seems that any genuine sympathy animal rights activists have been able to gain from the general public and the corporate and financial communities has been spoiled by such unethical behaviour. The extremists have ruined the case of genuine animal lovers who had managed to capture the ear of companies. Companies have improved the ways in which they deal with animals in experiments as a result of reasonable lobbying activity, but the extremists have now gone a long way to destroying the good that has been done.

Another influential institutional investor in the UK, Friends Provident, has chosen to pursue socially responsible investment proactively, in part because it believes that this leads to enhanced returns for shareholders. The institution's chief executive commented, for example, that:

Good corporate practice on human rights, child labour and environmental pollution is good for society, but it's also good for shareholders. As a large investor, it is right that we use our influence with companies to encourage responsible business practices while serving the financial interests of our customers.

(Quoted in *Financial Times*, 7 May 2000)

If corporate social responsibility is to grow, the importance of the institutional investment community's role cannot be exaggerated. The power that institutional investors can wield as a force for good has been frequently acknowledged as:

> ... what we need is a means by which we can wield our influence over businesses to act responsibly ... Ethical and environmental investment is that means.
>
> (Hancock, 1999, p. 8)

Latest figures indicate that the current value of assets managed by the global institutional investment community is in excess of 42 trillion dollars, with US and UK pension fund investments alone totaling 7.4 trillion dollars (Freshfields Bruckhaus Deringer, 2005). This demonstrates the size of the sword which may be wielded for good or evil! Indeed, given the financial size of the portfolios held by institutional investors, it is clear that the investment decisions made by these investors have a considerable impact on the environment and on society as a whole.

As discussed in earlier chapters, institutional investors hold the majority of UK shares. Consequently, unless they endorse corporate social responsibility through socially responsible investment, there will be little incentive for companies to act in a socially responsible manner. It is the pressure that these influential investors, the providers of finance, exert on the companies they own that decides corporate strategy to a certain extent. If these major shareholders put companies under pressure to behave in a socially responsible way then companies are likely to respond. If institutional investors reject socially responsible investment as an investment strategy, then companies will be unlikely to prioritize social and environmental issues in their business decisions. There is therefore a strong link between socially responsible investment and corporate social responsibility. Institutional shareholders are in a position to pressure companies to behave in a more socially responsible manner and should, according to Monks' (2001) discourse on global investment, act as responsible owners. As early as the 1930s the influence of large investment institutions on society was acknowledged by John Maynard Keynes, who commented that:

> Of the maxims of orthodox finance none, surely, is more anti-social than the fetish of liquidity, the doctrine that it is a positive virtue on the part of investment institutions to concentrate their resources upon the holding of 'liquid' securities. It forgets that there is no such thing as liquidity of investment for the community as a whole. The social object of skilled investment should be to defeat the dark forces of time and ignorance which envelop our future.
>
> (Keynes, 1936, p. 155)

Therefore, even in the early 20th century, the ability of large shareholders to degrade or enhance social welfare was clearly acknowledged. We now turn to establishing a working definition of socially responsible investment.

## Terminology and definitions

Over time the term used to describe what we now know as socially responsible investment has varied substantially. The most common term in general usage in the UK has tended to be 'ethical investment'. However, in recent years socially responsible investment has taken over as the primary term in theory and in practice. It implies a broader remit of definition, covering social and environmental issues. It is also more user-friendly than ethical investment, as the word ethical implies some subjective decision on the part of the investor. The term 'socially responsible' attempts to describe a form of investment that is less subjective and that 'should' be instigated by a 'responsible' society. The following definition of socially responsible investment illustrates the wide array of terms used to refer to the process of socially responsible investment:

> Social investing, socially responsible investing, socially aware investing, ethical investing, values-based investing, mission-based investing ... all describe the same concept. These terms tend to be used interchangeably within the investment industry to describe an approach to investing that integrates personal values and societal concerns into the investment decision-making process.
>
> (Steve Scheuth, Social Investment Forum, quoted in the *AccountAbility Primer*)

Another definition of the process of socially responsible investment, given in the *Primer* and quoted from the UK Social Investment Forum is that:

> Socially responsible investment combines investors' financial objectives with their commitment to social concerns such as justice, economic development, peace or a healthy environment.

This quote brings one of the most important issues in socially responsible investment to the fore: Is it possible to be ethical and still to make a profit? When we discussed corporate governance in earlier chapters we alluded to the importance of increasing corporate profitability by improving corporate governance. The discussion stipulated that unless better corporate governance resulted in better financial performance, there would be little incentive to further the agenda for corporate governance reform. Chapter 9 provided evidence from the extant literature that suggests that corporate social responsibility leads to higher financial performance for companies. The same argument applies to socially responsible investment. However moral and ethical investors are, they do not tend to welcome a reduction in their investment return. Few people are prepared to accept a lower return to investment from investing in a socially responsible manner. Indeed, such a choice would be impractical, given that the majority of institutional investment involves pension funds and lower returns would result in impoverished pensioners in the future. Again, unless socially responsible investment produces returns that are at least equivalent to non-socially responsible investment, socially responsible investment is unlikely to grow and prosper. This issue is considered later in this chapter. First, we discuss the type

**Table [10.1]**   Issues of traditional importance to the ethical investor

| Alcohol | Military/MOD contracts | Poor workplace conditions |
|---|---|---|
| Animal testing | Arms exports to oppressive regimes | Third World concerns |
| Gambling | Nuclear power | Tobacco |
| Greenhouse gases | Ozone depletion | Water pollution |
| Health and safety breaches | Pesticides | Tropical hardwoods |
| Human rights abuses | Pornography and adult films | Genetically modified food |
| Intensive farming | Road use/construction | Gene patenting |

of issues with which 'ethical' investors have traditionally been concerned. The issues that are important to socially responsible investors are shown in Table 10.1.

Nevertheless, a salient issue for institutional investors who wish to take account of social and environmental factors in their portfolio investment decisions is the extent to which a consensus can be reached on the relative importance of these factors. There is a general tendency for people to behave according to the philosophical concept of 'ethical subjectivism'. By this we mean that everyone has a different view of 'right' or 'wrong', and 'good' or 'bad'. It is therefore very difficult to decide on a set of ethical principles that may be applied to investments for a wide selection of investors. Indeed, by practising socially responsible investment investors are forcing a set of ethical principles on companies and by default on society as a whole. This is an interesting philosophical issue and one that is being explored in the academic work in order to appreciate the process of socially responsible investment and corporate social responsibility (Solomon and Solomon, 2003).

## From SEE to ESG

The last couple of years has seen an evolution in the terminology used to refer to the factors relevant to socially responsible investment. In the same way that ethical investment has become socially responsible investment (termed SRI) over time, so have the issues covered evolved and converged. When socially responsible investment was starting to move into the mainstream in the UK at the turn of the century, institutional investors were concerned with the extent to which they were incorporating social and environmental factors into their investment decisions. As socially responsible investment has become more firmly established as one of the mainstream considerations in institutional investment, the terminology has broadened to include environmental, social and governance factors, referred to as ESG factors. This implies that social and environmental factors have now caught up with more central corporate governance issues in their importance for investment institutions. These three areas taken together are

**Table [10.2]**   Issues associated with ESG investment

| Climate change | Environmental management | Sustainability |
|---|---|---|
| Corporate conventions | Globalization | Terrorism |
| Corporate governance | Health issues in emerging markets | Water |
| Employee relations | Human rights | |

now becoming central to institutional investment strategy, as we shall see from the following discussion. Although no definitive list of ESG issues has been compiled, Mercer Investment Consulting (2006) suggested a number of issues upon which ESG seems to be converging (see Table 10.2). Comparing Table 10.1 with Table 10.2 we can see how the area of socially responsible investing is changing and becoming more focused over time.

There has been some indication from recent research as to which of these ESG factors are viewed as more important among the global institutional investment community. Mercer Investment Consulting (2006) found from their survey of fund managers that globalization and corporate governance were the ESG factors viewed as most relevant to mainstream institutional investment analysis. They also found that a high proportion of fund managers expect clean water, climate change and environmental management to have a material impact on investment performance over the next five years. Terrorism was also one of the most relevant ESG factors according to survey participants.

The emergence of the concept of 'universal ownership' has also encouraged the integration of ESG issues into mainstream institutional investment. Universal owners have been defined as large investors who hold a wide range of investments in different listed companies as well as other assets and are therefore tied to the performance of markets of whole economies, rather than to the performance of individual assets. This implies that universal owners are forced to be concerned about long-term economic prosperity, and therefore forced to consider ESG issues (Mercer Investment Consulting, 2006). The implication is that most large investment institutions are starting to fall under this classification and are therefore not in a position to avoid taking ESG issues seriously.

## Some recent statistics on socially responsible investment

In 2003, European fund managers anticipated that ethical investment would continue to grow. Indeed, half of those interviewed claimed to manage 10 % or more of their assets on an SRI basis (*Ethical Investor*, 2003). The UK has witnessed a substantial increase in socially responsible investment in recent years. £4 billion was invested in 'ethical' funds in August 2001. However, this is only a drop in the ocean when we consider that ethical funds are a minor area of socially responsible investment. Socially responsible investment now implies institutional investors taking account of social and environmental issues in their portfolio decisions, as an overarching umbrella investment criterion. Indeed, market research has indicated that 77 % of the British public would like their pension funds to be invested in a socially responsible way, provided this did not harm financial returns

(Targett, 2000). The extent of UK socially responsible investment has increased significantly in recent years, evidenced by the growth in the number of socially responsible investment funds offered by institutional investors. Recent evidence has suggested that almost 80 % of pension scheme members require their schemes to operate a socially responsible investment policy (*The Ethical Investor*, November/December 1999). This trend toward more socially responsible investment has had a substantial impact on the institutional investment community, on pension fund trustees, on the managers of UK listed companies and on society in a wider context. As discussed in Chapter 5, pension funds hold the largest stake in the UK stock market, which shows the significant role they play in all areas of investment strategy, including social responsibility. Friedman and Miles (2001) and Sparkes (2002) showed that institutional investors have embraced socially responsible investment as part of their mainstream portfolio investment strategies. The recent report by Freshfield Bruckhaus Deringer (2005) affirms that as public awareness of business impact on the environment and society has grown, the attitudes of capital markets to environmental, social and governance issues have also evolved, such that investment with respect to environmental, social and governance performance is becoming increasingly mainstream. Importantly, a recent survey by Mercer Investment Consulting of 195 fund managers around the world, found that 70 % of fund managers believe that the integration of environmental, social and ethical factors into investment analysis will become mainstream in investment management within the next three to ten years. The survey also found that 60 % of fund managers consider that screening for social, ethical and environmental factors will be mainstream within the next three to ten years (Ambachtsheer, 2005). The findings of this survey have been significantly strengthened by Mercer Investment's latest survey (2006) which canvassed the views of 157 international institutional investors. The survey confirmed that socially responsible investment is continuing to expand at a global level. Specifically, 38 % of fund managers surveyed anticipated increased client demand for the integration of ESG analysis in to mainstream institutional investment over the next three years.

# Socially responsible investment strategies

*Screening*
Until relatively recently the primary strategy for socially responsible investment had been screening. In making their portfolio investment decisions the fund managers of ethical funds within investment institutions 'screened' companies according to socially responsible criteria. There are two types of social screening, positive and negative. Positive (or aspirational) screening involves deciding what sort of companies would be a 'good' addition to the investment portfolio (Dobson, 1994). Negative screening involves fund managers avoiding companies that pursue certain activities. These may include: companies with negative environmental impacts; companies that provide strategic goods to repressive political regimes; companies that produce tobacco products, alcoholic

beverages and weaponry; and companies involved in nuclear weapons or the production of nuclear power. Dobson commented that:

> Of all the social screens, environmental ones cause the least controversy . . . generally it is agreed that clean air, clean water and safe working conditions are desirable.
>
> (Dobson, 1994, p. 163)

As we saw in the area of environmental reporting in the previous chapter, the environment is the most mature form of non-financial, sustainability-oriented disclosure. This also seems to be the case in the area of socially responsible investment analysis.

*Best in sector*

Although socially responsible investment originally consisted of a screening strategy, more recent strategies have focused on a 'best in class' approach (Mansley, 2000), which means that socially responsible funds do not exclude whole sectors from their portfolios but include those companies in previously excluded sectors that are making the most effort to improve their social responsibility. The FTSE4Good index and other socially responsible investment indices around the world, such as the Jantzi index in Canada, which have been introduced in the last couple of years, adopt a best in class approach. This represents a realistic approach for socially responsible investment and one that is open to a much larger group of investors. However, from a 'deep green' perspective such an approach may be considered a cop-out, as shareholders can invest in a company in any industry, no matter what it produces, provided it has the best corporate social responsibility policies related to its industry peers. Having said that, the best in sector approach is perhaps the only socially responsible stance possible for pension fund investment managers who are bound by legislation to provide stable returns without reducing the potential for portfolio diversification. It allows trustees to adopt socially responsible investment policies without compromising their fiduciary duties.[1] As mentioned earlier a central issue for investors is whether socially responsible investment funds perform financially as well as, or better than, funds invested according to socially responsible investment criteria. However strongly investors desire to invest in a socially responsible manner, the prospect of lower financial returns on socially responsible funds would act as a disincentive for socially responsible investment.

## The financial performance of socially responsible investment funds

> There is no clear evidence from experience that the investment policy which is socially advantageous coincides with that which is most profitable . . .
>
> (Keynes, 1936, p. 157)

---

[1]  Fiduciary duties are imposed by common law jurisdictions on a person who exercises some discretionary power in the interests of another person in circumstances that give rise to a relationship of trust and confidence (Freshfields Bruckhaus Deringer, 2005, p. 8).

An essential issue for institutional investors is whether socially responsible investment funds perform as well financially as funds without socially responsible characteristics. Despite a desire to invest responsibly, investors are likely to avoid investing where this could lead to lower return. As socially responsible investment is rising it is likely that investors believe they will make equal, if not higher, returns from socially responsible investment than from non-socially responsible investment. Certainly, in interviews that we have performed with fund directors this belief prevails, especially among the largest funds. Solomon and Solomon (2002) found strong evidence of a growing perception among the institutional investment community that socially responsible investment, as part of the mainstream investment strategy, enhances financial returns in the long term. Drexhage (1998) considered that investors and fund managers believe it is possible to make a difference while making a profit.

Boatright (1999) discussed the theoretical arguments underlying socially responsible investment. From a theoretical perspective there is some support for socially responsible funds outperforming non-socially responsible funds. First, from simple economic theory of demand and supply it is reasonable that if demand for socially responsible companies increases, then so will their price (i.e., the share price and therefore the market value of the company will rise). Similarly, if demand for shares in companies that are not socially responsible falls, so will their market value. This impact has been summarized as follows:

> ... investment demand for shares in institutions with such products as 'natural cosmetics' or positive employment policies may be stimulated. From the purely financial view, growth in such investor sentiment may be expected to produce gains in shares with a 'positive' ethical rating and losses on others ...
>
> (Luther et al., 1992, p. 57)

Second, from a free market perspective, socially responsible investment is an important issue, as it implies that funds may not be so easily raised by companies that are not socially responsible in their activities. Ultimately, if socially responsible screening continues to grow at its current rate we may see Adam Smith's (1838) 'invisible hand' distributing more funds to socially responsible companies and diverting funds from companies that do not act in a socially responsible manner (Boatright, 1999).

On the contrary, there are also a number of reasons from a theoretical perspective why socially responsible funds may indeed underperform non-socially responsible funds. Luther et al. (1992) suggested from a portfolio theory perspective that socially screened funds will attract lower returns because of a lack of diversification potential and higher transaction costs. Second, efficient markets theory also presents reasons for socially responsible fund underperformance. It is generally accepted that the UK stock market is semi-strong form-efficient, implying that all publicly available information is completely, immediately and accurately incorporated in share prices. This in turn implies that all share prices are a true representation of their inherent risks. This means that no investor can consistently beat the market by obtaining more, or alternative, information about a specific company or indeed about wider economic issues. Therefore, the only way in which an investor can obtain a higher return is by taking on greater risk or by gaining access to, and acting on, private/inside information, which is illegal. The implications for socially responsible investment are that actively evaluating company shares by any specific criterion (e.g., social responsibility) is a waste of resources as the traditionally accepted investment strategy for investors is to passively select a balanced portfolio, mirroring the market as a whole, rather than selecting shares actively according to such subjective criteria as socially responsible objectives. Only if the stock market is inefficient can there be potential gains from socially responsible investment as:

> The case for SRI, then, must be based on the claims that the market is inefficient and that the source of this inefficiency is a failure to recognize the significance of socially responsible activity in the evaluation of stock price.
>
> (Boatright, 1999, p. 111)

Existing academic empirical research has failed to find any statistically significant difference in the returns of socially responsible funds (e.g., Mallin et al., 1995). A number of empirical studies have been performed to evaluate the financial performance of UK socially responsible funds. Luther et al. (1992) isolated a sample of socially responsible unit trusts and found that five of the trusts offered a higher total return than the FT-All Share index. They found overall that half of the trusts studied out-performed the market and half underperformed. However, the use of an appropriate benchmark in such empirical work has provided cause for concern (see Luther and Matatko, 1994). Mallin et al. (1995) attempted to overcome this problem by using improved techniques to compare the performance of UK socially responsible investment funds not only with a market benchmark but also with non-socially responsible investment funds. Overall, they found that both socially responsible and non-socially responsible trusts seemed to underperform the market. However, they provided some weak evidence that socially responsible trusts outperformed non-socially responsible trusts. They attributed their findings to a type of 'bandwagon' effect:

> The weakly superior performance of ethical funds evidenced in the sample may have been a temporary phenomenon caused by an increased awareness and interest in ethical investment. This in turn led to increasing levels of demand for appropriate investment products establishing a premium in realised rates of return. Indeed, this phenomenon may still be continuing as ethical investment gains in acceptance.
>
> (Mallin et al., 1995, p. 495)

Using similar techniques, the most recent academic study by Gregory et al. (1997) showed that both socially responsible and non-socially responsible trusts underperformed the market but that underperformance was worse for socially responsible trusts.

From a more practical perspective, the development of benchmark indices for evaluating socially responsible fund performance should provide clarification on this issue. Williams

(1999) stated that one of the future trends in UK socially responsible investment will be the development of dedicated performance benchmarks. Indeed, there has been a recent emergence of socially responsible investment stock exchange indices in the UK. The Ethical Investment Research Service (EIRIS) has developed five socially responsible indices, each of which indicates financial returns roughly equivalent to the FTSE-All Share Index for the period 1991 to 1998. Also, in 1998 the NPI Social Index was launched. It is likely that the emergence of new socially responsible investment indices will:

> ... explode the myth that green and ethical investors have to accept that their investment performance will be disappointing.
>
> (Holden-Meehan, 1999, p. 35)

Williams (1999) stated that one of the future trends in UK socially responsible investment will be the development of dedicated performance benchmarks. The launch of the FTSE4Good indices in 2001[2] has represented an encouraging development for supporters of the socially responsible investment movement. Indeed, Williams' (1999) predictions were quite visionary, given the growth of socially responsible investment indices in the UK and elsewhere. A new study has examined the financial performance of the FTSE4Good and investigated perceptions about its indices (Cobb, Collison, Power and Stevenson, 2005). Cobb et al. examined daily returns of the indices and compared these to their mainstream (non-SRI) equivalents from 1996 to 2003. They concluded that,

> Investors are unlikely to be worse off by restricting their investment universe, and may well be better off.
>
> (Cobb et al., p. 5)

The researchers partly attributed this finding to the high proportion of mainstream (and therefore financially successful) companies represented in the indices. They also conducted interviews and a questionnaire survey with constituent companies. The qualitative evidence suggested that being included in the FTSE4Good indices was having a limited impact on the participants generally. However, inclusion was found to be contributing significantly to stakeholder relations, as well as to internal processes such as reporting and management systems on social and environmental issues. The work did, however, raise questions about the genuine intentions of the FTSE4Good initiative to improve corporate accountability as,

> ...calls have been made for increased corporate accountability through mandatory disclosures on a range of social and environmental issues, and for a broadening of directors' duties of care beyond their duty to shareholders. Could FTSE4Good be seen as implementing the spirit of such calls? Alternatively, could it be viewed as a means

[2] The FTSE4Good comprises several indices which focus on companies that meet globally accepted corporate social responsibility standards.

of superficially placating them and maintaining the status quo, while, for good measure obscuring the influence of the traditional SRI sector? Should it be seen as neither of these but as a workable compromise that is achieving incremental improvements across a range of business sectors?

(Cobb et al., 2005, p. 6)

This is a deep series of contemplative questions, beyond the scope of the study itself. The issues raised here delve into the philosophical motivations underlying social and environmental corporate accountability. Certainly the findings of this important research lead the way for further work into underlying motivation of high profile initiatives in corporate social responsibility.

## The drivers of socially responsible investment

There is a broad range of factors driving socially responsible investment. Identifying the forces driving socially responsible investment is important, as it helps those who want to push the socially responsible investment agenda further identify which parties require more encouragement. My own research has attempted to discover what forces were principally motivating the socially responsible investment movement in the UK (see Solomon et al., 2002c). Were they drivers internal to companies or were they external drivers such as lobby groups? Lobby groups have been acknowledged as important drivers of socially responsible investment in the literature (Parkinson, 1994; Mansley, 2000). Was the church, for example, a significant driver of socially responsible investment? Non-passive and more socially oriented investment has been encouraged by church bodies as long ago as the Middle Ages (Monks, 2001). Indeed, the church developed some of the first ethical funds in the USA and the UK, and is still active in investing according to 'ethical' criteria (Parkinson, 1994). Many writers consider that socially responsible investment is being driven in part by an increase in interest in social responsibility in society in general, for example:

... growing awareness among the public at large of the broader consequences of how their investments are managed ...

(Mansley, 2000, p. 2)

Institutional investors themselves are likely to drive socially responsible investment as they are beginning to recognize the significant financial impacts in such areas as liability or reputation that environmental and social issues can have on investment portfolios (Mansley, 2000). The Government has also played an important role in driving socially responsible investment with its introduction of the new socially responsible investment disclosure requirement for pension fund trustees. This has already encouraged trustees to develop socially responsible investment policies for their pension funds and is acknowledged as a means of furthering corporate social responsibility (ACCA, 2000; Cowe, 2001; Solomon and Solomon, 2001). Trade associations such as the National Association of Pension Funds (NAPF) and the ABI are also involved in encouraging their members to be more proactive in corporate governance and socially responsible investment (NAPF, 1995; Cowe, 2001). Similarly, the recent Green Paper produced by the European Commission pressures for greater corporate social responsibility and emphasizes the important role that socially responsible investment has to play in furthering the corporate social responsibility agenda. A more cynical view suggests that an increase in consumerism in society resulting from a more luxurious standard of living has resulted in consumers requiring ethical funds as part of their desire for greater choice in commodities (Harte et al., 1991).

Figure 10.1 presents a theoretical model that shows the various drivers of socially responsible investment and the importance of socially responsible investment as a

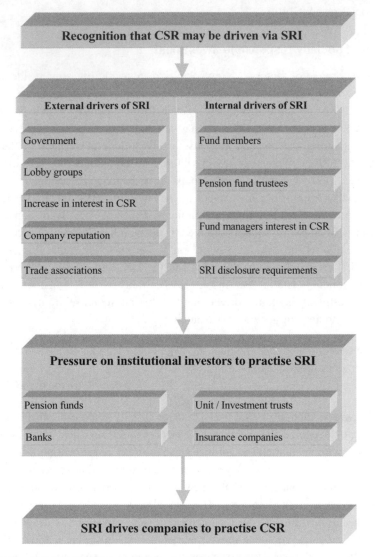

**Figure [10.1]** Drivers of SRI and its role in CSR
Reproduced by permission of the Braybrooke Press Ltd

driver of corporate social responsibility. In the model, a distinction is made between internal drivers and external drivers of socially responsible investment. Internal drivers include fund managers themselves, clients of the institutional investors (such as pension fund members) and (for pension funds) the actions of trustees. External drivers include lobby groups, the Government (and political parties competing for power), society's interest in corporate social responsibility, companies themselves wanting to promote socially responsible investment and such external bodies as the NAPF and the ABI.

As discussed earlier, one of the most important drivers of corporate social responsibility has to be socially responsible investment, as unless corporate owners require socially responsible behaviour from companies it is unlikely that companies will take corporate social responsibility seriously. The importance of the role of socially responsible investment in corporate social responsibility is represented by the arrow flowing from institutional investors to companies in Figure 10.1. The model does not attempt to rank the relative importance of each of these drivers but simply proposes a relationship. This empirical evidence from institutional investors sheds light on which drivers are considered to be of more/less importance in promoting the socially responsible investment agenda. The findings arose from a postal questionnaire survey and face to face interviews. The questionnaire survey was conducted between August and December 2000 and involved distribution of a detailed questionnaire to the whole population of pension fund trustees who are members of the NAPF, amounting to a total of 891 organizations. We received responses from 162 pension fund trustees, providing a total response of 18 %. Of the respondents 89 (10 %) completed the questionnaire. Of the respondent institutions 83 % had developed a socially responsible investment policy for their pension fund. The rest were either in the process of developing one or had decided not to develop a socially responsible investment policy. Also, 10 interviews were conducted in the summer of 2001. Table 10.3 summarizes the pension fund trustees' responses to a question about the extent to which they agreed/disagreed with a number of statements concerning the motivation of pension funds for developing a socially responsible investment policy.

The statistics show that the impact of environmental and social lobby groups was considered to be by far the most important driver behind the development of socially responsible investment policy by pension funds. Lobby group involvement in BP Amoco's interests in Alaska is a typical example of the way in which shareholders can be pressured and influenced by lobbyists' activities. Illustration 10.3 discusses the role of lobby groups in environmental issues, focusing on the case of BP Amoco. However, there was also some indication that a general increase in interest in social responsibility in society in general is motivating socially responsible investment policy development. Thus we can see from these findings that the parties involved in socially responsible investment who are internal to the investment institutions are not driving the socially responsible investment agenda; it is external parties, such as the Government and lobbyists. This is not encouraging as it implies that the people who are most closely involved in socially responsible investment do not appear to be interested in driving it forward. Lastly, the

**Table [10.3]** The drivers of SRI policies

| Rank | I believe that the development of SRI policy by pension funds is motivated by | Mean |
|---|---|---|
| 1 | The impact of environmental and social lobby groups | Agreement |
| 2 | A general increase in interest in social responsibility in society in general | Some agreement |
| 3 | Political parties competing for power | Some agreement |
| 4 | Companies seeking to improve their reputation and corporate identity | Some agreement |
| 5 | The actions of the NAPF | Weak agreement |
| 6 | European Union legislation | Disagreement |
| 7 | The social dimension of European Union membership | Disagreement |
| 8 | The growing interest of pension fund trustees in SRI issues | Disagreement |
| 9 | The growing interest of pension fund managers | Disagreement |
| 10 | A demand from active pension fund members | Disagreement |
| 11 | A demand from retired pension fund members | Disagreement |
| 12 | The religious beliefs of the general public | Strong disagreement |

Reproduced by permission of the Braybrooke Press Ltd

total rejection of religious beliefs as a socially responsible investment driver is interesting, given the church's involvement in early ethical investments. This demonstrates a complete transformation of society's ethics and values over the past hundred years, since the early years of ethical investment. People may pursue similar aims over time, such as social responsibility, but for allegedly different reasons.

## Illustration 10.3

### The role of lobby groups in corporate environmental issues: the case of BP Amoco in Alaska

The environment is a cause for serious concern to most people worldwide. Depletion of natural resources and pollution of the environment are considered by some to represent a time bomb that could ultimately render the Earth uninhabitable by humans, not to mention the millions of other species that share the planet with us. The debate about global warming and its potential consequences is well known. The destruction of the Earth's ozone layer due to pollution is undisputed, although the eventual impact is debatable. Certainly, many animal species are becoming extinct as a result of human interaction with the natural environment. Weather patterns are altering around the world. Although there have been global efforts to reduce pollution and 'clean up' industry, this is a difficult and controversial process. The usual problems apply. To what extent are we prepared to sacrifice high levels of corporate profitability, high rates of economic growth and wide choices in consumer goods in order to reduce our impact on the environment? People who make efforts to change their lifestyles to become more 'environmentally friendly' tend to be ridiculed by the majority and called 'greenies', 'tree-huggers' and the like. Some even consider such people wash less and have bad breath as a result of avoiding chemical products and eating organic, vegetarian food; but the dismissal of such a worthy cause through derision is worrying, given that its aims are for humankind, not the individual. Nevertheless, would most of us be satisfied with solar heating that worked intermittently? Would we be happy to sell our bright red sports car, trading it in for a bicycle? Somehow the local bus network does not give the same kick as revving the engine of a high-performance vehicle and speeding away from the traffic lights. How would we feel about not using our favourite deodorant anymore or doing without a cupboard full of expensive, exotic perfumes and face creams? The majority of people are satisfied with their high quality of life in the UK and elsewhere and would be unlikely to accept such changes. Going to work, bringing up children, cooking meals, coping with the everyday stresses – these constitute most people's everyday lives. It is hard in our hectic world to find the time to reflect on such imponderables as environmental degradation and sustainability. But the battle continues. The 'greenies' do not give up. There are many lobby groups that are influential worldwide, comprising individuals who believe passionately in preserving the planet for future generations. They are no longer in the background but have succeeded in influencing government policy in countries around the world. Things are changing. The Kyoto Protocol represented a worldwide attempt to combat the emission of greenhouse gases (Heal, 2000). However, withdrawal of the USA from this agreement was a massive step backward for lobbyists and reformers.

Nowhere are lobby groups more active and forceful than in the area of the environment. Greenpeace is a worldwide organization that has fought for environmental protection for many years. Oil companies are one of their many targets and BP Amoco's interests in Alaska represent one example of the most significant environmental issues in recent years. Not only did BP Amoco's presence in Alaska lead to forceful behaviour by lobby groups but it also resulted in one of the only cases of shareholder revolution in the UK. The Arctic National Wildlife Refuge (ANWR) in Alaska was deemed the largest unexplored, potentially productive onshore petroleum-producing basin in the nation in a report by the Energy Information Administration. However, it is also the last undisturbed area in the USA. The ANWR represents 8.9 million acres of land, designated a protected area by Public Law 2214 in 1960. The Alaska National Interest Lands Conservation Act created an additional 16 national wildlife refuges in 1980, which extended the area to 19 million acres. The area was also classified in 1980 as 'wilderness', which means that all types of development, including road building, are prohibited (Financial Times, 27 June 2000). Thousands of caribou live in the area of wilderness (Heal, 2000). In April 2000 a multinational alliance of environmental groups, including Greenpeace and the World Wildlife Fund, attended the AGM of BP Amoco in an attempt to prevent the company from drilling for oil in a remote area of Alaska (Financial Times, 11 April 2000). Sentiment was so strong that nine Greenpeace activists were arrested for trespassing at a BP Amoco oil exploration site in Alaska in a single week the same month (Financial Times, 13 April 2000). Indeed, environmental campaigners claimed 'unprecedented' support from shareholders, with about 13% of votes being cast at the AGM in favour of a Greenpeace-backed shareholder resolution. The resolution urged BP Amoco to cancel plans to exploit oil in Alaska's ANWR and to increase investment in solar energy (Ward, 2000). Despite such support, the resolution was at the time unsuccessful. However, BP Amoco has reduced the scale of its operations in Alaska (Buchan and Earle, 2002). Yet, the company's image was blighted. Oil spills in Alaska, due to ageing pipelines, have not enhanced BP Amoco's image. In July 2001 a corroded pipeline erupted, spilling over 400 gallons of crude oil onto the tundra (Earle, 2001). Since the problems in Alaska, BP Amoco has made a significant attempt to improve its image, becoming a pioneer company in environmental management, advertising its aims to develop new, renewable energy sources, such as solar power and wind energy. Indeed, the environment has become vastly important as a reputational issue for all UK companies and indeed for companies around the world (Fombrun and Shanley, 1990; Fombrun, 2000). As we have seen in Chapter 8, Corporate Environmental Reporting (CER) has grown significantly in recent years and there is evidence of a positive relationship between corporate environmental and financial performance. The Alaskan case has continued to be a centre of controversy, becoming a political football. Even before he became President, George W. Bush stated emphatically that he wanted to develop the oilfield. This proposal was inspired mainly by his concerns about reliance on oil imported from the Gulf. He proposed opening around 8% of the ANWR to exploration and drilling (Durgin and Wolffe, 2000). However, energy analysts were not at all confident that this proposal would be successful, as falling energy prices would not provide enough funding to develop the required infrastructure to support the developments.

Overall, the questionnaire data from my research indicated that there are a large number of significant socially responsible investment drivers, as suggested by Figure 10.1. However, there was a consensus on the overriding influence of lobby groups (which is related to society in general) and the Government (which again should theoretically represent the people). Overall, it was clear from our results that internal drivers of socially responsible investment that are closely involved in institutional investment, such as fund managers themselves, their members and trustees of pension funds, are not as interested in socially responsible investment as external parties. There are many possible explanations of this. One is that pension fund managers in particular are concerned about alienating corporate sponsors by pressuring them through active socially responsible investment engagement. This could lead to them losing their fund management contracts (e.g., Coffee, 1991). Another explanation in relation to pension funds is the concern of trustees about potential conflict between their fiduciary duties and socially responsible investment. Whatever the reason, the primary force for socially responsible investment is arising from outside the investment institutions. This means that fund managers are in effect having socially responsible investment thrust on them. If socially responsible investment is to have a sound future, it is necessary for the driving force to also come from within the institutions themselves. Unless fund managers, trustees and fund members believe that socially responsible investment is in their financial interests as well as perhaps their normative, ethical interests (which have to be subordinated to their fiduciary duties and need to meet financial return targets), then socially responsible investment will not progress substantially. As discussed earlier socially responsible investment is necessary if corporate social responsibility is to be encouraged further. Therefore, a clear policy recommendation for promoting socially responsible investment is to target the internal drivers of socially responsible investment. By making fund managers and trustees more aware of the financial (and non-financial) benefits of socially responsible investment they will be encouraged to take a proactive rather than reactive stance. In other words, fund managers need to be pursuing socially responsible investment actively as part of their own long-term investment strategy rather than merely to satisfy the expectations of Government and lobbyists. Without this sort of change, socially responsible investment will remain a box-ticking strategy that is more in form than in substance.

We now consider whether there is evidence of a significant demand for social and environmental disclosure by companies arising from the interest of the institutional investment community in socially responsible investment.

## A growing demand for social, ethical and environmental disclosure

Chapter 6 acknowledged the importance of corporate transparency as a means of reducing the agency problem and reducing information asymmetries. The disclosure function is just as important in the social and environmental area as in other areas.

Linked to the growth of socially responsible investment is the need for adequate social and environmental information. The emerging emphasis on greater corporate accountability through greater disclosure of all types of risk to shareholders (as well as to the wider stakeholder community) is a clear indication that social-oriented information is becoming more important. From the perspective of socially responsible investment, the importance of recent disclosure recommendations, such as those stemming from the Cadbury Report (1999) and the Turnbull Report (1999), is the shift of focus away from solely financial aspects of internal control and toward consideration of non-financial risks, as:

> An effective risk management process addresses both financial risks (such as credit, market and liquidity risk) and non-financial risks (such as legal and environmental risk).
>
> (Stock et al., 1999, p. 41)

You may recall that we discussed the importance of non-financial risks in Chapter 6. It is likely that companies that do not behave in a socially responsible manner will be at risk from investor sentiment as well as potential unanticipated reputation risks, such as environmental disasters. It is now generally acknowledged that increased and improved information disclosure is not only essential for purely financial investment decisions but also for socially responsible investment. One signal that social and environmental disclosure is growing in importance is the recent publication of a new standard for companies, the AA1000 Standard (AccountAbility 1000, 1999), which provides a framework for companies to improve and disclose their performance as socially responsible companies. Other initiatives include recommendations from the Association of British Insurers (ABI) (Cowe, 2001) and the Global Reporting Initiative (GRI, 2000). This area has been covered in some detail in the previous chapter. The ABI has also published a set of guidelines on social and environmental disclosure directed at companies. This set of guidelines was prepared by a number of important institutional investor groups and attempts to represent the information requirements of the institutional investor community. Specifically, the guidelines stated that they would like company boards of directors to state in their annual reports whether or not the board:

- takes regular account of the significance of social and environmental matters to the business of the company;

- has identified and assessed the significant risks to the company's short- and long-term value arising from social and environmental matters, as well as the opportunities to enhance value that may arise from an appropriate response;

- has received adequate information to make this assessment and that account is taken of social and environmental matters in the training of directors;

- has ensured that the company has in place effective systems for managing significant risks, which where relevant incorporate performance management systems and appropriate remuneration incentives.

Further, with respect to policies, procedures and verification, the ABI stated that they would like to see the following in the annual report:

- information on social and environmental-related risks and opportunities that may significantly affect the company's short- and long-term value and how they might impact on the business;

- description of the company's policies and procedures for managing risks to short- and long-term value, arising from social and environmental matters, and if the annual report and accounts state that the company has no such policies and procedures the Board should provide reasons for their absence;

- information about the extent to which the company has complied with its policies and procedures for managing risks arising from social and environmental matters;

- description of the procedures for verification of social and environmental disclosures. The verification procedure should be such as to achieve a reasonable level of credibility.

The needs of institutional investors and other shareholders for more disclosure of social and environmental information have been clarified in many institutional investor's written policy documents. For example, one institution provided the following in a document entitled *Responsible Shareholders: A Guide to Our Corporate Governance Views and Policies* (August 1998):[3]

---

[3] Confidentiality is maintained here as we are unsure whether or not this document is distributed in the public arena.

We expect the boards of the companies in which we invest to pay due regard to ethical and environmental issues and thereby protect and enhance long-term shareholder value. Companies should be able to demonstrate their commitment to responsible environmental policies. We believe that shareholders have a right to know about the activities of companies in the area of ethical and environmental issues. We will, therefore, support proposals for disclosure as long as the costs involved are reasonable.

In relation to corporate social disclosure and socially responsible investment, Harte et al. (1991) researched the sources of information used by socially responsible fund managers. The corporate annual report was found to be of little use in socially responsible investment decisions. The fund managers indicated that annual reports do not contain adequate information for screening companies on a socially responsible basis. The researchers concluded that there was a need for accounting policy makers to give a higher priority to issues of socially responsible information disclosure. Indeed, the fund managers suggested that companies should include more information in their annual reports on environmental impact, animal experimentation, community and social issues and trading interests in countries with repressive regimes. However, although these findings have substantial policy implications, the work has not been readdressed by the academic community until relatively recently. Friedman and Miles (2001) found from their research that the City of London was taking social and environmental issues far more seriously. My research has found evidence from extensive interviews within the institutional investment community that social and environmental matters are being treated as a mainstream issue and that fund managers are dissatisfied with the level of corporate disclosure of social and environmental information (Solomon and Solomon, 2003a). This is clearly an area where new research is needed to discover whether companies have responded in spirit, as well as in form, to information requirements of the ever-growing socially responsible investor population.

As well as greater disclosure of information on social responsibility issues, the development of longer and stronger communication and decision links between institutional investors and investee companies should help to improve information flows and increase the potential for socially responsible investment to continue growing. The role of fund managers within investment institutions is essential to the development of socially responsible investment, as:

Now a third way has emerged – a positive, proactive policy of communication between institutions, fund managers and companies. This trend towards 'active dialogue' is very exciting ... Engaging in constructive discussions with companies on their ethical and environmental activities is what will ultimately make a sustainable difference.

(Holden-Meehan, 1999, p. 25)

Solomon and Solomon (2002) argued that improvements in quality and quantity of social and environmental disclosure constitute part of a 'virtuous circle' of corporate social responsibility, arising from initiatives encouraging the development of socially responsible investment. As institutional investors take increasing account of social responsibility issues in their portfolio investment decisions, they will demand more information and companies will have to provide the information.

## Private social and environmental reporting: Institutional investor engagement on environmental, social and governance issues

Chapter 9 discussed the engagement process that is evolving between companies and stakeholders. Chapter 5 discussed engagement between institutional investors and companies on a range of issues. A sophisticated process of engagement and dialogue is also developing between institutional investors and their investee companies in the area of social and environmental information. Indeed, this type of engagement is becoming one of the most influential strategies used in socially responsible investment. Sparkes (2002) highlighted the growth in social and environmental engagement as a main indicator that socially responsible investment is moving away from the margin and into mainstream investment. My own research has provided evidence from a series of interviews with institutional investors that indicated that the process of engagement in this area has become formalized (Solomon and Solomon, 2006). The interviews showed that engagement by institutional investors on social and environmental issues is evolving into a two-way process, with companies asking institutional fund managers questions as well as questions being directed toward companies by shareholders. As we saw in Chapter 5 engagement and dialogue between institutional investors and their investee companies now plays a major role in corporate governance. Such an investment strategy is equally important and effective for corporate governance in its broadest context, where it embraces corporate social responsibility. It is a more proactive approach for socially responsible investment than screening, as companies are pressured by their core investors to improve their social and environmental performance. Engagement represents a particularly important approach for index-tracking investors who cannot divest shares if they are dissatisfied with investee companies and, therefore, use engagement as a means of influencing company management.

As well as pressure from social and environmental lobby groups, the clients of investment institutions are also calling for their fund managers to engage on social and environmental issues. As mentioned earlier on p. 266, company reputation is significantly affected by risks in the social and environmental area and institutional investors want to pre-empt the negative effects of such risks materializing wherever possible. Where risks materialize, significant financial losses can be incurred and social and environmental risks become financial risks. Often, in such cases, the institutional fund managers can no longer rely on engagement with the investee company but eventually turn to selling shares. A salient example of ethical problems within a company becoming public knowledge and leading to mass divestment of the company's shares by institutional shareholders is the case of Huntingdon Life Sciences. Refer to Illustrations 10.1 and 10.2 for a full discussion of this case and its repercussions on shareholders and the company.

There is an ever-expanding range of issues covered by the remit of institutional investors' engagement on social and environmental issues. One of the most salient concerns at present is that of climate change. The response of the institutional investment community to the challenge of climate change is discussed in Illustration 10.4.

## Illustration 10.4

### The Role of Pension Fund Trustees in Climate Change

In 2005, three organizations collaborated to produce a report to guide pension fund trustees in understanding and addressing risks associated with climate change.[1] The report aimed to raise awareness among trustees about climate change with respect to their fiduciary duty. It also aimed to show trustees how to address climate change in their investment strategy decision (The Carbon Trust, 2005).

#### The Issue of Climate Change

Climate change is probably the most important environmental risk facing the human race. There is now consensus that human intervention, especially business activity, is leading to global warming, as a result of carbon emissions (greenhouse gases) from the burning of fossil fuels filling the atmosphere. In fact, dealing with climate change is quintessential to the survival of the planet and humanity. The Intergovernmental Panel on Climate Change (IPCC) was set up in 1988 to assess the situation for climate change. The IPCC estimates that by the end of the 21st century, global temperatures will have risen by 1.5 to 5.8 degrees centigrade. They predict changes such as the thawing of permafrost, declines of some plant and animal populations, earlier flowering of trees, emergence of insects and egg-laying in birds. These changes will accelerate as temperatures continue to rise. Sea levels will rise and weather patterns will become extreme. These events will lead to flooding, droughts and storms, which will have direct, unpredictable and possibly devastating consequences on life as we know it. But why is climate change an issue for institutional investors? In particular, why is it an issue for pension fund trustees?

#### Why Climate Change Matters to Pension Fund Trustees

As we have seen in previous chapters, institutional investment has the dominant role in influencing corporate activity in UK companies, as a result of ownership structure. Of institutional investors, pension funds are the largest, and most influential group, who can potentially engage with companies. Therefore, if climate change is raised as an issue for trustees, then they can integrate it into their investment strategy, fund managers will engage with companies on these issues and, hopefully, they will change their behaviour with respect to carbon emissions. As stated in the report,

[1] A group of organizations collaborated in 2005 to produce this report into trustees' duties and climate change, namely the Carbon Trust, Mercer Investment Consulting and the Institutional Investor Group on Climate Change (IIGCC). The Carbon Trust is an independent not-for-profit company established by the UK Government to lead low carbon technology and innovation within the public and private sectors in the UK. Mercer Investment Consulting are a leading global provider of investment consulting services. They are dedicated to developing intellectual capital related to socially responsible investment and the integration of ESG factors into investment processes. The IIGCC is a forum for collaboration between pension funds and other institutional investors on issues relating to climate change.

Considering that both the physical and mitigation-related policy impacts of climate change will influence the ability for companies to create and maintain wealth for shareholders ... pension trustees will want to ensure that these risks ... are being addressed in relation to the funds in their care

There is increasing evidence that climate change can constitute a material risk. For example, Innovest Strategic Value Advisors estimated that up to 5.1% of market capitalization could be at risk from climate change, and maybe far more than this.

In order to take climate change risk into account, the Carbon Trust (2005) report advises trustees to:

(i) Assess their understanding of climate change risk and determine whether or not it could have a material impact on the assets in their care.

(ii) Explore the current approach of the fund to check whether it reflects their policy regarding climate change risk.

(iii) Behave as an active owner, by encouraging fund managers to engage with companies on climate change risks, and by participating in the public policy debate.

Overall, the report leads the way for trustees to act as an important key to unlocking a way forward for tackling the problems of global warming.

*Climate Change and Shareholder Value*

Following their work on trustees and climate change, the Carbon Trust has focused its efforts on identifying ways in which climate change can actually impact on shareholder value (Carbon Trust, 2006). They developed a model and a methodology for analysing shareholder value at risk from climate change. The industries which had significant potential value at risk, according to the analysis, were the building materials and bulk commodity chemicals sectors. For building materials, the risk was mainly related to weather-linked construction delays. The implications of the study's findings for senior management and investors were as follows:

(i) Companies need to look beyond their own emissions and energy use in order to assess their sensitivity to climate change, as carbon emissions may be involved in raw material extraction for example.

(ii) Although climate change risk seems at first sight material, the risk can be mitigated by effective risk management.

(iii) Institutional investors need to ensure that climate change risk constitutes an important part on their agenda for dialogue and engagement with investee companies. They need to satisfy themselves that companies are managing climate change risks effectively within their internal control systems.

The recent report by Freshfields Bruckhaus Deringer (2005) concluded that shareholder engagement on ESG issues would be considered prudent from a legal perspective, as long as it is properly motivated, transparent, informed and objective. Indeed, they state that,

... targeted and constructive engagement would be acceptable (and in some cases mandatory) where it is aimed at improving the financial performance of an investment over the relevant time horizon, for example by encouraging better environmental accountability or more forward-thinking management.

(Freshfields Bruckhaus Deringer, 2005, pp. 100–101)

This clearly demonstrates that engagement and dialogue on social, ethical, environmental and governance issues are being actively encouraged as a mainstream component of contemporary institutional investment.

## Private social and environmental reporting: mythicizing or demythologizing reality?

Solomon and Darby (2005) explored whether or not private social and environmental reporting was mythicizing or demythologizing reality. In other words, was the dialogue between companies and their institutional investors breaking down barriers and misconceptions about social and environmental risks and impacts by business, or was it simply helping companies to create a myth that they were environmentally aware all the time? From a series of interviews, we found that companies and institutional investors seemed to be creating and disseminating a 'green' myth, which suggested to society that both companies and investors were proactively working toward improvements in social and environmental management.

## Pension fund trustees and socially responsible investment

You may recall that Chapter 5 discussed the complicated web of ownership that arises from the existence of pension funds. This ownership structure has important implications for corporate governance and control. A diagram showed the accountability relationships between companies and their shareholders, where the shareholder is in fact the member (client) of a pension fund (Figure 5.1). The intermediaries include the pension fund trustee who is responsible for the investment of the financial assets on behalf of the pension fund member. There is then also a fund manager, appointed by the trustee on behalf of the pension fund member, who manages the assets on a daily basis. From an agency theory perspective, it is difficult for the individual member of the pension fund to influence the investment strategy and decision making of the fund manager. Accountability from fund managers to their clients is an area where significant advances are required. The case of the University Superannuation Scheme (USS), however, does indicate that pension fund members can influence the strategic management of the fund. A group of university professors in accounting joined forces and have succeeded in recent years in pressuring the USS to adopt an umbrella socially responsible investment policy for the whole pension fund. Indeed, a specialist socially responsible investment manager has been appointed to the fund whose sole responsibility is to monitor the extent to which the fund's investments comply with socially responsible investment criteria. However, this is probably an exception. Public sector pension funds such as the USS are traditionally more interested in society's needs and are more likely to adopt a stakeholder-oriented approach than private sector pension funds (see Monks, 2001 for a full discussion of the role and responsibilities of private and public sector pension funds).

The interesting question is whether or not pension fund trustees have a responsibility to adopt a socially responsible investment policy for their pension funds? We can see from the complexity of pension fund share ownership that the pension fund trustee has ultimate responsibility for the way in which the pension fund is invested. It is the pension fund trustee who decides on the investment strategy and who makes the investment allocation decision – the proportion of the fund to be invested in different financial assets (e.g., what proportion should be invested in equity and debt). If a socially responsible investment strategy is to be implemented, it is the trustee who has to make that decision and instruct the fund managers to pursue this strategy. The fund managers are simply employed by the trustee to manage the fund's assets. However, trustees seem in many cases to pass the responsibilities of equity ownership to their fund managers, stating that such responsibility has been 'delegated' to the fund managers and arguing that they are the ones with the expertise in the field. However, many will now argue that this does not exonerate them of all ownership responsibilities. Monks (2001) makes the point that the trustees are the true owners of the pension fund's investee companies and as such should ensure that they act as 'responsible owners'. As you can see this is a controversial and very complicated area of finance and corporate governance. What emerges from current research is that the trustees themselves appear to be confused as to their role in corporate governance and especially in the area of socially responsible investment.

One issue that remains unresolved at the moment is the role of pension fund trustees in corporate governance and in socially responsible investment. Trustees are extremely important people as they are ultimately responsible for the way in which workers' pensions are invested. Whether or not people have money to live on in their retirement is a result of decisions made by trustees. However, the amount of funds invested by pension funds is immense and represents the idle balances of most people in the UK. This financial power can be used for good or can be simply invested for financial return. It is evident from the earlier discussion that people are uncomfortable about their money being invested in companies that do not act in a socially responsible manner. There is a growing consciousness in society that buying shares in unethical businesses represents tacit support for unethical business practices. This appears to be increasingly unacceptable in the world we live in. The question therefore is whether or not pension fund trustees have a responsibility to society (as well as to their pension fund members) to ensure that funds are invested in a socially responsible manner. However, even if pension fund trustees want to adopt a socially responsible investment policy for the pension fund, they are faced with a significant problem: their fiduciary duty.

Trustees are concerned about breaching their fiduciary duties. Legal cases have found trustees guilty of not pursuing financial returns to the exclusion of all other investment motives. Trustees can be liable if they invest according to any criterion other than shareholder wealth maximization – in their terms of reference, the maximization of pension receivables for the members of the pension funds. If socially responsible investment results in suboptimal levels of pension payments then it would be in breach of the trustees' fiduciary duties as an investment strategy. However, it may be considered that trustees hide behind their fiduciary duty, as Monks stated:

> Under the rubric of 'fiduciary duty' much is justified. The unexceptionable fiduciary
> requirement that trustees may consider 'solely' the interests of beneficiaries is

adduced to justify non-involvement in 'social' or 'political' investments. Activism is
dismissed as being unrelated to adding long-term value to the trust portfolio.

(Monks, 2001, p. 125)

This issue is very much a matter for debate at the moment and is very important to the
pension fund community.

The *Cowan v Scargill* legal case spread fear in the hearts of trustees on social
responsibility issues.[4] This was the first legal case where ethical investment was
considered. The case arose from the actions of the National Union of Mineworkers
(NUM) Pension Scheme. Arthur Scargill, the notorious (or heroic) leader of the NUM
decided that the fund should not invest in non-UK companies and should not invest in
such other areas of the energy sector as oil and gas. However, this strategy was not
adopted as there was substantial opposition from the trustee board. The main problem
with this sort of proposed investment strategy is that it restricts the investment universe.
As you will recall from the theoretical discussion in the last chapter, for optimum risk and
return combinations the diversification of an investment portfolio is essential. Any
restriction on investment choices due to an ethical (or other) investment policy restricts
the risk reduction potential from portfolio diversification. Such a policy is therefore
considered to contravene trustees' fiduciary duties as it makes the portfolio more risky
and therefore potentially less profitable for the pension fund members. The judge Sir
Robert Megarry concluded that, '... It is the duty of trustees, in the interest of
beneficiaries, to take advantage of the full range of investments authorised by the
terms of the trust, instead of resolving to narrow that range.'

However, this argument is not as valid for socially responsible investment now as it was
in previous years. The increasing use of best in sector investment approaches rather than
screening strategies has allowed institutional fund managers to invest ethically without
restricting their investment universe. This new investment approach has made socially
responsible investment available to a far wider range of investors.

The trustees' fiduciary duty to maximize pension fund return to investment is not the
only restriction on their behaviour. The activities of company pension schemes are
influenced to a great extent by the sponsoring company itself. The sponsoring company is
the company whose employees are members of the scheme. For example, Marks &
Spencer's (M&S) employees[5] are all members of the M&S Pension Scheme. M&S is the
sponsoring company. The trustees of the M&S pension scheme appoint an institutional
investment company. If the investment managers place too much pressure on companies

---

[4] A full discussion of this case can be found in Mansley (2000).

[5] As from March 2002 M&S decided to join many other companies in discontinuing final
salary pensions to new pension fund members. This is a trend that is currently sweeping
the pension market and is of great concern to most workers in the country. It does have
implications for socially responsible investment – if companies cannot afford to run basic
traditional pension schemes, how can they afford to take risks by experimenting with
socially responsible investment strategies? This is certainly one possible argument
against socially responsible investment.

to improve their performance (e.g., in the area of corporate social responsibility) through active engagement and dialogue, this could lead to companies turning against the investment managers. The sponsoring company may dismiss the fund manager as a result. It is not in the interests of the investment managers to lose clients, and they will therefore avoid any investment strategy that could upset relations with companies. This is a problem inherent in private sector pension funds due to their relationship with the sponsoring company, an issue discussed in Coffee (1991).

Sponsoring companies have also been affected by the new accounting regulation (FRS17) that forces them to disclose the details of their pension funds. In many cases (due in part to the slowdown in the stock market) corporate pension schemes have been making substantial losses in recent years. This is not something they relish revealing in their financial reports. A socially responsible investment policy may be seen as a further risk to pension fund performance that they would rather not take at present.

The discussion of the *Cowan v Scargill* case brings us back to the burning issue in socially responsible investment (and indeed in corporate governance), which has been made many times throughout this book. Does the adoption of a socially responsible investment policy lead to a reduction in investment return? In other words: Does ethical investment mean unprofitable investment? We have considered some empirical evidence from the academic literature that suggested in the main that socially responsible investment does not reduce financial returns. However, there is no definitive consensus on this subject. From interviews that I carried out, there was a strong feeling from the professional investment community that not only does socially responsible investment not reduce returns to investment, it can also improve investment return. By encouraging companies to act in a more socially responsible way they can instead perform better financially. By avoiding reputational risks arising from socially irresponsible behaviour (such as environmental incidents or human rights abuses) companies can ensure more stable profitability. Better corporate performance leads to higher share values and therefore to better financial returns from investment. This scenario is perhaps a Utopian view of the results of socially responsible investment, and it remains to be seen whether or not such a 'virtuous circle' effect will manifest itself in practice.

Another way of looking at the trustee's role in socially responsible investment is as follows. If socially responsible investment improves investment performance over the long term, then it would actually be in breach of trustees' fiduciary duties *not* to pursue a socially responsible investment strategy. This is a very different approach. Although a little revolutionary it seems to be the approach that is rapidly being adopted by many core financial institutions at present.

Emerging evidence from new research is indicating that this view may not be as revolutionary as previously thought. The recent report (Freshfields Bruckhaus Deringer, 2005) into the importance of environmental, social and governance factors for institutional investment has taken the considered view that the *Cowan v Scargill* case (discussed above) has had a misguided impact on trustee behaviour. Indeed, the report suggests that,

... *Cowan v Scargill* cannot be relied upon to support the single-minded pursuit of profit maximization, or indeed any general rule governing investment decision-making ... Megarry's decision has been distorted by commentators over time to support the view that it is unlawful for pension fund trustees to do anything but seek to maximize profits for their beneficiaries ... Read carefully, his decision stands for an uncontroversial position that trustees must act for the proper purpose of the trust, and not for extraneous purposes.

(Freshfields Bruckhaus Deringer, 2005, p. 9)

The report goes on to explain that the judge, Megarry, revisited his own judgement, asserting that the outcome of the case did not in any way support the view that the fiduciary duties of pension fund trustees were only consistent with profit maximization. Clearly, where the trustees' fiduciary investment powers are to achieve the best possible financial return for the clients of the fund, then that has to be the primary motivation underlying investment decisions. However, the report explains that there are two instances where environmental, social and governance considerations must be included as part of the institutional investor's fiduciary responsibilities. First, if there is a consensus among the fund beneficiaries that social, ethical, environmental and governance factors should be taken into account, then they must be included in the investment strategy, alongside other considerations.[6] Second, if the environmental, social and governance considerations are reasonably expected to have a material impact on the financial performance of the investment, then again these factors must be taken into account together with all other relevant considerations. Failure in either of these cases to incorporate such factors into the investment strategy would represent a breach in fiduciary duty. This approach alters the whole view of social responsibility and fiduciary duty.

The report (Freshfields Bruckhaus Deringer, 2005) describes several powerful reasons why the *Cowan v Scargill* case does not support the sole pursuit of financial return maximization, including:

- The case focused on a narrow issue and is thus limited to specific circumstances.

- Scargill represented himself, so there is no equality of argument.

- Technical legal points were not made as Scargill was not a lawyer.

- There was no proper discussion of the case.

- The trustees involved had an ulterior motive for their actions, supporting the failing coal industry.

- Scargill was thought not to have acted with integrity.

- The investment plan concerned had nothing in common with a modern ESG strategy.

---

[6] The problems of ascertaining a consensus among beneficiaries have, however, been acknowledged (Freshfields Bruckhaus Deringer, 2005).

From July 2000 all private occupation pension schemes have been subject to new pension fund regulation. Since then pension fund trustees have been required by law to disclose the extent to which (if at all) they apply socially responsible investment criteria to their pension fund. The Government had intended to introduce this regulation for a number of years. Why? This is the big question. It seems obvious that the Government feels that this sort of regulation could affect practice. It seems that they could only have introduced the regulation with the intention of encouraging further socially responsible investment. If the Government felt that socially responsible investment contradicted trustees' fiduciary duties, it is unlikely that they would have taken such steps. If socially responsible investment did conflict with trustees' duties, then it would be more likely that they pass a regulation making socially responsible investment illegal – this is not at all the case. Over the last decade the Government has been pressured by lobby groups to encourage corporate social responsibility and to improve social responsibility in all areas, as well as accountability.

It is quite possible that the recent requirement to disclose whether or not pension funds adopt a socially responsible investment policy will actually act as an incentive for trustees to adopt such a policy. They will probably be embarrassed to state in their statement of investment principles that they do not adopt any type of socially responsible investment policy, given current sentiment. A report by the ACCA on the wider aspects of risk considered that:

> This [the SRI disclosure requirement] affects several hundred billion pounds of pension assets and is likely to cause a number of major pension funds to require their fund managers to give much greater emphasis to these issues.
>
> (ACCA, 2000, p. 7)

Further, it has been suggested that the Pensions Act amendment had a substantial effect, as:

> This requirement [the SRI disclosure requirement] has had a significant and wide-ranging impact on the investment community. The majority of trustees have incorporated reference to social, ethical and environmental (SEE) issues in their annual statements in 2001. Most of them have delegated responsibility for implementing this to fund managers which has added significantly to the growing Socially Responsible Investment movement.
>
> (Cowe, 2001, p. 8)

Overall, it seems that by introducing the regulation the Government has succeeded in not only initiating further debate in the area, bringing socially responsible investment onto the agenda for pension funds but it has also encouraged pension fund trustees to adopt a socially responsible investment policy. Mathieu (2000) found, from surveying large and small pension funds, that shortly after the Government introduced the legislation over half had incorporated socially responsible investment factors into their investment decisions.

Some institutional fund managers, however, objected strongly and considered that such policies are a back door means of influencing the City.

It seems from the evidence that trustees are somewhat confused about their role in socially responsible investment. Trustees' views seem to vary strongly depending on a number of organizational factors. Socially responsible investment is an important issue and one that is unlikely to go away. Indeed, given recent changes in institutional investors' strategies and policies it is more likely that socially responsible investment will increase in coming years. It is vital that trustees are made more aware of their role and that discussions take place in order to clarify their responsibilities. However, as Myners (2001) concluded, trustees are in a responsible position and have ultimate decision-making power for institutional investment strategy. He qualified this by showing that they were generally untrained, unprepared for their role and unpaid. Mainly as a result of Myners' conclusions, trustees are under increasing pressure to gain training in financial affairs and to devote more time and energy to their role as trustees. Surely, with the mounting pressures on trustees, social responsibility will represent simply another problem that they have to deal with. It may be more than they can take on at present. This issue was discussed in Solomon et al. (2002d). One solution to this and other problems may be to increase trustee remuneration, which would help them to treat their role in a more professional manner, as discussed in Chapter 3.

The recent report by Freshfields Bruckhaus Deringer (2005)[7] on the relevance of ESG factors for pension fund managers and other institutional investors, arises from an in-depth piece of research into the impact of changes in pension fund regulation in a group of countries. Following the amendment to UK pension fund law forcing pension fund trustees to disclose the extent to which they operate a socially responsible investment policy, a number of countries have made similar changes to their legislation, namely Australia, France, Germany, Italy and the USA.

This research provides groundbreaking evidence that trustees should not only be taking account of social, ethical, environmental and governance issues in their investment strategy decisions, but that *they are in breach of their fiduciary duty if they do not*. The study stated that it aimed to help dispel the all-too-common misunderstanding that fiduciary responsibility is restricted by law, in a narrow sense, to seeking maximization of financial returns. Specifically, the research was required to respond to the question,

> Is the integration of environmental, social and governance issues into investment policy ... voluntarily permitted, legally required or hampered by law and regulation; primarily as regards public and private pension funds, secondarily as regards insurance company reserves and mutual funds?
>
> (Freshfields Bruckhaus Deringer, 2005, p. 6)

This question certainly represents a tall order for any piece of research to answer. In order to respond to this question, the research analysed the legal frameworks underlying

---

[7] Freshfields Bruckhaus Deringer (2005) produced this report at the behest of the Asset Management Working Group of the UNEP Finance Initiative.

institutional investment in France, Germany, Italy, Japan, Spain, the UK and the USA. Time horizon was an important issue for the research, as institutional investors taking a longer-term view are more likely to take account of environmental and social factors as these represent significant material risks over the long term.

Another important point raised by the Freshfields Bruckhaus Deringer report was that institutional investors (and companies) have tended to use the excuse that social, ethical and governance factors are not quantifiable and cannot therefore be taken into account in investment analysis and strategy. This view is clearly outdated, as,

> ... it is increasingly difficult for investment decision-makers to claim that ESG [environmental, social and governance] considerations are too difficult to quantify when they readily quantify business goodwill and other equivalently nebulous intangibles.
>
> (Freshfields Bruckhaus Deringer, 2005, p. 11)

Although the report admits that there is a diverse range of views among the international institutional investment community towards the incorporation of environmental, social and governance factors into investment, their report shows that socially responsible investment in the form of consideration of environmental, social and governance factors within the pension fund investment is growing.

# Socially responsible investment in an international context

Socially responsible investment is not solely a UK concern and is increasingly important at a global level. We consider below some countries where socially responsible investment is growing in importance.

*Socially responsible investment in the USA*
The USA is a strong advocate of socially responsible investment. It is considered that ethical investment originated in the USA among a number of church groups and grew in importance with public reaction to the Vietnam War in the 1970s. In 1992 over US$500 billion of US institutional investment was invested accorded to some level of social screening. The latest figures indicate that more than $2 trillion (about 13 %) of all US investment follows socially responsible criteria. Indeed, growth of socially responsible investment in recent years has been exponential. A 1999 report by the Social Investment Forum in the USA found that, since 1997, total assets under management in screened portfolios rose 183 %. Another sign of the growing importance of socially responsible investment in the USA has been the development of the Domini 400 Social Index (DSI), used as a benchmark for measuring the performance of socially responsible portfolios. It includes the shares of 400 companies that have satisfied a multitude of social screens. From May 1990 to September 1992 the DSI was found to outperform the S&P500. The conclusion at that time was that socially responsible investing could produce higher

returns than investment without social constraints but that these returns were riskier. Guerard (1996) found that there was no significant difference between the average monthly returns of US funds that were screened according to socially responsible criteria and those that were not for the period 1987 to 1994. Further, Guerard (1997) extended his earlier work and found no significant difference in the mean returns of socially unscreened and screened investment funds between 1987 and 1996. He took the implications of his findings further by suggesting that social screens may be a signal of better management and the generation of higher financial returns. Also, Kessler and Gottsman (1998) compared the total financial returns of companies in the S&P500 over a number of years with a series of subsets of the S&P500 over the same period. Environmental performance indicators were used as the basis for selecting the various subsets analysed, and those companies with apparently better environmental performance showed a slightly higher return than the overall return of the S&P500 companies as a whole.

Freshfields Bruckhaus Deringer (2005) explain that there is an ongoing debate in the USA concerning the consideration of ESG factors in investment decision-making in relation to the 'prudent investor rule'.[8] The current view in the US institutional investment community seems to be that ESG considerations may be incorporated into investment strategy, provided that they are pursued for genuine reasons and that they do not compromise the return to investment.

### Socially responsible investment in Canada

Several years ago 60 Canadian companies were chosen to constitute Canada's first index comprising 'socially responsible' companies (*The Economist*, 1 June 2000) called the Jantzi Social Index (after Michael Jantzi who developed it). The aim of the Index was to encourage managers to incorporate social and environmental considerations in their business decision making. The DSI screens out companies involved in tobacco, alcohol, gambling, weapons or nuclear power generation, whereas the new Jantzi does not screen out alcohol or gambling companies. Similarly, it does not exclude mining companies and forestry – as these represent the backbone of Canada's industrial activities. The index therefore represents a compromise, as the Jantzi is adopting the new 'best in class' approach, already evident in socially responsible investment funds in the UK.

Freshfields Bruckhaus Deringer (2005) explained that there is little common law jurisprudence regarding pension fund investment in Canada, with trustees being only bound to duty of care in the same way as any other investor. Canada tends to refer to the

---

[8] The US prudent investor rule states that trustees should 'observe how men of prudence, discretion and intelligence manage their own affairs not only in regard to speculation, but in regard to the permanent disposition of their funds, considering the probable outcome, as well as the probable safety of the capital to be invested' (*Harvard College v Amory*, 26 Mass. (9 Pick.) 446 (1830)). The rule has been updated recently to incorporate modern portfolio theory and to merge it with duties applicable to trustees such as loyalty and diversification (Freshfields Bruckhaus Deringer, 2005).

*Cowan v Scargill* case as a reference point for trustee responsibilities. This, as we have seen from the earlier discussion, has had misleading repercussions for socially responsible investment. Although there is currently no legislation encouraging trustees to take ESG issues into account, some pension funds have included these issues within the context of profit maximization, for example the Ontario Municipal Employees Retirement System (OMERS) and the Ontario Teachers' Pension Plan Board. Further, the state of Manitoba has amended pension fund law to specify that pursuit of ESG factors in investment strategy does not represent a breach of fiduciary duty.

*Socially responsible investment in Australia*
Research indicates that socially responsible investment is financially viable in Australia. Indeed, Knowles (1997) found that there were over $200 million invested in Australian socially responsible investment funds. Further, Spiller (1997) showed that financial returns from portfolios invested according to socially responsible criteria could be just as high as from conventional investment portfolios. Further, a large institutional investor, Australian Ethical Investment Ltd, which currently manages over $40 million states that it can offer investors competitive financial returns from four different socially responsible unit trusts. Of these unit trusts, one has returned 7.6% per year, while another has returned 8.3% per year.

Despite this evidence, traditionally, Australian fund managers have considered that socially responsible investment is incompatible with fiduciary duty. The report by Freshfields Bruckhaus Deringer (2005) indicated that Australia has been slower than the USA, for example, in embracing and integrating ESG issues into portfolio investment. This has, in their view, led to relatively slow growth of ESG in Australia. Factors which have hindered the growth of socially responsible investment have been: confusion over what constitutes ESG factors; a perception that socially responsible investment leads to underperformance; confusion as to whether ESG investment is consistent with fiduciary duty; and, lack of demand from fund beneficiaries. Despite this, Australia's first corporate social responsibility index was introduced in 2004, which includes 150 top companies (Corporate Governance Update, July, 2004).

*Socially responsible investment in continental Europe*
Butz and Blattner (1999) examined the hypothesis that, by adopting environmentally and socially responsible business practices, companies can achieve a higher than market return. The study compared the financial performance of 65 European securities over a two-year period with measures of their environmental and social performance. They found a significant positive correlation between environmental and financial performance but not between social and financial performance. However, they concluded that overall socially responsible investment should provide rates of return at least as high as those provided by traditional equity investment.

The issue of integrating of environmental, social and governance factors into investment decision-making has been aired in relation to sustainable development and corporate social responsibility at a European level. Indeed, the European Commission has endorsed socially responsible investment as an important instrument for encouraging corporate social responsibility (Freshfields Bruckhaus Deringer, 2005). The work of the European Social Investment Forum (Eurosif), for example, has helped to promote the importance and value of socially responsible investment to the international institutional investment community. Eurosif is a European, non-profit organization aiming to inform, educate and provide a European forum for debate on sustainable and socially responsible financial services. The relevance of ESG factors to business has also been highlighted at the European level by the work of CSR Europe, a European business network.

*Socially responsible investment in Japan*
In the last couple of years socially responsible investment has become an issue in Japan and other East Asian countries. The Japanese have been shocked by a number of cases of unethical business practice, and the investment institutions in Japan have now reacted by taking some account of social and environmental issues in their portfolio investment decisions. Instances of meat contaminated with BSE (commonly referred to as 'mad cow disease') being passed off to customers have been highlighted in the media across Japan. The growth of socially responsible investment in Japan is outlined in Solomon et al. (2003c).

Unlike the UK, the USA, Australia and Canada, Japan is a civil law country. This means that law does not depend on cases such as the *Cowan v Scargill* case. Trust law in Japan stipulates that trustees have a 'duty of loyalty' to carry out their responsibilities in good faith on behalf of their beneficiaries and to avoid conflicts of interest (Freshfields Bruckhaus Deringer, 2005). At present, there is no legislation encouraging ESG issues to be integrated into institutional investment. Indeed, the extremely complicated laws relating to various forms of institutional investment tend to hamper rather than encourage socially responsible investment. There is currently an intention to amend legislation relating to institutional investment, but the proposed amendment does not involve integrating ESG issues into the investment decision. Despite progress, the evaluation by Freshfields Bruckhaus Deringer (2005) concludes that the ESG discourse in Japan is in its very early stages. This, they consider, is because the investment market is dominated by the profit maximization incentive, with only the mutual funds industry starting to discuss ESG issues.

Solomon, Solomon and Suto (2004) reviewed the growth of socially responsible investment in Japan, comparing it with the UK experience., They acknowledged that the legal framework surrounding portfolio investment in Japan represented a significant impediment to these potential routes for more effective socially responsible investment.

*Socially responsible investment in South Africa*
South Africa established its first socially responsible investment index in 2004. The initiative arose from collaboration between the FTSE Group and the Johannesburg Securities Exchange. Specifically relevant issues which will be considered include black empowerment, labour standards, HIV reporting and stakeholders dialogue (Corporate Governance Update, October, 2004). South Africa has been prominent in the way the

country has incorporated stakeholder and accountability issues into corporate governance through the two King Reports, and the development of this new index bears witness to the country's commitment to corporate social responsibility.

## Chapter summary

This chapter has outlined the growth of socially responsible investment. The discussion has shown that there is growing evidence in the academic and professional literature that socially responsible investment is no longer marginal but has become a mainstream strategy implemented by UK institutional investors across the board. Specifically, the chapter has examined the drivers of socially responsible investment, showing that they are mainly situated outside the financial community. The problems faced by pension funds if they choose to implement a socially responsible investment strategy, due to their obligation to fulfil their fiduciary duty, have been raised. However, having provided some evidence that socially responsible investment may enhance, rather than reduce, investment return, the suggestion that trustees should adopt socially responsible investment in order to fulfil their fiduciary duty may have a genuine empirical foundation. Indeed, the recent report from Freshfields Bruckhaus Deringer (2005) provides strong evidence to support this suggestion. The most important aspect of this chapter has been to demonstrate that the institutional investment community, as well as the corporate community (as discussed in Chapter 9) are embracing issues of social and environmental accountability. Indeed, the recent evolution of terminology from SEE (social, ethical and environmental) to ESG (environmental, social and governance) factors shows that social and environmental issues are now being integrated into the heart of corporate governance concerns for the institutional investment community. This represents a deep change in the attitudes of business and financial institutions toward social responsibility, endorsing a broader remit for corporate governance than that encapsulated by pure agency theory. We can see from the discussion in Part III, that a broader agenda for corporate governance, which embraces a stakeholder theory approach, may no longer be viewed as inconsistent with value creation in the long run. As discussed in Chapter 1, the gulf between a shareholder and a stakeholder approach to corporate governance may be less exaggerated than has been considered in the past.

## Questions for reflection and discussion

1   The new socially responsible investment disclosure requirement for pension fund trustees has had a substantial impact on trustees' attitudes towards, and practice of, socially responsible investment. This impact is, through a virtuous circle effect, likely to lead to increased corporate social responsibility. Explain and discuss the above statement with reference to the findings of academic papers and other published sources that you have read.

**2** Investigate one of the following cases: Nike, Huntingdon Life Science, Shell and Brent Spar; or BP and renewable energy. Discuss the implications of these cases for the socially responsible investment movement. Did they have a positive or a negative impact on the attitudes of institutional investors toward socially responsible investment?

**3** Spend some time developing your own diagrammatic image of the links between socially responsible investment, corporate social responsibility and the potential impact of socially responsible investment. Is yours a virtuous or a vicious circle?

**4** Do you think that the institutional investment community will take an increasing interest in socially responsible investment? Or do you think socially responsible investment is a fashionable trend that will be dismissed in the near future?

**5** Do you agree with the findings of the Freshfields Bruckhaus Deringer (2005) report? Do you think their findings set the scene for a completely new direction in pension fund investment at an international level?

**6** To what extent do you think companies within the FTSE4Good are benefiting from their inclusion in these SRI benchmarking indices? Refer to the report by Cobb et al. (2005).

# Chapter 11

# Future directions for corporate governance and accountability

In this book I have attempted to show how corporate governance has evolved in recent times into a discipline in its own right. Part I discussed the fall of the US giant Enron as well as the failure of Parmalat, the 'European Enron', and showed how these cases of corporate governance failure focused global attention on corporate governance issues. The text then analysed the process of corporate governance reform that has taken place in the UK over the last decade, paying special attention to the series of codes of practice and policy documents that this process has generated. The focus was on the UK system of corporate governance, showing that the traditional separation of ownership and control, on which agency theory was constructed, has been transformed in recent times into a system characterized by institutional ownership concentration. Specifically, the growth in institutional ownership and the recognition that institutional investors need to acknowledge their power and responsibility in society has been a driving force in this transformation. Institutional investors are no longer passive shareholders but have become active drivers of corporate governance reform. In an agency theory framework, institutional investors have been transformed from shareholders whose existence engendered agency problems to a corporate governance mechanism, efficient at monitoring company management, thereby solving agency problems to a certain extent.

Part II explored the diversity of corporate governance systems around the world. The categorization of systems into the insider and outsider models was examined. Further, the concept of a global convergence in corporate governance was introduced. I then used a selection of countries to illustrate the wide range of different corporate governance systems around the world, the many factors determining these traditional systems and the gradual transformation of these systems due to a worldwide agenda for corporate governance reform.

Part III showed that companies are concerned increasingly not just with their shareholders' demands but also with the needs of a wide range of stakeholders. Company directors are discharging accountability to shareholding and non-shareholding stakeholders through the disclosure process and through stakeholder engagement programmes. There is a gradual broadening of the corporate governance agenda, characterized by a move away from a narrow agency theory view toward a broader, stakeholder-oriented view that embraces concepts of corporate social responsibility and sustainability.

In summary, this book has attempted to cover corporate governance on a number of levels. First, the text summarizes the historical development of corporate governance initiatives in a global context, but with an emphasis on UK corporate governance reform. Second, the impact of corporate governance failures, especially those of Enron and Parmalat are used to endorse a growing need for corporate governance reform. Thirdly, and despite the risk of sounding somewhat evangelical, this book attempts to highlight the importance of accountability and ethics within the corporate governance framework. The overarching aim in this regard is to demonstrate that these factors contribute to a goal of long-term financial prosperity and do not detract from it. 'Good', socially responsible finance and business are synonymous with 'good' financial performance.

The question for discussion in this last chapter is therefore: *Where do we go from here?* A number of issues are considered below, including: the future path for institutional investor activism, the future route for corporate governance from a global perspective and ways in which a broader agenda for corporate governance may continue to develop. Lastly, I explore the question of whether corporate governance reform has gone too far, or whether it has not gone far enough, providing a personal viewpoint on the future direction for corporate governance initiatives.

### The future of institutional investor activism
It is clear from the evidence presented in this book that institutional investors are no longer passive, back-seat owners of companies. They can no longer ignore their responsibilities as shareholders. In the UK the investment institutions have realized that passive shareholding is not the route to shareholder wealth maximization. The actions of LENS and California Public Employees' Retirement System (CalPERS) in the USA and Hermes in the UK *inter alia* have shown that active shareholding and involvement in investee companies is financially rewarding. This type of instrumental ethics approach is a way of owning shares ethically and satisfying obligations to the ultimate beneficiaries of investment. Increasing shareholder activism (e.g., in the area of directors' remuneration) is clearly a case of ethical activism, as excessive remuneration is an ethical as well as a financial issue. Institutional investors through portfolio investment are discharging an accountability first and foremost to their own clients but also to society as a whole. The free rider effect of their activism applies not only to all shareholders but also to society. Indeed, the writing of Monks (2001) and Sparkes (2002) *inter alia* has set a clear ethical agenda for institutional investors. From the discussion in Chapters 9 and 10 institutional investors have a clear mandate to grasp the nettle of socially responsible investment and corporate social responsibility. As owners of listed companies in the UK and around the world they need to act as socially responsible owners, satisfying the needs of a broad range of stakeholders as well as seeking maximum returns to investment for shareholders. It is vital that the trust in financial institutions that has been so sorely dented by recent scandals in the financial and corporate communities is restored. It is only by embracing greater shareholder activism and socially responsible investment that financial institutions can recapture

this trust. Society needs to see change continuing. Without change, fewer and fewer people will choose to pay into a private pension or invest in the stock market, and capitalism as we know it today could decline immeasurably. The new report by Freshfields, Bruckhaus and Deringer provides a solid mandate for pension funds and especially their trustees, to adopt a socially responsible investment policy. Consideration of environmental, social and governance, 'ESG', factors is becoming an essential element of institutional investment.

Another area where improvements are clearly needed is in the accountability of institutional investors to their clients. The disclosure by institutional fund managers to their clients, who are the ultimate shareholders, is not standardized and is generally not public. It is difficult for clients to influence their institutional fund managers. However, there have been growing calls from clients for greater shareholder activism by their institutional fund holders. This should continue to grow, with pension fund members, for example, receiving more transparent and understandable information from their fund managers on a regular basis.

## A global convergence in corporate governance

One of the most important issues for corporate governance is the extent to which harmonization in corporate governance standards will genuinely be achieved at an international level. Chapter 7 considered the possibility that countries may be moving toward a global convergence in corporate governance as well as toward some of the initiatives aimed at international harmonization of corporate governance, such as the OECD (1999; 2004) Principles. At the moment, the future is uncertain, although there is increasing evidence that corporate governance standardization at a global level is desirable, in order to increase cross-border institutional investment and to reduce costs of capital for multinational companies.

As some of the cases in Chapter 8 demonstrated, reform may be taking place around the world, but in many cases improvements may only be skin deep. In many cases, change has been instigated too quickly, as a knee-jerk reaction to events such as the 1997 Asian Crisis or the collapse of Enron. If reform is desirable, it needs to take place as part of a long-term strategy, rather than in the context of a quick fix. Ultimately, it remains to be seen whether countries' systems of corporate governance will harmonize their standards in line with the Anglo-Saxon model of corporate governance or whether a different, more individualistic model will be chosen. There is certainly a danger at present of Anglo-American-style governance being grafted onto corporate governance systems around the world, when the roots are not in place to support this model. There is a danger that countries with extremely different traditional styles of governance will be engulfed by a tide of market-oriented initiatives that may not be appropriate for their legal frameworks, their economies, their individual markets and their culture. A clear policy recommendation that arises naturally from this discussion is for governments and policy makers around the world to look carefully at the eventual model they would like to see in their countries, before leaping into an inappropriate system and embracing a model that is not sustainable over the long term.

*A continuing broadening of the corporate governance agenda*

Throughout this book there has been a focus on the broadening agenda for corporate governance. The text has provided plenty of evidence that companies are embracing a broader approach to corporate governance by discharging accountability to a wider range of stakeholders. Further, institutional investors are encouraging corporate social responsibility though active socially responsible investment strategies of engagement and dialogue with their investee companies. This raises the question: Are we really moving towards a more accountable, socially responsible world? Perhaps corporate governance reform, corporate social responsibility and socially responsible investment are all signs that a moral consensus is forming around a more ethical approach to business. However, the continuing voluntary nature of social and environmental reporting remains a cause for concern. It is clear from the discussion in Part III that recent research has revealed a market failure in the area of social and environmental information. Some level of standardization of social and environmental reporting seems overdue. Companies need guidance on the type and form of information that their shareholders and other stakeholders require. Similarly, shareholders and other stakeholders require information that is standardized and therefore comparable for accountability and decision-making purposes. Even if there is to be no mandatory disclosure, which is looking unlikely in the current environment given the views expressed in the recent review of company law, it may still be possible to issue a policy document, similar in strength to corporate governance documents, such as the Higgs Report (2003) and the Turnbull Report (1999), which focus specifically on corporate accountability in the social and environmental domain. Unless a more formalized approach is adopted in this area, massive resources will be wasted by shareholders and stakeholders, who will continue to seek information on social and environmental issues by other means, given the unreliability of the public disclosure process. The abolition of the mandatory Operating and Financial Review has, as we saw from Chapter 6, dealt a heavy blow for hopes that social and environmental reporting would become part of mandatory narrative disclosure.

A more radical way of furthering social and environmental accountability arises naturally from the Higgs Report. Higgs' recommendations for one non-executive director in every listed company to assume the role of a senior independent director, or SID, who should represent shareholders' interests, could be extended to embrace social responsibility. Perhaps one non-executive director could take on the role of championing the interests of non-shareholding stakeholders (e.g., employees, local communities, environmental concerns). Higgs pointed out that there was little connection between non-executive directors and institutional investors. There is likely to be far less connection between non-executive directors and other stakeholders. This is a radical suggestion but one that could help companies to achieve greater stakeholder accountability by improving the board's understanding and appreciation of stakeholder concerns. It may be a more direct and more effective means of furthering stakeholder accountability than the process of stakeholder engagement which, as we have shown, has been criticized heavily for falling short of genuine improvements to stakeholder accountability. At present, it is highly unlikely that non-executive directors are involved in companies' programmes of stakeholder engagement. Perhaps encouraging one of the non-executive directors to attend meetings between the company and various stakeholder groups would be an effective means of improving corporate accountability within a broader corporate governance agenda. However, this suggestion is likely to be met with strong reactions from corporate lobby groups. If they considered a SID would be divisive by introducing different objectives to the boardroom, this suggestion would be explosive.

*Has corporate governance reform gone too far? Or has it gone far enough?*
This book has attempted to show why corporate governance is *the system of checks and balances, both internal and external to companies, that ensures that companies discharge their accountability to all their stakeholders and act in a socially responsible way in all areas of their business activity.* As we saw in Chapter 8 the South African King Report (2002) drew a distinction between accountability to shareholders and responsibility to stakeholders, which seemed to lessen any impact the report may have on corporate social responsibility. Nevertheless, I feel that the approach embodied in the report carries the most forward-looking and progressive approach to corporate governance adopted by any code of practice. The Report summarized its philosophy as follows:

> ... successful governance in the 21st century requires companies to adopt an *inclusive and not an exclusive approach.* The company must be open to institutional activism and there must be greater emphasis on the sustainable or non-financial aspects of its performance. *Boards must apply the tests of fairness, accountability, responsibility and transparency to all acts or omissions and be accountable to the company but also responsive and responsible towards the company's identified stakeholders.*
>
> (King Report, 2002, p. 19, emphasis added)

This corporate governance policy document is admirable in its attempt to address a genuine stakeholder approach to corporate governance. The extent to which this approach is operationalized by boards of directors remains to be seen. It is not an unrealistic expectation that countries around the world will incorporate a similar approach to corporate governance and social responsibility in their core principles and codes of practice. Furthermore, voluntary codes of practice need to be accompanied by an agenda for modernizing company law, which attempts to support and encourage a broader, more inclusive system of corporate governance at a global level.

The last decade has witnessed vast changes in the definition and remit of corporate governance in the UK and around the world. The question is, therefore, *has corporate governance gone too far or has it gone far enough?*

On a cosmetic level, there has been a proliferation of codes, policy documents and corporate governance guidelines but this is superficial unless they are taken on in spirit. Taking a broad view of what corporate governance is, leads us to the question of whether the ongoing agenda for corporate governance reform has had a genuine impact on accountability and especially on accountability to a broad group of stakeholders. All the rhetoric has to be founded in a genuine desire by directors, managers and institutions to pursue greater accountability and transparency.

Corporate governance entails far more than adherence to sets of principles and codes of practice. Good corporate governance requires manage and investors to take the codes to heart. Corporate governance in the 21st century is about human behaviour and the role of business in society. It is about ethics and accountability. In relation to ethics, the law may be seen to represent the lowest common denominator, with ethics involving far more than simply respecting the law:

> Ethical conduct by financial market participants is often thought of as being synonymous with not breaking the law. But ethical conduct is more than not being crooked. That is why ethics exists, to help us decide what is right and what is good.
>
> (Freshfields Bruckhaus Deringer, 2005, p. 3, Foreword)

In the same way, corporate governance is about far more than compliance. Codes of practice represent the lowest common denominator for good corporate governance. Good corporate governance is far broader than all the current rhetoric implies. Corporate governance is about a deep change in attitude. It is about the way in which businesses are run and the way in which they relate to their principal stakeholders. It is about engagement and dialogue. It is about restoring and maintaining trust in society and confidence in institutions and companies.

Corporate governance is not about box-ticking and boilerplate disclosures. It is about meaningful, quality reporting and transparency. As Sir Adrian Cadbury emphasized in 1992, corporate governance is about complying 'in spirit'. Corporate governance is not about the single-minded pursuit of shareholder value. It is not merely about monitoring directors and introducing independence in the boardroom, in an agency theory framework. Corporate governance is not just about identifying the occasional 'bad apple' or deviant individual.

In these respects, although significant progress has been made, corporate governance has not gone far enough. As we have seen from discussions throughout this text, the institutional investment community is more active, but the resources being channelled into activism are insufficient for the job in hand. The abolition of the mandatory Operating and Financial Review represented a backward step in underpinning the importance of social and environmental reporting, *inter alia*.

Do we have any evidence that change is under way? A significant emerging trend in UK corporate governance is the recent move towards a more reflexive, self-evaluative corporate community. As we have seen from the emerging issues discussed in this text, companies are being asked to produce governance reporting and risk reporting which evaluates board performance in the areas of corporate governance and internal control. Cosmetic disclosures simply summarizing compliance and areas of non-compliance with codes of practice are no longer acceptable. Boards of directors are being called upon by investors to evaluate their own performance, to consider whether they are improving governance and internal control. They are then being asked to disclose their reflections.

This is a very new and revolutionary way of reporting. It does not simply represent a move towards more forward-looking disclosure, but rather involves reflection and evaluation of processes and performance, communicating the results of these analyses to stakeholders. This may represent the beginnings of a genuine, meaningful dialogue between companies and their external constituencies. This may represent the emergence of more genuine accountability and stakeholder inclusion. Or it may not. Only time will tell.

We have, on the face of it, good corporate governance structures and processes in place in the UK, the USA and elsewhere, yet momentous corporate collapses continue to occur, in an unexpected way. Why? Surely if codes of practice were enough and the corporate governance mechanisms in place were adequate to act as monitoring tools, then such examples of corporate failure would not occur. Evidently, codes are not enough. They are essential in establishing an effective framework for corporate governance and it should never be argued that codes, principles and guidelines are unnecessary. But they are not enough on their own. There needs to be a genuine change among the actors in corporate governance. Boards, institutional investors need to take the codes to heart and comply in spirit.

As a final reflection, environmental, social and governance issues are rapidly becoming not just a concern for long-term shareholder value but can now affect value in the short term, or instantaneously, where sudden events occur, thanks to the all-pervasive impact of the media. The recent arguments supporting a more stakeholder-oriented approach to business have been founded on a belief that social, environmental and governance issues affect long-term performance. If they are beginning to be material in relation to short-term performance then their inclusion and consideration becomes far more urgent.

# Appendix A

# The Combined Code on Corporate Governance (July 2003)

## Preamble

1.  This Code supersedes and replaces the Combined Code issued by the Hampel Committee on Corporate Governance in June 1998. It derives from a review of the role and effectiveness of non-executive directors by Derek Higgs and a review of audit committees by a group led by Sir Robert Smith.

2.  The Financial Services Authority has said that it will replace the 1998 Code that is annexed to the Listing Rule with the revised Code and will seek to make consequential Rule changes. There will be consultation on the necessary Rule changes but no further consultation on the Code provisions themselves.

3.  It is intended that the new Code will apply for reporting years beginning on or after 1 November 2003.

4.  The Code contains main and supporting principles and provisions. The existing Listing Rules require listed companies to make a disclosure statement in two parts in relation to the Code. In the first part of the statement, the company has to report on how it applies the principles in the Code. In future this will need to cover both main and supporting principles. The form and content of this part of the statement are not prescribed, the intention being that companies should have a free hand to explain their governance policies in the light of the principles, including any special circumstances applying to them which have led to a particular approach. In the second part of the statement the company has either to confirm that it complies with the Code's provisions or – where it does not – to provide an explanation. This 'comply or explain' approach has been in operation for over 10 years, and the flexibility it offers has been widely welcomed both by company boards and by investors. It is for shareholders and others to evaluate the company's statement.

5.        While it is expected that listed companies will comply with the Code's provisions most of the time, it is recognized that departure from the provisions of the Code may be justified in particular circumstances. Every company must review each provision carefully and give a considered explanation if it departs from the Code provisions.

6.        Smaller listed companies, in particular those new to listing, may judge that some of the provisions are disproportionate or less relevant in their case. Some of the provisions do not apply to companies below FTSE 350. Such companies may nonetheless consider that it would be appropriate to adopt the approach in the Code and they are encouraged to consider this. Investment companies typically have a different board structure, which may affect the relevance of particular provisions.

7.        While recognizing that directors are appointed by shareholders who are the owners of companies, it is important that those concerned with the evaluation of governance should do so with common sense in order to promote partnership and trust, based on mutual understanding. They should pay due regard to companies' individual circumstances and bear in mind in particular the size and complexity of the company and the nature of the risks and challenges it faces. While shareholders have every right to challenge companies' explanations if they are unconvincing, they should not be evaluated in a mechanistic way and departures from the Code should not be automatically treated as breaches. Institutional shareholders and their agents should be careful to respond to the statements from companies in a manner that supports the 'comply or explain' principle. As the principles in Section 2 make clear, institutional shareholders should carefully consider explanations given for departure from the Code and make reasoned judge-ments in each case. They should put their views to the company and be prepared to enter a dialogue if they do not accept the company's position. Institutional shareholders should be prepared to put such views in writing where appropriate.

8.        Nothing in this Code should be taken to override the general requirements of law to treat shareholders equally in access to information.

9.        This publication includes guidance on how to comply with particular parts of the Code: first, *Internal Control: Guidance for Directors on the Combined Code*, produced by the Turnbull Committee, which relates to Code provisions on internal control (C.2 and part of C.3 in the Code); and, second, *Audit Committees: A Report and Proposed Guidance*, produced by the Smith Group, which relates to the provisions on audit committees and auditors (C.3 of the Code). In both cases, the guidance suggests ways of applying the relevant Code principles and of complying with the relevant Code provisions.

10.    In addition, this volume also includes suggestions for good practice from the Higgs Report.

11.    The revised Code does not include material in the previous Code on the disclosure of directors' remuneration. This is because 'The Directors' Remuneration Report Regulations 2002' are now in force and supersede the earlier Code provisions. These require the directors of a company to prepare a remuneration report. It is important that this report is clear, transparent and understandable to shareholders.

## Code of best practice

**Section 1    Companies**

*A*          *Directors*

*A.1*        *The board*

MAIN PRINCIPLE

**Every company should be headed by an effective board, which is collectively responsible for the success of the company.**

SUPPORTING PRINCIPLES

The board's role is to provide entrepreneurial leadership of the company within a framework of prudent and effective controls which enables risk to be assessed and managed. The board should set the company's strategic aims, ensure that the necessary financial and human resources are in place for the company to meet its objectives and review management performance. The board should set the company's values and standards and ensure that its obligations to its shareholders and others are understood and met. All directors must take decisions objectively in the interests of the company. As part of their role as members of a unitary board, non-executive directors should constructively challenge and help develop proposals on strategy. Non-executive directors should scrutinize the performance of management in meeting agreed goals and objectives and monitor the reporting of performance. They should satisfy themselves on the integrity of financial information and that financial controls and systems of risk management are robust and defensible. They are responsible for determining appropriate levels of remuneration of executive directors and have a prime role in appointing, and where necessary removing, executive directors and in succession planning.

CODE PROVISIONS

A.1.1    The board should meet sufficiently regularly to discharge its duties effectively. There should be a formal schedule of matters specifically reserved for its decision. The annual report should include a statement of how the board operates, including a high-level statement of which types of decisions are to be taken by the board and which are to be delegated to management.

A.1.2    The annual report should identify the chairman, the deputy chairman (where there is one), the chief executive, the senior independent director and the chairmen and members of the nomination, audit and remuneration committees. It should also set out the number of meetings of the board and those committees and individual attendance by directors.

A.1.3    The chairman should hold meetings with the non-executive directors without the executives present. Led by the senior independent director, the non-executive directors should meet without the chairman present at least annually to appraise the chairman's performance (as described in A.6.1) and on such other occasions as are deemed appropriate.

A.1.4    Where directors have concerns which cannot be resolved about the running of the company or a proposed action, they should ensure that their concerns are recorded in the board minutes. On resignation, a non-executive director should provide a written statement to the chairman, for circulation to the board, if they have any such concerns.

A.1.5    The company should arrange appropriate insurance cover in respect of legal action against its directors.


A.2    *Chairman and chief executive*

MAIN PRINCIPLE

**There should be a clear division of responsibilities at the head of the company between the running of the board and the executive responsibility for the running of the company's business. No one individual should have unfettered powers of decision.**

SUPPORTING PRINCIPLE

The chairman is responsible for leadership of the board, ensuring its effectiveness on all aspects of its role and setting its agenda. The chairman is also responsible for ensuring that the directors receive accurate, timely and clear information. The chairman should ensure effective communication with shareholders. The chairman should also facilitate the effective contribution of non-executive directors in particular and ensure constructive relations between executive and non-executive directors.

CODE PROVISIONS

A.2.1    The roles of chairman and chief executive should not be exercised by the same individual. The division of responsibilities between the chairman and chief executive should be clearly established, set out in writing and agreed by the board.

A.2.2    The chairman should on appointment meet the independence criteria set out in A.3.1 below. A chief executive should not go on to be chairman of the same company. If exceptionally a board decides that a chief executive should become chairman, the board should consult major shareholders in advance and should set out its reasons to shareholders at the time of the appointment and in the next annual report.


A.3    *Board balance and independence*

MAIN PRINCIPLE

**The board should include a balance of executive and non-executive directors (and in particular independent non-executive directors) such that no individual or small group of individuals can dominate the board's decision taking.**

SUPPORTING PRINCIPLES

The board should not be so large as to be unwieldy. The board should be of sufficient size that the balance of skills and experience is appropriate for the requirements of the business and that changes to the board's composition can be managed without undue disruption. To ensure that power and information are not concentrated in one or two individuals, there should be a strong presence on the board of both executive and non-executive directors. The value of ensuring that committee membership is refreshed and that undue reliance is not placed on particular individuals should be taken into account in deciding chairmanship and membership of committees. No one other than the committee chairman and members is entitled to be present at a meeting of the nomination, audit or remuneration committee, but others may attend at the invitation of the committee.

CODE PROVISIONS

A.3.1    The board should identify in the annual report each non-executive director it considers to be independent. The board should determine whether the director is independent in character and judgement and whether there are relationships or circumstances which are likely to affect, or could appear to affect, the director's judgement. The board should state its reasons if it determines that a director is independent notwithstanding the existence of relationships or circumstances which may appear relevant to its determination, including if the director:

— has been an employee of the company or group within the last five years;
— has, or has had within the last three years, a material business relationship with the company either directly, or as a partner, shareholder, director or senior employee of a body that has such a relationship with the company;
— has received or receives additional remuneration from the company apart from a director's fee, participates in the company's share option or a performance-related pay scheme, or is a member of the company's pension scheme;
— has close family ties with any of the company's advisers, directors or senior employees;
— holds cross-directorships or has significant links with other directors through involvement in other companies or bodies;
— represents a significant shareholder; or
— has served on the board for more than nine years from the date of their first election.

A.3.2    Except for smaller companies, at least half the board, excluding the chairman, should comprise non-executive directors determined by the board to be independent. A smaller company should have at least two independent non-executive directors.

A.3.3    The board should appoint one of the independent non-executive directors to be the senior independent director. The senior independent director should be available to shareholders if they have concerns which contact, through the normal channels of chairman, chief executive or finance director, has failed to resolve or for which such contact is inappropriate.

*A.4        Appointments to the board*

MAIN PRINCIPLES

**There should be a formal, rigorous and transparent procedure for the appointment of new directors to the board.**

SUPPORTING PRINCIPLES

Appointments to the board should be made on merit and against objective criteria. Care should be taken to ensure that appointees have enough time available to devote to the job. This is particularly important in the case of chairmanships. The board should satisfy itself that plans are in place for orderly succession for appointments to the board and to senior management, so as to maintain an appropriate balance of skills and experience within the company and on the board.

CODE PROVISIONS

A.4.1 There should be a nomination committee which should lead the process for board appointments and make recommendations to the board. A majority of members of the nomination committee should be independent non-executive directors. The chairman or an independent non-executive director should chair the committee, but the chairman should not chair the nomination committee when dealing with the appointment of a successor to the chairmanship. The nomination committee should make available its terms of reference, explaining its role and the authority delegated to it by the board.

A.4.2 The nomination committee should evaluate the balance of skills, knowledge and experience on the board and, in the light of this evaluation, prepare a description of the role and capabilities required for a particular appointment.

A.4.3 For the appointment of a chairman, the nomination committee should prepare a job specification, including an assessment of the time commitment expected, recognizing the need for availability in the event of crises. A chairman's other significant commitments should be disclosed to the board before appointment and included in the annual report. Changes to such commitments should be reported to the board as they arise and included in the next annual report. No individual should be appointed to a second chairmanship of a FTSE 100 company.

A.4.4 The terms and conditions of appointment of non-executive directors should be made available for inspection. The letter of appointment should set out the expected time commitment. Non-executive directors should undertake that they will have sufficient time to meet what is expected of them. Their other significant commitments should be disclosed to the board before appointment, with a broad indication of the time involved, and the board should be informed of subsequent changes.

A.4.5 The board should not agree to a full-time executive director taking on more than one non-executive directorship in a FTSE 100 company, nor the chairmanship of such a company.

A.4.6 A separate section of the annual report should describe the work of the nomination committee, including the process it has used in relation to board appointments. An explanation should be given if neither an external search consultancy nor open advertising has been used in the appointment of a chairman or a non-executive director.

A.5            *Information and professional development*

MAIN PRINCIPLES

**The board should be supplied in a timely manner with information in a form and of a quality appropriate to enable it to discharge its duties. All directors should receive induction on joining the board and should regularly update and refresh their skills and knowledge.**

SUPPORTING PRINCIPLES

The chairman is responsible for ensuring that the directors receive accurate, timely and clear information. Management has an obligation to provide such information, but directors should seek clarification or amplification where necessary. The chairman should ensure that the directors continually update their skills and the knowledge and familiarity with the company required to fulfil their role both on the board and on board committees. The company should provide the necessary resources for developing and updating its directors' knowledge and capabilities. Under the direction of the chairman, the company secretary's responsibilities include ensuring good information flows within the board and its committees and between senior management and non-executive directors, as well as facilitating induction and assisting with professional development as required. The company secretary should be responsible for advising the board through the chairman on all governance matters.

CODE PROVISIONS

A.5.1        The chairman should ensure that new directors receive a full, formal and tailored induction on joining the board. As part of this, the company should offer to major shareholders the opportunity to meet a new non-executive director.

A.5.2        The board should ensure that directors, especially non-executive directors, have access to independent professional advice at the company's expense where they judge it necessary to discharge their responsibilities as directors. Committees should be provided with sufficient resources to undertake their duties.

A.5.3        All directors should have access to the advice and services of the company secretary, who is responsible to the board for ensuring that board procedures are complied with. Both the appointment and removal of the company secretary should be a matter for the board as a whole.

*A.6*        *Performance evaluation*

**The board should undertake a formal and rigorous annual evaluation of its own performance and that of its committees and individual directors.**

Individual evaluation should aim to show whether each director continues to contribute effectively and to demonstrate commitment to the role (including commitment of time for board and committee meetings and any other duties). The chairman should act on the results of the performance evaluation by recognizing the strengths and addressing the weaknesses of the board and, where appropriate, proposing new members be appointed to the board or seeking the resignation of directors.

A.6.1      The board should state in the annual report how performance evaluation of the board, its committees and its individual directors has been conducted. The non-executive directors, led by the senior independent director, should be responsible for performance evaluation of the chairman, taking into account the views of executive directors.

*A.7*        *Re-election*

**All directors should be submitted for re-election at regular intervals, subject to continued satisfactory performance. The board should ensure planned and progressive refreshing of the board.**

A.7.1      All directors should be subject to election by shareholders at the first annual general meeting after their appointment and to re-election thereafter at intervals of no more than three years. The names of directors submitted for election or re-election should be accompanied by sufficient biographical details and any other relevant information to enable shareholders to take an informed decision on their election.

A.7.2      Non-executive directors should be appointed for specified terms subject to re-election and to Companies Acts provisions relating to the removal of a director. The board should set out to shareholders in the papers accompanying a resolution to elect a non-executive director why they believe an individual should be elected. The chairman should confirm to shareholders when proposing re-election that, following formal performance evaluation, the individual's performance continues to be effective and to demonstrate commitment to the role. Any term beyond six years (e.g., two three-year terms) for a non-executive director should be subject to particularly rigorous review and should take into account the need for progressive refreshing of the board. Non-executive directors may serve longer than nine years (e.g., three three-year terms), subject to annual re-election. Serving more than nine years could be relevant to the determination of a non-executive director's independence (as set out in provision A.3.1).

B   *Remuneration*

*B.1*   *The level and make-up of remuneration*

MAIN PRINCIPLES

**Levels of remuneration should be sufficient to attract, retain and motivate directors of the quality required to run the company success-fully, but a company should avoid paying more than is necessary for this purpose. A significant proportion of executive directors' remuneration should be structured so as to link rewards to corporate and individual performance.**

SUPPORTING PRINCIPLE

The remuneration committee should judge where to position their company relative to other companies. But they should use such comparisons with caution, in view of the risk of an upward ratchet of remuneration levels with no corresponding improvement in performance. They should also be sensitive to pay and employment conditions elsewhere in the group, especially when determining annual salary increases.

CODE PROVISIONS

REMUNERATION POLICY

B.1.1  The performance-related elements of remuneration should form a significant proportion of the total remuneration package of executive directors and should be designed to align their interests with those of shareholders and to give these directors keen incentives to perform at the highest levels. In designing schemes of performance-related remuneration, the remuneration committee should follow the provisions in Schedule A to this Code.

B.1.2  Executive share options should not be offered at a discount save as permitted by the relevant provisions of the Listing Rules.

B.1.3    Levels of remuneration for non-executive directors should reflect the time commitment and responsibilities of the role. Remuneration for non-executive directors should not include share options. If, exceptionally, options are granted, shareholder approval should be sought in advance and any shares acquired by exercise of the options should be held until at least one year after the non-executive director leaves the board. Holding of share options could be relevant to the determination of a non-executive director's independence (as set out in provision A.3.1).

B.1.4    Where a company releases an executive director to serve as a non-executive director elsewhere, the remuneration report should include a statement as to whether or not the director will retain such earnings and, if so, what the remuneration is.

SERVICE CONTRACTS AND COMPENSATION

B.1.5    The remuneration committee should carefully consider what compensation commitments (including pension contributions and all other elements) their directors' terms of appointment would entail in the event of early termination. The aim should be to avoid rewarding poor performance. They should take a robust line on reducing compensation to reflect departing directors' obligations to mitigate loss.

B.1.6    Notice or contract periods should be set at one year or less. If it is necessary to offer longer notice or contract periods to new directors recruited from outside, such periods should reduce to one year or less after the initial period.

*B.2*    *Procedure*

MAIN PRINCIPLE

**There should be a formal and transparent procedure for developing policy on executive remuneration and for fixing the remuneration packages of individual directors. No director should be involved in deciding his or her own remuneration.**

SUPPORTING PRINCIPLES

The remuneration committee should consult the chairman and/or chief executive about their proposals relating to the remuneration of other executive directors. The remuneration committee should also be responsible for appointing any consultants in respect of executive director remuneration. Where executive directors or senior management are involved in advising or supporting the remuneration committee, care should be taken to recognize and avoid conflicts of interest. The chairman of the board should ensure that the company maintains contact as required with its principal shareholders about remuneration in the same way as for other matters.

CODE PROVISIONS

B.2.1     The board should establish a remuneration committee of at least three, or in the case of smaller companies two, members, who should all be independent non-executive directors. The remuneration committee should make available its terms of reference, explaining its role and the authority delegated to it by the board. Where remuneration consultants are appointed, a statement should be made available of whether they have any other connection with the company.

B.2.2     The remuneration committee should have delegated responsibility for setting remuneration for all executive directors and the chairman, including pension rights and any compensation payments. The committee should also recommend and monitor the level and structure of remuneration for senior management. The definition of 'senior management' for this purpose should be determined by the board, but should normally include the first layer of management below board level.

B.2.3     The board itself or, where required by the Articles of Association, the shareholders should determine the remuneration of the non-executive directors within the limits set in the Articles of Association. Where permitted by the Articles, the board may however delegate this responsibility to a committee, which might include the chief executive.

B.2.4     Shareholders should be invited specifically to approve all new long-term incentive schemes (as defined in the Listing Rules) and significant changes to existing schemes, save in the circumstances permitted by the Listing Rules.

C     *Accountability and audit*

C.1     *Financial reporting*

MAIN PRINCIPLE

**The board should present a balanced and understandable assessment of the company's position and prospects.**

SUPPORTING PRINCIPLE

The board's responsibility to present a balanced and understandable assessment extends to interim and other price-sensitive public reports and reports to regulators as well as to information required to be presented by statutory requirements.

CODE PROVISIONS

C.1.1    The directors should explain in the annual report their responsibility for preparing the accounts and there should be a statement by the auditors about their reporting responsibilities.

C.1.2    The directors should report that the business is a going concern, with supporting assumptions or qualifications as necessary.

*C.2       Internal control*

MAIN PRINCIPLE

**The board should maintain a sound system of internal control to safeguard shareholders' investment and the company's assets.**

CODE PROVISION

C.2.1    The board should, at least annually, conduct a review of the effectiveness of the group's system of internal controls and should report to shareholders that they have done so. The review should cover all material controls, including financial, operational and compliance controls and risk management systems.

*C.3       Audit committee and auditors*

MAIN PRINCIPLE

**The board should establish formal and transparent arrangements for considering how they should apply the financial reporting and internal control principles and for maintaining an appropriate relationship with the company's auditors.**

CODE PROVISIONS

C.3.1    The board should establish an audit committee of at least three, or in the case of smaller companies two, members, who should all be independent non-executive directors. The board should satisfy itself that at least one member of the audit committee has recent and relevant financial experience.

C.3.2    The main role and responsibilities of the audit committee should be set out in written terms of reference and should include:

—        to monitor the integrity of the financial statements of the company and any formal announcements relating to the company's financial performance, reviewing significant financial reporting judgements contained in them;

—    to review the company's internal financial controls and, unless expressly addressed by a separate board risk committee composed of independent directors or by the board itself, to review the company's internal control and risk management systems;

—    to monitor and review the effectiveness of the company's internal audit function;

—    to make recommendations to the board, for it to put to the shareholders for their approval in general meeting, in relation to the appointment, reappointment and removal of the external auditor and to approve the remuneration and terms of engagement of the external auditor;

—    to review and monitor the external auditor's independence and objectivity and the effectiveness of the audit process, taking into consideration relevant UK professional and regulatory requirements;

—    to develop and implement policy on the engagement of the external auditor to supply non-audit services, taking into account relevant ethical guidance regarding the provision of non-audit services by the external audit firm, and to report to the board, identifying any matters in respect of which it considers that action or improvement is needed and making recommendations as to the steps to be taken.

C.3.3    The terms of reference of the audit committee, including its role and the authority delegated to it by the board, should be made available. A separate section of the annual report should describe the work of the committee in discharging those responsibilities.

C.3.4    The audit committee should review arrangements by which staff of the company may, in confidence, raise concerns about possible improprieties in matters of financial reporting or other matters. The audit committee's objective should be to ensure that arrangements are in place for the proportionate and independent investigation of such matters and for appropriate follow-up action.

C.3.5    The audit committee should monitor and review the effectiveness of the internal audit activities. Where there is no internal audit function, the audit committee should consider annually whether there is a need for an internal audit function and make a recommendation to the board, and the reasons for the absence of such a function should be explained in the relevant section of the annual report.

C.3.6    The audit committee should have primary responsibility for making a recommendation on the appointment, reappointment and removal of external auditors. If the board does not accept the audit committee's recommendation, it should include in the annual report, and in any papers recommending appointment or re-appointment, a statement from the audit committee explaining the recommendation and should set out reasons why the board has taken a different position.

C.3.7    The annual report should explain to shareholders how, if the auditor provides non-audit services, auditor objectivity and independence is safeguarded.

D        *Relations with shareholders*

D.1      *Dialogue with institutional shareholders*

MAIN PRINCIPLE

**There should be a dialogue with shareholders based on the mutual understanding of objectives. The board as a whole has responsibility for ensuring that a satisfactory dialogue with shareholders takes place.**

SUPPORTING PRINCIPLES

While recognizing that most shareholder contact is with the chief executive and finance director, the chairman (and the senior independent director and other directors as appropriate) should maintain sufficient contact with major shareholders to understand their issues and concerns. The board should keep in touch with shareholder opinion in whatever ways are most practical and efficient.

CODE PROVISIONS

D.1.1    The chairman should ensure that the views of shareholders are communicated to the board as a whole. The chairman should discuss governance and strategy with major shareholders. Non-executive directors should be offered the opportunity to attend meetings with major shareholders and should expect to attend them if requested by major shareholders. The senior independent director should attend sufficient meetings with a range of major shareholders to listen to their views in order to help develop a balanced understanding of the issues and concerns of major shareholders.

D.1.2    The board should state in the annual report the steps they have taken to ensure that the members of the board, and in particular the non-executive directors, develop an understanding of the views of major shareholders about their company (e.g., through direct face-to-face contact, analysts' or brokers' briefings and surveys of shareholder opinion).

D.2      *Constructive use of the AGM*

MAIN PRINCIPLE

**The board should use the AGM to communicate with investors and to encourage their participation.**

CODE PROVISIONS

D.2.1      The company should count all proxy votes and, except where a poll is called, should indicate the level of proxies lodged on each resolution and the balance for and against the resolution and the number of abstentions, after it has been dealt with on a show of hands. The company should ensure that votes cast are properly received and recorded.

D.2.2      The company should propose a separate resolution at the AGM on each substantially separate issue and should in particular propose a resolution at the AGM relating to the report and accounts.

D.2.3      The chairman should arrange for the chairmen of the audit, remuneration and nomination committees to be available to answer questions at the AGM and for all directors to attend.

D.2.4      The company should arrange for the Notice of the AGM and related papers to be sent to shareholders at least 20 working days before the meeting.

## Section 2    Institutional Shareholders

*E*      *Institutional shareholders*

*E.1*      *Dialogue with companies*

MAIN PRINCIPLE

**Institutional shareholders should enter into a dialogue with companies based on the mutual understanding of objectives.**

SUPPORTING PRINCIPLES

Institutional shareholders should apply the principles set out in the Institutional Shareholders' Committee's 'The Responsibilities of Institutional Shareholders and Agents – Statement of Principles', which should be reflected in fund manager contracts.

*E.2*      *Evaluation of governance disclosures*

MAIN PRINCIPLE

**When evaluating companies' governance arrangements, particularly those relating to board structure and composition, institutional shareholders should give due weight to all relevant factors drawn to their attention.**

SUPPORTING PRINCIPLES

Institutional shareholders should consider carefully explanations given for departure from this Code and make reasoned judgements in each case. They should give an explanation to the company, in writing where appropriate, and be prepared to enter a dialogue if they do not accept the company's position. They should avoid a box-ticking approach to assessing a company's corporate governance. They should bear in mind in particular the size and complexity of the company and the nature of the risks and challenges it faces.

*E.3        Shareholder voting*

MAIN PRINCIPLES

**Institutional shareholders have a responsibility to make considered use of their votes.**

SUPPORTING PRINCIPLES

Institutional shareholders should take steps to ensure their voting intentions are being translated into practice. Institutional shareholders should, on request, make available to their clients information on the proportion of resolutions on which votes were cast and non-discretionary proxies lodged. Major shareholders should attend AGMs where appropriate and practicable. Companies and registrars should facilitate this.

## Schedule A Provisions on the design of performance-related remuneration

1.      The remuneration committee should consider whether the directors should be eligible for annual bonuses. If so, performance conditions should be relevant, stretching and designed to enhance shareholder value. Upper limits should be set and disclosed. There may be a case for part payment in shares to be held for a significant period.

2.      The remuneration committee should consider whether the directors should be eligible for benefits under long-term incentive schemes. Traditional share option schemes should be weighed against other kinds of long-term incentive scheme. In normal circumstances, shares granted or other forms of deferred remuneration should not vest and options should not be exercisable, in less than three years. Directors should be encouraged to hold their shares for a further period after vesting or exercise, subject to the need to finance any costs of acquisition and associated tax liabilities.

3.      Any new long-term incentive schemes which are proposed should be approved by shareholders and should preferably replace any existing schemes or at least form part of a well-considered overall plan, incorporating existing schemes. The total rewards potentially available should not be excessive.

4.      Payouts or grants under all incentive schemes, including new grants under existing share option schemes, should be subject to challenging

performance criteria reflecting the company's objectives. Consideration should be given to criteria which reflect the company's performance relative to a group of comparator companies in some key variables such as total shareholder return.

5. Grants under executive share option and other long-term incentive schemes should normally be phased rather than awarded in one large block.

6. In general, only basic salary should be pensionable.

7. The remuneration committee should consider the pension consequences and associated costs to the company of basic salary increases and any other changes in pensionable remuneration, especially for directors close to retirement.

## Schedule B Guidance on liability of non-executive directors: care, skill and diligence

1. Although non-executive directors and executive directors have as board members the same legal duties and objectives, the time devoted to the company's affairs is likely to be significantly less for a non-executive director than for an executive director and the detailed knowledge and experience of a company's affairs that could reasonably be expected of a non-executive director will generally be less than for an executive director. These matters may be relevant in assessing the knowledge, skill and experience which may reasonably be expected of a non-executive director and therefore the care, skill and diligence that a non-executive director may be expected to exercise.

2. In this context, the following elements of the Code may also be particularly relevant. (i) In order to enable directors to fulfil their duties, the Code states that:

— the letter of appointment of the director should set out the expected time commitment (Code provision A.4.4); and

— the board should be supplied in a timely manner with information in a form and of a quality appropriate to enable it to discharge its duties. The chairman is responsible for ensuring that the directors are provided by management with accurate, timely and clear information (Code principles A.5).

(ii) Non-executive directors should themselves:

— undertake appropriate induction and regularly update and refresh their skills, knowledge and familiarity with the company (Code principle A.5 and provision A.5.1);

—   seek appropriate clarification or amplification of information and, where necessary, take and follow appropriate professional advice (Code principle A.5 and provision A.5.2);

—   where they have concerns about the running of the company or a proposed action, ensure that these are addressed by the board and, to the extent that they are not resolved, ensure that they are recorded in the board minutes (Code provision A.1.4);

—   give a statement to the board if they have such unresolved concerns on resignation (Code provision A.1.4).

3.   It is up to each non-executive director to reach a view as to what is necessary in particular circumstances to comply with the duty of care, skill and diligence they owe as a director to the company. In considering whether or not a person is in breach of that duty, a court would take into account all relevant circumstances. These may include having regard to the above where relevant to the issue of liability of a non-executive director.

## Schedule C Disclosure of corporate governance arrangements

The Listing Rules require a statement to be included in the annual report relating to compliance with the Code, as described in the preamble. For ease of reference, the specific requirements in the Code for disclosure are set out below. The annual report should record:

—   a statement of how the board operates, including a high-level statement of which types of decisions are to be taken by the board and which are to be delegated to management (A.1.1);

—   the names of the chairman, the deputy chairman (where there is one), the chief executive, the senior independent directors and the chairmen and members of the nomination, audit and remuneration committees (A.1.2);

—   the number of meetings of the board and those committees and individual attendance by directors (A.1.2);

—   the names of the non-executive directors whom the board determines to be independent, with reasons where necessary (A.3.1);

—   the other significant commitments of the chairman and any changes to them during the year (A.4.3);

—   how performance evaluation of the board, its committees and its directors has been conducted (A.6.1);

—   the steps the board has taken to ensure that members of the board, and in particular the non-executive directors, develop an understanding of the views of major shareholders about their company (D.1.2).

The report should also include:

— a separate section describing the work of the nomination committee, including the process it has used in relation to board appointments and an explanation if neither external search consultancy nor open advertising has been used in the appointment of a chairman or a non-executive director (A.4.6);

— a description of the work of the remuneration committee as required under the Directors' Remuneration Reporting Regulations 2002, and including, where an executive director serves as a non-executive director elsewhere, whether or not the director will retain such earnings and, if so, what the remuneration is (B.1.4);

— an explanation from the directors of their responsibility for preparing the accounts and a statement by the auditors about their reporting responsibilities (C.1.1);

— a statement from the directors that the business is a going concern, with supporting assumptions or qualifications as necessary (C.1.2);

— a report that the board has conducted a review of the effectiveness of the group's system of internal controls (C.2.1);

— a separate section describing the work of the audit committee in discharging its responsibilities (C.3.3);

— where there is no internal audit function, the reasons for the absence of such a function (C.3.5);

— where the board does not accept the audit committee's recommendation on the appointment, reappointment or removal of an external auditor, a statement from the audit committee explaining the recommendation and the reasons why the board has taken a different position (C.3.6); and

— an explanation of how, if the auditor provides non-audit services, auditor objectivity and independence is safeguarded (C.3.7).

**The following information should be made available (which may be met by making it available on request and placing the information available on the company's website):**

— the terms of reference of the nomination, remuneration and audit committees, explaining their role and the authority delegated to them by the board (A.4.1, B.2.1 and C.3.3);

— the terms and conditions of appointment of non-executive directors (A.4.4); and

— where remuneration consultants are appointed, a statement of whether they have any other connection with the company (B.2.1).

**The board should set out to shareholders in the papers accompanying a resolution to elect or re-elect:**

—        sufficient biographical details to enable shareholders to take an informed decision on their election or re-election (A.7.1);

—        why they believe an individual should be elected to a non-executive role (A.7.2);

—        on re-election of a non-executive director, confirmation from the chairman that, following formal performance evaluation, the individual's performance continues to be effective and to demonstrate commitment to the role, including commitment of time for board and committee meetings and any other duties (A.7.2).


**The board should set out to shareholders in the papers recommending appointment or reappointment of an external auditor:**

—        if the board does not accept the audit committee's recommendation, there should be a statement from the audit committee explaining the recommendation and another from the board setting out reasons why they have taken a different position (C.3.6).

# Appendix B

# The OECD Principles of Corporate Governance

## Preamble

The Principles are intended to assist OECD and non-OECD governments in their efforts to evaluate and improve the legal, institutional and regulatory framework for corporate governance in their countries, and to provide guidance and suggestions for stock exchanges, investors, corporations, and other parties that have a role in the process of developing good corporate governance. The Principles focus on publicly traded companies, both financial and non-financial. However, to the extent they are deemed applicable, they might also be a useful tool to improve corporate governance in non-traded companies, for example, privately held and state-owned enterprises. The Principles represent a common basis that OECD member countries consider essential for the development of good governance practices. They are intended to be concise, understandable and accessible to the international community. They are not intended to substitute for government, semi-government or private sector initiatives to develop more detailed "best practice" in corporate governance.

Increasingly, the OECD and its member governments have recognised the synergy between macroeconomic and structural policies in achieving fundamental policy goals. Corporate governance is one key element in improving economic efficiency and growth as well as enhancing investor confidence. Corporate governance involves a set of relationships between a company's management, its board, its shareholders and other stakeholders. Corporate governance also provides the structure through which the objectives of the company are set, and the means of attaining those objectives and monitoring performance are determined. Good corporate governance should provide proper incentives for the board and management to pursue objectives that are in the interests of the company and its shareholders and should facilitate effective monitoring. The presence of an effective corporate governance system, within an individual company and across an economy as a whole, helps to provide a degree of confidence that is necessary for the proper functioning of a market economy. As a result, the cost of capital is lower and firms are encouraged to use resources more efficiently, thereby underpinning growth.

Corporate governance is only part of the larger economic context in which firms operate that includes, for example, macroeconomic policies and the degree of competition in product and factor markets. The corporate governance framework also depends on the legal, regulatory, and institutional environment. In addition, factors such as business ethics and corporate awareness of the environmental and societal interests of the communities in which a company operates can also have an impact on its reputation and its long-term success.

While a multiplicity of factors affect the governance and decision-making processes of firms, and are important to their long-term success, the Principles focus on governance problems that result from the separation of ownership and control. However, this is not simply an issue of the relationship between shareholders and management, although that is indeed the central element. In some jurisdictions, governance issues also arise from the power of certain controlling shareholders over minority shareholders. In other countries, employees have important legal rights irrespective of their ownership rights. The Principles therefore have to be complementary to a broader approach to the operation of checks and balances. Some of the other issues relevant to a company's decision-making processes, such as environmental, anti-corruption or ethical concerns, are taken into account but are treated more explicitly in a number of other OECD instruments (including the *Guidelines for Multinational Enterprises* and the *Convention on Combating Bribery of Foreign Public Officials in International Transactions*) and the instruments of other international organisations.

Corporate governance is affected by the relationships among participants in the governance system. Controlling shareholders, which may be individuals, family holdings, bloc alliances, or other corporations acting through a holding company or cross shareholdings, can significantly influence corporate behaviour. As owners of equity, institutional investors are increasingly demanding a voice in corporate governance in some markets. Individual shareholders usually do not seek to exercise governance rights but may be highly concerned about obtaining fair treatment from controlling shareholders and management. Creditors play an important role in a number of governance systems and can serve as external monitors over corporate performance. Employees and other stakeholders play an important role in contributing to the long-term success and performance of the corporation, while governments establish the overall institutional and legal framework for corporate governance. The role of each of these participants and their interactions vary widely among OECD countries and among non-OECD countries as well. These relationships are subject, in part, to law and regulation and, in part, to voluntary adaptation and, most importantly, to market forces.

The degree to which corporations observe basic principles of good corporate governance is an increasingly important factor for investment decisions. Of particular relevance is the relation between corporate governance practices and the increasingly international character of investment. International flows of capital enable companies to access financing from a much larger pool of investors. If countries are to reap the full benefits of the global capital market, and if they are to attract long-term "patient" capital, corporate governance arrangements must be credible, well understood across borders and adhere to internationally accepted principles. Even if corporations do not rely primarily on foreign sources of capital, adherence to good corporate governance practices will help improve the confidence of domestic investors, reduce the cost of capital, underpin the good functioning of financial markets, and ultimately induce more stable sources of financing.

There is no single model of good corporate governance. However, work carried out in both OECD and non-OECD countries and within the Organisation has identified some common elements that underlie good corporate governance. The Principles build on these common elements and are formulated to embrace the different models that exist. For example, they do not advocate any particular board structure and the term "board" as used in this document is meant to embrace the different national models of board structures found in OECD and non-OECD countries. In the typical two tier system, found in some countries, "board" as used in the Principles refers to the "supervisory board" while "key executives" refers to the "management board". In systems where the unitary board is overseen by an internal auditor's body, the principles applicable to the board are also, *mutatis mutandis,* applicable. The terms "corporation" and "company" are used interchangeably in the text.

The Principles are non-binding and do not aim at detailed prescriptions for national legislation. Rather, they seek to identify objectives and suggest various means for achieving them. Their purpose is to serve as a reference point. They can be used by policy makers as they examine and develop the legal and regulatory frameworks for corporate governance that reflect their own economic, social, legal and cultural circumstances, and by market participants as they develop their own practices.

The Principles are evolutionary in nature and should be reviewed in light of significant changes in circumstances. To remain competitive in a changing world, corporations must innovate and adapt their corporate governance practices so that they can meet new demands and grasp new opportunities. Similarly, governments have an important responsibility for shaping an effective regulatory framework that provides for sufficient flexibility to allow markets to function effectively and to respond to expectations of shareholders and other stakeholders. It is up to governments and market participants to decide how to apply these Principles in developing their own frameworks for corporate governance, taking into account the costs and benefits of regulation.

The following document is divided into two parts. The Principles presented in the first part of the document cover the following areas: I) Ensuring the basis for an effective corporate governance framework; II) The rights of shareholders and key ownership functions; III) The equitable treatment of shareholders; IV) The role of stakeholders; V) Disclosure and transparency; and VI) The responsibilities of the board. Each of the sections is headed by a single Principle that appears in bold italics and is followed by a number of supporting sub-principles. In the second part of the document, the Principles are supplemented by annotations that contain commentary on the Principles and are intended to help readers understand their rationale. The annotations may also contain descriptions of dominant trends and offer alternative implementation methods and examples that may be useful in making the Principles operational.

**Part I**

# The OECD Principles of Corporate Governance

# I. Ensuring the Basis for an Effective Corporate Governance Framework

**The corporate governance framework should promote transparent and efficient markets, be consistent with the rule of law and clearly articulate the division of responsibilities among different supervisory, regulatory and enforcement authorities.**

A. The corporate governance framework should be developed with a view to its impact on overall economic performance, market integrity and the incentives it creates for market participants and the promotion of transparent and efficient markets.

B. The legal and regulatory requirements that affect corporate governance practices in a jurisdiction should be consistent with the rule of law, transparent and enforceable.

C. The division of responsibilities among different authorities in a jurisdiction should be clearly articulated and ensure that the public interest is served.

D. Supervisory, regulatory and enforcement authorities should have the authority, integrity and resources to fulfil their duties in a professional and objective manner. Moreover, their rulings should be timely, transparent and fully explained.

# II. The Rights of Shareholders and Key Ownership Functions

**The corporate governance framework should protect and facilitate the exercise of shareholders' rights.**

A. Basic shareholder rights should include the right to: 1) secure methods of ownership registration; 2) convey or transfer shares; 3) obtain relevant and material information on the corporation on a timely and regular basis; 4) participate and vote in general shareholder meetings; 5) elect and remove members of the board; and 6) share in the profits of the corporation.

B. Shareholders should have the right to participate in, and to be sufficiently informed on, decisions concerning fundamental corporate changes such as: 1) amendments to the statutes, or articles of incorporation or similar governing documents of the company; 2) the authorisation of additional shares; and 3) extraordinary transactions, including the transfer of all or substantially all assets, that in effect result in the sale of the company.

C. Shareholders should have the opportunity to participate effectively and vote in general shareholder meetings and should be informed of the rules, including voting procedures, that govern general shareholder meetings:

1. Shareholders should be furnished with sufficient and timely information concerning the date, location and agenda of general meetings, as well as full and timely information regarding the issues to be decided at the meeting.

2. Shareholders should have the opportunity to ask questions to the board, including questions relating to the annual external audit, to place items on the agenda of general meetings, and to propose resolutions, subject to reasonable limitations.

3. Effective shareholder participation in key corporate governance decisions, such as the nomination and election of board members, should be facilitated. Shareholders should be able to make their views known on the remuneration policy for board members and key executives. The equity component of compensation schemes for board members and employees should be subject to shareholder approval.

4. Shareholders should be able to vote in person or in absentia, and equal effect should be given to votes whether cast in person or in absentia.

D. Capital structures and arrangements that enable certain shareholders to obtain a degree of control disproportionate to their equity ownership should be disclosed.

E. Markets for corporate control should be allowed to function in an efficient and transparent manner.

1. The rules and procedures governing the acquisition of corporate control in the capital markets, and extraordinary transactions such as mergers, and sales of substantial portions of corporate assets, should be clearly articulated and disclosed so that investors understand their rights and recourse. Transactions should occur at transparent prices and under fair conditions that protect the rights of all shareholders according to their class.

2. Anti-take-over devices should not be used to shield management and the board from accountability.

F. The exercise of ownership rights by all shareholders, including institutional investors, should be facilitated.

1. Institutional investors acting in a fiduciary capacity should disclose their overall corporate governance and voting policies with respect to their investments, including the procedures that they have in place for deciding on the use of their voting rights.

2. Institutional investors acting in a fiduciary capacity should disclose how they manage material conflicts of interest that may affect the exercise of key ownership rights regarding their investments.

G. Shareholders, including institutional shareholders, should be allowed to consult with each other on issues concerning their basic shareholder rights as defined in the Principles, subject to exceptions to prevent abuse.

## III. The Equitable Treatment of Shareholders

**The corporate governance framework should ensure the equitable treatment of all shareholders, including minority and foreign shareholders. All shareholders should have the opportunity to obtain effective redress for violation of their rights.**

A. All shareholders of the same series of a class should be treated equally.

   1. Within any series of a class, all shares should carry the same rights. All investors should be able to obtain information about the rights attached to all series and classes of shares before they purchase. Any changes in voting rights should be subject to approval by those classes of shares which are negatively affected.

   2. Minority shareholders should be protected from abusive actions by, or in the interest of, controlling shareholders acting either directly or indirectly, and should have effective means of redress.

   3. Votes should be cast by custodians or nominees in a manner agreed upon with the beneficial owner of the shares.

   4. Impediments to cross border voting should be eliminated.

   5. Processes and procedures for general shareholder meetings should allow for equitable treatment of all shareholders. Company procedures should not make it unduly difficult or expensive to cast votes.

B. Insider trading and abusive self-dealing should be prohibited.

C. Members of the board and key executives should be required to disclose to the board whether they, directly, indirectly or on behalf of third parties, have a material interest in any transaction or matter directly affecting the corporation.

## IV. The Role of Stakeholders in Corporate Governance

**The corporate governance framework should recognise the rights of stakeholders established by law or through mutual agreements and encourage active co-operation between corporations and stakeholders in creating wealth, jobs, and the sustainability of financially sound enterprises.**

A. The rights of stakeholders that are established by law or through mutual agreements are to be respected.

B. Where stakeholder interests are protected by law, stakeholders should have the opportunity to obtain effective redress for violation of their rights.

C. Performance-enhancing mechanisms for employee participation should be permitted to develop.

D. Where stakeholders participate in the corporate governance process, they should have access to relevant, sufficient and reliable information on a timely and regular basis.

E. Stakeholders, including individual employees and their representative bodies, should be able to freely communicate their concerns about illegal or unethical practices to the board and their rights should not be compromised for doing this.

F. The corporate governance framework should be complemented by an effective, efficient insolvency framework and by effective enforcement of creditor rights.

## V. Disclosure and Transparency

**The corporate governance framework should ensure that timely and accurate disclosure is made on all material matters regarding the corporation, including the financial situation, performance, ownership, and governance of the company.**

A. Disclosure should include, but not be limited to, material information on:

1. The financial and operating results of the company.

2. Company objectives.

3. Major share ownership and voting rights.

4. Remuneration policy for members of the board and key executives, and information about board members, including their qualifications, the selection process, other company directorships and whether they are regarded as independent by the board.

5. Related party transactions.

6. Foreseeable risk factors.

7. Issues regarding employees and other stakeholders.

8. Governance structures and policies, in particular, the content of any corporate governance code or policy and the process by which it is implemented.

B. Information should be prepared and disclosed in accordance with high quality standards of accounting and financial and non-financial disclosure.

C. An annual audit should be conducted by an independent, competent and qualified, auditor in order to provide an external and objective assurance to the board and shareholders that the financial statements fairly represent the financial position and performance of the company in all material respects.

D. External auditors should be accountable to the shareholders and owe a duty to the company to exercise due professional care in the conduct of the audit.

E. Channels for disseminating information should provide for equal, timely and cost-efficient access to relevant information by users.

F. The corporate governance framework should be complemented by an effective approach that addresses and promotes the provision of analysis or advice by analysts, brokers, rating agencies and others, that is relevant to decisions by investors, free from material conflicts of interest that might compromise the integrity of their analysis or advice.

## VI. The Responsibilities of the Board

**The corporate governance framework should ensure the strategic guidance of the company, the effective monitoring of management by the board, and the board's accountability to the company and the shareholders.**

A. Board members should act on a fully informed basis, in good faith, with due diligence and care, and in the best interest of the company and the shareholders.

B. Where board decisions may affect different shareholder groups differently, the board should treat all shareholders fairly.

C. The board should apply high ethical standards. It should take into account the interests of stakeholders.

D. The board should fulfil certain key functions, including:

1. Reviewing and guiding corporate strategy, major plans of action, risk policy, annual budgets and business plans; setting performance objectives; monitoring implementation and corporate performance; and overseeing major capital expenditures, acquisitions and divestitures.

2. Monitoring the effectiveness of the company's governance practices and making changes as needed.

3. Selecting, compensating, monitoring and, when necessary, replacing key executives and overseeing succession planning.

4. Aligning key executive and board remuneration with the longer term interests of the company and its shareholders.

5. Ensuring a formal and transparent board nomination and election process.

6. Monitoring and managing potential conflicts of interest of management, board members and shareholders, including misuse of corporate assets and abuse in related party transactions.

7. Ensuring the integrity of the corporation's accounting and financial reporting systems, including the independent audit, and that appropriate systems of control are in place, in particular, systems for risk management, financial and operational control, and compliance with the law and relevant standards.

8. Overseeing the process of disclosure and communications.

E. The board should be able to exercise objective independent judgement on corporate affairs.

1. Boards should consider assigning a sufficient number of non-executive board members capable of exercising independent judgement to tasks where there is a potential for conflict of interest. Examples of such key responsibilities are ensuring the integrity of financial and non-financial reporting, the review of related party transactions, nomination of board members and key executives, and board remuneration.

2. When committees of the board are established, their mandate, composition and working procedures should be well defined and disclosed by the board.

3. Board members should be able to commit themselves effectively to their responsibilities.

F. In order to fulfil their responsibilities, board members should have access to accurate, relevant and timely information.

# References

ABI (1997) *ABI Member Companies Mailing List*, Association of British Insurers, London.

ABI (2001) *Disclosure Guidelines on Socially Responsible Investment*, Association of British Insurers, London.

Abraham, S. and Cox, P. (2006) 'Analysing the Determinants of Risk Information Disclosure in UK FTSE 100 Annual Reports', Working Paper, University of Exeter.

ACBE (1996) *Sixth Progress Report to and Responses from the President of the Board of Trade and the Secretary of State for the Environment*, Advisory Committee of Business and the Environment, London.

ACCA (2000) *Turnbull, Internal Control and Wider Aspects of Risk* (commissioned by the Association of Chartered Certified Accountants' Social and Environmental Committee), Certified Accountants Educational Trust, London.

AccountAbility 1000 (AA1000) (November 1999) *Accountability 1000 Framework: Exposure Draft*, AccountAbility, London.

AccountAbility (2003) *AA1000 Assurance Standard*, AccountAbility, London, UK.

Accountancy Age (5 January, 2004) Grant Thornton May Sever Ties with Italian Arm, *Accountancy Age*.

Accountancy Age (4 February, 2005) Parmalat Doubles Profits, *Accountancy Age*.

Adams, C. A. (2002) 'Internal organisational factors influencing corporate social and ethical reporting: Beyond current theorising', *Accounting, Auditing & Accountability*, **15**(2), 223–250.

Adams, C. A. and Evans, R. (2004) 'Accountability, Completeness, Credibility and the Audit Expectations Gap' *The Journal of Corporate Citizenship*, **14**, 97–115.

Adams, C. A., Hill, W. Y. and Roberts, C. B. (1995) *Environmental, Employee and Ethical Reporting in Europe* (ACCA Research Report No.41), Association of Chartered Certified Accountants, London.

Adams, R. (1992) 'Why is the environmental debate of interest to accountants and accountancy bodies?', in: D. Owen (ed.), *Green Reporting: Accounting and the Challenge of the Nineties*, Chapman & Hall, London.

Agrawal, A. and Knoeber, C. R. (1996) 'Firm performance and mechanisms to control agency problems between managers and shareholders', *Journal of Financial and Quantitative Analysis*, **31**(3), September, 377–397.

Al-Busaidi, H. S. (2005) 'The Role of the Corporate Governance System in Improving the Functioning of Company Boards in Oman – Perceptions of Directors', *Masters of Business Administration Dissertation*, Cardiff Business School.

Alexander, G. J. and Buchholz, R. A. (1978) 'Corporate social responsibility and stock market performance', *Academy of Management Journal*, **21**(3), 479–486.

Al-Harkan, A. A. M. (2005) *An Investigation into the Emerging Corporate Governance Framework in Saudi Arabia*, PhD Thesis, Cardiff University.

Alkhafaji, A. F. (1989) *A Stakeholder Approach to Corporate Governance: Managing in a Dynamic Environment*, Quorum Books, Westport, CT.

Allen & Overy (2006) 'The Business Review and Director Liability for Narrative Reporting: The Latest', Bulletin, *Allen & Overy LLP*, May, 1–3, London, UK.

Al-Mulhem, A. (1997) *An Empirical Investigation of the Level of Financial Disclosure by Saudi Arabian Corporations*, PhD Thesis, University of Hull.

Alrawi, M. (2003) 'New Arab Council to Zero In on Corporate Governance', *Jordan Times*, 1 July.

AlTonsi, F. (2003) *A Cross-Firm Analysis of the Impact of Corporate Governance Practices on Corporate Performance in Saudi Arabia*, Conference on Corporate Governance, Al-Gassim University, Saudi Arabia.

Alves, C. and Mendes, V. (2004) 'Corporate Governance Policy and Corporate Performance: The Portuguese Case', *Corporate Governance: An International Review*, **12**(3), July, 290–301.

Ambachtsheer, J. (2005) *Socially Responsible Investing – Moving into the Mainstream*, 23 June 2005, www.merceric.com.

Anglo American (2004) *Creating Enduring Value: Report to Society*, Anglo American plc, London, UK.

Apreda, R. (2001) 'Corporate governance in Argentina: The outcome of economic freedom', *Corporate Governance: An International Review*, **9**(4), October, 298–310.

Arlow, P. and Gannon, M. J. (1982) 'Social responsiveness, corporate structure and economic performance', *Academy of Management Review*, **7**, 235–241.

Arnold, G. (1998) 'Corporate Financial Management', *Financial Times,* Pitman Publishing, London.

Arthur Andersen (1996) 'What's the story? A survey of narrative reporting in annual reports', *Arthur Andersen*, Binder Hamlyn, London.

ASB (1996) *Derivatives and Other Financial Instruments* (discussion paper), Accounting Standards Board, Milton Keynes, UK.

ASSC (1975) *The Corporate Report* (Accounting Standards Steering Committee), Institute of Chartered Accountants in England and Wales, London.

Ball, A., Owen, D. L. and R. Gray (2000) 'External Transparency or Internal Capture? The Role of Third-Party Statements in Adding Value to Corporate Environmental Reports', *Business Strategy and the Environment*, **9**, 1–23.

Ball, S. and Bell, S. (1995) *Environmental Law* (3rd edn), Blackstone Press, London.

Barreveld, D. J. (2002) *The Enron Collapse: Creative Accounting, Wrong Economics or Criminal Acts?*, Writers Club Press, iUniverse Inc., USA.

Barrionuevo, A. and Evans, T. (2006) 'Witness in Enron Trial Struggles with Emotions', *Los Angeles Times* (LATIMES.com), 7 February.

Beaver, W. H. (1989) *Financial Reporting: An Accounting Revolution* (2nd edn), Prentice Hall International Editions, Upper Saddle River, NJ.

Beck, U. (1992) *Risk Society: Towards a New Modernity*, Sage Publications Ltd., London, UK.

Beck, U. (1999) *World Risk Society*, Polity, Blackwell Publishers Ltd., Oxford, UK.

Belcher, A. (2002) 'Corporate killing as a corporate governance issue', *Corporate Governance: An International Review*, **10**(1), January, 47–54.

Belkaoui, A. (1976) 'The impact of disclosure of the environmental effects of organizational behaviour on the market', *Financial Management*, **5**(4), 26–31.

Benston, G. J. (1982) 'Accounting and corporate accountability', *Accounting, Organisations and Society*, **7**(2), 87–105.

Berglof, E. and Perotti, E. (1994) 'The governance structure of the Japanese financial keiretsu', *Journal of Financial Economics*, **36**, 259–284.

Berle, A. and Means, G. (1932) *The Modern Corporation and Private Property*, New York.

Bethel, J. E., Liebeskind, J. P. and Opler, T. (1998) 'Block share repurchases and corporate performance', *Journal of Finance*, **53**, 605–635.

Bison, T. A. (1954) *Zaibatsu Dissolution in Japan*, Greenwood Press, Westport, CT.

Blackburn, S. (1999) 'Managing risk and achieving Turnbull compliance', *Accountants' Digest*, **417**, October, 1–51.

Blanchard, K. H. and Peale, N. V. (1988) *The Power of Ethical Management*, Morrow, New York.

Blitz, R. (2003) 'UK Survey Shows Wide Distrust of Directors', *Financial Times*, 29 June.

Boatright, J. R. (1999) *Ethics in Finance*, Blackwell, Oxford.

Bolger, A. and Jenkins, P. (2002) 'Animal Activists Target Marsh', *Financial Times*, 13 August.

Boritz, J. E. (1990) *Approaches to Dealing with Risk and Uncertainty* (CICA Research Report), Canadian Institute of Chartered Accountants, Toronto.

Bosch Report, The (1995) 'Corporate practices and conduct', *Information Australia* (3rd edn), Woodslane Pty Ltd, Melbourne.

Bosch, H. A. O. (1993) 'Corporate practices and conduct: Setting standards for corporate governance in Australia', *Corporate Governance: An International Review*, **1**(4), 196–198.

Bostock, R. (1995) 'Company responses to Cadbury', *Corporate Governance: An International Review*, **3**(2), April, 72–77.

Bowman, E. H. and Haire, M. (1975) 'A strategic posture toward corporate social responsibility', *California Management Review*, **18**(2), 49–58.

Boxell, J. (14 July 2003) 'Fat Cat" Pay Issue Set to Dominate AGMs', *Financial Times*, 14 July.

Boxell, J. (18 June 2003) 'Whitbread "Fat Cat" Protest Vote', *Financial Times*, 18 June.

Bradley, N. (2004) 'Corporate Governance Scoring and the Link between Corporate Governance and Performance Indicators: In Search of the Holy Grail', *Corporate Governance: An International Review*, **12**(1), January, 8–10.

Bream, R. (2003) 'AWG to Stop Special Bonuses', *Financial Times*, 9 July.

Brewer, J. (1997) 'The state of corporate governance in Hong Kong', *Corporate Governance: An International Review*, **5**(2), April, 77–82.

Briston, R. J. and Dobbins, R. (1978) *The Growth and Impact of Institutional Investors* (a report to the Research Committee of the ICAEW), The Institute of Chartered Accountants in England and Wales, London.

Brown, P. (2003) 'Use of Monkeys in Research "Can Be Reduced"', *The Guardian*, 2 July.

Buchan, D. and Earle, J. (2002) 'BP Puts $600 million Alaska Oilfield in Cold Storage', *Financial Times*, 8 June.

Buck, J. (1992) 'Green awareness: An opportunity for Business', in: D. Owen (ed.), *Green Reporting: Accounting and the Challenge of the Nineties*, Chapman & Hall, London.

Burgess, A. (1962) *A Clockwork Orange*, Penguin Books, Harmondsworth, UK.

Burgess, K. (2006) 'Top Executives See 18% Fall in Overall Remuneration Packages', *Financial Times*, 30 November, 3.

Burgess, K. (2006) 'Benefits of Code Compliance Doubted', *Financial Times*, 23 January, 3.

Bushman, R. M. and Smith, A. J. (2001) 'Financial accounting information and corporate governance', *Journal of Accounting and Economics*, **32**, 237–333.

Bushman, R., Indjejikian, R. and Smith, A. (1995) 'Aggregate performance measurement in business unit compensation: The role of intrafirm interdependencies', *Journal of Accounting Research*, **33**(Suppl.), 101–128.

Business Roundtable (September 1997) *Statement on Corporate Governance*, The Business Round-table, Washington, DC.

Butz and Blattner (1999) *Socially Responsible Investment: A Statistical Analysis of Returns* (Sarasin Basic Report), Basle, Switzerland.

Byrd, J. W. and Hickman, K. A. (1992) 'Do outside directors monitor managers?', *Journal of Financial Economics*, **32**, 195–221.

Cadbury Code, The (December 1992) *Report of the Committee on the Financial Aspects of Corporate Governance: The Code of Best Practice*, Gee Professional Publishing, London.

Cadbury, A. (2002) *Corporate Governance and Chairmanship: A Personal View*, Oxford University Press, Oxford.

CalPERS (April 1998) *Corporate Governance Market Principles*, California Public Employees' Retirement System, Sacramento, CA.

CalPERS *Corporate Governance Guidelines, The* (1999) Part published in *Corporate Governance: An International Review*, **7**(2).

Cannon, T. (1994) *Corporate Responsibility. A Textbook on Business Ethics, Governance, Environment: Roles and Responsibilities*, Pitman, London.

Carbon Trust, The (2005) *A Climate for Change: A Trustee's Guide to Understanding and Addressing Climate Risk*, The Carbon Trust, UK, August.

Carbon Trust, The (2006) *Climate Change and Shareholder Value*, The Carbon Trust, UK, March.

Cardon Report, The (1998) *Report of the Belgium Commission on Corporate Governance*, Brussels Stock Exchange, Brussels.

Carlyle, T. (1909) *Past and Present*, R. A. Kessinger Publishing, London.

CBI (1994) *Introducing Environmental Reporting Guidelines for Business*, Confederation of British Industry, London.

CEPS (1995) *Corporate Governance in Europe* (CEPS Working Party Report No. 12), Brussels.

CERES (1992) *The CERES Principles*, Coalition for Environmentally Responsible Economies, Washington, DC.

Chang, C. Z. and Chan, L. S. (2002) 'TSMC Establishes First Audit Committee', *Economy Daily*, 26 July [in Mandarin Chinese].

Charkham, J. (1994) *Keeping Good Company: A Study of Corporate Governance in Five Countries*, Clarendon Press, Oxford.

Charkham, J. and Simpson, A. (1999) *Fair Shares: The Future of Shareholder Power and Responsibilities*, Oxford University Press, Oxford.

Cheffins, B. R. (2003) 'Will executive pay globalise along American lines?', *Corporate Governance: An International Review*, **11**(1), January, 8–24.

Cheng, S. and Firth, M. (2005) 'Ownership, Corporate Governance and Top Management Pay in Hong Kong', *Corporate Governance: An International Review*, **13**(2), March, 291–302.

Child, J. and Rodrigues, S. B. (2004) 'Repairing the Breach of Trust in Corporate Governance', *Corporate Governance: An International Review*, **12**(2), April, 143–152.

Choi, C. J. and Wright, N. (1994) *How to Achieve Business Success in Korea: Where Confucius Wears a Three-Piece Suit*, Macmillan, Basingstoke, UK.

CICA (1994) *Reporting on Environmental Performance*, Canadian Institute of Chartered Accountants, Toronto.

CII (April 1998) *Desirable Corporate Governance: A Code*, Confederation of Indian Industry, New Delhi.

CII (March 1998) *Core Policies*, Council of Institutional Investors, Washington, DC.

Claessens, S., Djanklov, S. and Lang, L. H. P. (2000) 'The separation of ownership and control in East Asian corporations', *Journal of Financial Economics*, **58**, 81–112.

CMVM, The Portuguese Securities Market Commission (1992) *Recommendations on Corporate Governance*, http://www.CMVM.pt.

Coase, R. H. (1937) 'The nature of the firm', *Economica*, **4**, 386–405.

Cobb, G., Collison, D., Power, D. and L. Stevenson (2005) *FTSE4Good: Perceptions and Performance*, ACCA Research Report No. 88, Certified Accountants Educational Trust, London, UK.

Cochran, P. L. and Wood, R. A. (1984) 'Corporate social responsibility and financial performance', *Academy of Management Journal*, **27**(1), 42–56.

Coffee, J. C. (1996) 'Institutional investors in transitional economies: Lessons from the Czech experience', in: R. Frydman, C. W. Gray and A. Rapaczynski (eds), *Corporate Governance in Central Europe and Russia*. Volume 1: *Banks, Funds, and Foreign Investors* (pp. 111–186), Central European University Press, London.

Coffee, J. C., Jr (1991) 'Liquidity versus control: The institutional investor as corporate monitor', *Columbia Law Review*, **91**(6), October, 1277–1368.

Collett, P. and Hrasky, S. (2005) 'Voluntary Disclosure of Corporate Governance Practices by Listed Australian Companies', *Corporate Governance: An International Review*, **13**(2), March, 188–196.

Collier, P. A. (1992) *Audit Committees in Large UK Companies*, London: Research Board of the Institute of Chartered Accountants in England and Wales.

Collier, P. A. (1996) 'Audit Committees in UK Quoted Companies: A Curious Phenomenon?', *Accounting and Business History*, **6**, 121–140.

Collier, P. and Zaman, M. (2005) 'Convergence in European Corporate Governance: The Audit Committee Concept', *Corporate Governance: An International Review*, **13**(6), November, 753–768.

*Combined Code, The* (1998) The London Stock Exchange Limited, June, London, UK.

*Combined Code on Corporate Governance, The* (2003) Financial Reporting Council, July, London.

Commission of the European Communities (2001) *Promoting a European Framework for CSR*, Green Paper, Brussels.

Company Law (2001) *Company Law* (amended on 12 November 2001), translated into English by Lee & Li, Attorneys-at-Law, Taipei, Taiwan.

Conger, J. A. and Lawler, E. (2001) 'Building a High-Performing Board: How to Choose the Right Members', *London Business School Business Strategy Review*, Vol. 12.

Conyon, M. J. and Mallin, C. A. (1997) 'A review of compliance with Cadbury', *Journal of General Management*, **2**(3), spring, 24–37.

Cooke, T. E. and Sawa, E. (1998) 'Corporate governance structure in Japan: Form and reality', *Corporate Governance: An International Review*, **6**(4), 217–223.

Core, J. E. (2001) 'A review of the empirical disclosure literature: discussion', *Journal of Accounting and Economics*, **31**, 441–456.

Core, J. E., Holthausen, R. W. and Larcker, D. F. (1999) 'Corporate governance, chief executive officer compensation, and firm performance', *Journal of Financial Economics*, **51**, 371–406.

*Corporate Governance: A Practical Guide* (2004) London Stock Exchange and RSM Robson Rhodes LLP, August.

Corporate Governance Committee (May 1998) *Corporate Governance Principles*, Corporate Governance Forum of Japan, Tokyo.

Corporate Governance Forum of Japan (1999) 'Corporate governance principles – a Japanese view', *Corporate Governance: An International Review*, **7**(2), April.

*Corporate Governance Handbook, The* (1996) 'Supplement 1 on operating and financial review', Gee Professional Publishing, London.

Corporate Governance Report (1997) 'Corporate governance in the Netherlands', *Corporate Governance: An International Review*, **5**(4), October, 236–238.

Corporate Governance Update (January, 2004) *Corporate Governance: An International Review*, 119–124.

Corporate Governance Update (April, 2004) *Corporate Governance: An International Review*, 233–238.

Corporate Governance Update (July, 2004) *Corporate Governance: An International Review*, 408–414.

Corporate Governance Update (October, 2004) *Corporate Governance: An International Review*, 575–581.

Corporate Governance Update (January, 2005) *Corporate Governance: An International Review*, 101–105.

Corporate Governance Update (March, 2005) *Corporate Governance: An International Review*, 345–350.

Corporate Governance Update (May, 2005) *Corporate Governance: An International Review*, 458–461.

Corporate Governance Update (September, 2005) *Corporate Governance: An International Review*, 723–727.

Corporate Report, The, *see* ASSC (1975).

Courtis, J. K. (1993) 'Recent developments and frustrations in the corporate reporting process', *Corporate Governance: An International Review*, **1**(1), 18–25.

Cowe, R. (1992) 'Green issues and the investor: Inadequacies of current reporting practice and some suggestions for change', in: D. Owen (ed.), G*reen Reporting: Accounting and the Challenge of the Nineties*, Chapman & Hall, London.

Cowe, R. (2001) *Investing in Social Responsibility: Risks and Opportunities* (ABI Research Report), Association of British Insurers, London.

Croft, J. (2003) 'HSBC Shrugs Off Shareholder Protest', *Financial Times*, 12 May.

Croft, J. (24 July 2003) 'Anger at Nationwide Executive's Pay-Off', *Financial Times*, 24 July.

Cromme, G. (2005) 'Corporate Governance in Germany and the German Corporate Governance Code', *Corporate Governance: An International Review*, **13**(3), May, 362–367.

Crozier, M. (1964) *The Bureaucratic Phenomenon*, University of Chicago Press, Chicago.

Cruver, B. (2002) *The Unshredded Truth from an Enron Insider: Enron, Anatomy of Greed*, Arrow Books, London.

Cuervo, A. C. (2002) 'Corporate Governance Mechanisms: A Plea for Less Code and More Market Control', *Corporate Governance*, **10**, 84–93.

Cyert, R. M. and March, J. G. (1963) *A Behavioural Theory of the Firm*, Prentice Hall, Englewood Cliffs, NJ.

Dahya, J., McConnell, J. J. and Travlos, N. G. (2002) 'The Cadbury Committee, corporate performance, and top management turnover', *Journal of Finance*, **57**(1), February, 461–483.

Daily, C. M. and Dalton, D. R. (1997) 'Separate, but not independent: Board leadership structure in large corporations', *Corporate Governance: An International Review*, **5**(3), 126–136.

Daniels, R. J. and Morck, R. (1996) 'Canadian corporate governance policy options' (Discussion Paper No. 3), Industry Canada, March.

Daniels, R. J. and Waitzer, E. (1993) 'Corporate governance: A Canadian perspective', *Corporate Governance: An International Review*, **1**(2), April, 66–75.

De Andres, P., Azofra, V. and Lopez, F. (2005) 'Corporate Boards in OECD Countries: Size, Composition, Functioning and Effectiveness', *Corporate Governance: An International Review*, **13**(2), March, 197–210.

Deakin, S. and Konzelmann, S. J. (2004) 'Learning from Enron', *Corporate Governance: An International Review*, **12**(2), April, 134.

Deegan, C. and Rankin, M. (1996) 'Do Australian companies report environmental news objectively? An analysis of environmental disclosures by firms prosecuted successfully by the Environmental Protection Authority', *Accounting, Auditing and Accountability Journal*, **9**(2), 50–67.

Demirag, I. and Tylecote, A. (1992) 'The effects of organisational culture, structure and market expectations on technological innovation: A hypothesis', *British Journal of Management*, **3**(1), 7–20.

Deutsche Bundestag (March 1998) 'Law on Control and Transparency in the Corporate Sector', *Deutsche Bundestag*.

Dey Report, The (December 1994) *Where Were the Directors?*, Toronto Stock Exchange Committee on Corporate Governance in Canada, Toronto.

Diamond, D. and Verrecchia, R. (1991) 'Disclosure, liquidity, and the cost of capital', *Journal of Finance*, **66**, 1325–1355.

Diamond, D. W. (1984) 'Financial intermediation and delegated monitoring', *Review of Economic Studies*, **51**(3), 393–414.

Digital Korea Herald (27 April 2000) 'Top Financial Regulator Rejects Chaebol Demands for Regulation'.

Dobson, G. R. (1994) *The Global Investor*, Probus Europe, Cambridge.

Dombey, D. (2003) 'The Long March to Shareholder Democracy', *Financial Times*, 16 June.

Donaldson, L. and Davies, J. H. (1994) 'Boards and company performance – Research challenges the conventional wisdom', *Corporate Governance: An International Review*, **2**(3), July, 151–160.

Donaldson, T. and Preston, L. (1995) 'A stakeholder theory of the corporation: Concepts, evidence, and implications', *Academy of Management Review*, **20**(1), 65–91.

Draghi, M. (1998) 'Le Proposte della Commissione Draghi' (The Proposals of the Draghi Commission), *Il Sole 24 Ore On Line*, July.

Drexhage, G. (1998) 'There's money in ethics', *Global Investor*, **109**, 56.

Drucker, P. (1982) 'The new meaning of corporate social responsibility', *California Management Review*, **26**, 53–63.

DTI (1999) *Creating Quality Dialogue between Smaller Quoted Companies and Fund Managers*, Department of Trade and Industry, London.

DTTI (1993) *Coming Clean. Corporate Environmental Reporting*, Deloitte Touche Tohamatsu International, International Institute for Sustainable Development and SustainAbility Ltd, London.

Du, J. and Dai, Y. (2005) 'Ultimate Corporate Ownership Structures and Capital Structures: Evidence from East Asian Economies', *Corporate Governance: An International Review*, **13**(1), January, 60–71.

Durgin, H. and Wolffe, R. (2000) 'Oilman Bush Focuses on a Burning Issue: But Not All Analysts Are Convinced by His Plans to Drill in an Alaskan Wildlife Reserve', *Financial Times*, 12 October.

Durkheim, E. (1952) *Suicide*, Routledge & Kegan Paul, London (first published in French in 1897).

Eagle, J. (2000) 'Chemical Attack on Animal Researcher', *Birmingham Post*, 23 December.

Earle, J. (2001) 'Alaska Oil Spill Ahead of Vote', *Financial Times*, 24 July.

Earle, J. S., Kucsera, C. and Telegdy, A. (2005) 'Ownership Concentration and Corporate Performance on the Budapest Stock Exchange: Do Too Many Cooks Spoil the Goulash?', *Corporate Governance: An International Review*, **13**(2), March, 254–264.

*Economist, The* (26 February 1998) 'Electric Avenues'.

*Economist, The* (23 April 1998) 'Not As Billed'.

*Economist, The* (30 July 1998) 'Wet Behind the Ears'.

*Economist, The* (1st June 2000) 'The Energetic Messiah'.

*Economist, The* (15 June 2000) 'Buying a Financial Umbrella'.

*Economist, The* (8 February 2001) 'The Slumbering Giants Awake'.

*Economist, The* (28 June 2001) 'A Matter of Principals'.

*Economist, The* (1 November 2001) 'Houston, We Have a Problem'.

*Economist, The* (15 November 2001) 'See You In Court'.

*Economist, The* (29 November 2001) 'Upended'.

*Economist, The* (6 December 2001) 'The Amazing Disintegrating Firm'.

*Economist, The* (20 December 2001) 'Who Fiddled What?'.

*Economist, The* (7 February 2002) 'The Lessons from Enron'.

*Economist, The* (7 February 2002) 'When the Numbers Don't Add Up'.

*Economist, The* (2 May 2002) 'Badly In Need of Repair'.

*Economist, The* (9 May 2002) 'Bad News, Good News'.

*Economist, The* (21 May 2002) 'Picking Over Andersen'.

*Economist, The* (13 June 2002) 'Designed by Committee'.

*Economist, The* (13 June 2002) 'Prosecutor's Dilemma'.

*Economist, The* (15 August 2002) 'I Swear. . . '.

*Economist, The* (3 October 2002) 'But Not Forgotten'.

*Economist, The* (31 October 2002) 'Cleaning Up the Boardroom'.

*Economist, The* (15 November 2002) 'Executive Pay: The Background'.

*Economist, The* (28 November 2002) 'Investor Self-Protection'.

Edwards, J. and Fischer, K. (1994) *Banks, Finance and Investment in Germany*, Cambridge University Press, New York.

Eisenhardt, K. (1989) 'Agency Theory: An Assessment and Review', *Academy of Management Review*, **14**, 57–74.

Elkington, J. (1998) *Cannibals with Forks*, New Society, Gabriola Island, BC.

Elliott, A. L. and Schroth, R. J. (2002) *How Companies Lie: Why Enron is Just the Tip of the Iceberg*, Nicholas Brealey, London.

*Ethical Investor, The* (November/December 1999) Newsletter produced by the Ethical Investment Research Service (EIRIS), London.

*Ethical Investor, The* (Autumn, 2003) 'Fund Managers Get the Message', 2.

European Commission (2001) *Promoting a European Framework for Corporate Social Responsibility* (Green Paper), European Commission, Brussels.

European Financial Services Regulation (2003) 'Bolkestein outlines top priorities for FSAP and corporate governance', *European Financial Services Regulation*, **4**, July, 1–2.

Ezzamel, M. and Watson, R. (1997) 'Wearing Two Hats: The Conflicting Control and Management Roles of Non-Executive Directors', In K. Keasey, S. Thompson and M. Wright (eds) *Corporate Governance: Economic, Management and Financial Issues*, Oxford University Press, Oxford, UK.

Faccio, M. and Lasfer, M. A. (2000) 'Do occupational pension funds monitor companies in which they hold large stakes?', *Journal of Corporate Finance*, **6**, 71–110.

Fama, E. F. (1970) 'Efficient capital markets: A review of theory and empirical work', *Journal of Finance*, **25**, 383–417.

Fama, E. F. (1980) 'Agency problems and the theory of the firm', *Journal of Political Economy*, **88**, 288–307.

Fama, E. F. and Jensen, M. C. (1983) 'Separation of ownership and control', *Journal of Law and Economics*, **27**, 301–325.

Farrar, J. H. and Hannigan, B. M. (1998) *Farrar's Company Law* (4th edn), Butterworths, London.

FEE (2000) *Towards a Generally Accepted Framework for Environmental Reporting*, European Federation of Accountants, Brussels.

Financial Reporting Council (FRC) (2005) *Internal Control: Revised Guidance for Directors on the Combined Code*, FRC, October.

*Financial Times* (2 September 1998) 'Huntingdon Investors Approve Refinancing'.

*Financial Times* (11 April 2000) 'Eco-Shareholders Target BP'.

*Financial Times* (13 April 2000) 'Five Protesters Arrested'.

*Financial Times* (7 May 2000) 'Friends Provident Backs Ethics'.

*Financial Times* (27 June 2000) 'Alaska Oil: The Debate Heats Up Again'.

*Financial Times* (4 June 2003) 'Curbing Failure's Rotten Reward'.

*Financial Times* (26 January 2006) 'All Power to the Shareholders: Action by Investors is Preferable to Government Intervention'.

*Financial Times* (4 March 2006) 'Junking Fatty Foods and Fizzy Drinks: But a Lot More Exercise is Needed for a Healthy Lifestyle', 8.

Firn, D. (2000) 'Huntingdon to Lose NYSE Listing', *Financial Times*, 22 December.

Firn, D. (2002) 'Silent Message to Animal Rights Activists', *Financial Times*, 10 January.

Firn, D. and Guerrera, F. (2000) 'Bank Drops Its Holding in Animal Tests Group', *Financial Times*, 12 December.

Firn, D. and Jenkins, P. (2003) 'Animal Activists Expand Campaign Against HLS', *Financial Times*, 14 March.

Fitzpatrick, N. (2003) 'Shareholders Targeted by New Code', *Pensions Week*, 28 July, 40.

Flanagan, M. (2003) 'Higgs Challenge as Davis to Step Up at Sainsbury', *The Scotsman*, 15 March.

Florence, S. (1961) *Ownership, Control and Success of Large Companies*, Sweet & Maxwell, London.

Fombrun, C. J. (2000) 'The Value to be Found in Corporate Reputation: The Public's View of a Company Not Only Acts as a Reservoir of Goodwill but also Boosts the Bottom Line', *Financial Times*, 4 December.

Fombrun, C. J. and Shanley, M. (1990) 'What's in a name? Reputation-building and corporate strategy', *Academy of Management Journal*, **33**, 233–258.

Fox, L. (2003) *Enron: The Rise and Fall*, John Wiley & Sons Inc, Hoboken, NJ.

Franks, J. and Mayer, C. (1994) 'The ownership and control of German corporations' (manuscript), London Business School, London.

Freeman, E. (1984) *Strategic Management: A Stakeholder Approach*, Pitman Press, Boston.

Freire, P. (1996) *Pedagogy of the Oppressed*, Pelican, London.

Frémond, O. and Capaul, M. (May 2003) *Corporate Governance Country Assessment: Chile* (World Bank Report on the Observance of Standards and Codes). Available online at http://worldbank.org/ifa/rosc_chlcg.pdf

French, P. (1979) 'The corporation as a moral person', *American Philosophical Quarterly*, **16**(3), 207–215.

French, P. (1984) *Collective and Corporate Responsibility*, Columbia University Press, New York.

Freshflieds Bruckhaus Deringer (2005) A Legal Framework for the Integration of Environmental, Social and Governance Issues into Institutional Investment, UNEP Finance Initiative, produced for the Asset Management Working Group of the UNEP Finance Initiative, October.

Friedman, A. L. and Miles, S. (2001) 'Socially responsible investment and corporate social and environmental reporting in the UK: An exploratory study', *British Accounting Review*, **33**, 523–548.

Friedman, M. (1962) *Capitalism and Freedom*, University of Chicago, Chicago.

Friedman, M. (1970) 'The Social Responsibility of Business is to Increase its Profits', *New York Times Magazine*, 13 September. Reprinted in Beauchamp, T. L. and Bowie, N. (1988) *Ethical Theory and Business* (pp. 87–91), Prentice Hall, Englewood Cliffs, NJ.

*Frontline* (2002) 'In Harshad Mehta's Wake: Harshad Mehta is Dead, but the Trail Goes On', (India's National Magazine).

Fukuyama, F. (1995) *Trust: The Social Virtues and the Creation of Prosperity*, Penguin Books, Harmondsworth, UK.

Fusaro, P. C. and Miller, R. M. (2002) *What Went Wrong at Enron: Everyone's Guide to the Largest Bankruptcy in US History*, John Wiley & Sons, Hoboken, NJ.

Garratt, B. (1996) *The Fish Rots from the Head*, HarperCollins Business, London.

Garratt, B. (2005) 'A Portrait of Professional Directors: UK Corporate Governance in 2015', *Corporate Governance: An International Review*, **13**(2), March, 122–126.

Giddens, A. (1990) *The Consequences of Modernity*, Stanford University Press, Stanford, California, USA.

Giddens, A. (1991) *Modernity and Self-Identity, Self and Society in the Late Modern Age*, Polity Press, Oxford.

Gilson, R. J. and Mnookin, R. (1985) 'Sharing among the Human Capitalists: An Economic Inquiry into the Corporate Law Firm and How Partners Split Profits', *Stanford Law Review*, **37**, January, 313–397.

GM Board of Directors (June 1997) *GM Board of Directors Corporate Governance Guidelines on Significant Governance Issues* (2nd edn), General Motors, Detroit.

Goodpaster, K. E. (1982) 'Kohlbergian Theory: A Philosophical Counterinvitation', *Ethics*, April, 491–498.

Goodpaster, K. E. (1987) 'The Principle of Moral Projection: A Reply to Professor Ranken', *Journal of Business Ethics*, **6**, 329–332.

Goswami, O. (2000) 'The Tide Rises, Gradually: Corporate Governance in India', *Informal Workshop on Corporate Governance in Developing Countries and Emerging Economies*, OECD Headquarters, Paris.

Government Commission (2001) *German Corporate Governance Code* (translation), Government Commission, Dusseldorf.

Government Update, A. (2004) 'Corporate Social Responsibility: A Government Update', www.societyandbusiness.gov.uk/pdf/dti_csr_final.pdf, accessed May 2004.

Grant, P. (2006) 'Despair as Consultation on OFR Descends into "Farce"', *AccountancyAge*, 9th February, p.1.

Graves, S. B. and Waddock, S. A. (1994) 'Institutional owners and corporate social performance', *Academy of Management Journal*, **37**(4), August, 1034–1046.

Gray R., Bebbington, J. and Walters, D. (1993) *Accounting for the Environment*, Paul Chapman Publishing, London.

Gray, R. H. (1992) 'Accounting and environmentalism: An exploration of the challenge of gently accounting for accountability, transparency and sustainability', *Accounting, Organizations and Society*, **17**(5), 399–426.

Gray, R., Owen, D. and Adams, C. (1996) *Accounting and Accountability*, Prentice Hall, London.

Gray, R., Owen, D. and Maunders, K. (1987) *Corporate Social Reporting: Accounting and Accountability*, Prentice Hall, London.

Greenbury Report, The (July 1995) *Directors' Remuneration* (report of a study group chaired by Sir Richard Greenbury), Gee Professional Publishing, London.

Gregory, A., Matatko, J. and Luther, R. (1997) 'Ethical unit trust financial performance: small company effects and fund size effects', *Journal of Business Finance and Accounting*, **24**(5), June, 705–725.

GRI (2000) 'Sustainability reporting guidelines', available at the Global Reporting Initiative website, www.globalreporting.org

Griffin, J. and Mahon, J. F. (1997) 'The corporate social performance and corporate financial performance debate: Twenty-five years of incomparable research', *Business and Society*, **36**(1), 5–31.

Griffin, P. (2000) 'Wreath-Laying Marks Anniversary of Guinea Pig Raid', *Birmingham Post*, 2 September.

Groves, J. (1999) 'Identifying, developing and effectively implementing a risk management methodology which suits your company's operating strategy and corporate culture', *IIR Conference on Proactively Managing Business Risk and Ensuring Effective Internal Control in the Light of the Combined Code and the New Turnbull Committee Report*, London, May.

Guan, E. (2002) 'News Focus: SFC Sticks to Strengthen Corporate Governance', *Taiwan Business News*.

*Guardian, The* (29 August 2000) 'NIMAL Lab Staff Cars Set on Fire'.

Guerard, J. B. (1996) 'Is there a cost to being socially responsible in investing?', *Social Investment Forum Research*.

Guerard, J. B. (1997) 'Additional evidence of the cost of being socially responsible in investing', *Journal of Investing*, **6**(4), 31–36.

Guerrera, F. (2000a) 'Animal Rights Hit HLS Investors', *Financial Times*, 26 June.

Guerrera, F. (2000b) 'Huntingdon Seeks £34 million Lifeline in US. Drug Testing Group Says Attacks by Animal Rights Protesters Prompted it to Look Abroad', *Financial Times*, 16 August.

Hampel Report, The (1998) *The Final Report*, The Committee on Corporate Governance and Gee Professional Publishing, London.

Hancock, J. (1999) *Making Gains with Values: The Ethical Investor*, Financial Times/Prentice Hall, London.

Hansen, G. S. and Hill, C. W. L. (1991) 'Are institutional investors myopic? A time series study of four technology driven industries', *Strategic Management Journal*, **12**, 1–16.

Harris, C. (2003) 'WPP Shareholders Challenge Sorrell Contract', *Financial Times*, 30 June.

Hart, O. D. (1983) 'The market mechanism as an incentive scheme', *Bell Journal of Economics*, **14**, 366–382.

Harte, G. and Owen, D. (1992) 'Current trends in the reporting of green issues in the annual reports of United Kingdom companies', in: D. Owen (ed.), *Green Reporting: Accountancy and the Challenge of the Nineties* (pp. 166–200), Chapman & Hall, London.

Harte, G., Lewis, L. and Owen, D. (1991) 'Ethical investment and the corporate reporting function', *Critical Perspectives on Accounting*, **2**, 227–253.

Heal, G. (2000) 'Environmental Disaster: Not All Bad News', *Financial Times*, 30 October.

Healy, P. M. and Palepu, K. G. (2001) 'Information asymmetry, corporate disclosure, and the capital markets: A review of the empirical disclosure literature', *Journal of Accounting and Economics*, **31**, 405–440.

Healy, P. M., Hutton, A. and Palepu, K. (1999) 'Stock performance and intermediation changes surrounding sustained increases in disclosure', *Contemporary Accounting Research*, **16**, 485–520.

Hemmings, D. B. and Solomon, J. F. (1998) 'Corporate governance and stock market duration for South Korea and the USA', *Global Economic Review*, **27**(3), Autumn, 76–92.

Hermalin, B. E. and Weisbach, M. S. (1988) 'The determinants of board composition', *Rand Journal of Economics*, **19**, winter, 589–606.

Hermanson, H. M. (2000) 'An analysis of the demand for reporting on internal control', *Accounting Horizons*, **14**(3), September, 325–341.

Higgs Report, The (January 2003) *Review of the Role and Effectiveness of Non-Executive Directors*, Department of Trade and Industry, London.

High Level Finance Committee on Corporate Governance (February 1999) *The Malaysian Code on Corporate Governance* (High Level Finance Committee Report on Corporate Governance, Chapter 5), High Level Finance Committee on Corporate Governance, Kuala Lumpur.

Hill, C. W. and Jones, T. M. (1992) 'Stakeholder–agency theory', *Journal of Management Studies*, **29**, 134–154.

Hillman, A. J. and Keim, G. D. (2001) 'Shareholder value, stakeholder management, and social issues: What's the bottom line?', *Strategic Management Journal*, **22**, 125–139.

*Hindu, The* (12 January 2002) 'Cases Against Harshad Mehta to Continue'.

Hirschman, A. O. (1970) '"Exit", "voice" and "the elusive optimal mix of exit and voice"', *Exit, Voice and Loyalty: Responses to Decline in Firms, Organizations, and States*, Harvard University Press, Cambridge, MA.

HKSA (December 1997) *A Guide for the Formation of an Audit Committee*, Hong Kong Society of Accountants, Hong Kong.

Holden-Meehan (1999) *The Millennium Guide to Ethical and Environmental Investment*, Holden-Meehan, Bristol.

Holland, J. (1998) 'Private disclosure and financial reporting', *Accounting and Business Research*, **28**(4), Autumn, 255–269.

Holland, J. and Stoner, G. (1996) 'Dissemination of price sensitive information and management of voluntary corporate disclosure', *Accounting and Business Research*, **26**(4), 295–313.

Hooghiemstra, R. and Manen, J. V. (2004) 'The Independence Paradox: (Im)possibilities Facing Non-Executive Directors in the Netherlands', *Corporate Governance: An International Review*, **12**(3), July, 314–324.

Hoshi, T. and Kashyap, A. (2001) *Corporate Financing and Governance in Japan: The Road to the Future*, MIT Press, Cambridge, MA.

Hoshi, T., Kashyap, A. and Scharfstein, D. (1991) 'Corporate structure, liquidity, and investment: Evidence from Japanese industrial groups', *Quarterly Journal of Economics*, **106**, 33–60.

Humphrey, C., Moizer, P. and Turley, S. (1992) *The Audit Expectations Gap in the United Kingdom*, Institute of Chartered Accountants in England and Wales, London.

Hussain, S. H. and Mallin, C. (2002) 'Corporate governance in Bahrain', *Corporate Governance: An International Review*, **10**(3), 197–210.

Hutton, W. and Giddens, A. (2001) *On the Edge: Living with Global Capitalism*, Vintage, London.

Hutton, W. (1995) *The State We're In*, Vintage Books, London.

ICAEW (1998) *Financial Reporting of Risk: Proposals for a Statement of Business Risk*, Institute of Chartered Accountants in England and Wales, London.

IMF (July 2001) *Czech Republic: Financial System Stability Assessment* (IMF Country Report), International Monetary Fund, Washington, DC.

Independent Audit Limited (2006) *Better Governance Reporting*, Independent Audit Limited, London, UK.

*Independent, The* (16 September 2000) 'Government to Keep Animal Testing Secret'.

*Independent, The* (18 November 2000) 'Blair Tells Violent Eco-Warriors They Can't Stop Science'.

Ingley, C. B. and van der Walt, N. T. (2004) 'Corporate Governance, Institutional Investors and Conflicts of Interest' *Corporate Governance: An International Review*, **12**(4), October, 534–551.

*International Investment Management Directory* (1993/94), Euromoney Books/Global Investor, London.

ISC (1993) *Report on Investigation of Use of Voting Rights by Institutions*, Institutional Shareholders Committee, London.

ISC (2002) *The Responsibilities of Institutional Shareholders and Agents – Statement of Principles*, Institutional Shareholders Committee, London.

Jenkins, P. (2001) 'Huntingdon Set to Begin Trading on US Market', *Financial Times*.

Jensen, M. (1991) 'Corporate control and the politics of finance', *Journal of Applied Corporate Finance*, **4**(2), 13–33.

Jensen, M. (1993) 'The modern industrial revolution, exit, and the failure of internal control systems', *Journal of Finance*, **48**, 831–880.

Jensen, M. and Ruback, R. S. (1983) 'The market for corporate control: The scientific evidence', *Journal of Financial Economics*, **11**, 5–50.

Jensen, M. C. and Meckling, W. H. (1976) 'Theory of the firm: Managerial behaviour, agency costs and ownership structure', *Journal of Financial Economics*, **3**, October, 305–360.

Jesover, F. (2001) 'Corporate governance in the Russian Federation: The relevance of the OECD Principles on shareholder rights and equitable treatment', *Corporate Governance: An International Review*, **9**(2), April, 79–88.

Jesover, F. and Kirkpatrick, G. (2005) 'The Revised OECD Principles of Corporate Governance and their Relevance to Non-OECD Countries', *Corporate Governance: An International Review*, **13**(2), March, 127–136.

Johnson, R. A. and Greening, D. W. (1994) 'Relationships between corporate social performance, financial performance and firm governance', *Best Paper Proceedings of the Academy of Management*, 314–319.

Johnson, S., Boone, P., Breach, A. and Friedman, E. (2000) 'Corporate governance in the Asian financial crisis', *Journal of Financial Economics*, **58**, 141–186.

Jones, I. and Pollitt, M. (2002) 'Who Influences Debates in Business Ethics? An Investigation into the Development of Corporate Governance in the UK since 1990', in I. W. Jones and M. G. Pollitt (eds) *Understanding How Issues in Business Ethics Develop*. Basingstoke, Palgrave, UK.

Jones, I. and Pollitt, M. (2004) 'Understanding How Issues in Corporate Governance Develop: Cadbury Report to Higgs Review', *Corporate Governance: An International Review*, **12**(2), April, 162–171.

Jones, M. J. (1996) 'Accounting for biodiversity: A pilot study', *British Accounting Review*, **28**(4), 281–303.

Jones, M. J. (2006) 'Accounting for the Environment: Towards a Theoretical Perspective for Environmental Reporting', Paper presented at the *British Accounting Association conference*, Portsmouth, April.

Jones, M. J. and Solomon, J. F. (2006) 'Preliminary Thoughts on Social and Environmental Audit', paper presented at the *European Accounting Association conference*, Dublin, Ireland, March.

Jones, R. (2002) 'FTSE 100 Prepares for Shareholder Vote on Pay', *Investors Chronicle*, 25 January, 10.

Jonsson, E. I. (2004) The Icelandic Corporate Governance System, Unpublished working paper.

Jonsson, E. I. (2005) 'The Role Model of the Board: A Preliminary Study of the Roles of Icelandic Boards', *Corporate Governance: An International Review*, **13**(5), September, 710–717.

Judge, W. and Naoumova, I. (2004) 'Corporate Governance in Russia: What Model Will It Follow?', *Corporate Governance: An International Review*, **12**(3), July, 302–313.

Kamp-Roelands, N. (1996) *FEE Research Paper on Expert Statements in Environmental Reports*, Federation des Experts Comptables Europeens, Brussels, Belgium.

Kang, J. K. and Shivdasani, A. (1995) 'Firm performance, corporate governance, and top executive turnover in Japan', *Journal of Financial Economics*, **38**, 29–58.

Kaplan, R. S. and Norton, D. P. (1996) *The Balanced Scorecard: Translating Strategy into Action*, Harvard Business School Press, Boston.

Kaplan, S. N. and Minton, B. A. (1994) 'Appointments of outsiders to Japanese boards: Determinants and implications for managers', *Journal of Financial Economics*, **36**, 225–258.

Karpo, J. M., Malatesta, P. H. and Walkling, R. A. (1996) 'Corporate governance and shareholder initiatives: Empirical evidence', *Journal of Financial Economics*, **42**, 365–395.

Katz, D. and Kahn, R. L. (1978) *The Social Psychology of Organizations*, 2nd edition, John Wiley & Sons, Inc., New York.

Keasey, K. and Wright, M. (1993) 'Issues in corporate accountability and governance', *Accounting and Business Research*, **91a**, 291–303.

Keating, S. (1997) 'Determinants of divisional performance evaluation practices', *Journal of Accounting and Economics*, **24**, 243–273.

Kessler and Gottsman (1998) 'Smart screened investments: Environmentally screened funds that perform like conventional equity funds', *Journal of Investing*, **7**(3), 15–24.

Keynes, J. M. (1936) *The General Theory of Employment, Interest and Money*, Macmillan, Basingstoke, UK.

Kim, O. and Verrecchia, R. (1994) 'Market liquidity and volume around earnings announcements', *Journal of Accounting and Economics*, **17**, 41–68.

King Report, The (1994) *The King Report on Corporate Governance*, The Institute of Directors in South Africa, South Africa, 29 November.

King Report, The (2002) *The King Report on Corporate Governance for South Africa*, King Committee on Corporate Governance, Institute of Directors in Southern Africa, Parktown, South Africa.

Kingsley, C. (1984) *The Water Babies*, Puffin Books, Penguin Books, Harmondsworth, UK (first published in 1863).

Kirchgaessner, S. (2003) 'Telewest Fends Off Criticism by Shareholders', *Financial Times*, 13 June.

Kirkbride, J. and Letza, S. (2005) 'Can the Non-Executive Director be an Effective Gatekeeper? The Possible Development of a Legal Framework of Accountability', *Corporate Governance: An International Review*, **13**(4), July, 542–549.

Klein, P., Shapiro, D. and Young, J. (2005) 'Corporate Governance, Family Ownership and Firm Value: The Canadian Evidence', *Corporate Governance: An International Review*, **13**(6), November, 769–784.

KLSE (2002) *Malaysian Corporate Governance Survey*, Kuala Lumpur Stock Exchange and PricewaterhouseCoopers. Available online at http://www.pwcglobal.com/pdf/my/eng/survrep/cgsurvey2002execsummary.pdf

Knowles, R. (1997) *Ethical Investment*, Choice Books, Marrickville, New South Wales, Australia.

Koladkiewicz, I. (2001) 'Building of a corporate governance system in Poland: Initial experiences', *Corporate Governance: An International Review*, **9**(3), July, 228–237.

Kothari, S. P. (2001) 'Capital markets research in accounting', *Journal of Accounting and Economics*, **31**, 105–231.

Kotter, J. P. and Heskett, J. L. (1992) *Corporate Culture and Performance*, Free Press, New York.

KPMG (2002) *International Survey of Corporate Sustainability Reporting*, KPMG, Amsterdam.

Kula, V. (2005) 'The Impact of the Roles, Structure and Process of Boards on Firm Performance: Evidence from Turkey', *Corporate Governance: An International Review*, **13**(2), March, 265–276.

Lambert, R., Larker, D. and Weigelt, K. (1993) 'The structure of organisational incentives', *Administrative Science Quarterly*, **38**, 438–461.

La Porta, R., Lopez-de-Silanes, F. and Shleifer, A. (1999) 'Corporate ownership around the world', *Journal of Finance*, **54**, 471–518.

La Porta, R., Lopez-de-Silanes, F., Shleifer, A. and Vishny, R. W. (1997) 'Legal determinants of external finance', *Journal of Finance*, **52**(3), 1131–1150.

La Porta, R., Lopez-de-Silanes, F., Shleifer, A. and Vishny, R. W. (1998) 'Law and finance', *Journal of Political Economy*, **106**, 1113–1155.

Lawniczak, R. (1997) 'A Polish experiment in corporate governance – The National Investment Funds (NIFs)', *Corporate Governance: An International Review*, **5**(2), April, 67–76.

Lee, L. (2002) 'Time for Taiwan to Act on Non-Performing Loans', *Taipei Times*, 23 August.

Leftwich, R. (1983) 'Accounting information in private markets: Evidence from private lending agreements', *The Accounting Review*, **58**(1), 23–42.

Lehman, C. R. (1983) *Stalemate in Corporate Social Responsibility Research* (Working Paper No. 3), Public Interest Section, American Accounting Association, Sarasota, FL.

Longman (1984) *Dictionary of the English Language*, Longman, Harlow, UK.

Lozano, J. M. (2000) *Ethics and Organizations*, Kluwer Academic, Boston.

LSE (February 1994) *Guidance on the Dissemination of Price Sensitive Information*, London Stock Exchange, London.

Luther, R. G. and Matatko, J. (1994) 'The performance of ethical unit trusts: Choosing an appropriate benchmark', *British Accounting Review*, **26**, 77–89.

Luther, R. G., Matatko, J. and Corner, D. C. (1992) 'The investment performance of UK "Ethical" unit trusts', *Accounting, Auditing and Accountability Journal*, **5**(4), 57–70.

Mace, M. L. (1986) *Directors: Myth and Reality*, Harvard Business School Press, Boston.

MacKenzie, C. (2004) 'Don't Stop Rattling Those Boardroom Chains: Corporate Activists Are Key to Maintaining Shareholder Returns', *Financial Times*, 10 May, 6.

Macve, R. and Carey, A. (1992) *Business, Accountancy and the Environment: A Policy and Research Agenda*, Institute of Chartered Accountants in England and Wales, London.

Maitland, A. (2003) 'Importance of Training the NEDs', *Financial Times*, 7 July.

Maitland, A. (2006) 'Obesity Fears Carry Weight with Investors', *Financial Times*, 6 March, 2.

Mallin, C. (1999) 'Financial institutions and their relationship with corporate boards', *Corporate Governance: An International Review*, **7**(3), July, 248–255.

Mallin, C. A. (1996) 'The Voting Framework: A Comparative Study of Voting Behaviour of Institutional Investors in the US and the UK', *Corporate Governance: An International Review*, **4**(2), April, 107–122.

Mallin, C. A. (2001) 'Institutional investors and voting practices: An international comparison', *Corporate Governance: An International Review*, **9**(2), April, 118–126.

Mallin, C. A. and Jelic, R. (2000) 'Developments in Corporate Governance in Central and Eastern Europe', *Corporate Governance: An International Review*, **8**(1), January, 43–51.

Mallin, C. A., Saadouni, B. and Briston, R. J. (1995) 'The financial performance of ethical investment funds', *Journal of Business Finance and Accounting*, **22**, 483–96.

Mallin, C. (2002) 'Institutional Investors: The Growth of Global Influences', *Corporate Governance: An International Review*, **10**, 67–68.

Mallin, C. (2003) 'Editorial: Non-Executive Directors: Key Characteristics', *Corporate Governance: An International Review*, **11**(4), October, 287–288.

Mallin, C. (2005) 'Directors: How Training and Development Can Enhance Their Role', *Corporate Governance: An International Review*, **13**(6), November, 729.

Mallin, C., Mullineux, A. and Wihlborg, C. (2005) 'The Financial Sector and Corporate Governance: The UK Case', *Corporate Governance: An International Review*, **13**(4), July, 532–541.

Maltby, J. (1995) 'Environmental Audit, Theory and Practice. A Survey of Environmental Consultants' Views on the Purpose of Audit', *Managerial Auditing Journal*, **10**(8), 15–26.

Mansley, M. (2000) *Socially Responsible Investment: A Guide for Pension Funds and Institutional Investors*, Monitor Press, Sudbury, UK.

March, J. G. and Simon, H. A. (1958) *Organizations*, John Wiley & Sons Inc, New York.

Mathews, M. R. (1993) *Socially Responsible Accounting*, Chapman & Hall, London.

Mathieu, E. (2000) *Response of UK Pension Funds to the SRI Disclosure Regulation*, UK Social Investment Forum ('UKSIF') October.

Mayer, C. (2000) 'Ownership matters', inaugural lecture given in Brussels.

Mayo, C. and Young, M. (March 2002) *Cool for Cats: The DTI's Proposals on Directors' Remuneration*, Simmons & Simmons, London.

Mayson, S. W., French, D. and Ryan, C. (1998) *Company Law* (12th edn), Blackstone Press, London.

McBride, S. (2002) 'Heard in Asia: Corporate governance becomes a strong factor for investors', *The Asian Wall Street Journal*, 18 July.

McCann, L., Solomon, A. and Solomon, J. F. (2003) 'Explaining the recent growth in UK socially responsible investment', *Journal of General Management*, **28**(3), summer, 32–53.

McCarthy, D. and Puffer, S. (2002) 'Corporate Governance in Russia: Towards a European, US or Russian Model?' *European Management Journal*, **20**, 630–640.

McGuire, J. B., Sundgren, A. and Schneeweis, T. (1988) 'Corporate social responsibility and firm financial performance', *Academy of Management Journal*, **31**(4), 854–872.

McLaren, D. (2004) 'Global Stakeholders: Corporate Accountability and Investor Engagement', *Corporate Governance: An International Review*, **12**(2), April, 191–201.

McNulty, S. (2006a) 'Punches Start to Land on Lay and Skilling in Enron Trial', *Financial Times*, 24 February, 26.

McNulty, S. (2006b) 'Fastow's Tears Turn Tables in Enron Trial', *Financial Times*, 15 March, 26.

McNulty, S. (2006c) 'Prosecutors Keep it Simple in Enron Trial', *Financial Times*, 28 March, 26.

Melis, A. (1999) *Corporate Governance. Un'Analisi Empirica Della Realtà Italiana In Un'Ottica Europa.* Torino: Giappichelli.

Melis, A. (2000) 'Corporate Governance in Italy', *Corporate Governance: An International Review*, **8**(4), October, 347–355.

Melis, A. (2004) 'On the Role of the Board of Statutory Auditors in Italian Listed Companies', *Corporate Governance: An International Review*, **12**(1), January, 74–84.

Melis, A. (2005) 'Corporate Governance Failures: To What Extent is Parmalat a Particularly Italian Case?', *Corporate Governance: An International Review*, **13**(4), 478–488.

Melvin, C. (2006) 'Ownership, Conflict and the Universal Investor', presentation at the *Symposium on Shareholder and Stakeholder Relations*, ACCA, 9 February, London.

Mercer Investment Consulting (2005) *SRI: What Do Investment Managers Think?* 12 March, Mercer Human Resource Consulting LLC and Investment Consulting Inc., New York.

Mercer Investment Consulting (2006) *2006 Fearless Forecast: What Do Investment Managers Think About Responsible Investment?* March, Mercer Human Resource Consulting LLC and Investment Consulting Inc., New York.

Mertzanis, H. V. (2001) 'Principles of Corporate Governance in Greece', *Corporate Governance*, **9**, 89–100.

Meyrick-Jones, J. (1999) 'Effective strategies to ensure you overcome the barrier of corporate culture when adopting a proactive risk management approach', *IIR Conference on Proactively Managing Business Risk and Ensuring Effective Internal Control in the Light of the Combined Code and the New Turnbull Committee Report*, London, May.

Midgley, K. (1974) 'How much control do shareholders exercise?', *Lloyds Bank Review*, **14**, 24–37.

Mikkelson, W. H. and Ruback, R. S. (1985) 'An empirical analysis of the interfirm equity investment process', *Journal of Financial Economics*, **14**, 523–553.

Milliken, F. J. and Martins, L. L. (1996) 'Searching for Common Threads: Understanding the Multiple Effects of Diversity in Organisational Groups', *Academy of Management Review*, **21**, 402–433.

Minns, R. (1980) *Pension Funds and British Capitalism*, Heinemann, London.

Mintz, S. M. (2005) 'Corporate Governance in an International Context: Legal Systems, Financing Patterns and Cultural Variables', *Corporate Governance: An International Review*, **13**(5), September, 582–597.

Mitchell, A. and Sikka, P. (2005) 'Taming the Corporations', *Association for Accountancy & Business Affairs*, Essex UK.

*Modernising Company Law* (July 2002) White Paper presented to Parliament, Department of Trade and Industry, London.

Moher, B. (2004) 'Deloitte and Grant Thornton Face £5 Billion Parmalat Lawsuit', *Accountancy Age*, 19 August.

Monks, R. A. G. (1994) 'Tomorrow's corporation', *Corporate Governance: An International Review*, **2**(3), July, 125–130.

Monks, R. A. G. (2001) *The New Global Investors: How Shareholders Can Unlock Sustainable Prosperity Worldwide*, Capstone Publishing, Oxford.

Monks, R. A. G. and Minow, N. (2001) *Corporate Governance* (2nd edn), Blackwell, Oxford.

Monks, R. A. G. (2005) 'Corporate Governance – USA – Fall 2004 Reform – The Wrong Way and the Right Way', *Corporate Governance: An International Review*, **13**(2), March, 108–113.

Montagnon, P. (2004) 'The Governance Challenge for Investors', *Corporate Governance: An International Review*, **12**(2), April, 180–183.

Morck, R. and Stangeland, D. (1994) 'Large shareholders and corporate performance in Canada', unpublished manuscript.

Morck, R., Shleifer, A. and Vishny, R. W. (1988) 'Management ownership and market valuation: An empirical analysis', *Journal of Financial Economics*, **20**, 293–316.

Moskowitz, M. R. (1972) 'Choosing socially responsible stocks', *Business and Society Review*, **1**, 71–75.

Moules, J. (2005) 'Superstars Zoom Ahead in Pay Stakes', *Financial Times*, 6 September, 3.

Moxey, P. (2004) 'Corporate Governance and Wealth Creation', Occasional Research Paper No. 37, *Certified Accountants Educational Trust*, London.

Muller, K., de Frutos, J., Schussler, K-U. and Haarbosch, H. (1994) *Environmental Reporting and Disclosures: The Financial Analyst's View*, European Federation of Financial Analysts' Societies, Edinburgh.

Mulligan, M. and Munchau, W. (2003) 'Comment: Parmalat Affair Has Plenty of Blame to Go Round', *Financial Times*, 29 December.

Mulligan, T. S. (2006) 'Top Enron Figures Head to Court', *Los Angeles Times* (LATIMES.com), 25 January.

Mulligan, T. S. and Sanchez, J. (2006) 'Attorneys Spar in Enron Trial Opening Statements', *Los Angeles Times* (LATIMES.com), 31 January.

Murray, S. (2005) 'Business Continuity', Financial Times Report, *Financial Times*, 27 June, 2.

Myners, P. (2001) *Institutional Investment in the United Kingdom: A Review* (The Myners Report), London.

Myners, P. (July 2003) 'Trust is vital for good business', *Financial Times* Fund Management, 60.

Myners, P. (2005) 'Fixing the Hole in Britain's Investment Industry', *Financial Times*, 13 May, 19.

Myners Report, The (1995) *Developing a Winning Partnership*, Department of Trade and Industry, London.

NACD (November 1996) *Report of the NACD Blue Ribbon Commission on Director Professionalism*, National Association of Corporate Directors, Washington, DC.

NACD (November 1998) *Report of the NACD Blue Ribbon Commission on CEO Succession*, National Association of Corporate Directors, Washington DC.

Namgyal, T. (2001) 'AmCham Paper Calls for Pragmatic Cooperation', *Taipei Times*, 11 May.

National Association of Pension Funds (NAPF) (November 1995) *The Powerful Vote*, The National Association of Pension Funds Investment Committee, London.

National Association of Pension Funds (NAPF) (2005) *Pension Scheme Governance – Fit for the 21st Century*, NAPF Discussion Paper, July.

Nesbitt, S. L. (1994) 'Long-term rewards from shareholder activism: A study of the "CalPERS effect"', *Journal of Applied Corporate Finance*, **6**, 75–80.

Nicholson, G. J. (2004) 'A Framework for Diagnosing Board Effectiveness', *Corporate Governance: An International Review*, **12**(4), October, 442–460.

NYSE and NACD (December 1998) *Report of the NACD Blue Ribbon Commission on Improving the Effectiveness of Corporate Audit Committees*, New York Stock Exchange/National Association of Corporate Directors, New York.

O'Dwyer, B. and Owen, D. L. (2005) 'Assurance Statement Practice in Environmental, Social and Sustainability Reporting: A Critical Evaluation', *British Accounting Review*, **37**, 205–229.

Oakey, D. (2000) 'Share Price Shocks: An Active Interest', *Investors Chronicle*, 18 August.

OECD (1999) *OECD Principles of Corporate Governance*, OECD, Paris.

OECD (2004) *OECD Principles of Corporate Governance*, OECD, Paris.

Osborn, A. (2001) '50 Million Animals in Mass Test Plan', *The Guardian*, 27 October.

Ow-Yong, K. and Kooi Guan, C. (2000) 'Corporate governance codes: A comparison between Malaysia and the UK', *Corporate Governance: An International Review*, **8**(2), April, 125–133.

Owen, D. (1992) 'The implications of current trends in green awareness for the accounting function: An introductory analysis', in: D. Owen (ed.), *Green Reporting: Accounting and the Challenge of the Nineties*, Chapman & Hall, London.

Owen, D. L. (2003) 'Recent developments in European social and environmental reporting and auditing practice: A critical evaluation and tentative prognosis', Cardiff. University Staff Seminar Series in Accounting and Finance, 22 January.

Owen, D. L., Swift, T. and Hunt, K. (2001) 'Questioning the role of stakeholder engagement in social and ethical accounting, auditing and reporting', *Accounting Forum*, **25**(3), September, 264–282.

Owen, D. L., Swift, T. A., Humphrey, C. and Bowerman, M. (2000) 'The New Social Audits: Accountability, Managerial Capture of the Agenda of Social Champions?', *The European Accounting Review*, **9**(1), 81–98.

Parker, H. (1990) *Letters to a New Chairman*, Institute of Directors.

Parkes, C. (2005) 'Disney to Make Top Jobs Split Permanent', *Financial Times*, 7 January, 21.

Parkinson, J. E. (1994) *Corporate Power and Responsibility*, Oxford University Press, Oxford.

Pearce, J. A. (1982) 'The company mission as a strategic tool', *Sloan Management Review*, Spring, 15–24.

Peel, M. and O'Donnell, E. (1995) 'Board structure, corporate performance and auditor independence', *Corporate Governance: An International Review*, **3**(4), October, 207–217.

Pension Fund Corporate Governance Research Committee (June 1998) *Action Guidelines for Exercising Voting Rights*, Kosei Nenkin Kikin Rengokai, Tokyo.

*Pensions Week* (28 July 2003) 'Green Firms Perform Better Than Their Peers', 7.

Perks, R. W. (1993) *Accounting and Society*, Chapman & Hall, London.

Perotti, E. and Gelfer, S. (1998) Investment Financial in Russian Financial-Industrial Groups, Working Paper 42. William Davidson Institute.

Perotti, E. and Gelfer, S. (2001) 'Red Barons or Robber Barons? Governance and Investment in Russian Financial-Industrial Groups', *European Economic Review*, **45**, 1601–1617.

Peters Committee (June 1997) *Corporate Governance in the Netherlands – Forty Recommendations*, Secretariat Committee on Corporate Governance, Amsterdam.

PIAC (1998) *Corporate Governance Standards* (4th edn), Pensions Investment Association of Canada, Toronto.

Pistor, K. and Turkewitz, J. (eds) (1996) 'Coping with Hydra – State ownership after privatisation', in: R. Frydman, C. W. Gray and A. Rapaczynski (eds), *Corporate Governance in Central Europe and Russia*. Volume 2: *Insiders and the State*, Central European University Press.

Plender, J. (2003) 'Bank Bandwagon Hits a Bump', *Financial Times*, 16 March.

Potts, S. D. and Matuszewski, I. L. (2004) 'Ethics and Corporate Governance', *Corporate Governance: An International Review*, **12**(2), April, 177–179.

Power, M. (1991) 'Auditing and Environmental Expertise: Between Protest and Professionalism', *Accounting, Auditing and Accountability Journal*, **4**(3), 30–41.

Power, M. (1994) *The Audit Explosion*, Demos, London, UK.

Power, M. (1996) 'Making Things Auditable', *Accounting, Organisations and Society*, **21**(2/3), 289–315.

Power, M. (1997a) *The Audit Society: Rituals of Verification*, Oxford University Press, Oxford.

Power, M. (1997b) 'Expertise and the Construction of Relevance: Accountants and Environmental Audit', *Accounting, Organizations and Society*, **22**(2), 123–146.

Prais, S. (1976) *The Evolution of Giant Firms in Britain: A Study of the Growth of Concentration in Manufacturing in Britain 1909–1970*, Cambridge, UK.

Prowse, S. D. (1992) 'The structure of corporate ownership in Japan', *Journal of Finance*, **47**(3), July, 1121–1141.

Quinn, D. and Jones, T. (1995) 'An agent morality view of business policy', *Academy of Management Review*, **20**(1), 22–42.

Rae, D. (2004) 'Grant Thornton SpA Chairman Goes Over Parmalat', *Accountancy Age*, 2 January.

Race for Opportunity (2004) *RfO Benchmarking Report 2004*, Race for Opportunity (part of Business in the Community), London, UK.

Rajan, R. and Zingales, L. (1998) 'Which capitalism? Lessons from the East Asian Crisis', *Journal of Applied Corporate Finance*, **11**(3), fall.

Ramos, M. (2004) *How to Comply with Sarbanes-Oxley Section 404: Assessing the Effectiveness of Internal Control*, John Wiley & Sons Inc.

Randoy, T. and Jenssen, J. I. (2004) 'Board Independence and Product Market Competition in Swedish Firms', *Corporate Governance: An International Review*, **12**(3), July, 281–289.

Rao, P. S. and Lee-Sing, C. R. (1995) 'Governance structure, corporate decision-making and firm performance in North America', in: R. J. Daniels and R. Morck (eds) *Corporate Decision-Making in Canada* (Industry Canada Research Vol. V), University of Calgary Press, Ottawa.

Rho, H. K. (2004) 'From Civil Society Organization to Shareholder Activist: The Case of the Korean PSPD', Working Paper No.15, Brunel Research in Enterprise, Innovation, Sustainability, and Ethics (BRESE), Brunel University, 1–36.

Rio Tinto (2004) *Sustainable Development Review: Meeting Global needs for Minerals and Metals*, Rio Tinto plc and Rio Tinto Limited, London, UK.

Roberts, C. (1992) 'Environmental disclosures in corporate annual reports in Western Europe', in: D. Owen (ed.), *Green Reporting: Accountancy and the Challenge of the Nineties*, Chapman & Hall, London.

Roe, M. (1993) 'Some differences in corporate structure in Germany, Japan and the United States', *The Yale Law Review*, **102**, 1927–2003.

Rose, C. and Mejer, C. (2003) 'The Danish Corporate Governance System: From Stakeholder Orientation Towards Shareholder Value', *Corporate Governance: An International Review*, **11**(4).

Rosenstein, S. and Wyatt, J. (1990) 'Outside directors, board independence and shareholder wealth', *Journal of Financial Economics*, **26**, 175–191.

Ross, S. (1973) 'The economic theory of agency: The principal's problem', *American Economic Review*, **63**, 134–139.

RSA (1995) *Tomorrow's Company* (Royal Society for the Encouragement of Arts, Manufactures and Commerce), RSA-Gower, Aldershot, UK.

Ruskin, J. (1862) 'The veins of wealth', *Unto This Last and Other Writings* (an essay, pp. 180–189), Penguin Books, Harmondsworth, UK (1997).

Rutteman Working Group (December 1994) *Internal Control and Financial Reporting, Guidance for Directors of Listed Companies Registered in the UK*, Institute of Chartered Accountants in England and Wales, London.

Ryland, P. (2002) 'Enronmania Sweeps Britain', *Investors Chronicle*, 8 February, 9.

Sarkar, J. and Sarkar, S. (2000) 'Large shareholder activism in corporate governance in developing countries: Evidence from India', *International Review of Finance*, **1**(3), 161–195.

Scheuth, S. (accessed 2002) *AccountAbility Primer*, Social Investment Forum, downloaded from www.socialinvest.org

Schilling, F. (2001) 'Corporate governance in Germany: The move to shareholder value', *Corporate Governance: An International Review*, **9**(3), July, 148–151.

SEHK (September 1997) *Guide for Directors of Listed Companies*, Stock Exchange of Hong Kong, Hong Kong.

Seki, T. (2005) 'Legal Reform and Shareholder Activism by Institutional Investors in Japan', *Corporate Governance: An International Review*, **13**(3), May, 377–385.

SET (1998) *The SET Code of Best Practice for Directors of Listed Companies*, Stock Exchange of Thailand, Bangkok.

Shane, P. B. and Spicer, B. H. (1983) 'Market response to environmental information produced outside the firm', *The Accounting Review*, **58**(3), 521–538.

Shankman, N. A. (1999) 'Reframing the debate between agency and stakeholder theories of the firm', *Journal of Business Ethics*, **19**, 319–334.

Sherman, H. (2004) 'Corporate Governance Ratings', *Corporate Governance: An International Review*, **12**(1), January, 5–7.

Shi, S. and Weisert, D. (2002) 'Corporate governance with Chinese characteristics', *China Business Review*, **5**, 40.

Shleifer, A. and Vishny, R. W. (1997) 'A survey of corporate governance', *Journal of Finance*, **52**(2), June, 737–783.

Shome, D. K. and Singh, S. (1995) 'Firm value and external blockholdings', *Financial Management*, **24**, 3–14.

Short, H. (1996) 'Non-executive directors, corporate governance and the Cadbury Report: A review of the issues and evidence', *Corporate Governance: An International Review*, **4**(2), April, 123–131.

Short, H., Keasey, K., Hull, A. and Wright, M. (1998) 'Corporate governance, accountability, and enterprise', *Corporate Governance: An International Review*, **6**(3), 151–165.

Simon, H. (1957) *Models of Man*, John Wiley & Sons Inc, New York.

Skapinker, M. (2000) 'In the Line of Fire – from all Directions: The "New Economy" and Stakeholder Pressure Are Making Life Ever More Difficult for Company Boards', *Financial Times* Survey, 31 March.

Skapinker, M. (2003) 'When Push Comes to Shove – We Shove', *Financial Times*, 6 June.

Smith Report, The (January 2003) *Audit Committees: A Report and Proposed Guidance*, Financial Reporting Council, London.

Smith, A. (1838) *The Wealth of Nations*, Ward Lock, London.

Smith, M. P. (1996a) 'Shareholder activism by institutional investors: Evidence from CalPERS', *Journal of Finance*, **51**(1), March, 227–252.

Smith, T. (1996b) *Accounting for Growth* (2nd edn), Century Business Books, London.

Social Investment Forum (1999). Available online at http://www.socialinvest.org

Solomon, A. (2000) 'Could corporate environmental reporting shadow financial reporting?', *Accounting Forum*, **24**(1), March, 35–61.

Solomon, A. and Lewis, L. A. (2002) 'Incentives and disincentives for corporate environmental disclosure', *Business Strategy and the Environment*, **11**(3), May–June, 154–169.

Solomon, A. and Solomon, J. F. (1999) 'Empirical evidence of long-termism and shareholder activism in UK unit trusts', *Corporate Governance: An International Review*, **7**(3), July, 288–300.

Solomon, A. and Solomon, J. F. (2002) 'The SRI dilemma for pension fund trustees: Some perceptions of their evolving role', *Business Relationships, Accountability, Sustainability and Society (BRASS)*, Working Paper Series No. 7, 1–45.

Solomon, A. and Solomon, J. F. (2003b) 'Commentary: Pension fund trustee payment debate', *European Financial Services Regulation*, July, 14–16.

Solomon, J. F. (2005) 'Does Social and Environmental Reporting Nurture Trust and Stakeholder Engagement and Reduce Risk?', Cardiff University Working paper.

Solomon, J. F. and Darby, L. (2005) 'Is Private Social, Ethical and Environmental Disclosure Mythicizing or Demythologizing Reality?', *Accounting Forum*, **29**, 27–47.

Solomon, J. F., Hemmings, D. B. and Solomon, A. (November 1999) 'Evidence of a global compromise in corporate governance. Part II: Management of the crisis', in: Kap-Young Jeong and Jaewoo Choo (eds), *East Asian Economy Reconsidered*, ORUEN Publishing, South Korea.

Solomon, J. F. and Solomon, A. (2006) 'Private Social, Ethical and Environmental Disclosure', *Accounting, Auditing and Accountability Journal*, **19**(4), 564–591.

Solomon, J. F., Solomon, A., Joseph, N. L. and Norton, S. D. (2000a) 'Institutional investors' views on corporate governance reform: Policy recommendations for the 21st century', *Corporate Governance: An International Review*, **8**(3), July, 217–226.

Solomon, J. F., Solomon, A., Norton, S. D. and Joseph, N. L. (2000b) 'A conceptual framework for corporate risk disclosure emerging from the agenda for corporate governance reform', *British Accounting Review*, **32**(4), December, 447–478.

Solomon, J. F., Solomon, A. and Park, C. (2002a) 'A conceptual framework for corporate governance reform in South Korea', *Corporate Governance: An International Review*, **10**(1), January, 29–46.

Solomon, J. F., Solomon, A. and Park, C. (2002b) 'The role of institutional investors in corporate governance reform in South Korea: Some empirical evidence', *Corporate Governance: An International Review*, **10**(3), July, 211–224.

Solomon, J. F., Solomon, A. and Norton, S. D. (2002c) 'Socially responsible investment in the UK: Drivers and current issues', *Journal of General Management*, November 2001.

Solomon, J. F., Solomon, A., Joseph, N. L. and Norton, S. D. (2002d) Who would be a trustee? The growth of SRI in UK pension funds', *New Academy Review*, **1**(4), winter, 98–104.

Solomon, J. F., Lin, S. W., Norton, S. D. and Solomon, A. (2003b) 'Corporate governance reform in Taiwan: Empirical evidence from Taiwanese company directors', *Corporate Governance: An International Review*.

Solomon, J. F., Solomon, A. and Suto, M. (2003c) 'SRI in Japan: Lessons from the UK experience' (Working paper), unpublished.

Solomon, J. F. and Thomson, I. (2006a) 'An Illustration of Environmental Shadow Reporting in Victorian Britain', Paper presented at the European Accounting Association conference, Dublin, March.

Solomon, J. F. and Thomson, J. (2006b) 'Calling the 'Stink-and-Pest Breedes' to Account: William Morris' Role in Sowing the Seeds of Environmental Accountability', Working Paper, Cardiff University.

Song, B-N. (1997) *The Rise of the Korean Economy*, Oxford University Press, New York.

*South China Morning Post* (19 April 2002) 'Taiwan Template Tempts', 3.

Sparkes, R. (2002) *Socially Responsible Investment: A Global Revolution*, John Wiley & Sons Ltd, Chichester, UK.

Spiller, R. (1997) 'Death of the "Greed is Good" Era', in: R. Knowles (ed.), *Ethical Investment*, Choice Books, Marrickville, New South Wales, Australia.

Spira, L. F. and Bender, R. (2004) 'Compare and Contrast: Perspectives on Board Committees', *Corporate Governance: An International Review*, **12**(4), October, 489–499.

Sprenger, C. (2002) *Ownership and Corporate Governance in Russian Industry: A Survey*, Working Paper 70, European Bank for Reconstruction and Development.

Stapledon, G. P. (1995) 'Exercise of voting rights by institutional shareholders in the UK', *Corporate Governance: An International Review*, **3**(3), 144–155.

Stapledon, G. P. (1996) *Institutional Shareholders and Corporate Governance*, Clarendon Press, Oxford.

Sternberg, E. (October 1998) *Corporate Governance: Accountability in the Marketplace* (Hobart Paper No. 137), The Institute of Economic Affairs, London.

Stiles, P. and Taylor, B. (1993) 'Maxwell: The failure of corporate governance', *Corporate Governance: An International Review*, **1**(1), January.

Stiles, P. and Taylor, B. (2001) *Boards at Work*. Oxford University Press, Oxford, UK.

Stock, M., Copnell, T. and Wicks, C. (1999) *The Combined Code: A Practical Guide*, Gee Publishing, London.

Strachan, J. L., Smith, D. B. and Beedles, W. L. (1983) 'The price reaction to (alleged) corporate crime', *The Financial Review*, **18**(2), 121–132.

Strenger, C. (2004) 'The Corporate Governance Scorecard: A Tool for the Implementation of Corporate Governance', *Corporate Governance: An International Review*, **12**(1), January, 11–15.

Sykes, A. (1994) 'Proposals for internationally competitive corporate governance in Britain and America', *Corporate Governance: An International Review*, **2**(4), 187–195.

*Taipei Times* (18 July 2000) 'Corporate Scandal Old Hat in Asia'.

*Taipei Times* (15 July 2002) 'Asia Can Learn from Trials in the US'.

*Taiwan Business News* (3 December 2002) 'News Briefs: The Executive Yuan Decides to Improve the Island's Listed Firms' Corporate Governance'.

Tam, O. K. (2000) 'Models of corporate governance for Chinese companies', *Corporate Governance: An International Review*, **8**(1), January, 52–64.

Targett, S. (2000) 'Friends Plans to Give Ethical Lead' (Companies and markets), *Financial Times*, 8 May.

Targett, S. and Gimbel, F. (2003) 'Unpaid Trustees Run Most Company Pension Schemes', *Financial Times*, 6 January.

Targett, S. (2004) 'Banham Slates Fund Managers: Whitbread Chairman Says Corporate Governance Activists Should Carry a Health Warning', *Financial Times*, 12 April, 1.

Tassell, T. (31 January 2003) 'FTSE 100 Chiefs Question Boardroom Reform Plans', *Financial Times*, 4.

Tassell, T. (14 March 2003) 'Higgs Qualifies Boardroom Reform', *Financial Times*.

Tassell, T. (14 March 2003) 'Warning on Revisions to Corporate Governance Code', *Financial Times*.

Tassell, T. (9 July 2003) 'Executive Pay Under Review After Shareholder Activism', *Financial Times*.

Tassell, T. (24 July 2003) 'Investors Urged to Adopt Higgs Standards', *Financial Times*.

Tassell, T. (25 July 2003) 'Corporate Code Will Increase Disclosure Burden', *Financial Times*.

Tassell, T. (28 July 2003) 'Japanese Fund to Improve Standards', *Financial Times* Fund Management, 5.

Tassell, T. and Voyle, S. (2003) 'Promoting the Exception that Moves the Rule', *Financial Times*, 15 March.

Tassell, T., Bolger, A. and Parker, A. (2003) 'Fear of Board Splits Over Higgs Code: Critics Argue Proposal Could Lead to Division and Confusion', *Financial Times*, 20 January, 1.

Teather, D. and Bates, S. (2006) 'Enron Chiefs Face Rest of their Lives in Prison', *The Guardian* (online), 26 May.

Thomas, S. (1999) 'Proactively managing business risk', *IIR Conference on Proactively Managing Business Risk and Ensuring Effective Internal Control in the Light of the Combined Code and the New Turnbull Committee Report, London, May.*

Thompson, S. (2005) 'The Impact of Corporate Governance Reforms on the Remuneration of Executives in the UK', *Corporate Governance: An International Review*, **13**(1), January, 19–25.

Thomsen, S, and Rose, C. (2002) 'Foundation Ownership and Financial Performance – Do Companies Need Owners?' *Working Paper No. 9, Department of Finance*, Copenhagen Business School, Denmark.

Thomson, I. and Bebbington, J. (2005) 'Social and Environmental Reporting in the UK: A Pedagogic Evaluation' *Critical Perspectives on Accounting*, **16**, 507–533.

TIAA-CREF (October 1997) *TIAA-CREF Policy Statement on Corporate Governance*, Teachers Insurance and Annuity Association-College Retirement Equities Fund, New York.

Tran, M. and Jay, A. (2004) 'Parmalat: All You Need to Know About the Collapse of the Italian Dairy Giant', *Guardian Unlimited*, 6 October.

Tran, M. (2005) 'Parmalat Trial Gets Under Way', *Guardian Unlimited*, 28 September.

Treadway Commission, The (1987) *Report of the National Commission on Fraudulent Financial Reporting*, New York.

Tricker, R. I. (1984) *Corporate Governance: Practices, Procedures and Powers in British Companies and Their Boards of Directors*, Gower Press, Aldershot, UK.

Tsipouri, L. and Xanthakis, M. (2004) 'Can Corporate Governance be Rated? Ideas Based on the Greek Experience', *Corporate Governance: An International Review*, **12**(1), January, 16–28.

Tucker, S. (2005) 'Shareholder Group Switches its Focus', *Financial Times*, 10 February, 2.

Turley, S. and Zaman, M. (2004) 'Corporate Governance Effects of Audit Committees', *Journal of Management and Governance*, **8**, 305–332.

Turnbull Report, The (September 1999) *Internal Control: Guidance for Directors on the Combined Code*, Institute of Chartered Accountants in England and Wales, London.

Tyson Report, The (June 2003) *The Tyson Report on the Recruitment and Development of Non-Executive Directors*, A report commissioned by the Department of Trade & Industry following the publication of the Higgs Review of the role and effectiveness of non-executive directors in January 2003, London Business School.

Ullman, A. A. (1985) 'Data in search of a theory: A critical examination of the relationships among social performance, social disclosure, and economic performance of U.S. Firms', *Academy of Management Review*, **10**(3), 540–557.

UNEP (1996) *Engaging Stakeholders. 1: The Benchmark Survey*, SustainAbility Ltd/United Nations Environment Programme (Industry and Environment Office), London, UK.

Unerman, J. and O'Dwyer, B. (2004a) 'Theorising CSR/CSD as a Hegemonic Risk Discourse', Paper presented at the *International Congress on Social and Environmental Accounting*, Dundee, 1 September.

Ungson, G. R., Steers, R. M. and Park, S-H. (1997) *Korean Enterprise: The Quest for Globalization*, Harvard Business School Press, Cambridge, MA.

Vance, S. C. (1975) 'Are socially responsible corporations good investment risks?', *Management Review*, **64**, 18–24.

Vancil, R. F. (1987) *Passing the Baton: Managing the Process of CEO Succession*, Harvard Business School Press, Boston.

Van den Berghe, L. A. A. and Levrau, A. (2004) 'Evaluating Boards of Directors: What Constitutes a Good Corporate Board?', *Corporate Governance: An International Review*, Vol.12, No. 4, October, 461–477.

Voyle, S. and Tassell, T. (2003) 'Tesco Mulls One-Year Contracts for Chiefs', *Financial Times*, 14 June.

Waldmeir, P. (2006) 'The Simple Truth is that Accounting Fraud is Complicated', *Financial Times*, 4 February, 11.

Waldo, C. N. (1985) *Boards of Directors: Their Changing Roles, Structure, and Information Needs*, Quorum Books, New York.

Wan, D. and Ong, C. H. (2005) 'Board Structure, Process and Performance: Evidence from Public-Listed Companies in Singapore', *Corporate Governance: An International Review*, Vol.13, No. 2, March, 277–290.

Ward, A. (2000) '13% Back Greenpeace Move', *Financial Times*, 14 April.

Watts, R. L. and Zimmerman, J. L. (1986) *Positive Accounting Theory*, Prentice Hall International Editions, Upper Saddle River, NJ.

WCED (1987) *Our Common Future* (World Commission on Environment and Development, known as the Brundtland Commission), Oxford University Press, Oxford.

Weil, Gotshal & Manges LLP (January 2002) *Comparative Study of Corporate Governance Codes Relevant to the European Union and its Member States* (on behalf of the European Commission Internal Market Directorate General, Final Report), Weil, Gotshal & Manges LLP, Brussels.

Weisbach, M. S. (1988) 'Outside directors and CEO turnover', *Journal of Financial Economics*, **20**, 431–460.

Welford, R. and Gouldson, A. (1993) *Environment Management and Business Strategy*, Pitman, London.

Wendlandt, A. (2003) 'Kingfisher Bows to Shareholder Demands', *Financial Times*, 26 May.

Werder, A. V., Talaulicar, T. and Kolat, G. L. (2005) 'Compliance with the German Corporate Governance Code: An Empirical Analysis of the Compliance Statements by German Listed Companies', *Corporate Governance: An International Review*, **13**(2), March, 178–187.

Wheeler, D. and Sillanpää, M. (1997) *The Stakeholder Corporation*, Pitman, London.

Wheeler, D., Colbert, B. and Freeman, R. E. (2002) 'Focusing on value: Reconciling corporate social responsibility, sustainability and a stakeholder approach in a network world', paper Denver Meeting of the Academy of Management, August.

WICE (1994) *Environmental Reporting. A Manager's Guide* (World Industry Council for the Environment), International Chamber of Commerce, Paris.

Wiggins, J. (2006) 'Flat Lines as the Fizz Goes from Pop', *Financial Times*, 3 March, 21.

Williams, S. (1999) 'UK ethical investment: A coming of age', *Journal of Investing*, summer, 58–75.

Williamson, O. E. (1985) *The Economic Institutions of Capitalism*, Free Press, New York.

Williamson, O. E. (1996) *The Mechanisms of Governance*, Oxford University Press, New York.

Wymeersch, E. (1994) 'Aspects of corporate governance in Belgium', *Corporate Governance: An International Review*, **2**(3), July, 138–152.

Xstrata (2004) *Sustainability Report*, Xstrata, Switzerland.

Yasaki, A. G. A. (2001) 'Corporate governance in a Third World country with particular reference to Nigeria', *Corporate Governance: An International Review*, **9**(3), July, 238–253.

Yeh, K, S. (1997) 'Board network structural change before and after initial public offerings in Taiwan', *Sun Yat-sen Management Review*, International Issue, 93–114.

Yeltsin, B. (1996) *Decree on Measures to Ensure the Rights of Shareholders* (Parker School of Foreign and Comparative Law, Legal Matters, Release No. 28), Columbia University, New York.

Yermack, D. (1996) 'Higher market valuation for firms with a small board of directors', *Journal of Financial Economics*, **40**, 185–211.

Yoo, S. and Lee, S. (1987) 'Management style and practice in Korean chaebols', *California Management Review*, summer, 95–110.

Zeghal, D. and Ahmed, S. A. (1990) 'Comparison of social responsibility information disclosure media used by Canadian firms', *Accounting, Auditing and Accountability Journal*, **3**(1), 38–53.

Zun, W. M. (2002) 'The difficulties of improving Taiwanese corporate governance', *Economy Daily*, 2 September [in Mandarin Chinese].

Zysman, J. (1983) *Governments, Markets and Growth: Financial Systems and the Politics of Industrial Change*, Cornell University Press, Ithaca, NY.

# Index

Association of Chartered Certified Accountants
(ACCA) 147, 156, 252, 296
Association of Executive Search
Consultants 96
Association of Investment Trust Companies 119
audit
committees 43, 62, 174–5
expectations gap 171
external 50
fees 168
function, effectiveness of 175–6
independence considerations 172–5
role of 171–6
rotation considerations 173–4
Australia 193, 197–8, 297, 300
Australian Ethical Investment Ltd 300
Australian Investment Managers' Group
(AIMG) 198

B&Q 159
Bahrain 198
balance sheet 150
balanced scorecard 251
Ball, A. 258, 259
Ball, S. 244
Banham, Sir John 128, 129
Bank of America 44
banks 6
  see also under names
Barings Bank 58–60, 69, 151
Barrionuevo, A. 41
Bates, S. 42
Beatrice Foods 44
Beaver, W.H. 145
Bebbington, J. 260, 261
Beck, U. 245
Belcher, A. 158
Belgium 198
Belkaoui, A. 238
Bell, S. 244
benchmark indices 277–8
Bender, R. 83
Benston, G.J. 244
Berardino, Joseph 37
Berglof, E. 212
Berkowitz, Sean 40
Berle, A. 3–4, 5, 17, 110, 183, 186, 226
Bethel, J.E. 137

Bhopal disaster 251
BI 158
Bianchi, Maurizio 44
biodiversity and animal species 255
Bison, T.A. 210
Blackburn, S. 152
Blair, Tony 24, 235, 270
Blanchard, K.H. 28
Blattner 300
Blitz, R. 96, 120
Blockbuster Video 36
boards
  culture 81
  effectiveness 77–8, 103–5
  Enron 42
  future of 105–6
  role of 77–106
  size 81, 103
  as social phenomenon 104–5
  structures, unitary and two-tier 78–9
  types 78
Boatright, J.R. 17, 29, 235, 276, 277
Bolger, A. 268
Bolkestein, Frits 97, 191
Bondi, Enrico 44
Bonlat 44
Boritz, J.E. 151, 161
Bosch Report 198
Bostock, R. 98
bounded rationality 22
Bouton Code (2002) 205
Bowman, E.H. 238
box tickers 56, 126
  see also voting
BP 19, 65–6, 118, 149, 150, 165, 204, 252,
281, 282–4
BP-Amoco 19
Branson, Richard 69, 70, 73
Bravo, Rose Marie 97
Brazil 199
Bream, R. 97
Brent Spar incident 158, 266
Brewer, J. 207
Briston, R.J. 111
British Aerospace 152
British Gas 55, 138
British Merchant Banking and Securities
Houses Association 119